EXOMOLOGETARION

A MANUAL OF CONFESSION

The Works
of Saint Nikodemos the Hagiorite

Volume 1: Exomologetarion — A Manual of Confession

Volume 2: Concerning Frequent Communion

Volume 3: Confession of Faith

ΒΙΒΛΙΟΝ ΨΥΧΩΦΕΛΕΣΤΑΤΟΝ

ΔΙΗΡΗΜΕΝΟΝ ΕΙΣ ΤΡΙΑ ΜΕΡΗ.

ΩΝ

ΤΟ ΜΕΝ ΠΡΩΤΟΝ ΠΕΡΙΕΧΕΙ

ΔΙΔΑΣΚΑΛΙΑΝ ΣΥΝΤΟΜΟΝ ΚΑΙ ΠΡΑΚΤΙΚΗΝ
ΠΡΟΣ ΤΟΝ ΠΝΕΥΜΑΤΙΚΟΝ, ΠΩΣ ΝΑ
ΕΞΟΜΟΛΟΓῌ ΜΕ ΚΑΡΠΟΝ.

ΤΟ ΔΕΥΤΕΡΟΝ.

ΤΟΥΣ ΚΑΝΟΝΑΣ ΤΟΥ ΑΓΙΟΥ ΙΩΑΝΝΟΥ
ΤΟΥ ΝΗΣΤΕΥΤΟΥ ΑΚΡΙΒΩΣ ΕΞΗΓΗΜΕΝΟΥΣ,
ΜΕΤΑ ΚΑΙ ΤΙΝΩΝ ΑΛΛΩΝ ΑΝΑΓΚΑΙΩΝ.

ΤΟ ΔΕ ΤΡΙΤΟΝ.

ΣΥΜΒΟΥΛΗΝ ΓΛΑΦΥΡΑΝ ΚΑΙ ΣΥΝΤΟΜΟΝ
ΠΡΟΣ ΤΟΝ ΜΕΤΑΝΟΟΥΝΤΑ, ΠΩΣ ΝΑ
ΕΞΟΜΟΛΟΓΗΤΑΙ ΚΑΘΩΣ ΠΡΕΠΕΙ.

ΕΚ ΔΙΑΦΟΡΩΝ ΔΙΔΑΣΚΑΛΩΝ ΣΥΝΕΡΑΝΙΣΘΕΝ,
ΚΑΙ ΕΙΣ ΑΡΙΣΤΗΝ ΤΑΞΙΝ ΤΑΧΘΕΝ
ΠΑΡΑ ΤΟΥ ΟΣΙΟΛΟΓΙΩΤΑΤΟΥ

ΕΝ ΜΟΝΑΧΟΙΣ ΚΥΡΙΟΥ

ΝΙΚΟΔΗΜΟΥ

ΚΑΙ ΝΥΝ
ΠΡΩΤΟΝ ΤΥΠΟΙΣ ΕΚΔΟΘΕΝ, ΕΙΣ ΚΟΙΝΗΝ
ΤΩΝ ΑΝΑΓΙΝΩΣΚΟΝΤΩΝ ΩΦΕΛΕΙΑΝ.

❀❀❀   ❀❀❀
❀❀❀   ❀❀❀

αψϟδ. ΕΝΕΤΙῌΣΙ, 1794.

Παρὰ Νικολάῳ Γλυκεῖ τῷ ἐξ Ἰωαννίνων.
Con Licenza de' Superiori.

EXOMOLOGETARION

A MANUAL OF CONFESSION

by our Righteous God-bearing Father

Nikodemos the Hagiorite

A BOOK MOST PROFITABLE TO THE SOUL

CONTAINING

Concise instruction to the Spiritual Father on how
to conduct a fruitful confession, the Canons of
St. John the Faster meticulously interpreted, pleasing counsel
for the penitent on how to confess as one should, and a
homily on repentance profitable to the soul.

Gathered from various teachers and put into good order.

Translated by Fr. George Dokos

Uncut Mountain Press

EXOMOLOGETARION
A MANUAL OF CONFESSION

uncutmountainpress.com

This translation has been made from the Greek text of the sixth edition published by Nektarios Panagopoulos (Athens, 2002), while also checked against earlier editions.

Front Cover Photograph: Portable icon from the Holy Monastery of the Annunciation, Ormylia, Greece.
Back Cover Photograph: Portable icon from the Holy Monastery of St. Nikodemos the Hagiorite, Goumenissa, Greece.

Scriptural quotations are primarily taken from the King James Version. The translator to better reflect the original Greek text has emended some quotations. All citations of the Psalms are taken from The Psalter According to the Seventy, translated from the Septuagint Version of the Old Testament by the Holy Transfiguration Monastery, Brookline, MA.

Library of Congress Cataloging-in-Publication Data

Nikodemos the Hagiorite, Saint, 1749-1809
    Exomologetarion: A Manual of Confession / by Saint Nikodemos the Hagiorite: translated and annotated by Fr. George Dokos. —2nd ed.

ISBN (Hardcover): 978-1-63941-001-9
ISBN (Softcover): 978-1-63941-014-9

I. Christianity—Eastern Orthodox Spirituality
II. Christianity—Spiritual Instruction

If we confess our sins, He is faithful and just to forgive us our sins, and to cleanse us from all unrighteousness.

I John 1:9

Πνευματικοῖς Πατράσι μου εὐχαριστῶ,
Πρεσβεύσατε πρὸς Κύριον ἵνα σωθῶ,
Ὁ πρεσβύτερός Του ὁ ἀχρεῖος ἐγώ,
Ὦ Ἁγιορεῖτα καὶ σὲ παρακαλῶ.

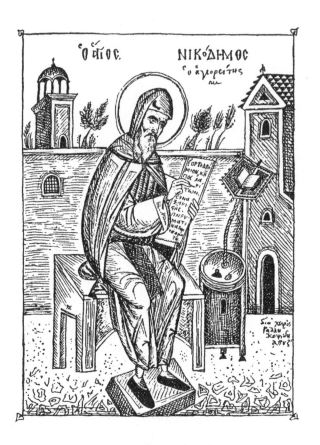

Apolytikion

Tone 3. Awed by the beauty.

Adorned were you O Father* by the grace of wisdom*
inspired you appeared as* a trumpet of the Spirit*
and as a teacher of virtues* Nikodemos who speaks of God*
for to all have you offered* teachings of salvation*
and of purity of life* pouring forth enlightenment*
by the richness of your virtuous writings*
through which as light you have illumined the world.

The Synodical Act of the Ecumenical Patriarchate Concerning the Registering in the Company of the Saints of the Righteous Monk Nikodemos the Hagiorite

---

Protocol Number 1717/31/5/55

+ ATHENAGORAS by the mercy of God Archbishop
of Constantinople
New Rome and Ecumenical Patriarch

It is right and most profitable for the whole body of the Church that they who excelled in virtuous deeds while in the body, and are now departed this life, be venerated and honored and glorified and celebrated yearly, in that the praise given to them that lived virtuously is directed to God Himself, from Whom is every virtue that comes to man, as Gregory the Theologian declaringly theologizes, and also because the praise of good deeds admonishes and stirs those who are slothful and idle to acquire virtue.

Insomuch therefore as Nikodemos the Hagiorite, in the beginning at the Sacred Royal Patriarchal and Stavropegic Monastery of Dionysiou, in which monastery he received the sacred monastic schema, then in the Sacred Royal Patriarchal and Stavropegic Monastery of Great Lavra and in other places, did excel in such eminent feats of virtue on the Holy Mountain, and by sanctity and holiness of life did make himself to be a pattern of the life in Christ, and a living icon of virtue, showing and poising himself to be a teacher of the Church and of the whole Christian body through his various Orthodox and edifying works, our Modesty together with the most sacred and most honorable Metropolitans with us, our beloved brethren and concelebrants in the Holy Spirit, recognizing his God-pleasing life and his works and achievements, and foreseeing the common benefit of the faithful, also taking into account all of his contributions to the Church, as Elder Ananias of the Cell of Lavriotes in Karyes personally submitted, along with all of the holy monks living in asceticism on the Holy Mountain, requesting that the anniversary of his death be established in honor of a Saint, we decree, in accord with the customary practice of the Church and our divine Fathers before us, to bestow upon him the honor due to holy men.

Wherefore we decree synodically, and do ordain, and in the Holy Spirit, direct that from this day forth and unto all ages Nikodemos the Hagiorite be numbered among the holy men and Saints of the Church and that he be honored with annual sacred and holy rites and venerated with hymns of praise on the fourteenth day of July, on which day he blessedly departed to the Lord.

In witness thereto, and confirmation, this our present Patriarchal and Synodical Act is made, drawn up, and signed in the Sacred Codex of our Holy and Great Church of Christ, and transmitted without change or alteration to the Sacred Community of the Holy Mountain that it be placed in their archives.

In the year of salvation 1955, on the 31st day
of the month of May, Eighth Indiction.
Patriarch ATHENAGORAS of Constantinople pronounces

+ Thomas of Chalcedon	+ Iakovos of Derkoi
+ Dorotheos of the Prince's Islands	+ Leontios of Theodoroupolis
+ Constantine of Eirenoupolis	+ Maximos of Sardis
+ Iakovos of Iconium	+ Meliton of Imbros and Tenedos
+ Jerome of Rhodopolis	+ Iakovos of Philadelphia

TABLE OF CONTENTS

PART THREE
COUNSEL FOR THE PENITENT

HOMILY ON REPENTANCE

INDICES

PREFACE

Almost all that were wounded by sin left hierarchs and confessors and ran to shabbily dressed Nikodemos, in order to find their cure and consolation from their afflictions; not only monks from monasteries, sketes and kellia, but also many Christians from various places.[1]

In his Introduction to the first English language publication of St Nikodemos' 'Handbook of Spiritual Counsel' (*Symbouleutikon Encheiridion*)[2] George S. Bebis wrote :"There is no doubt that 'The Manual of Confession' (*Exomologetarion*) is one of the most impressive of the books of St Nikodemos, an edifying and helpful spiritual book,"[3] and later mused that "an English translation of this book would be most beneficial."[4] The *Exomologetarion* to which he makes reference was first published in the year 1794 at the press of Nicholas Glykeus of Ioannina in Venice and has since seen numerous reprintings (e.g. 1804, 1818, 1868, 1893), including a 1799 translation published in Constantinople in the Turkish language (though in Greek characters) intended for the use of Turkish speaking Greek Orthodox

---

1   See the earliest *Vita* of St Nikodemos, written just four years after his repose by his fellow-struggler the Monk Euthymios: *Bios kai Politeia kai Agones tou Hosiologiotatou kai Makaritou kai Aoidimou Nikodemou Monachou* ("The Life, Conduct and Struggles of the Most Holy and Most Learned Monk Nikodemos of Blessed Memory") in the journal *Gregorios Palamas* (1920), 636-641 and (1921), 210-218. For an English-language translation of the *Vita* from his *Akolouthia* authored in Greek by the Monk Gerasimos Micragiannanitis, see Constantine Cavarnos, *Modern Orthodox Saints, Vol. 3, St Nicodemos the Hagiorite* (Belmont, MA: Institute for Byzantine and Modern Greek Studies, 1974), 64-95.

2   Peter A. Chamberas, trans., *Nicodemos of the Holy Mountain: A Handbook of Spiritual Counsel* (New York: Paulist Press, 1989).

3   Ibid., 41.

4   Ibid., 43.

Christians. Now, thanks to the inspired work of the Reverend George Dokos, who translated the work from Greek into English, and the devotion to the Patristic *phronema* by the Reverend Peter Heers of Uncut Mountain Press, we hold in our hands the long-awaited English translation of the *Exomologetarion* composed by our Venerable and Godbearing Father Nikodemos the Hagiorite.[5]

The son of Anthony Kallivourtsis and his wife Anastasia (Agatha in monasticism), St Nikodemos was born on the Aegean island of Naxos, one of the Cyclades, in 1749 and baptized with the name Nicholas. His first teacher was Archimandrite Chrysanthos Aitolos (+1785), brother of the New Martyr and Peer-of-the Apostles, St Cosmas Aitolos (1714-1779).[6] In 1764 young Nicholas was taken by his father to Smyrna where he was enrolled as a boarding student at the famous *Evangelike Schole* where he studied under the renowned educator Hierotheos Voulismas. Because of the violent persecution of Christians by the Turks which broke out in 1770, Nicholas fled Smyrna and returned to his native island of Naxos where, for the next five years, he served as *grammateus* (secretary) and *synkellos* (attendant) to Anthimos Vardis, the Metropolitan of Paros and Naxos. It was during this period of his life that he came into contact with three Athonite monks – Hieromonks Gregory and Niphon and Elder Arsenios the Peloponnesian – who, because they were *Kollyvades*,[7] were exiled from the Holy Mountain and had found refuge on Naxos. It was from these three monastics that Nicholas first learned of Athonite asceticism and spiritual life, including the practice of unceasing prayer and *hesychia*.

In the year 1775, Nicholas, now having an insatiable desire to be formed in the monastic life, traveled to the small island of Hydra in order to meet the greatest *Kollyvas*, St Makarios Notaras (1731-1835), the Metropolitan

---

5   The designation 'Hagiorite' indicates that St Nikodemos was a monk of the Holy Mountain (*Hagion Oros*), which is also known as Mount Athos.

6   See Constantine Cavarnos, *Modern Orthodox Saints, Vol. 1, St Cosmas Aitolos* (Belmont, MA: Institute for Byzantine and Modern Greek Studies, 1971). St Cosmas was glorified by the Oecumenical Patriarchate in 1961. His annual feast is kept on August 24.

7   For a brief but very fine description of the *Kollyvades* movement, see Chamberas, *Nicodemos of the Holy Mountain: A Handbook of Spiritual Counsel*, 11-13.

of Corinth.[8] Thus began his association with St Makarios which, over the next several decades, resulted in their collaborating to produce numerous soul-profiting works. While on Hydra, Nicholas also made the acquaintance of another experienced holy elder, Sylvester of Caesarea, whose life and counsels inspired in young Nicholas an even greater longing for a life of stillness and unceasing prayer. Thus, later that year, twenty-six year old Nicholas left Hydra for the Holy Mountain, bearing letters of recommendation from Elder Sylvester.

Arriving on the Holy Mountain, Nicholas went to the Sacred Monastery of Dionysiou where he made his metanoia before the holy Elder Makarios Dionysiatis and began his formal monastic formation. There he was tonsured a monk of the *Microschema*,[9] having his baptismal name of Nicholas changed to Nikodemos. He remained at Dionysiou for the next two years.

In 1777 his friend and spiritual guide, St Makarios of Corinth, visited the Holy Mountain. St Nikodemos met with him at Karyes, the capital of the Holy Mountain, and began what would become a lifelong collaboration of producing spiritual masterpieces by preparing for publication *The Philokalia* (first edition published in Venice in 1782), *The Evergetinos* (first edition published in Venice in 1783), and *Peri tes Synechous Metalepseos ton Theion Mysterion* or 'Concerning Continual Communion of the Divine Mysteries' (first edition published in Venice in 1783).[10] After St Makarios departed from the Holy Mountain, St Nikodemos was given hospitality at the *kelli* of St George commonly known as the *kelli* of the Skourtaioi. Here a bond of love was forged between St Nikodemos and that brotherhood

---

8   See Constantine Cavarnos, *Modern Orthodox Saints, Vol. 2, St Macarios of Corinth* (Belmont, MA: Institute for Byzantine and Modern Greek Studies, 1972). St Makarios' *Vita* and *Akolouthia*, authored by Nicephoros the Chian, were first published in 1863. His annual feast is kept on April 17.

9   The Lesser Schema. A monk or nun of this degree is known as being a Stavrophor or of the Mandyas.

10   For a listing of the more than one hundred published and unpublished works of St Nikodemos, see Cavarnos, *Modern Orthodox Saints, Vol. 3, St Nicodemos the Hagiorite,* 96-114.

which would nourish and sustain him (both spiritually and physically!) on many occasions through the remainder of his life.

Having learned of the spiritual giant and divinely-minded coenobiarch St Paissii Velichkovskii (1722-1794),[11] who, having been trained in *hesychasm* on the Holy Mountain, was serving as Schema-Archimandrite at the Moldavian Monastery of Neamts (in present day Romania) and spiritual father to over one thousand monks, St Nikodemos determined that he would visit him and receive spiritual sustenance. He began his journey to Neamts by boarding a ship, but shortly after its departure a violent storm arose at sea which forced the ship to moor at the island of Thassos. Abandoning his plans to visit St Paissii, St Nikodemos returned to the Holy Mountain and eventually settled at a skete near Pantocratoros where he placed himself under obedience to one of his first instructors in the ascetic life, the famous Elder Arsenios the Peloponnesian, who had returned to Athos from his exile on Naxos. In 1782, when Elder Arsenios again withdrew from the Holy Mountain, this time to the tiny and barren island of Skyropoula (south of Athos and across from Euboia), St Nikodemos accompanied him and struggled together with him in asceticism for one year, living, as St Nikodemos himself writes, "the life of a worker and laborer: digging, sowing, harvesting, and every day doing all the other things by which the toilsome life on barren islands is characterized."[12]

In 1783 St Nikodemos returned to the Holy Mountain where he was tonsured a monk of the *Megaloschema*[13] by the holy Elder Damascene Stavroudas. He then purchased and withdrew to the *kalyva* of Theonas near Pantocratoros, where he was joined by a fellow Naxian (named John in the world, but Hierotheos in monasticism) who served him for six years

---

11   See J.M.E. Featherstone, trans. *The Life of Paisij Velyčkovs'kyj* (Boston, MA: Harvard University Press, 1989). St Paissii was glorified by the Patriarchate of Moscow in 1988. His annual feast is kept on November 15.

12   See Gerasimos Micragiannanitis, *Akolouthia tou Hosiou kai Theophorou hemon Patros kai Didaskalou Nikodemou tou Hagioreitou* ("Akolouthia of our Venerable and Godbearing Father and Teacher Nikodemos the Hagiorite") in a *phyllada* (Athos, 1955).

13   The Great Schema. A monk or nun of this degree is known as being of the Great and Angelic Schema.

as his disciple and *synkellos*.[14] In 1784 his friend and patron, St Makarios of Corinth visited the Holy Mountain for a second time and encouraged St Nikodemos to correct and prepare for publication many edifying works. It was at this time that St Nikodemos began his composition of our present book, the *Exomologetarion* or 'The Manual of Confession' which is a compilation drawn from various works and *Exomologetaria* from libraries throughout the Holy Mountain, including that by Chrysanthos of Jerusalem, combined with the Saint's own inspired spiritual counsels.

St Nikodemos' *Exomologetarion* is a masterpiece of spiritual insight and direction which is composed of three distinct sections: the first being the qualifications of a true confessor, the second being the thirty-eight canons and seventeen penances of St John 'the Faster'[15] together with commentaries and interpretations, and the third being St Nikodemos' own fatherly counsels and a homily concerning the Mystery of Confession.

After spending two decades exploring the manuscript-rich monastic libraries on the Holy Mountain, editing and authoring scores of spiritual books, and composing sacred hymns for numerous saints, St Nikodemos returned in 1809 to the *kelli* of his beloved Skourtaioi brotherhood. On July 5 of that year he suffered a stroke from which he was never to recover. Knowing that the end of his earthly life was drawing near, St Nikodemos made his confession, was anointed with the *Euchelion* in the Mystery of Holy Unction and, each day, partook of the Immaculate Body and Precious Blood. On July 13 he asked that the sacred relics of two of his spiritual fathers, Saints Makarios and Parthenios, be brought to him. Having reverently kissed and embraced them, he made the sign of the Cross, crossed his hands on his breast, straightened his legs, and patiently awaited his falling asleep in Christ which came quietly early the next morning – July 14, 1809. He was buried at the *kelli* of the Skourtaioi.

In 1953 the Sacred Monastery of Megesti Lavra, oldest and first in rank among the twenty ruling monasteries of the Holy Mountain, of which

---

14   A cell-mate and attendant.
15   Patriarch John IV 'Nesteutes' of Constantinople (582-595). His annual feast is kept on September 2.

the *kelli* of the Skourtaioi is a dependency, petitioned the Holy Synod of the Oecumenical Patriarchate for the glorification of St Nikodemos. Two years later, on May 31, 1955, the Holy Synod issued the Synodical Decree whereby the "clarion of the Spirit and teacher of virtue,"[16] the "shabbily dressed" Nikodemos the Hagiorite was officially numbered among the saints of the One, Holy, Catholic and Apostolic Church.[17] May his blessings be upon this book to the glory of the All-holy Trinity and the upbuilding of Holy Orthodoxy, and by his intercessions may we all be saved.

+ B A S I L

Bishop of Wichita and Mid-America
Antiochian Orthodox Christian Archdiocese of North America

July 14, 2005
The Commemoration of St Nikodemos the Hagiorite

---

16   This is a phrase from the Apolytikion of St Nikodemos which, together with his *Vita* and *Akolouthia*, was composed by the late great contemporary hymnographer of the Great Church of Christ, the Monk Gerasimos Micragiannanitis (+1991). See footnote 12.
17   St Nikodemos' annual feast is kept on the date of his repose, July 14.

INTRODUCTION*

by Protopresbyter George Metallinos

I consider the translation and publication in the English language of the *Exomologetarion* of the great theologian and Father of the Church, Nikodemos the Hagiorite, to be a momentous event. It is an important pastoral work which has, from its very first appearance, been of tremendous help both to confessors and those confessing. The reading and study, however, as well as the pastoral use, of this book in our day and age require familiarization with the Patristic terminology of the author, so as to make an Orthodox understanding and interpretation possible. For this reason, then, I express my heartfelt gratitude to the publishers of the English language edition of the book for requesting of me the following instructive introduction, for the service of all who will read it, both clergy and laity.

The *Exomologetarion* or *Manual of Confession* of this great Neo-Hesychastic Father of our Church[1] has given rise to lengthy discussions.[2] Its language

---

* This text was originally translated by the staff of *Orthodox Tradition*. It appears here with slight changes and additions by the author and editors.

1   For a critical survey of his life, with all of his known writings, see Gerhard Podskalsky, *Griechische Theologie in der Zeit der Türkenherrschaft (1453- 1821)* (*Greek Theology during the Period of the Turkish Yoke (1453-1821)*) (Munich: 1988), pp. 377ff (Greek edition: Athens, 2005, translation by Fr. George Metallinos, *He Hellenike Theologia epi Tourkokratias: 1453-1821*, pp. 460ff)).

2   The Saint's biographer (see Monk Nikodemos Bilalis, *Ho prototypos bios tou Hagiou Nikodemou tou Hagioreitou* (*The Original Life of St. Nikodemos the Hagiorite*) (Athens, 1985)) notes: "He...[settled]...in...[his]...*kalyva* (an Anthonite hut) in 1774. There, he corrected and improved the *Euchologion* and composed the *Chrestoetheia* (*Christian Morality*), the second *Exomologetarion*, and (commentaries on) the fourteen Epistles of St. Paul and the seven Catholic Epistles, and edited the *Psalterion* of Euthymios Zygadinos (*sic*)...." What is meant by the second *Exomologetarion*? In all likelihood, it means that he was working on an already

and style pose challenges, and the question is often raised as to how one of the redactors of the *Philokalia*[3] could have composed such a work. However, if we are to interpret a text of this kind, we must first come to an understanding of its ecclesiological perspective. The aim of my introduction

---

existing work, and perhaps on what was later to be known as the first edition. See P.G. Nikolopoulos, *Bibliographike Epistasia ton Ekdoseon Nikodemou tou Hagioreitou (A Bibliographical Overview of the Publications of Nikodemos the Hagiorite), Epeteris Etaireias Kykladikon Meleton*, Vol. XVI (2000), pp. 489ff. The first edition of the work appeared in 1794, with the following subtitle and publication data: "A book most profitable to the soul, divided into three parts, of which the first contains concise and practical instructions for the Spiritual Father on how to perform a fruitful confession. The second part contains the Canons of St. John the Faster, meticulously interpreted, together with certain other necessary comments. The third part contains perceptive and concise advice for the penitent on how to confess as one should, gathered from various teachers and put into good order by the most reverend and learned among monks Nikodemos, and now published for the first time for the general benefit of readers." Venice, 1794. At the press of Nicholas Glykeus of Ioannina (see G.G. Ladas and A.D. Hatzedemos, *Hellenike Bibliographia ton eton 1791-1795 (Bibliography of Greek Publications from the Years 1791-1795)* (Athens, 1970), pp. 283-284, No. 161). The second edition appeared in 1804, with this subtitle and data: "A book most profitable to the soul, containing: concise instruction to the Spiritual Father on how to perform a fruitful confession; the Canons of St. John the Faster, meticulously interpreted, together with certain other necessary comments; pleasing counsel for the penitent on how to confess as one should, gathered from various teachers and put into good order by the least among monks, Nikodemos; published previously, and now expanded and published for the second time through the generosity and at the expense of His Eminence, Metropolitan Hierotheos of Ioannina, for the general benefit of Orthodox Christians." Venice, 1804. At the press of Nicholas Glykeus of Ioannina. With royal approbation. In 1799, between the first and second editions, a version of the work was printed in Constantinople in Turkish (though in Greek characters). The third edition was published in 1818, and was frequently reprinted. In this paper, I have used an undated reprint by the St. Nikodemos Society (Athens) of the edition published in Venice in 1868 (while all quotations and page number references correspond to the present English language edition). For excerpts from the work in Italian translation, see Angelo Amato, S.D.B., *Il Sacramento della Penitenza nella Teologia Greco-Ortodossa: Studi storico-dogmatici (The Sacrament of Confession in Greek Orthodox Theology: Historical and Dogmatic Studies)* (Thessaloniki, 1982), pp. 300-329. For comments on the *Exomologetarion*, see pp. 261ff.; *cf.* Podskalsky, *Griechische Theologie*, pp. 380f. (Greek edition: pp. 469f.); Monk Theokletos Dionysiates, *Hagios Nikodemos ho Hagioreites. Ho Bios kai ta erga tou (1749-1809) (St. Nikodemos the Hagiorite: His Life and Works (1749-1809))* (Athens, 1959), pp. 181-186; Chrestos Yannaras, *Orthodoxia kai Dyse ste neotere Hellada (Orthodoxy and the West in Modern Greece)* (Athens, 1992), pp. 201f. In the nineteenth and twentieth centuries, this work was reprinted more often than any other work by St. Nikodemos. For a very concise account of this work, see P. Eliou, *Hellenike (1801-1818) (Bibliography of Greek Publications in the Nineteenth Century: Books and Pamphlets (1801- 1818))* (Athens, 1997), Vol. I, pp. 95-96 (No. 13). This is a description of the 1804 reprint.

3   See Podskalsky, *Griechische Theologie*, pp. 379f. (Greek edition: pp. 469f.); Monk Theokletos, *Hagios Nikodemos ho Hagioreites*, pp. 96ff.

is not to analyze the work, but to provide a psychological and hermeneutical treatment of its overall structure and to ascertain its pastoral goals.

1. *Let us bear in mind the structure and lineaments of the work.* It begins with an address To the Most Reverend Spiritual Fathers in Christ (pp. 65-67), to which is added an Epigram for the Present Instruction (p. 69). There follows: Part One: Instruction to the Spiritual Father (pp. 71-211). In Part Two, after brief prefatory remarks about the author thereof, The Canons of St. John the Faster Together With Their Interpretation are set forth, with explanations by St. Nikodemos (pp. 213-263). To these are added Some Pertinent Subjects Outside of the Canons of the Faster (pp. 264-297). After a brief address (pp. 301-304), To The Brethren in Christ: Greeting, and an Epigram on the subject (p. 305), Part Three – Counsel for the Penitent (pp. 307-387) – commences. To this is attached a Homily on Repentance: Concerning the Audacity of Those Who Intentionally Sin with the Hope That They Can Confess and Repent (pp. 389-454).

St. Nikodemos composed the *Exomologetarion* after occupying himself with the writings of St. Symeon the New Theologian,[4] and therefore in a spiritual atmosphere that was purely Hesychastic and imbued with the precepts of the *Philokalia*; not only is it evident that the work is a compilation of texts, but the author himself clearly states this.[5] Consequently, there is no basis in reality for the idea that we are dealing with a genre thitherto completely unknown in the Church,[6] since this kind of work is not foreign to the literary output of the Greek nation during its enslavement to the Turks.[7] At any rate, it behooves us to locate the sources of this misunderstanding. Gerhard Podskalsky, evidently in order to explain the ostensibly scholastic nature of the work, characterizes it, in terms of its structure, as probably based on a Latin original.[8] But the notion that St. Nikodemos worked from Latin models – which, in the past, led to some preposterous speculations   ·

---

4   See Monk Theokletos, *Hagios Nikodemos ho Hagioreites*, pp. 175ff. (181).
5   See below.
6   Monk Theokletos, *Hagios Nikodemos ho Hagioreites*, p. 181.
7   See Amato, *Il Sacramento della Penitenza*.
8   Podskalsky, *Griechische Theologie*, p. 380. (Greek edition: pp. 469-470).

– has now been decisively laid to rest by Mr. Emmanuel Frangiskou,[9] who, in the wake of his critical intrusion into the debate, has contributed significantly to demolishing an essentially groundless attempt to make unjust war against this Saint; and for this, we theologians are grateful to him.

St. Nikodemos himself states that he used other works for his *Exomologetarion* (compiled from various sources,[10] compiled from different teachers[11]). He was translating not from a single text (written in Greek or some other language), but was drawing on diverse works of similar character, using the usual method of compilation that he employs in his writings.[12] In any case, with the exception of his wholly original liturgical commentaries, St. Nikodemos, following the mind of the Fathers,[13] did not consider it a defect to base oneself on the works of others, since in this way the traditional practice of the Church is rekindled and renewed and Her continuity is made manifest by a plurality of voices. Nonetheless, whatever the Saint took from some other writer was always passed through the spiritual transformer of his conscience and his purely Orthodox and ecclesiastical mind-set.[14] Hence, he does not hesitate to say: "[We] took great pains to gather together from various teachers the present concise counsel."[15] He states that he has before him the most accurate manuscripts of *Exomologetaria*

---

9   Emmanuel Frangiskou, *"Aoratos Polemos" (1796), "Gymnasmata Pneumatika" (1800). Patroteta ton "metaphraseon" tou Nikodemou Hagioreite* (*"Unseen Warfare* (1796) and *Spiritual Exercises* (1800): The Authorship of the Translations by Nikodemos the Hagiorite") (Athens, 1993) (reprinted from the periodical *Ho Eranistes*, Vol. XIX (1993), pp. 102-135). The picture that has hitherto been formed about Nikodemos the Hagiorite's relationship with the texts of Scupoli and Pinamonti and, beyond this, about the influence of Catholicism on his work, is undergoing a radical change. It is clear that this relationship was wholly indirect (p. 127).

10   *Exomologetarion*, p. 55.

11   *Exomologetarion*: see the title-page of the book and p. 239.

12   Panagiotis Chrestou (*Pateres kai theologoi tou Christianismou* (*Christian Fathers and Theologians*) (Thessaloniki, 1971), Vol. II, p. 324) considers it a demerit that Nikodemos did not apply himself more to composing original works, a view which is repeated also by Podskalsky (*Griechische Theologie*, p. 379 (Greek edition: p. 469)).

13   Concerning originality in the Patristic tradition, see the chapter *"To ergo ton Pateron kai to ergo ton Philosophon"* ("The Work of the Fathers and the Work of the Philosophers"), in S.G. Papadopoulos, *Patrologia* (*Patrology*) (Athens, 1977), Vol. I, pp. 58ff.

14   Hence, he makes everything Orthodox, such as, for example, the translations of Western works by Emmanuel Romanitis.

15   *Exomologetarion*, p. 239.

from the Holy Mountain, which are profitably used by all of the experienced spiritual Fathers on the Holy Mountain,[16] and he recommends spiritual Fathers to study the *Exomologetarion* by Chrysanthos of Jerusalem,[17] in conjunction with the Sacred Canons,[18] as well as the printed works of Emmanuel Romanitis, *Ho Pneumatikos Didaskomenos* (*Instructions for Spiritual Fathers*) and *Ho Metanoon Didaskomenos* (*Instructions for Penitents*),[19] the works of an author who, through his translations, provided Nikodemos with material for other of his writings.[20] He also uses an *Orthodoxos Homologia* (*Orthodox Confession*),[21] and he is familiar with the *Exomologetarion* printed many years ago by one Neophytos of Cyprus, surnamed Rhodinos, who was a heretic.[22] Hereby, he tacitly reproaches the Ecumenical Patriarch Kallinikos III, who republished this work, with his name on the title page, but without purging it of its erroneous ideas.[23] As well, he mentions a newly

---

16   *Ibid.*, p. 133.

17   *Ibid.*, p. 151. The work in question is *Didaskalia ophelimos peri metanoias kai exomologeseos* (*Beneficial Teaching on Repentance and Confession*), (Venice, 1724).

18   He recommends the study primarily of Canons 11 of the First Ecumenical Council; 102 of the Sixth Ecumenical Council; 2, 5, and 6 of Ancyra; 1 and 2 of Laodicea; 4, 5, 7, and 8 of St. Gregory of Nyssa; and 2, 3, 74, 84, and 85 of St. Basil the Great, because these Canons are particularly relevant to the vocation of a Spiritual Father (p. 168).

19   Concerning Emmanuel (or Manuel) Romanitis, Cretan by descent and Chancellor of Patmos (secretary of the island community), who flourished in the eighteenth century (he must have died between the years 1758 and 1762), see Frangiskou, *"Aoratos Polemos* (1796)...," pp. 127f. and n. 15. His works *Ho Pneumatikos Didaskomenos* and *Ho Metanoon Didaskomenos* (see Mile Legrand, *Bibliographie Hellnique* (*Bibliography of Greek Publications*), XVIIIth cent., Vol. I, No. 292, pp. 296-298) belong to Paolo Segneri (Frangiskou, *"Aoratos Polemos* (1796)...," pp. 109-110). See *Exomologetarion*, pp. 16, n. 9; 20, n. 14; 29, n. 52; 86, n. 15; and 108, n. 68.

20   See note 9 above.

21   *Exomologetarion*, pp. 67, 74, 81, 134, 155, and 328. According to Amato (*Il Sacramento della Penitenza*, p. 293), this is a reference to a work of the same title by Peter Mogila (1638-1642).

22   *Exomologetarion*, p. 128, n. 140. The work is: Neophytos Rhodinos, *Peri Exolomogeseos* (*Concerning Confession*) (Rome, 1630, 1671) (see Legrand, *Bibliographie Hellenique*, XVIIIth cent., Vol. I, No. 202, pp. 275f. and Vol. II, No. 500, p. 66).

23   *Ibid.* See Podskalsky, *Griechische Theologie*, p. 203 (and n. 846) (Greek edition: pp. 264-265, n. 94). Regarding its publication, see Legrand, *Bibliographie Hellenique*, XVIIIth cent., Vol. II, No. 1197, p. 472. See also the analysis by Amato (*Il Sacramento della Penitenza*, pp. 294f.

printed *Exomologetarion* for the sick,[24] which has recently been published
under the name of St. Nikodemos[25] (though His Eminence, Metropolitan
Paul of Sweden, considers this a misattribution,[26] asserting that the work
belongs to Methodios Anthrakitis (1736)[27]).

The *Exomologetarion* of St. Nikodemos is based, specifically, on the thirty-
eight Canons of St. John the Faster[28] and on his seventeen Penances, which
were discovered in manuscripts located in Athonite monasteries. He translates
these canonical texts, simplifying them linguistically, and also comments
on them, adding detailed footnotes, following the method that he employs
in the *Pedalion (The Rudder)*. He holds St. John the Faster in great esteem:
"The divine Faster established his Canons with the discernment of the
Holy Spirit..."[29] He recommends that Spiritual Fathers apply the Canons
in the way that St. John the Faster did,[30] and this because of the condescension
that the latter employed (a Spiritual Father should thus tell the person
confessing to him: "I have rather placed you under a rule according to the
lenient Faster."[31]). The criteria used by St. Nikodemos in selecting these
Canons are pastoral and, as well, purely ecclesiastical (criteria which the

---

24   *Exomologetarion*, p. 129, n. 140. The work is entitled *Episkepis pneumatike, etoi me
poion tropon chreostei ho pneumatikos na episkeptetai tous astheneis... (Spiritual Visitation, that is, how a
Spiritual Father should visit the sick...)* (Venice, 1780 and 1781) (see Legrand, *Bibliographie
Hellenique*, XVIIIth cent., Vol. II, No. 998, p. 328).
25   *Episkepsis Pneumatikou pros asthene (When a Spiritual Father Visits the Sick)* (Athens,
Hypakoë Publications, 1993).
26   Metropolitan Paul (Menevisoglou) of Sweden, "Peplanemene apodosis ergou
eis Nikodemon Hagioreiten" ("The Erroneous Ascription of a Work to Nikodemos the
Hagiorite"), *Kleronomia*, Vol. XXIX (1997), pp. 203-210.
27   *Ibid.*, pp. 205f. Concerning this author, see Podskalsky, *Griechische Theologie*, pp.
312ff (Greek edition: pp. 391ff). But see also Fr. B.E. Bouloudakis, *Peri tes patrotetos duo
anonymon ergon Hagiou Nikodemou tou Hagioreitou. Apantesis ston Metropoliten Souedias k. Paulon
(Concerning the Authorship of Two Anonymous Works by St. Nikodemos the Hagiorite: A Reply to
Metropolitan Paul of Sweden)*, (Athens, 2000).
28   Patriarch John IV of Constantinople (595). See the article by George
Mantzarides in the *Threskeutike kai Ethike Egkyklopaideia (Encyclopdia of Religion and Ethics)*
(Athens, 1965), Vol. VI, cols. 1210-1211.
29   *Exomologetarion*, p. 142.
30   *Ibid.*, p. 131.
31   *Ibid.*, p. 142.

entire Orthodox Church has generally accepted and does accept).[32] The great fall in the spiritual level of humanity rendered it imperative to use St. John's Canons, which were governed by a spirit of leniency greater than that of the ancient Fathers.[33] St. Nikodemos was also aware that the Faster was reproached for the small number of years that he prescribed for abstinence from Communion.[34] St. John provided a new yardstick for repentance: he shortened the period of abstinence from the Mystery of the divine Eucharist,[35] but he laid greater emphasis on the ascetical dimension, something which, for reasons that are easy to understand, Hesychasts like St. Nikodemos upheld. The Saint offers a masterly explanation of this shift in the Church's pastoral practice[36]; along with the Faster, he emphasizes an ascetical rule (*kanon*), which, more than anything else, keeps the penitent in a state of constant vigilance and guides him towards true repentance. There is thus a continuity between the category of mourners (penitents) that existed in Christian antiquity and those Faithful who put into practice and fulfill the ascetical rule given to them. The method changes, but the same spirit is preserved, a spirit which, in both cases, governs the process of repentance and the restoration of the believer to good standing in the Church.

2. *The ideas expressed in the* Exomologetarion *are at odds with the anti-Pietistic tendency that prevails in our day.*[37] The attempt to overstate the admittedly pernicious spirit of Pietism[38] little helps those who ardently apply their anti-Pietistic criteria to approach the work of St. Nikodemos with purely

---

32   *Ibid.*, p. 131, n. 142. See also his introductory remarks on St. John the Faster and his Canons (pp. 171-173).

33   *Ibid.*, p. 142.

34   *Ibid.*, p. 169, n. 213.

35   *Ibid.*, and pp. 173-174, n. 215. St. Nikodemos writes: "As I see it, the reason why the Fathers only prescribed abstinence from Communion as a penance for sinners is because the Christians of those times had such a desire to commune, that they thought it the worst possible thing to be deprived of Communion. For this reason, then, the Fathers of those times had nothing better with which to deter them from sin than the deprivation of Communion" p. 175, n. 215.

36   *Ibid.*, pp. 172-173, n. 214 (the subject of ecclesiastical *oikonomia* or economy).

37   See Yannaras, *Orthodoxia kai Dyse* (*Orthodoxy and the West*)

38   Regarding the essence of Pietism, see the important discussion by Chrestos Yannaras in his book *He eleutheria tou ethous* (Athens, 1979), 2nd rev. ed., pp. 151ff. (ET: *The*

Orthodox ecclesiological criteria. Somewhere along the line, a delicate balance is lost. At the same time, an evaluation of his works that proceeds from a realm in which asceticism takes priority leads to views that are at times equally hyperbolic; such views constitute a challenge from the right. Thus, two diametrically opposed assessments have been formulated.

The second view is expressed by the venerable Elder of blessed memory, Father Theokletos of Dionysiou.[39] "St. Nikodemos distinguishes himself," according to Father Theokletos, "as a confessor of rare talent... In this book, he proves to be an expert interpreter of the penances prescribed by the Sacred Canons, a truly Patristic preacher of repentance... He is so gentle and compunctionate in his exposition of the Mystery of repentance, confession, and forgiveness that he arouses those who are indifferent towards this Mystery to repentance and confession."[40] The first view is set forth by Professor Chrestos Yannaras,[41] who summarizes his critique of St. Nikodemos as follows: "It is, rather, inevitable that an ever-increasing number of people should sever their ties with the Church after just one experience of a traumatic confession based on the principles of a juridical transaction"[42] – and he has in mind, here, the *Exomologetarion* of St. Nikodemos. He concludes: "The God of Augustine, Anselm, and Nikodemos, the God Who terrorizes us with His sadistic demands for

---

Freedom of Morality, Crestwood, 1984, pp. 119ff). In theological terms, the author quite rightly calls Pietism a heresy in the realm of ecclesiology.

39   From his book *Hagios Nikodemos ho Hagioreites* (see n. 2).

40   *Ibid.*, p. 181.

41   See n. 2.

42   Yannaras, *Orthodoxia kai Dyse*, p. 206.

justice, is of no interest to humanity."[43] These opinions are shared by others, too.[44] How is one to respond to them?

It is undeniable that the language of the *Exomologetarion* appears intensely scholastic at many points, and this is something that cannot be overlooked.[45] Academic theology in our day has largely recovered its Orthodox identity – primarily in linguistic terms – and its style has been purged of scholastic influences; as such, it views the language of the *Exomologetarion* as repulsive and offensive. However, we should not forget that every artifact is a product of its era and embodies the characteristics of that era. The *Exomologetarion*,

---

43   *Ibid.* And he adds: "It cannot be proved, but it is reasonable to suppose that the juridical mentality of the *Exomologetarion* and the *Pedalion* – which has spread very rapidly, like a plague, in the pastoral practice of the Greek Church – was one of the reasons for the manifestation, even in Greece, of a reaction, at all levels of society, against religion, or secularization, as it is called, whereby great masses of the population cut themselves off from the life of the Church; this does not necessarily betoken their acceptance of atheistic ideas, but rather, an entrenched indifference towards all metaphysical problems, a transformation in the religious identity of the masses" (p. 206). In response to this it should be pointed out that the spirit of indifferentism, which Yannaras equates with secularization, was introduced by way of the Enlightenment and does not owe its origins to the works of St. Nikodemos, of which the proponents of the Enlightenment [in Greece – *Trans.*] were totally ignorant. All those who allowed themselves to be influenced by Pietism – whether positively or negatively – in studying the *Exomologetarion* and other related works did so because they were lacking in Orthodox criteria and attempted to interpret St. Nikodemos with purely Western criteria (deriving from the Enlightenment or from Pietism), being complete strangers to the ascetical (Neptic) tradition of Orthodoxy.

44   Prof. Chrestos Patrinelis, for example, in the *Historia tou Hellenikou Ethnous* (*History of the Greek Nation*), Athens edition (1975), Vol. XI, p. 132, observes: "It is difficult, therefore, to regard the teaching of the *Kollyvades* in its entirety as a ray of Orthodox spirituality, as it is often called. Furthermore, the *pietistic* and *casuistic* character of the popular works by Nikodemos, the *Exomologetarion* (1794) and the *Pedalion* (1800), are scarcely consistent with the mystical [*sic*] spirit." We have here, unfortunately, a clear confusion between Pietism (moralism) and the ascetical-Neptic tradition of Orthodoxy, something that is evident from the author's use of the term mystical instead of spiritual (Fr. John Romanides correctly suggests that we Orthodox make a distinction between mystical and secret). Orthodox Patristic spirituality has nothing in common with the mysticism of Neoplatonism.

45   See the communiqué of the Holy Community of the Holy Mountain, entitled, *"Anairesis ton peplanemenon theseon tou k. Chr. Giannara peri tou en hagiois Patros emon Nikodemou tou Hagioreitou"* (*A Refutation of the Erroneous Views of Mr. C. Yannaras Concerning our Father among the Saints Nikodemos the Hagiorite*), *Orthodoxos Martyria*, No. 40 (1993), pp. 2-10. The authors of this important document boldly aver: "...if certain expressions reminiscent of Scholastic theology, for historical reasons that are easy to understand, *inadvertently* slipped into his work, these in no way affect the generally Orthodox outlook and tenor of his work...."

too, is a product of the ecclesiastical idiom that was in vogue during the period of the Turkish domination,[46] and it echoes both the climate in which it was written and its Western influences,[47] reformulating the Tradition of the Church with the means provided by that period. This is all the more so because such a work was intended for a broad *stratum* of the people and was couched in terms that they could understand. However, we should not confuse language with the spirit of Holy Tradition, which is preserved, not simply by language and intellectual expressions, but above all by the practice of asceticism and the entire spiritual struggle. St. Nikodemos, despite the language of the *Exomologetarion* and other related works of his, is faithful to the Hesychastic tradition and is a successor to St. Gregory Palamas, by virtue of the ascetical experience to which he fully adhered.

Additionally, it is a fact, overlooked by the critics of St. Nikodemos, that his affinity with the juridical Western theory of satisfaction[48] is only a matter of terminology, and it is this terminological resemblance that allows such critics to put forth their familiar, but superficial, equation of his view with the Western view. Linguistically speaking, of course, the correspondence is easy to demonstrate. St. Nikodemos talks about an infinite offense, an eternal recompense, the gratification of divine righteousness, the wrath of God, and the like: "Do you wish to understand, sinner, the *infinite offense* that sin is against God? Understand it by the *infinite payment* that the Son of God made because of it, with so many sufferings and such a disgraceful

---

46   Angelo Amatos work (see n. 2) provides samples of this idiom, with particular reference to the practical aspect of Confession.

47   Regarding these influences and their magnitude, see the *Procs-Verbaux du premier Congrs de Thologie Orthodoxe Athnes (29 Nov.-6 Dc. 1936)* (*Proceedings of the First Congress on Orthodox Theology in Athens (29 Nov.- 6 Dec. 1936)*) (Athens, 1939) (especially the papers delivered by Chrysostomos Papadopoulos, Constantine Dyobouniotis, and Georges Florovsky), and the study by John Karmiris, *Logoi peri ton exoterikon epidraseon epi ten Orthodoxon Theologian* (*Discourses Concerning Foreign Influences on Orthodox Theology*) (Athens, 1938).

48   For the substance of this theory, see the entry by Nicholas Matsoukas in the *Threskeutike kai Ethike Egkyklopaideia* (Athens, 1965), Vol. VI, cols. 857-858. Matsoukas states in this article that the writings of Tertullian and Cyprian already contain references to the satisfaction of divine righteousness through human works (*satisfacere Deo*).

death."[49] And elsewhere: "According to the theologians, sin is infinite[50]; and as an offense to the infinite God,[51] no finite creature, especially an impure creature like a sinner, by works or by fulfilling a rule, can be loosed from it."[52] And there are many other similar expressions in the same vein.

Mortal sins, St. Nikodemos writes in another place, render one who commits them an enemy of God and liable to everlasting death in Hell.[53] Sin does not bring harm (only) to the sinner, but also to God.[54] Thus, God becomes a punisher and an avenger in order to restore order where it has been disturbed: "For the impartial righteousness of God is not pleased by any other means than by the very person who sinned, and for that person to be chastised."[55] Penances (that is, penitential canons or rules of prayer) are a small punishment whereby the penitent appeases the great wrath that God has towards him.[56]

Admittedly, if these phrases are detached from their context, they immediately take on a cruel, sadistic character, overturning the theology of divine love which permeates the spirit of Orthodox (ecclesiastical) soteriology (see Jn. 3:16, Rom. 5:8, etc.). For this reason, it is necessary to place them in the entire context of St. Nikodemos' thought and activity.

Now, if we study the *Exomologetarion* as a whole and put these phrases in its more general theological and pastoral context, we are easily led to a diametrically opposed understanding of them. The term *satisfaction* occurs very frequently in this work of St. Nikodemos,[57] but it has no connection

---

49   *Exomologetarion*, p. 283.
50   He means Orthodox theologians during the Turkish domination.
51   Only in this way does sin acquire infinite significance!
52   *Exomologetarion*, p. 140.
53   *Ibid.*, p. 67.
54   *Ibid.*, p. 245.
55   *Ibid.*, p. 261.
56   *Ibid.*, p. 259.
57   *Ibid.*, pp. 106, 141, 263-265, etc. For a history of the usage of this term, see Fr. B. Kalliakmanis, *"He didaskalia peri hikanopoieseos tes theias dikaiosynes neoellenike theologia"* (*The Teaching Concerning the Satisfaction of Divine Righteousness in Modern Greek Theology*), *Gregorios Palamas*, Vol. LXXI (1988), pp. 529-537. *Cf.* Fr. George D. Metallinos, *"He 'peri hikanopoieseos tes theias dikaiosynes' didaskalia kai he neoellenike katechetike kai keryktike praxe"* (*The*

with the vindictive attitude of some inexorable divine Judge; it has, rather, to do with the rule assigned to the penitent.[58] The meaning of the term is defined by the author himself as follows: It is the actual *fulfillment* of the rule given by the Spiritual Father. That is, it does not refer to any sadistic authority figure, but indicates the good pleasure and joy (loving satisfaction) of God over the fulfillment of a rule (the taking of ones spiritual medicine in its totality) by the spiritually ailing penitent, just as every doctor rejoices when his patient completes the treatment that he (the doctor) has prescribed. In other words, whereas the Western spirit consists in the vindictive demand on the part of God for the restoration of His wounded dignity, here the love of God is made manifest in the cure of His ailing child. After spending many anguished days examining the relevant passages, I have come to the conclusion that the idea of satisfaction (*hikanopoiesis*), in the *parlance* of St. Nikodemos, corresponds to the notion of being well-pleasing (or acceptable) and its cognates (*euarestein, euarestesis, euarestein to Theo*), which are very commonly encountered in ecclesiastical texts (*cf.* "[W]ithout faith [total self-surrender] it is impossible to please [God]" (Heb. 11:6); "For he that in these things serveth Christ is acceptable to God, and approved of men" (Rom. 14:18)). With regard to the sacrifice of Jesus Christ, the term *satisfaction* expresses what is meant by the Gospel phrase: "This is my beloved Son, in Whom I am well pleased" (Matt. 3:17, etc.). Aside from this, it is inconceivable, to put it mildly, that anyone – and especially a theologian – could accept that St. Nikodemos, who was very Patristic and Orthodox in his other works, was caught up in Western error in his *Exomologetarion* and elsewhere!

Moreover, it is significant that the Saint draws, in the *Exomologetarion*, not on Western sources, but on the work *Peri Mysterion* (*Concerning the Mysteries*), by Gabriel Severos of Philadelphia, an authoritative theologian from the

---

Teaching Concerning the Satisfaction of Divine Righteousness and Modern Greek Catechetical and Homiletic Practice), in *Logos hos Antilogos. Theologika dokimia* (*Thesis and Antithesis: Theological Essays*) (Athens, 1992), pp. 85-98.

58   *Exomologetarion*, pp. 259-262. See the relevant comments of Fr. Bouloudakis in his book *Orthodoxia kai Chr. Giannaras* (*Orthodoxy and Chrestos Yannaras*) (Athens, 1993), pp. 55ff.

period of the Turkish captivity.[59] In particular, he defines abstinence from divine Communion as the satisfaction of satisfactions,[60] which is a necessary constituent of true repentance.[61] In this context, satisfaction is divided into two aspects: the physical and the spiritual. The physical aspect consists in fasting, the eating of dry food, prostrations, and almsgiving to all and sundry. The spiritual aspect consists in compunctionate prayer.[62] That is to say, satisfaction is consummated within the boundaries of the process of repentance, and when it is put into practice, it takes on a purely spiritual and totally non-juridical character. Furthermore, it can be documented historically that the practical dimension of the Mystery of Repentance was formed by the Church's monastic practice, that is, by her ascetic practice.[63] As a Hesychast, St. Nikodemos remains absolutely faithful to this spirit.

3. *It is from this point on that St. Nikodemos' language begins to diverge from the Western Anselmian tradition.* Western legalism is defined by Chrestos Yannaras as an individualistic effort,[64] as a juridical activity of individual propitiation[65] by the sinner, who stands alone and guilty before an implacable Deity, a just and retributive judge, Who thirsts insatiably for the satisfaction of His righteousness, which human sin has offended.[66] Aroused by the boundless

---

59   *Exomologetarion*, p. 146. The work is entitled *Syntagmation peri ton hagion kai hieron mysterion (Treatise on the Holy and Sacred Mysteries)* (Venice, 1600) (Legrand, *Bibliographie Hellenique*, XVth and XVIth cent., Vol. II, No. 998, p. 328). There is a detailed analysis of this work in Amato, *Il Sacramento della Penitenza*, pp. 59ff. Concerning the author, see Podskalsky, *Griechische Theologie*, pp. 118ff. and *passim* (Greek edition: pp. 167ff.). With regard to his introduction of the term satisfaction, Amato remarks: "Severos bases satisfaction (*hikanopoiesis*) on Scriptural and Patristic teaching" (p. 67), that is to say, it is purely ecclesiastical (Orthodox) in character. We should pay particular attention to this statement by Amato, a Roman Catholic.

60   *I.e.*, the satisfaction *par excellence* (*cf.* the Song of Songs).

61   *Exomologetarion*, p. 264. *Cf.* Amato, *Il Sacramento della Penitenza*, pp. 285ff., 68f. (concerning Gabriel Severos, on whom Nikodemos is drawing).

62   *Exomologetarion*, pp. 133ff.

63   See Fr. John S. Romanides, "Man and His True Life According to the Greek Orthodox Service Book," *The Greek Orthodox Theological Review*, Vol. I (1954), p. 77

64   Yannaras, *Orthodoxia kai Dyse*, p. 201: The pastoral practice of the *Exomologetarion* based unreservedly on the Roman Catholic distortion of the Church's Gospel of salvation.

65   *Ibid.*, p. 203.

66   *Ibid.*, pp. 201-202.

sadism of His wounded ego,[67] God demands the punishment of the sinner. Penances are understood, not as an educative therapy provided by God in His lovingkindness for the healing of the sinner, but as a ransom which the sinner must pay.[68] These tendencies evolved in the framework of turning the true Church into a religion and reducing it to a form of individualistic moralism.[69]

It is impossible to identify St. Nikodemos with this mentality, even if only superficially,[70] for the following reasons: (1) he had no direct contact with Western sources, because at this stage he operated freely within the parameters of hagiographical and Patristic language and tradition; (2) and though his scholastic expressions derive from writers of his era,[71] they take on a purely hagiographical and Patristic meaning. For example, he observes that sin defiles the blood of Christ and insults His grace.[72] However, he accurately quotes Hebrews 10:29: "Of how much sorer punishment, suppose ye, shall he be thought worthy, who hath trodden underfoot the Son of God, and hath counted the blood of the Covenant, wherewith he was sanctified, an unholy thing, and hath done despite unto the Spirit of Grace?" Corresponding to the participle "treading underfoot" (the Son of God) is the application to God of the verb "to harm,"[73] in which his aim is to make

---

67   *Ibid.*, p. 202.

68   *Ibid.*, p. 203.

69   *Ibid.*, p. 209.

70   See Bouloudakis, *Orthodoxia kai Chr. Giannaras*, and especially his comments on St. Nikodemos (pp. 46ff., 68ff.); also, pp. 237ff., where he quite rightly emphasizes the spiritual unanimity of Sts. Nikodemos and Cosmas Aitolos.

71   *E.g.*, Gabriel Severos, George Koressios [a *savant*, physician, and theologian from Chios who flourished during the second half of the 16th century and the first half of the 17th century—*Trans.*], and Orthodox *Confessions* from the 17th century, etc.

72   *Exomologetarion*, p. 244.

73   *Ibid.* Human sin is ascribed to God because it cuts man off from communion with God. *Cf.* "Against Thee only have I sinned and done this evil before Thee" (Psalm 50:4), and also the prayer from the Kneeling Service at Pentecost, which is an expansion of this Psalm verse: "Against Thee only do we sin, but Thee alone do we worship...."

clear to the people, in their own everyday language, the gravity of sin, and especially of mortal sin.

Furthermore, when he writes that sin is forgiven through the infinite satisfaction of Christ's sacrifice,[74] he faithfully renders Titus 3:5: "Not by works of righteousness which we have done, but according to His mercy He saved us, by the washing of regeneration," which is parallel to I John 1:7, "...and the blood of Jesus Christ His Son cleanseth us from all sin;" in addition, Christ is "He Who taketh away the sin of the world (Jn. 1:29) – or, as St. Basil the Great puts it, "the forgiveness of sins is by the blood of Christ."[75]

St. Nikodemos wishes, hereby, precisely to avoid a twofold danger: (1) that the sinner be led into quaking with guilt and the threat of condemnation,[76] or (2) that he form the impression that a rule, in and of itself, leads one to salvation. Forestalling similar superficial assurances, he teaches that sins are not forgiven through performing our rule, but through the mercy of God and through the satisfaction (i.e., the blood) of Jesus Christ.[77] "God also punished sin in the Person of Jesus Christ with such a severe punishment, that all of the abovementioned punishments seem as but a shadow in comparison to it..."[78] The purpose of these words, formulated in such a way that ordinary people could understand them, is to show how important the sacrifice of Jesus Christ is and to dissociate the idea of a rule from any demand for recompense,[79] making the Faithful aware of the fact that an ascetical rule simply makes a man receptive to God's grace, by opening him

---

74   *Exomologetarion*, p. 140.
75   *Regulæ Brevius* 13, PG 31, 1089C. Even the description of carnal sin, which, at first sight, is reminiscent of a Scholastic penitential (*Exomologetarion*, p. 181, n. 225), is based on Patristic precedents (pp. 230-231).
76   Yannaras, *He eleutheria tou ethous*, p. 246.
77   *Exomologetarion*, p. 140.
78   *Ibid.*, p. 298.
79   "These good works, however, are not to be understood as natural in and of themselves... but inasmuch as they are united through faith with the supranatural grace of Jesus Christ, which brings them about and effects them and makes them worthy of divine acceptance" (p. 142). Inward faith, as this is understood in the *Philokalia*, endows deeds with salvific potential. A believer fulfills his rule in order to attain to divine grace.

up to it.[80] This is precisely what he means when he exhorts the sinner to propitiate divine righteousness with this temporal rule[81]: a man must become receptive to grace.

The use of the terms *wrath, chastisement, enemy of God, wrath of God, guilty, punishment,* and the like, is free, in the work of St. Nikodemos, from any juridical purport and makes it easy for readers to approach his teaching, which rests on firm hagiographical and Patristic foundations. We do not need to cite actual examples of every term. For the sake of argument, we will confine ourselves to a single passage from St. Gregory of Nyssa concerning the controversial term *punishment*: "As each shall receive his wages, just as the Apostle says (1 Cor. 3:14), according to his labor, so also each shall receive punishment according to the extent of their negligence."[82] This idiom, moreover, is customary in ecclesiastical worship and is therefore familiar to a believer who loves the divine services. Let us recall that the Prayer of Manasseh, King of Judah[83] is linguistically at odds with the Prayer of St. Basil the Great,[84] even though both are read at Great Compline. And these are certainly not the only examples.

4. *Any anachronistic hermeneutical approach to the* Exomologetarion, *and to St. Nikodemos more generally, does an injustice to the Saint and his theology.* I have already said that the language of the *Exomologetarion* is repugnant to today's believer; but it is all the more repugnant to one who moves on the fringes of the Church's life and experience. In this work, the Saint operates within the soteriological framework of the Church, in the spirit of the *Philokalia*. It is inadmissible to compartmentalize his personality, which remains forever

---

80   See Fr. George D. Metallinos, *Latreia kai askese* (*Worship and Ascesis*), in press. *Cf. idem, Theologike martyria tes ekklesiastikes latreias* (*The Theological Testimony of Ecclesiastical Worship*) (Athens, 1996), 2nd ed., pp. 184ff.

81   *Exomologetarion*, p. 261.

82   *Contra Eunomium* 12, PG 45, 912C. *Exomologetarion*, p. 72.

83   "Unbearable is the wrath of Thy threatening toward sinners; because I have provoked Thine anger; destroy me not with mine iniquities, neither in enmity for ever keep mine evils, nor condemn me to the nethermost parts of the earth."

84   "O Lord, O Lord, Who hast delivered us from every arrow that flieth by day..."

integrated, unified, and inseparable, in keeping with the Neptic tradition
of Orthodoxy (the prayer of the heart).[85]

St. Nikodemos' sole purpose is to make man aware of the essence of
sin and its devastating power, since it jeopardizes his very salvation, depriving
him of God's grace and, thereby, of the capacity for adoption into divine
sonship.[86] The true Gospel (Good News) is described by St. Nikodemos as
adoption into sonship: It is a special and distinctive gift and a charisma so
sublime that it makes the Holy Spirit dwell in you; He is present in you
and acts in you in a way that is peculiar and distinct from His presence and
activity in all other places, because He makes man a son of God and an
heir of His kingdom.[87] It is for this reason that St. Nikodemos wishes to
make man hate sin[88] (hate and abhor sin).[89] Hence, he covers every possible
shade of sin in his analysis of the *Decalogue* and, of course, those that are
most common in any age, such as sins of the flesh. Thereby, the Saint
presents the struggling believer of his time with a spiritual mirror, although
it is necessary that one be aware (and this includes the Spiritual Father, too)
of what the illnesses of the soul, that is, sins, are, so that he may know how
to cure them.[90] This is a matter, therefore, not of Latin casuistry, but rather
of a medical diagnosis that is the necessary prerequisite for any cure.[91]

Consequently, the author does not offer an impersonal legal code[92] but
a classification of spiritual diseases, so that a spiritual Father might determine
an appropriate prescription. St. Nikodemos always has in view the ideal
of the authentic Christian and how a penitent can attain to this ideal. A

---

85   The discussion of the Prayer of the Heart occupies a central place in the
Exomologetarion (pp. 97ff).

86   This is also the case in *Unseen Warfare*. See Bouloudakis, *Orthodoxia kai Chr.
Giannaras*, pp. 73ff.

87   *Exomologetarion*, pp. 245-246.

88   *Cf.* Monk Theokletos, *Hagios Nikodemos ho Hagioreites*, p. 185: "In this work, he is
at pains to persuade Christians to detest sin, sometimes through fear of punishment, and
at other times through the promise of good things in eternity."

89   *Exomologetarion*, p. 239.

90   *Ibid.*, p. 66.

91   Angelo Amato observes that Nikodemos combines a juridical scheme with a
therapeutic scheme (*Il Sacramento della Penitenza*, pp. 288f.).

92   As Yannaras admits (*Orthodoxia kai Dyse*, p. 205).

Christian who does not live a Christian life is not a Christian, he observes,[93] basing himself on the Fathers.[94] Nikodemos has no patience[95] for the idea of a Christian committing mortal sins; which is to say, this is, for the Saint, intolerable! Indeed, he trembles at the mere thought of it. Thus, he does not offer half measures in the war against sin, but very drastic measures. And there is no measure more drastic than *ascesis*, that is, the spiritual struggle, which is laid down and conveyed by the Tradition of the Church. One who is a Christian only intellectually, and does not cultivate asceticism, cannot understand the spirit of St. Nikodemos, since the Saint regards as legendary the defining characteristics of asceticism, which correspond to the experience of the monastic Saints (*e.g.*, St. Gerasimos, *et al.*).[96]

As we have already said, St. Nikodemos emphasizes the authority of St. John the Faster, because, in place of lengthy abstinence from divine Communion, he puts the weight of repentance on the rule (on satisfaction). St. Nikodemos underscores in particular the importance of the ascetical rule, because he wants to help the Faithful to approach divine Communion more frequently[97] without trivializing the Mystery in such a way that it

---

93   *Exomologetarion*, p. 284.

94   St. Athanasios: "A Christian is a true rational house of Christ, consisting of good works and correct dogmas" (*Liber de Definitionibus*, PG 28, 549C) (*Exomologetarion*, p. 284, n. 409); St. Nikodemos also cites other Patristic views.

95   *Exomologetarion*, p. 284.

96   It is, therefore, a very serious mistake to adduce the *Epistle to Diognetos* (Yannaras, *Orthodoxia kai Dyse*, pp. 208-209) in order to prove that St. Nikodemos supposedly deviated from the ancient Tradition of the Church. The spirit and tone of this text are absolutely identical to those of St. Nikodemos. The following phrase, "Christians are known to be in the world, but their godliness remains invisible" (VI.4) is to be interpreted historically and ecclesiologically: only their presence in society is known, but not their way of life. The term godliness (*theosebeia*) is completely identical to St. Paul's phrase to live in a godly manner (*eusebos zen*), with its ascetical and Neptic connotations. (*Cf*. "But I keep under my body, and bring it into subjection, lest by any means, when I have preached to others, I myself should be rejected" (I Cor. 9:27).) The same idea is contained in the phrase, "[T]hey surpass the laws by their own lives...They pass their days on earth, but they are citizens of Heaven" (V.10, 9; *cf*. Phil. 3:20). Ignorance of this spirit leads us to misinterpret the *Exomologetarion* and confirms our alienation [from the authentic Tradition of the Church—*Trans.*]. *Cf*. the comments of Fr. Bouloudakis on this point (*Orthodoxia kai Chr. Giannaras*, pp. 246f.).

97   This is evident from his work *Peri synechous theias metalepseos* (*Concerning Continual Divine Communion*) (Venice, 1777). Regarding the problem of the authorship of this work, see Podskalsky, *Griechische Theologie*, pp. 372f (Greek edition: pp. 461f). Nikodemos revised

loses its significance and place in the life of the Church. Indeed, the Jesuit Gerhard Podskalsky, in his assessment of the *Exomologetarion*, observes that its author is concerned, not only with the validity, but at the same time with the most fruitful possible reception of the Mysteries.[98] That is to say, we should avoid communing unworthily (I Cor. 11:27-29).[99]

Consequently, any attempt to interpret the sacred Canons in legalistic or moralistic categories is foreign to St. Nikodemos.[100] The penances, the satisfaction, and the rule imposed by a Spiritual Father are not, in the end, a punishment or a chastisement, but, as he points out, entail one's salvation. And here[101] he cites the divine Chrysostom, who writes: "These laws, then, of philanthropy let us learn also (which law of love Paul used on the fornicator). For if thou seest a horse hurrying down a precipice, thou appliest a bit and holdest him in with violence and lashest him frequently; although this is punishment, yet the punishment itself is the mother of safety. Thus act also in the case of those that sin. Bind him that hath transgressed until he have propitiated God; let him not go loose, that he be not bound the faster by the anger of God. If I bind, God doth not chain; if I bind not, the indissoluble chains await him. 'For if we judged ourselves, we should not be judged' (1 Cor. 11:31). Think not, then, that thus to act cometh of cruelty and inhumanity; nay, but of the highest gentleness and the most skillful leechcraft and of much tender care."[102]

This passage from St. John Chrysostom is, I believe, the key to understanding and vindicating St. Nikodemos' language, too. The Mystery of repentance, in all of its workings – as the Church's pastoral mechanism

---

and expanded the Venice edition of 1783. For the spiritual content of this work, see Monk Theokletos, *Hagios Nikodemos ho Hagioreites*, pp. 108ff.

98   *Griechische Theologie*, p. 380.

99   On this subject, see Metallinos, *Theologike martyria*, pp. 274ff.

100   According to the aforementioned communiqué of the Holy Community of the Holy Mountain (n. 45), St. Nikodemos lies, as do all of the Godbearing Fathers, between two extremes; that is, between a legalistic understanding of the Gospel versus antinomianism and between moralism versus moral license, which extremes alienate the Christian from salvation in Christ.

101   *Exomologetarion*, pp. 262-263, n. 374.

102   *On II Corinthians*, Homily 14, 3, PG 61, 502.

par excellence –, presents many parallels to medical science, in terms of its language and methods. It is the means by which the Church effects cures, and for this reason it functions in a manner as practical as surgery. To be sure, this kind of language does not belong in a mission to those outside the Church, nor is it suitable for use with neophytes who have not entered into the Church's spiritual life, since the results would be rather negative.[103] It is, however, the proper language for dealing with sinners who are conscious of the life of the Church and who sincerely seek to be readmitted into the body of the Church. In them, such language engenders joyful sorrow (*charmolype*). They feel sorrow and fear, for they are unworthy because of sin, but joy, on account of their salvation.[104]

The most important point, however, is that the *Exomologetarion* functions within the framework of the Church and orients the believer, not towards some individual justification, but towards readmittance into the life of the Church. Only through ascetical *praxis*, as an endeavor within the realm of this Mystery (and, consequently, one that is centered on the Church), can the believer become receptive to grace, and this grace is imparted by the Mystery of the Church. The *Exomologetarion* is not without an ecclesiological perspective, for it greets man in the narthex of the Church, in order to lead him to the Holy of Holies. Spiritual Fathers, according to St. Nikodemos, are those physicians and innkeepers whom the Lord established, in keeping with the Gospel parable, in the inn of the Church to care for the sick; that is, those sinners who are wounded by the noetic thieves, namely, the demons.[105] The *Exomologetarion* always presupposes the Church. She is the mother [of the believer]...who delivered the Faith to him.[106] Moreover, it frequently mentions the Saints, the angels, and especially the Theotokos, into whose fellowship the repentant sinner is reincorporated. The author does not neglect to remind us of the category of mourners, that is, the

---

103   On this point Prof. Yannaras is right.
104   *Doxastikon* of the Praises, Feast of the Universal Elevation of the Precious Cross, September 14.
105   *Exomologetarion*, p. 55.
106   *Ibid.*, p. 134.

penitents of the early centuries of Christianity,[107] who attest to the Church's abiding penitential practice.

Accordingly, the penitent is called to an awareness that he belongs to a society that is not worldly or secularized, but ecclesiastical. For this reason, in his interpretation of the Canons, St. Nikodemos often explains them in social terms. These explanations impress us even today by their progressiveness,[108] and they also liberate the penitent from any individualistic notion of himself. Thus, ascetical satisfaction becomes an ecclesiastical event and an act of communion.[109]

---

107   *Ibid.*, p. 172, n. 216 and p. 173-174.

108   *E.g*: "One who has forced his children to marry also errs in this commandment (the fifth), or has forced them to become monastics or put them in another state against their will" (*Exomologetarion*, p. 78, n. 37), "or did not teach them letters or some craft" (*ibid.*). He affirms and reprints the classic example from Romanitis' *Ho Pneumatikos Didaskomenos* (pp. 31f.) about the unsophisticated, but discerning, Spiritual Father and the king, who, when he had confessed his sins, told his spiritual Father, "I don't have anything else to say to you." "How so, O King?" replied the Elder. "How so? Have we finished your confession? No. You have told me the sins of Alexios (calling him by his personal name), if I may so put it; come now, tell me the sins of the King." By these words, this wise Spiritual Father wished to show that every ruler and leader, whether foreign or domestic, should not confess only as if he were a private individual, or be examined by a spiritual Father as a simple layman; but beyond the sins that he has committed as a man, he should also confess all of the good things which he could, as a ruler, have done for his people, but did not do, and all the bad things which happened to his subjects because of him, but which he did not correct, for which he will have to give an exact accounting to God (pp. 31-32).

109   Yannaras, *He Eleutheria tou Ethous,* p. 140.

ABBREVIATIONS

ACW   Ancient Christian Writers, Westminster, MD, 1946ff.

ANF   Ante-Nicene Fathers, Grand Rapids, MI, 2001.

Ascetical Homilies   *The Ascetical Homilies of Saint Isaac the Syrian*, Holy Transfiguration Monastery, Boston, MA, 1984.

CWS   The Classics of Western Spirituality, Mahwah, NJ.

GrPhilokalia   *Philokalia of the Sacred Neptic Fathers*, ed. St. Nikodemos the Hagiorite and St. Makarios Notaras, Venice, 1782.

The Ladder   *The Ladder of Divine Ascent*: Saint John Climacus, Holy Transfiguration Monastery, Boston, MA, 2001.

NPNF   Nicene and Post-Nicene Fathers of the Church, Grand Rapids, MI, 1979.

PG   Patrologia Graeca, ed. J.-P. Migne, Paris, 1857ff.

The Philokalia   *The Philokalia*: The Complete Text, trans. and ed. G. E. H. Palmer, P. Sherrard, K. Ware, London and Boston, 1979 (volume I), 1981 (volume II), 1984 (volume III), 1995 (volume IV).

SC   Sources Chrétiennes, Paris, 1941ff.

Ὁ ΕΝ ΜΟΝΑΧΟΙΣ ΔΙΔΑΣΚΑΛΟΣ ΝΙΚΟΔΗΜΟΣ ΑΓΙΟΡΕΙΤΗΣ, Ο ΕΚ ΤΗΣ ΝΗΣΟΥ ΝΑΞΟΥ, ΕΤΩΝ ξ΄. ΑΝΕΠΑΥΘΗ ΕΝ ΚΥΡΙΩ ΕΝ ΕΤΕΙ ͵αωθ΄, ΕΝ ΜΗΝΙ ΙΟΥΛΙΩ, ιδ΄. ✝

„ Τίς Νικόδημος ὗτος ὗ κλέος μέγα;
„ Ἐν ὀρδοδόξοις κὴ σοφοῖ; Ὅρ8ς Ἄδω;
„ Ὅς τήν δε βίβλον εὐφυῶς τάξεν φίλε;
„ Νάξιος ἀνήρ. εὖγε τῆς εὐφυΐας!

Ἀντεγράφη διὰ χειρός Φωτί8 Κόντογλ8 Κυδωνιέως.

͵αλμγ΄

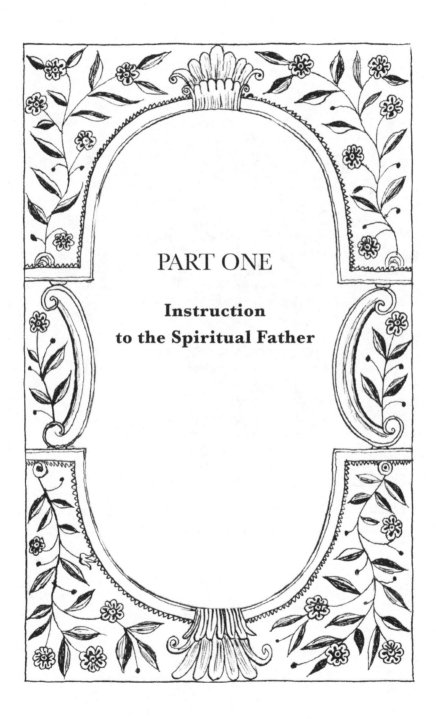

PART ONE

Instruction
to the Spiritual Father

"Brethren, if a man be overtaken in a fault, ye which are spiritual, restore such an one in the spirit of meekness"

(Gal. 6:1)

TO THE MOST REVEREND
SPIRITUAL FATHERS IN CHRIST
WITH FILIAL VENERATION

Inasmuch as the distinction of the Spiritual Father is great, so also is great labor required of him, so that from him may be produced beneficial results and fruit.

Indeed the Spiritual Father has received successively from the sacred and Spiritbearing Apostles the authority to bind and to loose the sins of men, according to the pronouncement of the Lord: "Whose soever sins ye remit, they are remitted unto them; and whose soever sins ye retain, they are retained" (Jn. 20:23), which authority is only proper to God Himself: "Who can forgive sins but God only?" (Mk. 2:7). It is, however, also necessary for Spiritual Fathers to labor in order to learn which sins must be loosed and which must be bound, as the Chief Apostle Peter said to Clement: "Bind what must be bound, and loose what must be loosed."[1] Having become mediators between God and men, they have reconciled, that is, brought men to friendship with God; but it is necessary for them to know exactly the manner and the science of this reconciliation, as blessed Paul said: "God was in Christ... and hath committed unto us the word of reconciliation" (2 Cor. 5:19). These are the physicians and those innkeepers which the Lord appointed to the inn of the Church, according to the parable of the Gospel (Lk. 10:25-37), in order to care for the sick, that is, those sinners who are wounded by the noetic thieves, the demons. But it is also necessary that they know which wounds need to be cauterized, which need to be incised, and which need to be wrapped in a cast, and upon

---

1   Epistola Clementis ad Jacobum 2, PG 2, 36B.

which ones to pour the wine and severity, and upon which ones to apply the oil and gentleness.

It has truly been afforded to Spiritual Fathers to be judges, judging the Christian people of the Lord; but it has also been afforded to them to scrutinize matters with much inquiry, in order to find through these judgments the hidden truth and that which is right, so that they may not happen to perform unjust judgment on account of partiality toward someone, or because of ignorance or some other passion, and so that which divine Paul said may be fulfilled in them: "But he that is spiritual judgeth all things, yet he himself is judged of no man" (1 Cor. 2:15).

To them it has been given to be like hunters, as the Prophet Jeremiah most appropriately calls them: "And after will I send for many hunters, and they shall hunt them... out of the holes of the rocks" (Jer. 16:16); and to be like the priests of the Old Law who cleansed the lepers: "Go shew yourselves unto the priests" (Lk. 17:14). And it has been given to them to know many skills and to perform great labors, so that they may be able to hunt among the forests and the thickets the sins of the unfortunate sinners and to take great care, so as to be able to discern which leprosy, that is, which sin is mortal and which is pardonable, which is to some degree a sin and which not at all, which is superficial and which is deeply rooted.

In brief, Spiritual Fathers have been appointed shepherds and herdsmen over the rational sheep of Christ. However, it is also necessary for them to shed much sweat, ascending the mountains, descending into the valleys, running and searching here and there, in order to find the stray sheep, the sinner, which is ensnared by the devil, and finding it, placing it upon their shoulders in order to offer it saved unto the Arch-shepherd Christ, as a most precious gift, according to the saying: "All that are round about Him shall bring gifts" (Ps. 75:10).

Therefore, in order that we may assist in this great labor of the Spiritual Fathers, we have taken care to bring together herein from various teachers the present concise and practical Instruction, and through it to facilitate whatever difficulty they will encounter in the work of their spiritual vocation. We have also added the Canons of St. John the Faster, explained with meticulousness, and some other things, in order for Spiritual Fathers to be able to place penitents under a rule (*kanon*) according to them.

Receive, therefore, most reverend Spiritual Fathers, with fatherly goodwill this small handbook, and read it and be aided. Do not cease to supplicate God on behalf of those sinful souls who have labored for this collection and composition, and for this publication, unto the common benefit of the Christian people.

Farewell!

The least among monks,
Nikodemos

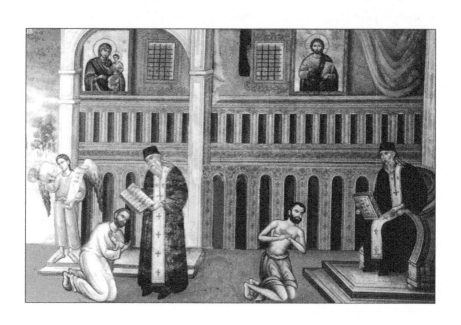

EPIGRAM

FOR THE

PRESENT INSTRUCTION

Rhadamanthys was an example, just as Plouton and Minos,
To the judge of spiritual cases.

Galenos was an example, as Apollo was to Hippocrates,
To the healer of spiritual maladies.

But the judge and healer of spiritual matters is the greatest of these,
Inasmuch as the spirit is greater than the body.

CHAPTER 1

What One Must Possess Before Becoming a Spiritual Father

Concerning the Virtue of the Spiritual Father

First of all, Father, you who intend to become a Spiritual Father, you must have exceptional and incomparable virtue and holiness from that of other men, and even from your fellow priests, from whom you intend to be chosen. And you need to have healed and conquered your passions in order that you may have an especial holiness from the others. For you who would be designated a Spiritual Father must live a spiritual life, being ruled by the grace and discernment of the Holy Spirit, if you wish to have the name of Spiritual Father in truth and in concord with the matter.[1]

Thereby Basil the Great writes emphatically what the Spiritual Father is: "For he, who no longer lives after the flesh, but, being led by the Spirit of God, is called a son of God, being conformed to the image of the Son

---

[1] Take note that there are three types of people found in the world: carnal (σαρκικοί), natural (ψυχικοί), and spiritual (πνευματικοί). The carnal are those who are against nature. The natural are those who are according to nature. The spiritual are those who are above nature. For example, a carnal person is someone who wrongs another; a natural person is someone who neither wrongs another, nor desires to be wronged by others; but a spiritual person is someone who, not only does not wrong another, but when he is wronged by others, endures gladly and does not seek revenge. Concerning these three types the Apostle Paul writes: "For whereas there is among you envying, and strife, and divisions, are ye not carnal, and walk as men?" (1 Cor. 3:3) (Behold the carnal person.) "But the natural man receiveth not the things of the Spirit of God: for they are foolishness unto him: neither can he know them, because they are spiritually discerned" (1 Cor. 2:14) (Behold the natural person.) "He that is spiritual judgeth all things, yet he himself is judged of no man" (1 Cor. 2:15), (that is, by no one who is natural or carnal), but by another spiritual one, as is stated: "Comparing spiritual things with spiritual" (1 Cor. 2:13). (Behold also the spiritual person.)

of God, is called spiritual."[2] While the divine Gregory of Sinai says: "To guide others is not for everyone, but for those who have been given divine discernment, what is called by the Apostle, the 'discernment of spirits' (1 Cor. 12:10), discerning the bad from the good by the sword of the Word."[3]

It is not alone sufficient to merely have a single charisma[4] of the Holy Spirit, but it is necessary for you to ask God that He may double (or may I even say multiply) the charismata of the Holy Spirit, just as Elissaios sought it from Elias: "Let a double portion of thy spirit be upon me" (4 Kg. 2:9), so that with it you may be able to rule both yourself and others. I also said that you, the future Spiritual Father, must have the passions healed and conquered, because if you unjustly seek to heal the passions of others before you have healed your own passions, you will hear the words: "Physician, heal thyself" (Lk. 4:23), and: "A physician of others, himself full of sores,"[5] the reason being, if you truly wish to be an enlightener and perfecter of others, you must first be enlightened and perfected yourself, so as to be able to also enlighten and perfect others. In short, you must first have and then afterward give to others: "For it is right to partake before imparting," as Dionysios the Areopagite says.[6] Lastly, you are to be a type

---

2   *De Spiritu Sancto* 26, SC 17[bis], p. 466.

3   *On Prayer, Philokalia*, Venice, 1782, p. 923. (Translator's note: Hereafter, the original Greek *Philokalia*, compiled by St. Nikodemos and St. Makarios Notaras of Corinth, will be referred to as *GrPhilokalia*, and the English language translation as *The Philokalia*.)

4   Translator's note: Charisma (χάρισμα), and its plural form, charismata (χαρίσματα), have been retained throughout this work to signify the divine grace or spiritual gift(s) of the Holy Spirit bestowed upon an individual (through the Holy Mysteries of the Church) in a unique and personal manner. It has nothing to do with the contemporary definitions, which have lost this original meaning (most dictionaries give such definitions as a powerful or attractive personality, allure, or appeal). See Rom. 12:4-8, 1 Cor. 12:4-13, 2 Tim. 1:6-7.

5   This proverb is cited by Gregory the Theologian in his *Apologetica* (*Oratio* 2, 13, PG 35, 424A).

Translator's note: The Theologian also says in this same work: "It is necessary first to be purified, then to purify; to be made wise, then to make wise; to become light, then to enlighten; to approach God, then to bring others to Him; to be sanctified, then to sanctify" (*Oratio* 2, 71, PG 35, 480B).

6   *De Ecclesiastica Hierarchia* 3, 14, PG 3, 445A; tr. *Pseudo-Dionysius: The Complete Works*, CWS, New York, 1987, p. 223.

Translator's note: St. Dionysios continues: "Whoever wrongfully dares to teach holiness to others before he has regularly practiced it himself is unholy and is a stranger to sacred norms. Just as the

and example of every good and virtue before the eyes of your spiritual children. If you fast, they will also fast; if you are humble, they will also be humble; and generally speaking, if you live modestly and according to Christ, they too will be motivated to live in this manner. If you only say, but do not do, know that they will not listen to your words. They believe more when they see you doing, rather than what they hear coming from your mouth with their ears: "For the eyes," according to the popular proverb, "are more trustworthy than the ears."

Next, you must respond to many dangerous subjects in confession. You will hear so many shameful sins of people and so many disgraces and pollutions on account of their passions. Therefore it is necessary that you are either like an impassible sun, which when passing through filthy places remains unspotted, or like that pure dove of Noah, which when passing over so many grimy bodies of those drowned from the flood did not perch upon any of them, or like a silver or gold wash basin, which washes and cleans the dirtiness of others while none of the dirt sticks to it. This is exactly how Symeon the New Theologian likens the worthy and dispassionate shepherd. Wherefore St. Meletios the Confessor also states how those who are passionate should not lead and be in charge of souls:

"As a lion cannot shepherd sheep,
As it is not befitting for a vulture to shepherd Hermes,
Likewise those who are passionate must not be leaders of souls,
Let it be necessary to present themselves to God free of passions."[7]

If then, being passionate, you seek to be a Spiritual Father, alas! Most certainly, having your intellect darkened from the passions you will not be able to discern the necessary correction which every sinner requires: "Thou hypocrite, first cast out the beam out of thine own eye; and then shalt thou

---

finest and the most luminous of beings are the first to be filled with the sun's rays, and then pass on the superabundant light to others after them, so if God's inspiration and choice have not summoned one to the task of leadership, if one has not yet received perfect and lasting divinization, one must avoid the arrogance of guiding others" (*ibid.*).

7   *Alphabetalphabetos* Degree 171, Thessaloniki, 1923.

see clearly to cast out the mote out of thy brother's eye" (Mt. 7:5). You will not be able to place them under a spiritual rule as is necessary for their good, but you will rather carry out exceedingly light-handed accommodations for those sinners who fall into the same passions as you also have: "For wherein thou judgest another, thou condemnest thyself; for thou that judgest doest the same things" (Rom. 2:1).[8]

You will not be able to turn sinners toward your counsel. Conversely, the sinners will turn you toward them. They will turn you toward their will, but you will not turn them toward your will. This is something which God forbids: "Let them return unto thee; but return not thou unto them" (Jer. 15:19). How much danger, then, and how much damage are brought upon the soul by these things, both to yours and to the penitent's! Who cannot see this?[9]

---

8   On this account we read in *Instructions for Spiritual Fathers* (p. 135), that a Christian once asked a wise man if the same sins exist in various places. The wise man answered him that they do, because God Himself is in various places. Then the Christian said to him, how is it, then, that when I committed the same sins in various places I was penanced in different ways? For when I was in one place, the Spiritual Father there did not reprove me thoroughly concerning drunkenness, but concerning fornication he rebuked me so greatly that the rebuke was sufficient to keep me from that sin. But when I was in another place, the Spiritual Father there did not even give me the slightest admonition concerning fornication, but concerning drunkenness he had much to say, reproving me thoroughly as being sacrilegious, and he gave me a penance. We learn from this that these Spiritual Fathers, with respect to the passions which they themselves had, carried out exceeding accommodation. With respect to the passions which they did not have, they carried out the appropriate reproof.

9   Thus Nikephoros the Archivist, answering questions from a certain Theodosios the Recluse, says: "For in truth, it is perilous to boldly bind and loose those who have fallen into offenses, and not to produce the appropriate medicines for the corresponding passions" (p. 343 of the *Juris Graeco-romanorum*). For this reason Basil the Great also likens the passionate and inept Spiritual Father and shepherd with the inept enchanter who does not know how to take hold of and pacify snakes and beasts, and when seeking to grab them is bitten by them and killed: "Do not undertake to chant as an expert would the incantations pronounced over persons who have been bitten by serpents, inexperienced as you are in the art of weaving spells, lest, perhaps, having attracted the reptiles and being caught fast in their coils, you become powerless to resist them and they destroy you mercilessly" (*De Renuntiatione Saeculi* 4, PG 31, 633B; tr. *Saint Basil: Ascetical Works*, Washington D. C., 1999, p. 21). The Saint says here "mercilessly," because that one is not merciful or compassionate to anyone, and is unworthy, having undertaken by himself to care for souls, as the wise Sirach said: "Who will pity a snake charmer bitten by a serpent, or any who go near wild beasts?" (Sir. 12:13). Symeon the New Theologian says that the passionate

CHAPTER 2

Concerning the Knowledge
of the Spiritual Father

Spiritual Father is like a clay or wooden wash basin which, while washing and cleaning others, is also itself dirtied. So, because the Spiritual Father is also required to be dispassionate, it is difficult to find one who is dispassionate in every place, especially in our generation, therefore the holy hierarchs must at least choose the most elderly and experienced priests to be Spiritual Fathers. These, on account of their age, are the most experienced in knowledge and they have more or less tamed the passions. They should not make young priests Spiritual Fathers on account of their age, being both inexperienced in knowledge and having active and untamed passions, unless only there happens to be found some young priest having virtue in his youth similar to elderly prudence. This one (in my opinion) is not prohibited from becoming a Spiritual Father for, according to Solomon: "Understanding is gray hair for men, and a blameless life is ripe old age" (Wis. 4:9). Some advise that it is safer and better for married priests to become Spiritual Fathers (worthy also in the other aspects, that is), rather than virgins and unmarried hieromonks, because the married have less of a battle with the flesh, the others a greater battle. Joseph Bryennios says that those who are better off financially should become priests, and even Spiritual Fathers, and not those who are poorer, so that they may not have the need to take money from Christians but, rather, give out money themselves (v. 3, ch. 39). St. John of the Ladder complies and says these things to the Shepherd: "There are some men who, beyond their strength, take upon themselves the burden of others by reason of their spiritual love (that is, not on account of vainglory or love of pleasure or greed or some other worldly end), recalling Him Who said, 'Greater than this love no one has, than to give his life for his friends.' But there are others who have perhaps even received from God the power to take spiritual responsibility for other men, yet who do not readily submit themselves to burdens for the sake of the salvation of their brethren. The latter, as ones who do not possess love, I called wretched; but concerning the former, I quoted that which is said somewhere, 'He that bringeth forth the precious from the worthless shall be as My mouth'" (*To the Shepherd*, PG 88, 1189C; tr. *The Ladder of Divine Ascent: Saint John Climacus*, Boston, 2001, p. 240. Translator's note: Hereafter, referred to as *The Ladder*). Again he says in the same book: "I have seen one infirm man, by reason of his faith, heal the infirmity of another infirm man by employing praiseworthy shamelessness before God for his sake, and in humility laying down his soul for that brother's soul; and through the healing of the latter, the former healed his own soul as well. But I have also seen a man who acted in the same manner, but out of pride, and heard these words of censure, 'Physician, heal thyself.'" (*To the Shepherd*, PG 88, 1193B; tr. *The Ladder*, p. 241).
Translator's note: St. Peter of Damaskos says: "If in this present generation no one possesses discernment, it is because no one has the humility that engenders it" (*Twenty-Four Discourses*, GrPhilokalia, p. 667; tr. *The Philokalia*, London, 1984, v. 3, p. 243).

Concerning Knowledge of the Divine Scriptures, of the Dogmas, and of the Sacred Canons

Secondly, you who will be a future Spiritual Father must have an especial knowledge and familiarity of the Old and New Testament beyond that of others; of the dogmas of the faith contained in the Creed; and especially of all the Apostolic, Synodical, and Patristic Canons, which are contained in the *Pedalion* (*The Rudder*). You must be engaged in the study of these day and night, to such an extent that you know them by heart. You should fall asleep reading these, as Alexander the Great did when reading the *Iliad* of Homer, and breathe them at every hour and moment. This is because you will be the ruler of the ship of the Holy Church, and you especially will hold in your hands those Canons, which are as a steering wheel of the Church. Therefore you are required to be trained beforehand in how to turn it and steer it knowledgably, so that at the suitable time, when you become a Spiritual Father, you will be able to liberate those poor sinners from the storm of sin on account of your adept control.[10]

CHAPTER 3

Concerning Mortal Sins, Pardonable Sins, and Sins of Omission

Concerning these you must know that, just as a physician is required to know what the illnesses of the body are in order to treat them, you who seek to be a Spiritual Father are obligated to know what the illnesses of the soul are, that is, sins, in order to treat them. Although the illnesses of the soul are many, they generally fall into the following three categories. Hence, you need to know which are mortal, which are pardonable and not mortal, and which are sins of omission or inaction.

---

10   One teacher said, this is a great thing: Physicians are always engaged in the reading of medical books to find some cure, so that they may prolong the present life of some sick person. Spiritual Fathers, however, either never or grudgingly open a spiritually profitable book in order to learn some cure, and through it give eternal life and salvation to sinners.

1. Concerning Mortal Sins

According to Gennadios Scholarios, George Koressios, the *Orthodox Confession*, and Chrysanthos of Jerusalem, mortal sins are those voluntary sins which either corrupt the love for God alone, or the love for neighbor and for God, and which render again the one committing them an enemy of God and liable to the eternal death of hell.[11] Generally speaking, they are: pride, love of money, sexual immorality, envy, gluttony, anger, and despondency, or indifference.[12]

---

11   Translator's note: St. Mark the Ascetic says: "Because God's righteousness is inescapable, it is hard to obtain forgiveness for sins committed with complete deliberation" (*On the Spiritual Law* 55); and again: "There is a sin which is always 'unto death' (1 Jn. 5:16): the sin for which we do not repent. For this sin even a saint's prayers will not be heard" (*No Righteousness by Works* 41); (*GrPhilokalia*, pp. 93; 102; tr. *The Philokalia*, London, 1979, v. 1, pp. 114; 129). And Elder Sophrony (Sakharov) writes: "Sin cuts us off from the God of Love" (*His Life Is Mine*, Crestwood, 1977, p. 41).

12   Take note that according to the *Orthodox Confession*, Gabriel of Philadelphia, and Nicholas Boulgaris, the effects and offspring of pride are these: vainglory, boasting, conceit, self-esteem, disobedience, scorn, hypocrisy, stubbornness, and others. Those of love of money are: greed, mercilessness or lack of charity, hardness of heart, theft, robbery, deceit, injustice, treachery, perjury, simony, sacrilege, unbelief, and taking interest on money. Those of sexual immorality are: adultery, sodomy, fornication, bestiality, incest, child molestation, virgin molestation, colluctation (Translator's note: An explanation of this word, συγκυλισμός, can be found in the *Interpretation* to Canon 19 of St. John the Faster. It implies the idea of "rolling around," "caressing," or "heavy-petting."), masturbation, insolence, blindness of the intellect, and fearlessness of God. Those of envy are: conspiracy, malice, spite, argumentation, slander, fraud, betrayal, murder, ingratitude, and grief over the good things of the one envied. Those of gluttony are: gormandizing, drunkenness, debauchery, stupor, lewdness, despondency, and others. Those of anger are: blasphemy, hate, remembrance of wrongs, argumentation, perjury, malediction, invectiveness, war, contention, and murder. Those of despondency are: cowardice, effeminacy, grief and indignation over the good that they should be doing, excuses for sins, despair, unbelief, and, in short, apathy and indifference concerning the good which they ought to do. Note also that these mortal sins are considered as passions and habits rooted in the soul, from which are born the above-mentioned offspring. Some of these are worse than others, and some are caused by others, while some are causes of others, as you saw. From gluttony is born gormandizing and despondency, and from these are brought forth various offspring, while others give birth to these same ones, just as both envy and anger give birth to murder and argumentation. Theophylact of Bulgaria says that self-love is the beginning and cause of all evils, wherefore the Apostle placed self-love before the others (Explanation of the verse, "For people shall be lovers of self, lovers of money, etc." 2 Tim. 3:2; PG 125, 116D-117A).

2. Concerning Pardonable Sins

Pardonable sins are those voluntary sins which do not corrupt the love for God or the love for neighbor, nor do they render the person an enemy of God and liable to eternal death, to which transgressions even the Saints are susceptible, according to the words of the Brother of God: "For in many things we all sin" (Jas. 3:2), and of John: "If we say that we have no sin, we deceive ourselves" (1 Jn. 1:8), and according to Canons 125, 126, and 127 of Carthage. These sins, according to Koressios and Chrysanthos, are: idle talk, the initial inclination and agitation of anger, the initial inclination of lust, the initial inclination of hate, a white lie, passing envy, or that which is commonly called jealousy, which is slight grief over the good fortunes of one's neighbor, and the like.[13]

---

13   It is difficult to distinguish the reason and exact difference between mortal sins and pardonable ones. Explaining the saying of John: "There is a sin unto death; and there is a sin not unto death" (1 Jn. 5:16, 17), Metrophanes of Smyrna says a sin unto death is every sin which was penalized by death under the Old Law, as was blasphemy against God, voluntary murder, bestiality, and others. A sin not unto death is that one which was not penalized by death, such as involuntary murder, and others. Anastasios of Sinai says that the sin unto death is that which is committed knowingly, and the sin not unto death is the one committed in ignorance; but blasphemy against God and a great sin committed knowingly, such as murder or adultery, is unto death (*Quaestiones LIV*, PG 89, 616C-617A). Canon 5 of the Seventh Ecumenical Council and Oikoumenios say that the sin unto death is the one which is not repented for and uncorrected. Similarly, George Koressios in his *Theology* (which seems to me the most accurate from the others because he noticed these differences), says that mortal sins may differ from pardonable sins according to their class, as for example a mortal deed differs from idle talk and from some vain thought, as there are three general classes of sin: the evil deed, the evil word, and the evil thought. All the evil deeds are of one class, differing among themselves according to their specific kind, and this goes also for all of the evil words and all of the evil thoughts. They may also differ according to the incompletion of the deed and act, just as the initial inclination of anger and hate differs from full-blown rage and remembrance of wrongs. Mortal sins may also differ from pardonable sins according only to the value of the content, for theft (which does not differ in itself from other theft, either in specific kind or content), if it involves a lot of money or capital, is mortal; if it involves a little, without resulting in much harm to the owner, is pardonable. Chrysanthos also says these things in his *Exomologetarion*. In addition to these, they may also differ according to the specific kind, just as perjury, being mortal, differs according to the kind of sin from idle talk. Gennadios Scholarios (in the *Exomologetarion* of Chrysanthos), dividing the mortal sins and the pardonable sins into the general areas where they are enacted, that is, evil thoughts to the intellect, evil words to the tongue, evil deeds to the body, says that every sin belonging

Know also, Spiritual Father, that the many sins which are generally called pardonable are not of one and the same degree, but they are of

---

to the intellect and being mortal according to its kind, then becomes mortal when it is given form and carried out, not however merely through assault or consent or struggle with the bad thought (concerning these see Canons 2, 3, and 4 of the Faster), but through consenting to its completion (as it is with pride, remembrance of wrongs, heresy, and others). Likewise, every sin belonging to the tongue and being mortal according to its kind, then becomes mortal when it is carried out (like blasphemy, perjury, false witness, and the like). Similarly, every sin belonging to the body and being mortal according to its kind, then becomes mortal when it is carried out (as it is with fornication, adultery, murder, etc.). Mortal sins belonging to the body become pardonable when they only appear to the intellect and reason. For example, when the mortal sin of sexual immorality is conceived in desire and in the intellect, or if it is spoken through obscenity, it is pardonable. Hence, the Brother of God said: "Then when lust hath conceived, it bringeth forth sin," pardonable sin, that is; for it produces, "sin, when it is finished (through the body and the act), bringeth forth death" (Jas. 1:15). Likewise, mortal sin belonging to the word, if it occurs only in the intellect, is pardonable. The mortal sin of blasphemy, for example, when it occurs involuntarily in the intellect alone, it is pardonable. Simply speaking, the mortal sins arising from the lower and grosser areas, when they occur in the higher and finer areas, are pardonable.

Worthy of attention and fear is that which the sacred Augustine says (*On the First Epistle of John* and *On the Saints*, Homily 41, taken from Koressios) which is in accord with many others: that many small sins create a large one. This is understood, according to Koressios, when a person dismisses small sins as small, because the one continuously stealing small things sins mortally. Wherefore also Basil the Great, knowing that according to the Holy Gospel there exists a difference between a gnat and a camel, straw and wood, but saying it more clearly, small and large sins, yet at the same time he says that in the New Testament there is no such distinction between large and small sins. First, because a small sin and a large one are equally transgressions of the Law, for according to John: "Sin is the transgression of the law" (1 Jn. 3:4) and defiance of the Son, as is said: "He that disobeyeth the Son shall not see life" (Jn. 3:36) (*Regulæ Brevius* 293, PG 31, 1288C-1289A). Second, because a small sin becomes a large one when it is master of the one committing the sin: "For of whom a man is overcome, of the same is he brought in bondage" (2 Pet. 2:19). The divine Chrysostom gives a third reason (*On I Cor.*, Homily 16, and *To Demetrios on Compunction*), saying that wood and straw, that is, the large sin and the small one, because they do not receive the same punishment, differ; but in so much as those committing sins (small or large) are put out of the kingdom of heaven, they do not differ. Wherefore the Apostle also says that both idol-worshippers, and sodomists, and revilers, equally will not inherit the kingdom of heaven (1 Cor. 6:9-10), that is, those who commit large and small sins. That which the aforementioned Koressios says is also worthy of note and awe, namely that desire becomes a mortal sin in two ways: either when it moves toward some severe sin (like murder, or another like it), or when it consents to do a sin, even if it is not carried out, because the movement of desire is threefold: involuntary, incompletely voluntary, and completely voluntary. The first movement is not called sin; the second is called a pardonable sin; the third is mortal. Accordingly, in *Instructions for Penitents* (p. 239), it is written that every hedonistic pleasure, when it is completely voluntary, is a mortal sin.

varying degrees, smaller and larger, lower and higher, and that pardonable sins and mortal sins are two extremes. For in between these extremes there are found varying degrees of sins, beginning from the pardonable ones and proceeding up to the mortal ones, which degrees were not given names by the Ancients, perhaps because they are many and varied according to the class and specific kind of sins, but could have named them if they so desired. Here we name some of them, for the benefit of clarity and for your knowledge, beginning from below: pardonable sins, those near the pardonable, those that are non-mortal, those near the non-mortal, those between the non-mortal and the mortal, those near the mortal, and finally, mortal sins. Here is an example of the sins of the incensive aspect of the soul: The initial movement of anger is pardonable; near to the pardonable is for someone to say harsh words and get hot-tempered. A non-mortal sin is to swear; near the non-mortal is for someone to strike with the hand. Between the non-mortal and the mortal is to strike with a small stick; near the mortal is to strike with a large stick, or with a knife, but not in the area of the head. A mortal sin is to murder. A similar pattern applies to the other sins. Wherefore, those sins nearer to the pardonable end are penanced lighter, while those nearer to the mortal end are more severely penanced.[14]

3. Concerning sins of omission

Those good works, or words, or thoughts, which are capable of being done or thought by someone, but through negligence were not done, or said, or thought, are called sins of omission,[15] and are brought forth from

---

14   Translator's note: St. Ambrose says: "Paul teaches us that we must not abandon those who have committed a sin unto death, but that we must rather coerce them with the bread of tears and tears to drink, yet so that their sorrow itself be moderated. For this is the meaning of the passage: 'Thou hast given them to drink in large measure' (cf. Ps. 79:6), that their sorrow itself should have its measure, lest perchance he who is doing penance should be consumed by overmuch sorrow, as was said to the Corinthians: 'What will ye? Shall I come to you with a rod, or in love and a spirit of meekness?' (1 Cor. 4:21). But even the rod is not severe, since he had read: 'Thou shalt beat him indeed with the rod, but shalt deliver his soul from death' (Pr. 23:13)" (*On Repentance*, Book I, ch. 13, NPNF (V2-10), p. 339).
15   Translator's note: St. Mark the Ascetic says: "Failure to do the good that is within your power is hard to forgive" (*On the Spiritual Law* 64, *GrPhilokalia*, p. 94; tr. *The Philokalia*, v. 1, p. 114).

the mortal sin of despondency, as we have said. I know very well that these sins of omission are not considered by people as full sins, because those are few who consider it a sin if they did not perform such and such a charity when they were able to, or had the means to either give good advice to their neighbor, or to do a certain amount of prayer, or do another virtue, and did not.

But this, however, I know for certain, that God will render an account on the day of judgment concerning these. Who verifies this for us? The example of that slothful servant who had the one talent and buried it in the ground, who was judged, not because he committed any sin or injustice with it (because he who gave the talent to him took it all back, as Basil the Great says in the Introduction of *The Long Rules*),[16] but because being able to increase it, was negligent and did not increase it: "Thou oughtest therefore to have put my money to the exchangers, and then at my coming I should have received mine own with usury" (Mt. 25:27). It is also verified for us by the example of the five foolish virgins who were condemned for nothing other than an absence of oil. And concerning the sinners placed at the left hand, they will be condemned, not because they committed any sin, but because they were lacking and were not merciful to their brother: "For I was an hungred, and ye gave me no meat: I was thirsty, and ye gave me no drink" (Mt. 25:42). The reason that God gave to man natural strength was not in order to leave it idle and useless, without results and fruit, just as that slothful servant left the talent of the Lord idle, as we said above, but He gave it to man in order for man to put it into action, and into practice, and for it to increase, doing good with it and the commandments of the Lord, and so to be saved through this. On this account Basil the Great said: "We have already received from God the power to fulfill all the commandments given us by Him, so that we may not take our obligation in bad part, as though something quite strange and unexpected were being asked of us, and that we may not become filled with conceit, as if we were paying back something more than had been given us."[17] And also in agreement with the above words, his brother, Gregory of Nyssa, says: "As

---

16   *Regulæ Fusius*, PG 31, 893A.

17   *Regulæ Fusius* 2, PG 31, 909A; tr. *Saint Basil: Ascetical Works*, pp. 233-234.

each shall receive his wages, just as the Apostle says (1 Cor. 3:14), according to his labor, so also each shall receive punishment according to the extent of their negligence."[18]

Those things which are also called sins of omission are those which we were able to prevent, by word or act, but did not prevent. On this account those who commit these are likewise penanced according to Canon 25 of Ancyra, Canon 71 of Basil the Great, and Canon 25 of St. John the Faster.[19]

Furthermore, Spiritual Father, you must know that the degrees of sin from the beginning until the end are twelve. The first degree is when someone does good, but not in a proper manner, mixing the good with the bad. This occurs in seven ways, as Basil the Great says, "As regards the place, the time, the person, the matter involved, or in a manner intemperate, or disorderly, or with improper dispositions."[20] An example of a sin of the first degree is when someone performs an act of mercy, or fasts, or does some other good deed, so that he might be glorified by people. The second degree of sin is complete idleness in regard to the good. The third degree is an assault of evil. The fourth is coupling. The fifth is struggle.[21] The sixth is consent.[22] The seventh is the sin according to the intellect, according to St. Maximos, which is when a person, having consented, plans carefully to accomplish that sin which is in his intellect so as to do the deed. The eighth is the deed itself and the sinful act. The ninth is the habit of someone committing the sin often. The tenth is the addiction to sin, which with violence and force compels the person to sin voluntarily and involuntarily. The eleventh is despair, that is, hopelessness. The twelfth is suicide, namely, for a person to kill himself, while having a sound intellect, being conquered

18   *Contra Eunomium* 12, PG 45, 912C.

19   A certain teacher compares sins of omission with the venom and bite of the asp, because, just as it kills without causing pain to the person (wherefore the Alexandrians killed those committing small crimes this way, as Galenos says), so also those transgressions kill the soul, without the sinners hurting or feeling anything.

20   *De Baptismo II*, Question 8, PG 31, 1600C; tr. *Saint Basil: Ascetical Works*, p. 408.

21   Struggle is considered common to all of the degrees of sin, because one struggles and wrestles in order to do good in a proper manner, and not to delay in doing good and so forth in all things.

22   Concerning these four (assault, coupling, struggle, consent) see the Canons of St. John the Faster.

by despair. So then, Spiritual Father, you must try assiduously in every way to turn the sinner around to smaller degrees of sin and to prevent him from proceeding to the greater degrees ahead. And most of all, you must endeavor to sever him from despair, no matter in how great a degree of sin he is found.[23]

---

23   The arguments with which you will be able to free the sinner from despair are these, Spiritual Father. 1) That despair is the greatest and worst of all evils, because it is opposite to and extremely opposed to God. And even though every sin is opposed to God in some way and partially, despair is entirely opposed to God and in every way, because it negates God, and by taking Him out of the picture it makes evil as another God, as well as the cause of evil, the devil. It would make evil stronger than the goodness of God, more infinite than His infinity, and for despair to even be in the place of wherever God is. What can be found that is more impious or more mindless? To believe that powerless sin is more powerful than Power Himself? That the finite is more infinite than the Infinite Himself? And for non-being to be above the Eternal Being? For this reason the *Orthodox Confession* writes that despair is opposed to the Holy Spirit. Therefore say to the sinner, Spiritual Father, that which Basil the Great says, that is, if it is possible to measure the fullness and the magnitude of the compassion of God, let the sinner then despair, comparing and measuring the amount and magnitude of his sin: "If it is possible to number the multitude of God's mercies and the greatness of God's compassion in comparison with the number and greatness of sins, then let us despair" (*Regulæ Brevius* 13, PG 31, 1089C). Even if one's transgressions are measured and counted, the mercy and compassion of God being immeasurable, why should one despair and not know the mercy of God and blame his transgressions: "But if, as is obvious, the latter are subject to measure and can be numbered, but it is impossible to measure the mercy or number the compassions of God, there is no time for despairing, but only for recognizing mercy and condemning sins; the remission of which is set forth in the blood of Christ" (*ibid.*). 2) Despair is opposed to common sense, because it does not have a proper place among people. For a sinner to live, even though he sins, is a sign that God accepts him and does not reject him, Who did not put him to death when he sinned as he deserved, but allowed him to live, for no other reason other than that he may repent. The great Gregory of Thessaloniki verifies this for us in this way: "This is why no one should give way to despair... because the time of this life is time for repentance, the very fact that a sinner still lives is a pledge that God will accept whoever desires to return to Him" (*To the Most Reverend Nun Xenia*, *GrPhilokalia*, p. 933; tr. *The Philokalia*, v. 4, London, 1995, p. 299). 3) Despair is a child of the devil, according to St. Ephraim. Before someone sins, the devil says to that person how the sin is nothing, and then when he does sin, he says to that person how his sin is terrible and unforgivable (*Evergetinos*, Venice, 1783, p. 11; also see the English language translation, *The Evergetinos: A Complete Text*, Etna, 1988, vol. I, book 1, p. 41). If we search more exactly, we find that despair sprouts both from pride and self-esteem. The prideful who speaks of himself as great in regards to virtue and holiness, when he falls into some mortal sin, he straightway despairs, thinking that that fall is unworthy of his virtue, according to John of the Ladder (Step 26, PG 88, 1032D-1033A; *The Ladder*, p. 175). It also sprouts from the inexperience which one has in the noetic warfare of the enemy. Just as Judas was inexperienced in this

CHAPTER 4

Concerning the Ten Commandments

Additionally, Father, you who will become a Spiritual Father, you must know the Ten Commandments and who are those that err in any of these, according to the *Orthodox Confession*.[24]

---

warfare and despaired, as one Father says, thus despairing he hanged himself. Peter being experienced, even though he denied, did not despair, but repented, again becoming Peter (the rock). (Translator's note: The 'Father' St. Nikodemos is referring to is St. John of Karpathos. See *Texts for the Monks in India* 85, *GrPhilokalia*, p. 255; *The Philokalia*, v. 1, p. 318). It also sprouts from the many sins one commits, just as Solomon says: "When an ungodly man comes into a depth of evils, he despises himself" (Pr. 18:3). It sprouts from other causes also, like the negligence and idleness in doing good works and not bearing fruits of repentance. Therefore, whoever desires not to fall into the webs of despair, let them remember its causes and correct them, learning the machination of the devil with which he tries to create despair, throwing away one's pride, becoming experienced in noetic warfare, abstaining from sins, and striving for their salvation with all of their strength. 4) Lastly, despair is opposed to the Old and New Scripture which in a thousand places portrays the immeasurable mercy of God with which He receives all sinners equally. It is opposed to so many examples of sinners, who were great transgressors, who were saved from the beginning of the world until the end without despairing: Lamech, Manasseh, Nebuchadnezzar, David, prostitutes, adulterers, tax collectors, prodigals, thieves, Peter, Paul. It is opposed to all of the words of the divine Fathers who taught sinners to hope in the mercy of God and to cast away despair, showing that there is not one sin which can conquer the philanthropy of God. See also the *Evergetinos*, vol. I, book 1, *Hypothesis I*.

These things having been said, we complete this footnote with the following. Just as despair is opposed to the Holy Spirit, as we said, likewise is exaggerated hope and boldness in the compassion of God opposed to the same Holy Spirit when one is so bold as to sin without fear, as the *Orthodox Confession* says (p. 221). Concerning this the word of the polymath George Koressios is very wise, saying that the life of Christians must stand between these two, between hope and despair: on the part of God they must hope in His goodness; but on their part they must despair on account of the multitude of their sins (from his *Theology*). (Translator's note: Concerning this last statement by George Koressios, these are the words told to St. Silouan by the Lord: "Keep thy mind in hell, and despair not" (Archimandrite Sophrony, *Saint Silouan the Athonite*, Crestwood, 1999, p. 460).)

24   We place here the Ten Commandments and those who err in them for two reasons, for the Spiritual Father and for the penitent: for the Spiritual Father, in order that, learning them, he may be able to question penitents during confession with ease if they have kept the commandments; for the penitent, so he may be able to examine his conscience to see whether he has kept each commandment, and so finding his sins easily, he may remember them in order to confess all of them properly.

1. Concerning the First Commandment

"I am the Lord thy God, which have brought thee out of the land of Egypt, out of the house of bondage. Thou shalt have no other gods before Me" (Ex. 20:2-3).

The atheists, polytheists, deniers of the providence of God, and believers in automation and fate, err in this commandment, as do all magicians and fortunetellers and superstitious people, and as many as resort to them.[25] Also the heretics, as many as do not believe in an orthodox manner in the One God in Trinity and, simply speaking, all those who hope more in man or in themselves, and in the things of the natural order, and in their acquired goods instead of God, err in this commandment.[26]

2. Concerning the Second Commandment

"Thou shalt not make unto thee any graven image, or any likeness of any thing that is in heaven above, or that is in the earth beneath, or that is in the water under the earth: Thou shalt not bow down thyself to them, nor serve them" (Ex. 20:4-5).

Those who err in this commandment are those who directly worship idols and bow down to the creation rather than the Creator, like the godless and idol-worshippers, or indirectly through the attachment they have to material goods and to the things of the world, like the covetous, concerning

---

25   See Canon 32 of St. John the Faster and the footnote to it.

26   One also errs in this commandment if he had voluntary thoughts of unbelief in any matter of the faith or said these things with his mouth; if he hated God or denied Him; if he tempted God, seeking from Him miracles without there being any need; if he stole a sacred or ecclesiastical object; if he sold or bought the grace of God with money; if he was negligent and did not learn the Mysteries of the Faith and the Christian Teaching; if he read books opposed to the Faith and virtue; if he did not have the correct piety toward divine things; if he did not confess with the proper examination of the conscience and with grief, and with the decision not to sin any more; if he received the immaculate Mysteries having committed a mortal sin; if he laid a hand upon clergy; if he lost hope in the compassion of God or intentionally sinned with too much boldness in that compassion, or decided to sin as far as he could and then to repent afterward; and if, finally, he advised or assisted someone in these transgressions, or if one were able to prevent them by word or deed, and did not.

whom the divine Paul said: "Mortify therefore your members which are upon the earth; fornication... and covetousness, which is idolatry" (Col. 3:5), and concerning the gluttonous he said: "Whose God is their belly" (Phil. 3:19). Simply speaking, as many as have hypocritical rather than true piety, and all those who confine piety to external things and neglect the weightier matters of the law, justice and mercy and faith (Mt. 23:23), err in this commandment.[27]

3. Concerning the Third Commandment

"Thou shalt not take the Name of the Lord thy God in vain; for the Lord will not hold him guiltless that taketh His Name in vain" (Ex. 20:7).

Blasphemers err in this commandment; as many as take oaths or violate oaths or make others take oaths;[28] as many as say in every instance: "O God!" or, "God knows!" and other things like these; as many as promise to God that they will do some good work, and afterward do not fulfill their promises;[29] false prophets and as many as ask from God improper things, according to their own will, err in this commandment.[30]

4. Concerning the Fourth Commandment

"Remember the sabbath day, to keep it holy. Six days shalt thou labour, and do all thy work: But the seventh day is the

---

27   As many as believe and trust in their dreams also err in this commandment. Also, as many as are passionate and lovers of pleasures who delight in and endeavor for the images and idols of their passions, which are pictured again in their minds.

28   See Canon 31 of St. John the Faster.

29   See Chapter 9 ahead on how the Spiritual Father should care for those who have made promises.

30   One also errs in this commandment when they use the words of Scripture pridefully and for jokes; if one does not endure the misfortunes and illnesses of the body with patience and thanksgiving, but rather complains and criticizes God as unjust; if one not only blasphemes against God or the Saints, but also causes others to blaspheme; if one says that Holy Scripture contains myths and contradictions within itself, and praises more the writings of the Gentiles.

sabbath of the Lord thy God" (Ex. 20:8-10).

As many as do not go to Church on Sunday err in this commandment, for the Lord transferred the old Sabbath to this day, and because He is the Lord of the Sabbath (Mt. 12:8), and not subject to any authority. Sunday is also the day on which occurred His resurrection and the renewal of the whole world.[31] Those also who do not go to Church on the Feasts of Christ or the Theotokos or other Saints in order to hear the divine words err in this commandment, or go to Church out of habit only, in order to pass time, not paying attention to the service, chatting and talking with others about their secular matters; as many as work on Feast Days or make others to work on them out of their immeasurable lust for money[32]; as many as have concerts and dances, eating and drinking parties and fights and other similar improprieties on these days; as many as are literate and do not read sacred books on Feasts; as many shepherds and leaders of the Church do not teach the people on these days[33]; as many as do not give from their possessions even a small amount to the collection for the poor during Feasts, concerning which the divine Paul writes (1 Cor. 16).

5. Concerning the Fifth Commandment

"Honour thy father and thy mother: that thy days may be long upon the land which the Lord thy God giveth thee" (Ex. 20:12).

Children who do not honor their parents with the following four things err in this commandment: honor, love, obedience, and thanksgiving; just

---

31   See Canon 92 of Basil the Great and Canon 1 of Theophilos.

32   See Canon 29 of Laodicaea. The sacred Ambrose also says that we are not to make holidays into feasts of lewdness. And the Apostles say in the *Apostolic Constitutions*: "Nor do we allow you on Sundays to say or do anything indecent" (Book V, ch. 10; SC 329, p. 240). For the Scripture says somewhere: "Serve ye the Lord with fear, and rejoice in Him with trembling, and your rejoicings should be in fear and trembling" (cf. Ps. 2:11). And John of the Ladder says: "The slave of his belly calculates with what dishes he will celebrate the feast" (Step 14, PG 88, 864D; tr. *The Ladder*, p. 98). And some other Father says: "Do not carry out feasts of wine-drinking knowingly, but renew the purity of mind and soul; for being filled and drunk rather infuriates the head of the feast" (*Scholion* 5 on Step 14, PG 88, 873A).

33   See Canon 58 of the Apostles and Canon 19 of the Sixth Ecumenical Council.

as children are to receive from their parents these six things: nurture, words of good counsel, a good example of living through works, protection from evil company, instruction in letters or in a craft from good teachers and craftsmen, and instruction through physical discipline unto correction. As many as do not honor their Spiritual Fathers, hierarchs, priests, teachers, and those who have become their elders through the angelic habit, err in this commandment[34]; slaves who do not honor their masters[35] or servants their kings and rulers[36]; and simply, as many as do not honor their benefactors.[37]

6. Concerning the Sixth Commandment

"Thou shalt not kill" (Ex. 20:13).

Those who physically kill someone, either by hand, or by another means, or by plotting, or through assistance and provocation; those who kill someone spiritually, like heretics, false teachers, and all those Christians who scandalize others by the evil example of their life; those who in time of plague, knowing they are infected, associate with others and thus infect them; those who kill themselves; and simply, all those who are reckless, err in this commandment.[38] To this are related both anger and envy and the other passions which are causes of murder.[39]

---

34   See Canons 55 and 56 of the Holy Apostles.
35   See Canon 82 of the Apostles.
36   See Canon 84 of the Apostles.
37   One who has forced his children to marry also errs in this commandment, or has forced them to become monastics or put them in another state against their will. And if one did not send them to Church or did not take care to teach them good morals or did not discipline them when they erred or did not teach them letters or some craft. Likewise if the children did not manage their parents when they were in need or care for them in their infirmity or against their parents' will promised to get married or did not forbear them when they aged and did strange things. The husband who did not care for his wife's spiritual and bodily needs also errs in this commandment, or scolded her beyond what was necessary or chastised her unjustly. Likewise, if the wife did not obey her husband. All masters and those in high places who do not take care for the spiritual and bodily needs of their slaves and servants also err in this commandment.
38   See Canon 20 of St. John the Faster.
39   One who wishes evil for his neighbor or rejoices in his neighbor's tragedy also errs in this commandment; if he envied him and was saddened by his good fortune; if he has animosity toward

7. Concerning the Seventh Commandment

"Thou shalt not commit adultery" (Ex. 20:14).
Those who not only commit adultery with the married wife of their neighbor, but also fornicate with the unmarried err in this commandment. For according to Canon 4 of St. Gregory of Nyssa, fornication is also considered to be adultery. Those monastics who fornicate or marry also err in this commandment, as do those who fall into spiritual adultery, that is, into heresy and dogmatic error. To this is related gluttony, carousing, licentious and erotic imagery, and as many other things that are related to adultery.[40]

8. Concerning the Eighth Commandment

"Thou shalt not steal" (Ex. 20:15).
Those who steal outright, like those who are thieves and dictators and robbers; as many as are thieves secretly, like those who steal using concealed methods;[41] as many as are fraudulent thieves, just as are merchants and all those who long to cheat the other, selling with false scales and measures and using a myriad of other means and lies, err in this commandment. That is why the Lord called merchants thieves and robbers, saying: "My house shall be called the house of prayer; but ye have made it a den of thieves" (Mt. 21:13). So also are those who charge interest.[42] Love of money is a transgression of this Commandment, as are the passions and

---

someone and seeks revenge; if one did not forgive his enemy or did not ask forgiveness from his enemy; if one turned away the poor with harsh words; if one employed herbs in order for a woman to abort a child; if one encouraged evil things; if one created scandals and caused fights; if one struck someone or wounded them; if one questioned someone unjustly on account of anger and not love; if one wielded the authority of teacher or judge or physician or priest or Spiritual Father or hierarch or ruler unworthily, or caused others to wield this authority; if one injured oneself through overeating and drunkenness or through carnal pleasures and other improprieties.

40   A man or woman also errs in this commandment if they dressed themselves up or adorned themselves or applied makeup and perfumes with an evil intent and scandalized another; if one encouraged someone to sin in the flesh or became a mediator to this end through letters, messages, manipulations, etc

41   See Canon 27 of the Faster.

42   See *Subject G* which follows the Canons of St. John the Faster.

sins related to it which are born from the love of money, as we have already said.[43]

9. Concerning the Ninth Commandment

"Thou shalt not bear false witness against thy neighbor" (Ex. 20:16).

Those who witness falsely and unjustly in order to damage or smear their brother err in this commandment,[44] as do those who have doubts and suspicions against their brother[45]; those who make fun of the physical

---

43   One also errs in this commandment if they knowingly buy stolen items in order to get them cheaper than their actual worth; if one passed counterfeit, worthless, or inferior money as true; if a worker did not work as he should have, or worked lazily, and took his pay; if one did not pay those who worked for him; if one found something and kept it without trying to find the one who lost it; if one did not keep the agreements he made; if one was negligent in the matters of supervising orphans or widows or Churches or schools or societies; if one gave gifts to a judge in order that he may judge unjustly, or if the judge took them; if one seeks alms without having need; if merchants sell a defective item as good, or they mix it with good; if they sell an item for more than it is worth, or buy it for less than it is worth; if they agree with other merchants to sell at an unjust price; if they sell goods for more to an uneducated buyer, or buy goods for less from an uneducated seller; if they do not sell according to how the authorities direct them; if they give gifts to the authorities to allow them to sell as they wish; if they do not give an accurate account to their partners; if they falsely claimed bankruptcy in order to keep another's money; if a slave sells goods for more than what his master tells him; if someone has somebody else's item or belonging and allows it to ruin or sells it; if one played cards or other games with children or other strangers in order to cheat them. One also errs in this commandment if he damaged an item or possession which was his brother's; if one extended the boundaries of his fields or of his houses in order to take a portion from the field or house of his neighbor; if one cut down the trees of his brother, whom the civil laws punish as a thief; if one stole his animals, whom the laws punish with exile or by the cutting off of the hand; if one demoralizes and takes the slave of another by promising higher wages; if one opens letters and reads them, or forges, or transcribes, or erases, or tears the signature of another, who is punished by the civil laws with exile and the seizure of his possessions. All these things are robbery and must be given back, if they wish to receive forgiveness.

44   See Canon 75 of the Apostles. And Solomon says: "A false witness will not go unpunished" (Pr. 19:5).

45   A lie is three-fold according to Abba Dorotheos: according to the intellect, when one has false suspicions against his brother; according to word, when he falsely accuses him; and according to his life and his works, as when he is one thing in reality and in his works, but falsely pretending and appearing to be another thing to people, thus called a hypocrite (*Doctrina IX, De Mendacio*, PG 88,

defects of the mind, or of the voice, or of the face, or of the other members of the body of their neighbor, for he is not the cause of those defects; and those judges who either on account of partiality, or gifts, or not examining into an issue well, make an unjust judgment.[46]

10. Concerning the Tenth Commandment

"Thou shalt not covet thy neighbour's house, thou shalt not covet thy neighbour's wife, nor his manservant, nor his maidservant, nor his ox, nor his ass, nor any thing that is thy neighbour's" (Ex. 20:17).

The preceding five Commandments, which teach duties toward one's neighbor,[47] forbid man from only exterior words and acts of sin. The

---

1716B-1716C). The Lord says that such ones resemble the devil: "Ye are of your father the devil, and the lusts of your father ye will do. He was a murderer from the beginning, and abode not in the truth, because there is no truth in him. When he speaketh a lie, he speaketh of his own: for he is a liar, and the father of it" (Jn. 8:44), that is, of lies, according to Theophylact. Hence, the sacred Augustine also says that lying is never allowed, regardless of how good the intent is of the one telling it (*Book Concerning Purpose and Aim*).

46   One who advised or compelled another to bear false witness also errs in this commandment; if with unjust accusations one prevented another from receiving any due recognition; if one was able to prevent accusations and false testimonies but did not wish to; if one spoke words unto the detriment of his neighbor; if one condemned another or spoke ill of another, or listened with pleasure while others were maligning someone, or praised the maligner. It is pardonable, however, to speak of the evils of another when one is counseling someone unto the correction of the sinner, and when trying to protect another from falling into that sin through ignorance, according to Basil the Great: "I think there are two occasions on which it is allowable to say something bad of a man: when a man is obliged to take counsel with others approved for this purpose as to how one who has sinned may be corrected; and again when there is need to secure the safety of some who may often through ignorance be likely to consort with evil as if it were good" (*Regulæ Brevius* 25, PG 31, 100C; tr. *The Ascetic Works of Saint Basil*, London, 1925, pp. 239-240). One errs in this commandment if they flattered or praised someone falsely.

47   The first four Commandments teach those duties toward God and were written on the first tablet, according to the *Orthodox Confession* (p. 231). The six after these teach those duties toward one's neighbor and were written on the second tablet. Therefore the Lord recapitulated the Ten Commandments in the Gospel with the love toward God and love toward neighbor, and concerning them He said: "One jot or one tittle shall in no wise pass from the law" (Mt. 5:18), from the Decalogue, that is, according to the *Orthodox Confession* (ibid.).

present Commandment also further forbids him from that interior evil of lust of the soul, that is, it forbids him from desiring any sin with his heart, insomuch as this lust of the heart is the cause and root of all exterior words and actions.[48] All those, then, err in this Commandment who, even though they do not physically take another's belonging, nevertheless desire to possess it with their soul and heart, whatever it may be, a wife, an animal, a possession, or any other thing.[49]

CHAPTER 5

Concerning the Circumstances of Sin

Furthermore, Father, the future Spiritual Father, you must know the so-called circumstances of sin, which are, according to Koressios, seven: 1) who, that is, who is the doer; 2) what, that is, what sin was committed; 3) why it was committed; 4) in what manner it was committed; 5) at what time it was committed; 6) where; and, 7) how many times it was committed. Examining, therefore, every sin by these seven circumstances, the sin will be determined to be greater or smaller. Related to these seven circumstances are also included the circumstances preceding the sin and following the sin.

1. Concerning Who

"Who" means the person considered in himself, whether Peter or Paul, or in relation to another, according to four ways: according to nature, as a

---

48   Therefore the Lord said in one place concerning lust: "Whosoever looketh on a woman to lust after her hath committed adultery with her already in his heart" (Mt. 5:28), and in another: "For out of the heart proceed evil thoughts, murders, adulteries, fornications, thefts, false witness, blasphemies" (Mt. 15:19). And Chrysostom says that: "Just as the flame ignites the torch, so also does lust ignite the soul. And just as smoke blinds and impairs the eye, so also does lust the intellect," and again: "The root of adultery is reckless lust," and again: "For this reason did Christ not only condemn adultery but also chastised lust" (De Poenitentia VI, 2, PG 49, 316).

49   We note two things here: 1) that the penitent need not repeat all of the errors which we have mentioned with each commandment, but only the ones actually committed, and to confess them; and 2) that although all those things mentioned are not mortal sins, they must all be revealed to the Spiritual Father just as they were committed.

father is related to a son; according to lot, as a hierarch, king, ruler, and simply every leader and head, is related to their subject people; according to will, as a friend in relation to another friend; according to occupation, as a teacher or mentor in relation to a student. "Who" also refers to the profession, such as monk or philosopher, and to age, like young or old. Simply speaking, "Who" refers to and extends to every condition of mind and ability in which one is, that is, bodily, spiritually, interiorly, and exteriorly.[50]

So then, examining the sin in relation to "Who," it is determined to be greater or smaller. For example, the error of a hierarch, a king, or a leader, on account of the bad example which they exhibit to the people, is greater than that same error committed by one of his subjects.[51] A child sins greater when he insults his parents, or a friend his friend, or a student his teacher or mentor, than when a stranger insults them. Likewise, a monk, philosopher, or elder sins greater when he adorns and beautifies himself, than when a secular, or an uneducated person, or a young person does the same. "Who" also pertains to the status of the person against whom the one confessing sinned, that is, if this person was ordained or a lay person, and the like, but without revealing that person's name.

---

50   Translator's note: "The spiritual condition and psychosynthesis of the penitent ought also to be seriously considered… [This] is the principle of 'individualization' ('*exatomikefsis*')… profusely invoked in the pastoral theology of the Fathers. This is in view of the fact that each member of the body is distinguishable by the different characteristics of his personality" (Lewis J. Patsavos, *Spiritual Dimensions of the Holy Canons*, Brookline, 2003, p. 47).

51   See p. 974 of v. 1 of the *Octateuch* where the divine Isidore says that the sin of a priest is greater than that of a layman, not by nature, but on account of the dignity of the priest who commits it. See also the divine Chrysostom (*On the Priesthood*, Book VI) who says the same thing. Amusing and curious is that account which is recorded in the booklet *Instructions for Spiritual Fathers*, that a king once happened to confess to a farmer, who was discreetly a Spiritual Father, and after having confessed his sins, said to the Spiritual Father: "I don't have anything else to say to you." "How so, O king?" said the Spiritual Father, "How? Have we finished the confession? No. You have said the sins of Alexis (stating the king's first name), say now the sins of the king." That wise Spiritual Father wanted to show by these words that every ruler and head, foreign or domestic, must not only confess as an individual or be examined by a Spiritual Father as a common person, but in addition to the sins he committed as a person, he must also confess those things he could have done as a ruler unto the good of his people but did not do, and as many bad things as happened to his subjects on his account which he did not correct, for which he will have to give an exact account to God. You must conduct confession with all those in authority according to this example, Spiritual Father.

2. Concerning What

Examining the sin in relation to "What" determines it to be greater or smaller, because mortal sins are graver than pardonable ones. Also, of the mortal sins, murder is greater than grand theft, and worse than all is denial of the faith and impiety. Sins of omission are also related to and examined by the question "What," as we have said. That is, as many good things as someone could have done, or said, or thought, and did not do them, or say them, or think them, and as many evil things as someone was able to prevent by word or act, and did not prevent them. In this instance the class of the sin is examined, that is, if it is an act, or a word, or a thought.[52] Likewise, of what specific kind is it, namely, which act, adultery or fornication or murder; and what word, gossip or perjury or false witness or blasphemy; and what thought, pride or heresy or intellectual blasphemy, and whether there occurred an assault, or coupling, or consent, and the others.[53]

3. Concerning Why

Examining the cause of why a person sinned increases or lessens the gravity of the sin. For example, if someone murdered a tyrant in order to free his city from his tyranny, or stole in order to give alms to the poor, or struck a rapist in order to free his daughter who was being raped by him, these are of less gravity than if someone murders or steals or strikes for his own evil purposes. Simply speaking, every act and sin is judged by its purpose and aim. Therefore sacred Augustine also says: "It differs greatly by what cause, purpose, and aim something occurs,"[54] because aim and purpose have great power over the acts of people, so that even according to the philosophers, every purpose must be analogous and in agreement with the act, and conversely, every act must be analogous with the purpose,

---

52   Translator's note: Ilias the Presbyter says: "A person may have sullied his soul with words even if he has not degraded it by actions; and he may still be impure in his thoughts even if he watches over his words. For there are three different ways of sinning" (*A Gnomic Anthology* 16, Gr*Philokalia*, p. 530; tr. *The Philokalia*, v. 3, pp. 35-36).

53   See Canons 2, 3, 4, and 5 of St. John the Faster.

54   *Book Concerning Purpose and Aim.*

namely, a good purpose will have good acts, and an evil one will have evil acts, and not vice-versa. The divine Maximos says in one place: "In everything that we do God searches out our purpose to see whether we do it for Him or for some other motive",[55] and in another place that: "The demons do not hate self-restraint, fasting, almsgiving, hospitality, the singing of psalms... or any of the other things which characterize a life lived according to God, so long as the aim and purpose of a person trying to live such a life are tilted in their direction."[56]

4. Concerning Manner

The manner in which a sin occurs increases or lessens its gravity. For example, the one who sins knowingly, or with premeditation, or with guile, or with evil intent, sins worse than the one who sins in ignorance, involuntarily, by enticement and circumstance, from frivolity and guilelessness. The manner is also related to every instrument and means with which someone sins, that is, whether someone murdered with wood or a knife, or carried out the sin through the means and assistance of people.

5. Concerning Time

The time according to which someone sinned lessens or increases the gravity of the sin. For example, if someone in a time of need and hunger steals bread or wheat, he sins less than the one stealing without this need.[57] And as many as sin after the grace of the Gospel have a greater offense than those who sinned under the Law. And women who take deadly herbs after the conception of a child sin greater than those who take them prior to conception. The same applies to other like things.

---

55   *Second Century on Love* 36, *GrPhilokalia*, p. 304; tr. *The Philokalia*, London, 1981, v. 2, p. 71.

56   *Fifth Century on Various Texts of Theology* 70, *GrPhilokalia*, p. 402; tr. *Third Century of Various Texts, The Philokalia*, v. 2, pp. 227-228.

57   See the end of Canon 86 of Basil the Great where he says that the one who eats a dog in a time of need and hunger does not sin.

6. Concerning Place

The place in which a sin occurs increases or lessens its gravity. For example, if someone murders or steals in a Church, he sins worse than someone who murders or steals in a house, for the one doing these things in the Church sins doubly by committing murder therein, showing both impiety and unbelief toward God, and by stealing therein he commits both robbery and sacrilege. And the one who sins in the desert sins worse than the one who sins in the world; the one in the monastery worse than the one in the city. The one who has many good examples of virtue in his life sins worse than the one in a village who does not have such examples. The one who sins in an open place sins worse than the one who sins in secret.[58]

7. Concerning Frequency

Finally, the gravity of a sin increases or lessens according to the frequency of committal, because the one who sins one or two times has a smaller penance than the one who committed that sin not only one or two or three times, but many times. See also Canon 8 of Ancyra.[59]

---

[58]   Therefore, the divine Chrysostom says that large sins committed in secret have a lesser punishment than those small sins which one commits openly unto the scandal of others: "But it is a wondrous thing, that when someone mistakenly commits a great sin without scandalizing anyone, he is judged less than the one who sins in a lesser degree and scandalizes many" (*Adversus eos qui apud se habent subintroductas Virgines* 7, PG 47, 506).

[59]   See also the divine Chrysostom who says that a greater punishment follows for those who fall again into the same transgression: "Though we have suffered severely for former sins, if we afterward fall into the same, we shall suffer much more severely" (*On John*, Homily 28, 1, PG 59, 211). Also note that because people drink sin as if it were water, they forget how many glasses they drink, as Job says: "Abominable and filthy is man, which drinketh iniquity like water" (Job 15:16). For this reason some who are experienced advise that in these cases, in order for the Spiritual Father to easily find out the number of sins, he must ask the one repenting how many times he committed the sin, and then how many times he fell during the week or the month, and from these things determine the number of times, as much as possible. That is why the Lord also asked the father of the demon-possessed: "How long is it ago since this came unto him? And he said, Of a child" (Mk. 9:21). And because this alone was not sufficient, the father further revealed

8. Concerning the Circumstances Preceding and Following a Sin

The life and attitude of the penitent, before and after a sin, must be examined, according to Canons 3, 5, and 7 of Ancyra, Canon 3 of Neocaesaria, and Canon 29 of Nikephoros, because the one leading a virtuous life prior to the sin is subject to a lesser penance than the one leading a negligent life.[60] The one who ceases from the sin prior to confession has a lesser penance than the one who ceases after confession. The one who on his own accord goes and confesses has a lesser penance than the one who is reproved to do so, according to Canon 7 of Basil the Great, and than the one who confesses out of the fear of death. And simply, the one who repents after the sin has a lesser penance than the one who does not repent. Therefore St. Isidore Pelousiotes says: "Concerning offenses, not only is the type of sin inquired about, but also the disposition of the sinner, and the character, and the time, and the cause. And the circumstances after the sin are inquired into, whether one was pleased, or remorseful, or

the frequency of the possession: "And ofttimes it hath cast him into the fire, and into the waters, to destroy him."

And this is also necessary for us to note, that you, Spiritual Father, who confess people that do not want to say how many times they have sinned on account of their shame, you must ask them if they have sinned a great and exaggerated number of times, rather than asking if they have sinned a small number of times. For example, ask if they have committed a particular sin a thousand times, or two thousand, so that hearing such a great number, they are relieved, and then are more easily able to come down from that number, rather than increasing it.

60   What Solomon said, then, is rather perplexing: "The lowliest man may be pardoned in mercy, but mighty men will be mightily tested" (Wis. 6:7), concerning which see Chapter 4 in the section, *Counsel for the Penitent,* wherein the opposite is seen, that those living virtuous lives and then sinning are penanced less than those living negligent lives and then sinning. As a solution to the quandary, we say there are two reasons for it: 1) because those who for the most part live virtuous lives fall into sin because of coercion or some other involuntary circumstance, and not deliberately or with complete voluntary conviction, as those living negligently do; and 2) because those living virtuous lives, after having committed a sin, are sorry for it until death, thinking about from what height of virtue they fell and from what grace they were deprived on account of the sin, so much that, according to Niketas Stethatos, if those days were not cut short, they would certainly fall into despair, but those living negligent lives would not be saddened (*On the Practice of the Virtues* 56, *GrPhilokalia*, pp. 796-797; *The Philokalia*, v. 4, p. 93).

was insensate, whether one remained as they were, whether one changed, and whether it was dependent on circumstance, whether done out of deceit, whether done by meditation, whether done out of evil habit and custom. And this examination entails many other things."

CHAPTER 6

Concerning Thoughts

Just as so-called diagnostic physicians not only know how to treat external and visible wounds of the body, but they also, by measuring the pulse, learn the internal and invisible maladies of the heart, of the bowels, and the other unseen workings of the human body, and are therefore able to treat them. Likewise, Spiritual Father, it is not enough for you only to know how to treat the external passions of the soul, those acts and deeds and effects of sin, but it is also necessary to know through the confession of the penitent the internal wounds of his soul, which are the hidden passions in his heart and the passionate and evil thoughts, and so treat them with great scrutiny and care. For this reason we thought it good to inform you a little about some general and vital matters concerning thoughts.

1. How many types of thoughts there are

Know then, Spiritual Father, that in general, all thoughts are of three types: some thoughts are good, some thoughts are vain and idle, and some thoughts are bad. Concerning good thoughts, it is not necessary to discuss here in detail how and from what aspects of the soul they arise, for we are satisfied that these are good and therefore beneficial and salvific to the soul. We say this only, Spiritual Father, that if someone says to you during confession that he has good thoughts, you should counsel him to take care to be humble and to never trust in himself and become prideful: 1) because a person on his own is not able to do a good work or say a good word or even think a good thought without the power and help of God: "Not that we are sufficient of ourselves to think any thing as of ourselves; but our sufficiency is of God" (2 Cor. 3:5); 2) because the devil is so cunning and evil, that many times he brings evil from good and through good thoughts throws those who are not careful into self-esteem, and conceit, and haughtiness, from which is caused the destruction and death of the soul. So says Paul: "Sin, that it might appear sin, working death in me by that which is good" (Rom. 7:13); 3) because man never remains in one state, but is so changing and so quickly alters that, with his thoughts, in one instant he is found in Paradise and in another instant he is in hell, as one Saint said. And St. Isaac says: "By the mind we improve, and by the mind we become unprofitable,"[61] hence the one who today has good thoughts may very well have evil ones tomorrow; and 4) tell him that the devil has greater envy and wages a fiercer battle against those who have good thoughts, so that he should have more fear and greater care over himself.

2. What vain thoughts are and how they are corrected

Those thoughts which are not profitable unto the purpose and aim of salvation, as much as to our own soul as to that of our neighbor, and do not look to the necessary requirements and constitution of our body, but to the superfluous and more-than-necessary things, even if they are good, I call vain and idle. According to the *Shorter Rules* of Basil the Great, vain and idle thoughts arise from the idleness of the intellect that is neither engaged in necessary things, nor believes that God is present and searches our hearts and thoughts: "Mental aberration comes from idleness of a mind not occupied in necessary things. For the mind is idle and careless from lack of belief in the presence of God Who tries the heart and reins... He who does this and what is like to it will never dare or have leisure to

---

61   *The Ascetical Homilies of Saint Isaac the Syrian*, Boston, 1984, Homily 69, p. 338. (Translator's note: Hereafter, referred to as *Ascetical Homilies*. It should be noted that, when quoting from this work of St. Isaac, St. Nikodemos references the Greek printed text of 1770 by Nikephoros Theotokis which numbers the Homilies differently than the English language translation of Holy Transfiguration Monastery. See the Table of Homily Equivalences in the Holy Transfiguration Monastery edition, pp. cxiii-cxv.)

think of any of those things that do not conduce to the edification of faith, even if they seem to be good."[62] Concerning these vain and idle thoughts, I say, advise the penitent not to allow his intellect to meditate upon or ponder over them: 1) because just as we have to give an account for idle words on the day of judgment, as the Lord said: "But I say unto you, That every idle word that men shall speak, they shall give account thereof in the day of judgment" (Mt. 12:36), so likewise we have to give an account on the day of judgment for idle and vain thoughts, and indeed, if we willfully left our intellect to go after them.[63] And it is thence apparent, because the Lord reproaches and condemns those servants who remain idle: "Why stand ye here all the day idle?" (Mt. 20:6); 2) because those vain thoughts deprive us from profitable and salvific thoughts, which we are able to have instead of them; and 3) because these idle thoughts are in themselves evil, as they are the cessation of good and become the beginning of evil, and as giving way and permission to the devil to sow in our idle intellect the tares of evil thoughts. Thus does Gregory the Theologian confirm this: "May evil and its original cause, the devil, be destroyed. For while we were idle, the evil one planted tares in us (cf. Mt. 13:25), in order that the neglect of good might become the beginning of evil, just as the beginning of darkness is the retreat of light."[64]

3. The causes of bad thoughts

Know that, in general, bad thoughts derive from two causes,[65] one external and the other internal. The external cause of bad thoughts is the sensible objects of the five senses, that is, those things seen, heard, smelled, tasted, and touched, like bad and indecent and theatrical sights, obscene words and lewd songs, scents and colognes and perfumes, luscious foods

---

62   *Regulæ Brevius* 21, PG 31, 1097B-1097C; tr. *The Ascetic Works of Saint Basil.*
63   Translator's note: Concerning thoughts, St. Mark the Ascetic says: "Never belittle the significance of your thoughts, for not one escapes God's notice" (*On the Spiritual Law* 89); and again: "When you sin, blame your thought, not your action. For had your intellect not run ahead, your body would not have followed" (*ibid.* 119); (*GrPhilokalia*, pp. 95; 96; tr. *The Philokalia*, v. 1, pp. 116; 118).
64   *Oratio* 19, 14, PG 35, 1060C.
65   Concerning bad thoughts, see the footnote of Canon 2 of the Faster.

and pleasurable drinks, fine and soft clothes and comfortable mattresses. All these things cause passionate and hedonistic thoughts in the soul, and then sinful and death-bearing thoughts. Thus, the Prophet Jeremiah on one hand says: "Death has come up into our windows" (Jer. 21:9), the windows meaning the five senses. On the other hand, Gregory the Theologian rather interpreted this saying in broader terms: "And it is kept until the fifth day (that is, the sacrificed Paschal Lamb), perhaps because the Victim, of Whom I am speaking, purifies the five senses, from which comes falling into sin, and around which the war rages, inasmuch as they are open to the incitements to sin."[66]

4. The internal causes of bad thoughts

The internal causes of bad thoughts are four:

1. The imagination, which is like a second sense and receives and records all of the images and perceptions which enter through the five senses, that is, of those things touched, tasted, smelled, and especially of those things heard and seen, is called an internal sense, because it portrays the things sensed so grossly and clearly, just as the external senses. It is a common sense, according to Aristotle, because it receives commonly the experiences of all the senses; and this naturally, because just as lines are disconnected at the perimeter of a circle but converge at its center, so also the five senses, which are disconnected on the outside, converge in the imagination of the soul, but they converge without confusion. So then, from the imagination are born bad thoughts in the soul, making it sense them as really present and to noetically conceptualize through memory those things that it should not have outwardly seen or heard or smelled or tasted or touched, even though it is sensibly far from these things and is settled peaceably in a deserted place. For this reason, in his tetrastich Iambic Poetry, the Theologian said:

---

66   *Oratio* 45, 14, PG 36, 641C; tr. NPNF (V2-07) p. 428. (Translator's note: For a thorough discussion on the guarding of the senses, the imagination, the intellect, and the heart, see the work by St. Nikodemos, *Symbouleutikon Encheiridion*, and the English language translation, *Nicodemos of the Holy Mountain: A Handbook of Spiritual Counsel*, CWS, New York, 1989.)

"A vision caught me, but was checked.
I set up no idol of sin.
Was an idol set up? The experience was avoided.
These are the degrees of deceit of the adversary."[67]

Do you hear? He says an idol of sin was set up and was not recorded in the imagination. The soul escaped the experience at once, that is, it escaped from consenting to the thoughts and from the committal of sin.

2. The passions are a cause of bad thoughts, which are generally two: love and hate, or pleasure and pain, for we are moved passionately either because we love something as pleasurable, or because we hate it as painful.[68] Specifically, the passions are divided into the three aspects of the soul: the intelligent, the appetitive, and the incensive. The passions of the intelligent aspect, according to Gregory of Sinai, are unbelief, blasphemy, evilness, curiosity, double mindedness, gossip, love of applause, pretension, pride, and others. The passions of the appetitive aspect are fornication, adultery, debauchery, greed, unchastity, incontinence, love of pleasure, self-love, and others. The passions of the incensive aspect are anger, bitterness, shouting, audacity, revenge, and others. From these passions of the soul, then, bad thoughts are generally and immediately born, these also being divided into three categories like the passions. From the passions of the intelligent aspect of the soul come bad thoughts, which are generally given the name blasphemous thoughts. From the passions of the appetitive aspect come the so-called obscene thoughts. From the passions of the incensive aspect come the so-called evil thoughts. For this reason the above-mentioned Gregory of Sinai said that: "The passions are the causes of thoughts,"[69]

---

67   *Carmina Moralia* 33, PG 37, 932A-933A.

68   Translator's note: St. Maximos the Confessor says: "Let us reject the pleasure and pain of this present life with what strength we have, and so free ourselves entirely from all thoughts of the passions and all machinations of the demons. For we love the passions because of pleasure and avoid virtue because of pain" (*Third Century on Various Texts of Theology* 52, *GrPhilokalia*, p. 369; tr. *First Century of Various Texts, The Philokalia*, v. 2, p. 175). On the interconnectedness of pleasure and pain, see especially *Sixth Century on Various Texts of Theology* 33-50, *GrPhilokalia*, pp. 412-416; *Fourth Century of Various Texts, The Philokalia*, v.2, pp. 243-248.

69   *On Commandments and Doctrines* 62, *GrPhilokalia*, p. 886.

and Abba Isaac also calls the passions assaults, because they attack within the soul and stir up passionate thoughts.[70]

3. An internal and initial cause of bad thoughts is the demons, for those accursed ones, being light spirits and found superficially around the heart, speak there through internal suggestion and whisper softly from inside all the blasphemous thoughts, all the obscene thoughts, all the evil thoughts, and simply all the bad thoughts. They train the imagination with obscene and impure idols from the senses, as much as when a person is sleeping as when awake. From these the aforementioned passions in the three aspects of the soul are stirred up and make the wretched soul to be a cave of thieves and a slum of the passions. For this reason the abovementioned Gregory of Sinai said: "Occasions give rise to thoughts, thoughts to imaginations, imaginations to the passions, and the passions give entry to the demons… but no one thing in the sequence is self-operative: each is prompted and activated by the demons. The imagination is not wrought into an image, passion is not energized, without unperceived hidden demonic impulsion,"[71] and in another place he says: "Thoughts are the promptings of the demons and precursors of the passions."[72] In agreement with this, St. Isaac says, "I hold as a truth, nevertheless, that our intellect, without the mediation of the holy angels, is able of itself to be moved toward the good uninstructed; however, our senses (the interior ones, that is) cannot come to know evil or be incited by it without the mediation of the demons."[73]

4. An internal cause of thoughts, however remote, is the passionate and corrupted condition of human nature which was brought about by the ancestral sin.[74] This condition remains in our nature also after baptism,

---

70   *Ascetical Homilies*, Homily 62.

71   *On Commandments and Doctrines* 70, *GrPhilokalia*, p. 887; tr. *The Philokalia*, v. 4, p. 224.

72   *Ibid.* 67, *GrPhilokalia*, p. 886; tr. *The Philokalia*, v. 4, p. 223.

73   *Ascetical Homilies*, Homily 28, p. 138.

74   Translator's note: St. Mark the Ascetic says: "When evil thoughts become active within us, we should blame ourselves and not ancestral sin" (*No Righteousness by Works* 120, *GrPhilokalia*, p. 106; tr. *The Philokalia*, v. 1, p. 135). And St. Diadochos of Photiki writes: "For although baptism removes from us the stain resulting from sin, it does not thereby heal the duality of our will immediately, neither does it prevent the demons from attacking us or speaking deceitful words to us. In this way we are led to take up the weapons of righteousness, and to preserve through the power of God what

not as ancestral sin *as such* (for this is removed through baptism, according to Canon 120 of Carthage), but as a consequence of the ancestral sin, for the exertion and test of our free will, and in exchange for greater crowns and rewards, according to the theologians. For after the fall the intellect lost its innocent memory and thought which it had fixed formerly only on the good; but now when it wishes to remember and think upon the good, it is immediately dispersed and also thinks upon the bad. For this reason the divine Gregory of Sinai said: "The source and ground of our thoughts is the fragmented state of our memory. The memory was originally simple and one-pointed, but as a result of the fall its natural powers have been perverted: it has lost its recollectedness in God and has become compound instead of simple, diversified instead of one-pointed."[75]

5. The treatments for bad thoughts

You have learned, Spiritual Father, from what causes come bad thoughts: learn now also how to treat them. Therefore, just as we said earlier how there are two general causes of bad thoughts, so also now we say that there are two general treatments for them, namely, the external and the internal. The external treatments are namely these: for you to advise the penitent not to let his eyes wander, nor to fix his eyes upon the beautiful faces of women, or of young men, because "from looking, lusting is born," according to the ancient proverb, and because the sting of pleasure enters into the soul through these sights, according to Basil,[76] and then follows rising waves of obscene and improper thoughts in the heart which ultimately drown the intellect. You should advise him to guard his ears so as not to hear any bad word, indeed, those erotic and obscene songs, just as the Theologian exhorts, saying: "Block your ears with wax, and foolish words hear not, nor pleasant songs or thrilling melodies,"[77] because from hearing these things the soul is disturbed and begins to recall

---

we could not keep safe through the efforts of our soul alone" (*On Spiritual Knowledge* 78, *GrPhilokalia*, p. 225; tr. *The Philokalia*, v. 1, p. 280).

75   *On Commandments and Doctrines* 60, *GrPhilokalia*, p. 886; tr. *The Philokalia*, v. 4, p. 222.

76   *Ad Adolescentes* 7, PG 31, 581C.

77   *Carmina Moralia* 33, PG 37, 933A.

obscene idols in its imagination and to think immoral thoughts in its heart.

You should advise him to protect his sense of smell from pleasant scents and perfumes because these things are not proper to men but to women, and not modest or prudent women, but immodest and imprudent women. He should protect his sense of taste from the various and luscious foods and keep his tongue from speaking obscene, abusive, and improper words, because according to the Theologian, there is little difference between the word and the act: "There is little difference between 'to hear' and 'to do'."[78] He should protect the sense of touch and his hands from soft clothes and fine garments and should not touch something when there is no need to do so, not only other bodies but also his own body, just as St. Isaac exhorts. The more these are protected the more the bad thoughts diminish from the soul; just as contrarily, the less these are protected the more bad thoughts are engendered. For, if only plain, natural, sensible objects engender neutral thoughts, according to the well-versed Gregory of Sinai: "The raw material of actions generates neutral thoughts,"[79] how will passionate and hedonistic sensible objects not bring about hedonistic and passionate thoughts in the soul?

Advise those, then, Spiritual Father, who have blasphemous thoughts or obscene thoughts or evil thoughts to first treat the passions of the three aspects of their soul, from which arise those bad thoughts, as we have already said. For example, as many as are warred upon by blasphemous thoughts[80] must purify the intelligent aspect of their soul through the sacred prayer, according to St. Maximos, by shedding tears and by abstaining from the reading of heretical books, according to St. Isaac,[81] through spiritual knowledge of the divine Scriptures, according to the divine Serapion, and especially through humility. Having healed the intelligent aspect of the soul through these things, it follows that thoughts of blasphemy and unbelief which arise from this intelligent aspect will also be healed. As many as are warred upon by obscene thoughts must wither the appetitive

---

78   *Ibid.*

79   *On Commandments and Doctrines* 68, *GrPhilokalia*, p. 886; tr. *The Philokalia*, v. 4, p. 224.

80   Look ahead to the footnote and the separate treatment which we have written for you, Spiritual Father, concerning advice for you to give to those having blasphemous thoughts (pp. 146-148).

81   *Ascetical Homilies*, Homily 4, p. 33.

aspect of their soul (from which these types of thoughts arise) through the
practice of threefold self-control with respect to sleep, the stomach, and
bodily comfort, according to St. Maximos and Mark the Ascetic. As many
as are warred upon by evil thoughts, with which they deliberate about how
they will injure and take revenge upon their enemy, must calm the passions
of the incensive aspect of the soul (from which area these thoughts arise)
by love, just as St. Maximos says, by supplicating God on behalf of their
enemies, just as the Lord said: "Pray for them which despitefully use you,
and persecute you" (Mt. 5:44), and by reconciling with their enemies if
they are present, and by imagining mentally the face of their enemy when
he is absent, sweetly and lovingly kissing it and embracing him, according
to St. Diadochos.

By these things are the passions of the three aspects of the soul purified,
quenched, and bridled. It then follows that the bad thoughts sprouting
from these passions are also purified and withered, for it is obvious that
when the causes are quenched the effects are always co-quenched. Testifying
to these things is the Godbearing Maximos who says: "Bridle your soul's
incensive power with love, quench its desire with self-control, give wings
to its intelligence with prayer, and the light of your intellect will never be
darkened,"[82] and the divine Serapion who says verbatim: "The intellect
drunk with spiritual knowledge is perfectly purified; love treats the inflamed
parts of the incensive aspect of the soul; self-control stops the flow of the
appetitive aspect of the soul."

6. The internal treatments for bad thoughts

The internal treatments for bad thoughts are the following three: prayer, rebuttal,
and disregard, just as St. John of the Ladder says: "It is one thing to pray for
deliverance from bad thoughts, another to contradict them, another to despise
and disregard them."[83] The first is characteristic of those who are ill, the second
is characteristic of those struggling, and the third is characteristic of contemplatives.

---

82   *Fourth Century on Love* 80, *GrPhilokalia*, pp. 328-329; tr. *The Philokalia*, v. 2, p. 110.
83   Step 26, PG 88, 1029B; tr. *The Ladder*, p. 173.

A. Prayer, especially noetic prayer,
as a treatment for bad thoughts

Advise, then, Spiritual Father, those who lack the strength to rebut bad thoughts and who still fear the noetic and invisible war of the thoughts, of the demons, and of the passions, to keep silent when passionate thoughts come to them and not to dispute with them with the so-called rebuttal method, but to noetically flee to God alone through prayer, calling upon His aid. This is why the divine Maximos advises this, saying: "Those who still fear the war against the passions and dread the assaults of invisible enemies (like Israel once feared those of Pharaoh) must keep silent; in their struggle for virtue they must not enter into disputes with their enemies but through prayer must entrust all anxiety about themselves to God. To them apply the words of Exodus: 'The Lord will fight for you, and you must be silent' (Ex. 14:14)."[84] They are to flee to God through prayer, not only through prayer which is said with the mouth, but more rather through noetic prayer spoken in the heart with the inner word of the heart. This prayer means that they who are warred upon by demonic thoughts are to keep the inner and esoteric word of the heart silent from every other thought, in order for the inner word to repeat and say this short and so-called single-phrased prayer: "Lord Jesus Christ Son of God have mercy on me." And while the inner word below is repeating this prayer, the intellect is to bring down its noetic energy into the heart and noetically concentrate with all of its might on the words spoken by the inner word of prayer, without imagining anything noetic or sensible, just as all the divine Fathers, ancient and new, commonly teach.[85] This noetic prayer is the only mighty, the only helpful, and the only victorious weapon in the noetic war of the thoughts, and this is necessarily so, for the war is noetic, and noetic weapons are required to be victorious. Notice how this single-phrased prayer treats all of the causes for bad thoughts. 1) The intellect, becoming accustomed to turning into itself and noetically conversing with God through prayer, neither sees those sensible objects which it desires nor

---

84   *First Century on Theology* 30, *GrPhilokalia*, p. 334; tr. *The Philokalia*, v. 2, p. 120.

85   See *GrPhilokalia*, pp. 1178-1202; *The Philokalia*, v. 4, pp. 67-75; 275-286.

are its senses moved, according to the maxim: "Those who make most use
of the intellect make little use of the senses."[86] 2) The inner word of the
heart, always repeating and saying the prayer, "Lord Jesus Christ," ceases
from being an organ of the evil spirits and from speaking some other
obscene or blasphemous or evil word; and because the imagination, being
the bridge of the demons by which they mingle with the soul, according
to the divine Fathers,[87] is purified, I say, from every passionate idol by
lowering the energy of the intellect into the heart, naked and cleansed of
every shape and form of the imagination, for on account of the narrowness
of the place of the heart the imagination is filtered and stripped and leaves
outside every gross image, just as the serpent, when passing through narrow
places, is stripped of its old skin.[88] 3) The warmth generated in the heart
from the continual repetition of the sacred prayer chases away and scorches
the assaults of evil thoughts like a fly, according to the great Gregory of
Thessaloniki,[89] and it scatters the passions of the intellectual aspect of the
soul like clouds and smoke and causes it to become bright and radiant, it
placates and calms the passions of the incensive aspect, it scatters the
passions of the desirable aspect, and draws all of that loving power to itself
and to the love of the one being repeated, Jesus Christ. 4) Always repeating
the sweet and very name of Jesus Christ in the heart flogs, wounds, and
drives away the demons from the heart, those leaders and creators of all

---

86   Plutarch, *Moralia, De Curiositate* 521; (cf. Plato, *Phaedo* 66A). (Translator's note: And St.
Basil says: "Thus the intellect, saved from dissipation from without and not thrown upon the world
through the senses, falls back upon itself and thereby ascends to the contemplation of God" (*Epistulae*
II, 2, PG 32A, 228A).)

87   See *GrPhilokalia*, p. 1068; *Writings from the Philokalia on Prayer of the Heart*, London, 1951, pp.
234-236.

88   Translator's note: In his *Aoratos Polemos* (*Unseen Warfare*), St. Nikodemos adds to this same
illustration the following one: "And just as water which is compressed and concentrated through a
narrow hose gains pressure and shoots all the more powerfully upward, in like manner the more the
intellect is occupied with the narrow prayer of the heart and with contemplation of itself, the more
concentrated and powerful it becomes, and the higher it rises above every passion and assault of the
thoughts, and above every sensory and noetic shape and form, all of these things remaining outside
and unable to enter in" (Athens, 2003, p. 116).

89   Cf. *Homily 11, On the precious and lifegiving Cross*, PG 151, 129A; *The Homilies of Saint Gregory
Palamas*, v. 1, South Canaan, 2002, p. 118.

the bad thoughts and passions of the soul. That is why the divine John of the Ladder said: "Flog your enemies with the name of Jesus."[90] And 5) the manifold memory of bad thoughts, brought about by the Fall of Adam, becomes simple and is healed through the unified memory of Jesus Christ, according to Gregory of Sinai who says: "The memory is restored above all by constant mindfulness of God consolidated through prayer, for this spiritually elevates the memory from a natural to a supranatural state."[91]

Why say more? The sweetest name of Jesus, repeated continuously, and with compunction, and with desire and faith, in the depth of the heart, lulls all bad thoughts. And where in the past "out of the heart proceeded evil thoughts, murders, adulteries, fornications, thefts, false witness, blasphemies" (Mt. 15:19), as the Lord said, afterward come good thoughts, spiritual reflections, words of wisdom, judgments, analyses, and discernment, as it is written: "The thoughts of the righteous are right" (Pr. 12:5). Therefore, teach, advise, and prompt penitents and all Christians, Spiritual Father, to repeat continuously in their heart the name of Jesus Christ through the prayer above, because this noetic and uninterrupted prayer in the heart was not given only to ascetics and monks, but also to all the Christians in the world. Therefore the Apostle Paul commands and says to those in the world to pray always: "Pray without ceasing" (1 Th. 5:17), because it is possible for them to pray continuously: when they work, when they eat and drink, when they are at home, when they are outside, when they are sitting, and when they are walking, if only they wish to forsake vain chatter and rather gather their intellect into their heart.

B. Rebuttal as a treatment for bad thoughts

Those things say to the ill and the weak, Spiritual Father. To those who struggle and have some strength to fight against bad thoughts and invisible demons and the passions, you are to advise them, Spiritual Father, to stand against their evil and obscene and blasphemous thoughts with incensive rebuttal and contradiction, in order that through this noetic warfare of

---

90   Step 21, PG 88, 945C; tr. *The Ladder*, p. 131.

91   *On Commandments and Doctrines* 61, *GrPhilokalia*, p. 886; tr. *The Philokalia*, v. 4, p. 223.

rebuttal they may receive crowns from God, as John of the Ladder says: "As our conflicts increase, so do our crowns."[92] This is how the Prophet David rebutted and stood against the invisible demons which warred against him through thoughts, saying: "So shall I give an answer to them (with a word of rebuttal, that is) that reproach me" (Ps. 118:42).

Thus, through rebuttal did our Master Jesus Christ conquer the three great battles with which the devil assaulted Him on the mountain: He conquered love of pleasure by saying: "Man shall not live by bread alone, but by every word that proceedeth out of the mouth of God" (Dt. 8:3; Mt. 4:4); He conquered love of glory by saying: "Thou shalt not tempt the Lord thy God" (Dt. 6:16; Mt. 4:7); and He conquered love of money by saying: "Thou shalt worship the Lord thy God, and him only shalt thou serve" (Dt. 6:13; Mt. 4:10). In this way many of the Ascetic Holy Fathers, especially those of Tabenessi, as is written in the *Gerontikon*, fought through rebuttal and conquered bad thoughts and the passions, thereby being crowned. You should teach them, however, not to only battle through rebuttal, but also with prayer to God; because according to St. Maximos, as many as war against thoughts through prayer and are weak, are not able to also rebut them, but as many as are strong and rebut thoughts are also able to pray against them: "The one who speaks against thoughts is also able to pray against them; but the ones who pray against them, not at leisure to speak against them, can only in one manner pray against them."[93]

St. Isaac, however, says that for both strugglers and strong ones, it is better and safer not to rebut the thoughts sown by the enemy, but to flee to God through prayer and tears: 1) because the soul does not always possess the strength to fight, so that many times when seeking to strike and conquer the demonic thoughts, we are rather struck and conquered by them; 2) because when someone is fighting bad thoughts and the thoughts fight back with their impure shapes and passionate idols, after they are conquered their pollutions remain in his intellect and the stench in his noetic nostrils for a long time. I also say, 3) that whoever flees to God and to Jesus alone in the time of battle against thoughts and considers himself unworthy and

---

92   Step 26, PG 88, 1069A; tr. *The Ladder*, p. 187.
93   *Scholion* on Step 26.

unable to fight, but that only Jesus is strong and mighty in this invisible warfare, avoids pride and exhibits humility: "The Lord strong and mighty, the Lord, mighty in war" (Ps. 23:8); and again: "Be of good cheer; I have overcome the world" (Jn. 16:33), that is, the passions, and thoughts, and the devil. "The man who does not contradict the thoughts sowed in us by the enemy, but who severs any conversation with them by means of his supplication to God, may have this fact as a sign that his intellect has found the wisdom which is of grace, and that his true knowledge has freed him of many labours... For we do not have the strength to gainsay at all times every thought that opposes us, so that they may be silenced; and it often happens that they inflict a severe wound upon us which is long in healing... Yet even if you conquer them, the filth of such thoughts will pollute your mind and their stench will linger long in your nostrils. By the first method, however (that is, by fleeing to God through prayer), you will be free of all this and of fear; for there is no helper like God."[94]

C. Disregard as a treatment for bad thoughts

Thirdly and lastly, Spiritual Father, say to those who have received weapons and arms from the grace of God, in order that they may be victorious in the noetic and invisible warfare, to disregard the bad thoughts which the devil sows in them as the barking of a small dog, as worthless beasts and as vermin, and as nothing. Tell them also not to fear the threats which are raised against them or to be drawn to the pleasures offered to them, but to struggle: 1) believing completely and hoping in the infinite strength of the Almighty God and in the invincible aid of our great Commander Jesus Christ: "This is the victory that overcometh the world, even our faith. Who is he that overcometh the world, but he that believeth that Jesus is the Son of God?" (1 Jn. 5:4-5); and 2) believing and knowing that after the Cross and the death of our Lord the devil has no power over us, but has become most weak and powerless, as it is written: "The swords

---

94   *Ascetical Homilies*, Homily 54, p. 269. See also Homily 6, p. 58, where Abba Isaac says: "It is better to elude the passions by the recollection of the virtues than by resisting and disputing with them."

of the enemy have utterly failed" (Ps. 9:6). Fortunate indeed is whoever received a sovereign intellect and which was equipped and armed by grace, and thus armed disregards all obscene and blasphemous and evil thoughts as nothing. One reason is because there is no greater victory over and shame of the demons than this disregard, as St. Maximos says: "Those ignored in this way, are always and forever despised, for the one ignoring is prepared, already equipped by grace."[95] Another is because these people, by means of this disregard, remain perfectly elusive to bad thoughts and demons, saying with the Prophet David: "I was dumb and opened not my mouth" (Ps. 38:12), and: "I set a guard for my mouth, when the sinner stood up against me" (Ps. 38:2).

7. How harmful bad thoughts are and how beneficial their treatment is

We have set these things out for you in the present chapter in detail, Spiritual Father, and see to it that you read it continuously, because you have a great need for knowledge of these things. Know that the most difficult and fine work of your vocation is the spiritual understanding and knowledge of the thoughts and passions of the soul and the scientific treatment of them. Therefore, do not take after those mindless ones who say: "Thoughts are not sin; man is not punished because of thoughts," and other like things. Rather, be convinced and informed that every sin, and hell itself, has as its beginning and root and center a bad thought[96]; and again conversely, a bad thought is the beginning and root and center of every sin and of hell itself, because, just as a small pebble or rock, when it happens to fall into some well, first causes a small circle, then the small circle causes another large one, and the large one another larger one, and so on until it reaches the edge of the well. Likewise, an assault from one

---

95   *Scholion* on Step 26.

96   Translator's note: St. Philotheos of Sinai says: "The person who gives himself over to evil thoughts cannot keep his outer self free from sin; and if evil thoughts have not been uprooted from the heart, they are bound to manifest themselves in evil actions" (*Texts on Watchfulness* 33, *GrPhilokalia*, p. 524; tr. *The Philokalia*, v. 3, p. 29).

bad thought begets a passionate coupling with the thought; coupling begets consent; consent begets the act; the act begets habit; habit begets addiction; addiction begets unrepentance; unrepentance begets hell. Do you see this long and intertwined chain, how it obtained its beginning and center from a bad thought, so that the whole stands upon a thought? For this reason the divine Gregory of Thessaloniki said that the intellect is the first victim of all sins, because the intellect first suffers and is wounded from a thought of sin.[97] His namesake, Gregory the Theologian, calls passionate thoughts the firstborn of Egypt, that is, of sin, because from passionate thoughts are born second and third and fourth children of sin. Passionate thoughts are the seed of the Chaldeans, that is, of the demons, because from this seed of thoughts are conceived and born evil deeds, infants of the daughter of Babylon, that is, of sin, of the one born from confusion, as Niketas explains, because these infants of the thoughts grow and become men through action: "And Egypt mourns the firstborn of her own thoughts and actions which are also called in the Scripture the seed of the Chaldeans removed, and the infants of Babylon dashed against the rocks and destroyed."[98]

Therefore, Spiritual Father, if you kill the passionate thoughts of the penitent through your counsel, you will become another angel destroying the firstborn of Egypt, concerning which it is written in Exodus (12:23). You will become like God, Who says to blot out the seed of the Chaldeans: "The Lord hath loved him: he will do his pleasure on Babylon, and his arm shall be on the Chaldeans" (Is. 48:14), and if you smash those infants of bad thoughts before they can grow up, you will become worthy of that Beatitude which the divine David says: "Blessed shall he be who shall seize and dash thine infants against the rock" (Ps. 136:12). Not only will you be blessed, but also the penitent will be blessed, because through confession[99]

---

97   *To the Most Reverend Nun Xenia*, *GrPhilokalia*, p. 940; *The Philokalia*, v. 4, p. 309.

98   *Oratio* 45, 15, PG 36, 644B.

99   Although it is very good and beneficial for one to confess all the thoughts (if it is possible) with which the devil assaults him, some of the Fathers, however, say in the *Gerontikon* that it is not necessary for us to confess all of our thoughts, but only those which disturb us and which war upon us the most. That we are required to confess not only the evil works which we did and the evil words which we spoke but also the bad thoughts which we thought upon in our heart, the Old Law also bears witness, inasmuch as it commands that not only the right shoulder of the animal to be

he smashes his bad thoughts on the Rock, that is, on Christ, running to Him through prayer and calling upon His aid.

Why should I say so much? Whoever has passionate and bad thoughts in his heart is before the "God that searchest out the hearts and reins" (Ps. 7:9), repulsive and an adulterer and unclean. This is what God Himself decided, saying concerning evil thoughts: "These are the things which defile a man" (Mt. 15:20). And Solomon says: "The thoughts of the wicked are an abomination to the Lord" (Pr. 15:26). If you then, Spiritual Father, liberate the penitent from these thoughts, you cleanse the inside of his soul from impurity, and when it becomes pure, certainly all of his outward works and actions will also be pure, just as the Lord said: "Cleanse first that which is within the cup and platter, that the outside of them may be clean also" (Mt. 23:26); and if you sanctify the root, which is his heart, the branches will certainly also be holy, which are his offspring and works: "If the root be holy, so are the branches" (Rom. 11:16).

---

sacrificed be given to the priests, but also its breast: "And the priest shall burn the fat upon the altar: but the breast shall be Aaron's and his sons'. And the right shoulder shall ye give unto the priest for an heave offering of the sacrifices of your peace offerings" (Lev. 7:31-32). This revealed symbolically and enigmatically that through confession we must bring to the priests and Spiritual Fathers all of our actions, of which the shoulder is a symbol, and all the thoughts of our heart, of which the breast is a symbol, being the heart's protector. This is how the wise Niketas allegorizes this passage, in his explanation of Gregory the Theologian's *Oration on Baptism*: "The law designated the shoulder and the breast as a priestly portion of every sacrifice, obscurely signifying the necessity of placing the heart in the hands of the priests through confession, for this is the symbol of the breast, being the protector of the heart; actions are indicated by the shoulder, which, through the priests, are related to God." (See chapter 1 of part three of this book, *Counsel for the Penitent*, especially the footnotes there, in which is discussed how one is to examine his conscience, and also Chapter 4, Precaution 3, *Frequent Confession*, Benefit 5). Concerning this, Makarios the Great of Egypt also says: "There are always those who say that the Lord requires only visible fruits from men. The interior ones God will rectify. But this is not the way things are. For as one defends himself against the exterior man, so also he must enter into the lists and do battle against his thoughts. For the Lord demands of you that you be angry with yourself and engage in battle with your mind, neither consenting to or taking pleasure in wicked thoughts" (*Homiliæ Spirituales 50*, Homily 3, PG 34, 469B-469C; tr. *Pseudo-Macarius: The Fifty Spiritual Homilies and the Great Letter*, CWS, New York, 1992, p. 48).

CHAPTER 7

Concerning the Mystery of Repentance

After the knowledge of these things, you, who are to become a Spiritual Father, must also know the Mystery of Repentance well, which is the more common matter you will be engaged in. Likewise, you are also to know the aspects of repentance, which are: contrition, confession, and satisfaction. We judged it more fitting, however, to write about these things in Part Three, *Counsel for the Penitent*, and you may read about them there.

So, if you know well the things which we have said up to this point, you will be able to undertake the vocation of spiritual direction, possessing these things and also what we have to say in the following eighth chapter. If you know that you are still lacking and inept in the knowledge of these things, keep yourself, for the sake of the Lord, from becoming a Spiritual Father. For one, because not having the necessary knowledge, instead of becoming a physician, you will become a murderer of so many souls, not one of which the whole world is worthy, and you will likewise become a murderer of your own soul. Another reason is because the Lord will not only not accept you to become a Spiritual Father[100] without this knowledge, but not even to become a priest at all, for as He says through Hosea: "Because you have rejected knowledge, I reject you from being a priest to me" (Hos. 4:6). Nor will it avail you to say, "I was tested in these things by my hierarch," because the examination of the hierarch presupposes that you already possess this knowledge on your own, and not that he gives it to you; neither does he give you eyes to see if you are blind.

---

100   God does not accept you to become a Spiritual Father because He wants the one who intends to be appointed a steward of the souls of His people to be not only faithful (that is, virtuous, according to Theophylact), but also prudent and knowledgeable, for He says: "Who then is that faithful and wise steward, whom his lord shall make ruler over his household, to give them their portion of meat in due season?" (Lk. 12:42). The sacred Theophylact interprets this passage saying: "Both faithfulness and wisdom are required. I myself know many who appear zealous in virtue and are God-fearing and faithful, but because they are not able to manage wisely the affairs of the Church, they cause damage not only to property but to souls as well" (PG 123, 900D; tr. *The Explanation by Blessed Theophylact of the Holy Gospel According to St. Luke*, 1997, p. 156).

CHAPTER 8

Concerning an Active Priesthood and
Permission to Become a Spiritual Father

We said in the beginning what type of life and virtue you must have, Father, you who intend to become a Spiritual Father. Then we spoke about the matters about which you must have knowledge. Now we tell you a third thing, that you must be a canonically and lawfully ordained priest: not a deposed priest because of your manifest transgressions, not one who has resigned from the priesthood because of your hidden and degrading transgressions, not one suspended for a time, but an active priest having ordination.[101] Fourthly, and above all, you must have the blessing (through the laying on of hands) and the permission by an *Entalterion* (letter of authorization) from the local hierarch for you to be a Spiritual Father.[102]

---

101   That one manifestly deposed is not able to be a Spiritual Father is witnessed to by: 1) the response of John, Bishop of Kitros, in which he says that: "Whoever is a Spiritual Father, and commits some transgression worthy of deposition, is deposed from the priesthood and from the vocation of the Spiritual Father"; and 2) Symeon of Thessaloniki says that: "The one who hears confessions of thoughts must both bless and recite the prayer of forgiveness, and liturgize, and give Communion to those who have confessed, and intercede to God on behalf of those having repented; the one who is deposed cannot perform any of these things" (*Responsa as Gabrielem Pentapolitanum*, Question 11, PG 155, 854C). That the one who resigned from the priesthood because of his unworthiness also cannot become a Spiritual Father is obvious: 1) from the same John Kitros, where in one response (preserved in manuscripts) he explicitly says: "The one who willingly or against his will resigns from the priesthood cannot hear confessions of thoughts"; 2) from Canon 8 of Nicholas the Patriarch which says that: "Whoever on his own accord resigns from the priesthood is not able to say either, 'Blessed is our God,' or "May Christ our true God,' nor can he receive Communion inside of the altar, nor can he cense with the censer." Thus, if one is prevented from doing these things, how much more is one prevented from becoming a Spiritual Father? And 3) from common sense, because if they resign from the priesthood, how can they hear confession, which is an active power of the priesthood? That the one who has resigned from the priesthood is also not able to perform the other sacred duties of the priesthood, look ahead to the end of Chapter 9 in the footnote of the section entitled, *How to care for ordained clergymen who have sinned* (pp. 160-162).

102   The *Entalterion* is written this way: "Our Humbleness by the grace of the All-holy and Perfecting Spirit appoints to you, the Very Reverend among hieromonks (or priests) Father (*name*), as an honorable man, and worthy of reverence, the liturgical office of Spiritual Father. Therefore, you are obliged to receive the thoughts of all those who come to you to confess their transgressions, and to

CHAPTER 9

What One Must Do When He Becomes a Spiritual Father

1. How to conduct confession

Possessing these things and thus being prepared, you ascend, Spiritual Father, and are seated on the lofty chair of confession, with piety, gladdened

---

question them, and to search the depths of their hearts, and their ruminations, and to find out their actions; by this you have the principles and grounds and the canonical responsibility to inhibit and to weigh the results and actions of those who come to you, and to apply to them medicines for their addictions and their dispositions, and to become all things to all men, in order to win all men; now reproving, now penancing, and supplicating, and by every means actualizing their salvation. Thus, binding what must be bound, and loosing those things worthy of being loosed. You are also obliged to inspect and finely examine those approaching the dignity of the priesthood, as the divine and sacred Canons demand, so as not to communicate in others' sins, and your own soul inherit the eternal fire together with theirs. You are also to tonsure monks with examination and in the presence of their sponsors, according to the Canons, as usual. And above all you are obliged to behave in all piety and modesty, as is proper to spiritual men, as having to give account to God. Thus our present *Entalterion* is given to you as a declaration." Note that the hierarch giving the *Entalterion* must lay his hand upon the head of the future Spiritual Father. This laying on of hands is necessary: 1) because even though we may suppose it, a priest, as a priest, neither has the power nor the faculty to bind and to loose sins, as some would like; and if we suppose that he has the power, he does not however have the faculty, as others would like. The laying on of hands of the hierarch must always occur in order for the power and the faculty to be given through it, or just the faculty; 2) because through this laying on of hands the Spiritual Father receives the spirit of prudence, in order to worthily administer his vocation, and to wisely care for the souls of sinners, just as through the laying on of Moses' hands Joshua the son of Nun also received the spirit of prudence, as it is written: "And Joshua the son of Nun was full of the spirit of wisdom; for Moses had laid his hands upon him" (Dt. 34:9). Therefore the Acts of the Apostles also says that through the hands of the Apostles was the Holy Spirit given (Acts 8:18). And to say it simply, this laying on of hands is good, as communicating a blessing. And because Tarasios the Patriarch (as the first Act of the Seventh Ecumenical Council states) received a blessing by the aforementioned laying on of hands, in accordance with Canon 8 of the First Ecumenical Council. Whatever priest conducts confession without the permission of the hierarch, is deposed, according to Michael of Constantinople, just as those who exercise the priesthood away from their parish are deposed by the Canons, according to Balsamon (Explanation of Canon 7 of Carthage, PG 138, 48A-48C). Symeon of Thessaloniki says that such a person, on account of sin, is like a layman or someone profane conducting the things of the priesthood (*Responsa as Gabrielem Pentapolitanum*, Question 11, PG 155, 860A-864D).

and sweetened in soul and appearance, and through your character exhibiting divine love, according to Symeon of Thessaloniki.[103] Seated there, you must be mindful of the fact that toward the penitent you represent three persons: father, physician, and judge. As father, you must receive the sinner with open arms, as the heavenly Father received that Prodigal Son without deriding or rejecting him on account of his sins. As physician, you must treat his wounds with oil and wine, that is, with philanthropy and penance,[104] according to the example of the one who fell among the thieves. As judge, your decision must be most just and not swayed on account of bribes,[105]

---

103   *De Poenitentia*, ch. 257, PG 155, 481B.

104   Translator's note: "Penances in the Orthodox tradition have a pedagogical, philanthropic, therapeutic, and ecclesiastical characteristic. The use of penances is not for the punishment of the sinner, but for his healing from the illness of sin. The superficial appearance of penances gives the impression that they are intended as penalties. The Fathers of the Church, however, stress and emphasize that the aim of penances is the healing and the therapeutic care of the sinner. The Spiritual Father who has the charisma of discernment takes care of matters. Sometimes he adheres to the exact observance of the commandments and of the Canons, while other times he applies "κατ᾽ οἰκονομίαν," the principle of economy," Protopresbyter Vasileios Kalliakmanes, *Methodologika protera tes poimantikes* (*A Priori Methodologies of Pastoral Care*), Thessaloniki, 2000, pp. 176-177 (in Greek). See also, Lewis J. Patsavos, *Spiritual Dimensions of the Holy Canons*, esp. pp. 41-49. Note that *oikonomia* (*economy*) is defined by Patriarch Nicholas Mystikos as "an imitation of the divine philanthropy" (*Epistulae XXXII*, PG 111, 213A). And St. Gregory the Theologian says: "For whom the Lord loveth He chasteneth (Prov. 3:12), and a penance is a fatherly action; while every soul which is unchastised, is unhealed (*Oratio* 16,15, PG 35, 956A).

105   See Canon 23 of the Sixth Council which says that whoever seeks money or any other compensation, however small, in return for imparting the divine Mysteries, such as divine Communion, is deposed, because grace is not sold nor is sanctification acquired with money. Therefore, it is apparent that those Spiritual Fathers must be deposed who seek money from the Christians who confess to them, and so give them permission to commune even if they are unworthy. The most-wise Joseph Bryennios deplores this greatest impiety in one of his homilies, saying that it is the reason for the slavery of our race under the atheist Muslim Turks. "What will you give me to forgive you so you can receive Communion?" This is nothing other than that which Judas said to the Jews when he betrayed the Lord: "What will ye give me, and I will deliver him unto you?" (Mt. 26:15). Holy hierarchs, see to it, for the love of God, that such a great evil be eradicated from your Sees, that which causes sweetest Jesus to be sold daily, He Who was sold once for the race of man. Brother Christians, guard yourselves well for the sake of the Lord, so as not to give money to those insulters of Christ and simoniac Spiritual Fathers, falsely receiving forgiveness from them. Know for certain that you are not forgiven, even if you give all of the money in the world: 1) because Spiritual Fathers are not lords and masters of the Mysteries of God, but only servants and stewards, as the divine Paul says (1 Cor. 4:1); and 2) because they loose those things which are proper and legitimate, but never

or fear, or friendship, or any other passion, so that it may be immovable upon the earth and in heaven, according to the saying: "Whatsoever ye shall bind on earth shall be bound in heaven: and whatsoever ye shall loose on earth shall be loosed in heaven" (Mt. 18:18); and because the judgment of the Spiritual Father, which is the judgment of God, must be unbiased and above all partiality, just as it is written: "Ye shall not respect persons in judgment; but ye shall hear the small as well as the great; ye shall not be afraid of the face of man; for the judgment is God's" (Dt. 1:17).

And so having a time and place established for sacred confession—the time being in the morning,[106] the place being mainly the Church, or as occasion demands, a modest house, clean and peaceful, as Symeon of Thessaloniki says,[107] in which there also must be an icon of our Master Christ and certainly of His Crucifixion—you bring the one to confess there. Beginning the service with, "Blessed is our God," say the *Trisagion* prayers and the 50th Psalm, and then turn to the penitent saying the following:

---

those things which are improper and illegitimate. Therefore, as the Apostle Peter said to Clement of Rome, and as the Church, which gives the *Entalterion* to the Spiritual Father, ordains: "Bind what must be bound, and loose what must be loosed" (*Epistola Clementis ad Jacobum* 2, PG 2, 36B). Even if those Spiritual Fathers forgive sins, God condemns you; and if they loose you here on earth, God has you bound in heaven, both in this age and in the future one, if you do not seek another Spiritual Father to rectify you with God, without a bribe. In addition, the holy hierarchs are not to take money, but are to appoint Spiritual Fathers without bribery, so that the Spiritual Fathers do not have a pretext to take gifts from penitents for confession.

106   Although all times are suitable for confession (especially in a time of need), according to Job in his *Concerning the Mysteries*, the most suitable time is the morning, because at that time the intellect, of both the Spiritual Father and the penitent, is more clear and collected. That which David says also bears witness to this: "In the morning I slew all the sinners of the land, utterly to destroy out of the city of the Lord all them that work iniquity" (Ps. 100:9), namely, in the morning I killed through confession all those evil thoughts of my heart and destroyed from my soul all the lawless demons and passions. According to Timothy (Canon 18), some should start confessing from ten years old, others from an older age. According to Balsamon, children should confess after six years of age (*Responsa ad Interrogationes Marci*, Question 48, PG 138, 996C-997A).

107   *De Poenitentia*, ch. 257, PG 155, 481B.

2. Pre-confession counsel of the Spiritual Father
to the penitent

"Behold, child, Christ (gesturing toward His icon) is invisibly present, awaiting your confession; do not therefore be ashamed, or afraid, and hide any of your sins, but from your whole heart confess them, so that you may receive forgiveness for them from Christ Himself. If you hide any, know that the unconfessed sin will not only stand marked upon your conscience, like letters printed on paper, so that it will appear on the day of judgment before all the angels and all men, but you will also bring upon yourself another sin, that of sacrilege. Therefore, because you have come to a physician, see to it that you are healed completely and do not remain unhealed, because this harm will be upon yourself."

Then, having the penitent kneel before the icon of Christ, or sit on a stool, ask him who he is (if you do not know him), how long it has been since his last confession, and if he is prepared to confess, having examined himself properly.[108]

After these things, and having asked him if he believes absolutely and unwaveringly in all of the Dogmas of the Eastern Church, in the contents of the Symbol of Faith (Creed), and in the proclamations of the Seven Holy and Ecumenical Councils, of the local councils, and of the Holy Fathers, without any addition or subtraction,[109] say to him:

---

108   If the penitent is literate, and if the occasion affords itself, tell him, Spiritual Father, to read the counsel for the penitent which is in this book, in order that he may learn from it how to prepare for confession, and so let him come for you to hear his confession.

109   It is a most profitable thing and necessary for salvation, Spiritual Father, to make sure that you impress upon the intellect of penitents, especially those who are illiterate and villagers, the two primary and catholic Dogmas of our Faith, namely, the Dogma of the Theology of the Holy Trinity, and the Dogma of the Incarnate Economy. Concerning the Dogma of the Holy Trinity you can say the following: You must believe, my child, that the One God in which we believe is Three according to Persons—Father, Son, and Holy Spirit—and that the Father alone begets the Son and alone issues forth the Holy Spirit; the Son is begotten from the Father alone and the Holy Spirit proceeds from the Father alone. Although there are Three Persons, there is One God according to nature, just as the disk of the sun and the ray and the light are three, yet the sun remains one. You must believe that this God made all visible creatures, the sky, the earth, the sea, and all that is in them; He also made all the invisible creatures, angels, demons, and souls. Concerning the Incarnate Economy you

3. That properly, the Spiritual Father is not to question

"Know, child, that according to other criteria, whoever reveals himself to be an offender is chastised; but according to the criterion of confession, whoever first reveals his sin on his own is forgiven. For this reason the Spiritual Father has no need to question the one confessing about what he did, for then the penitent is examined rather than confessed. However, the one confessing must by himself say his sins in order to receive forgiveness for them, for so God also commands: 'A righteous man accuses himself at the beginning of his speech, until the other comes and examines him' (Pr. 18:17), and: 'First say your transgressions, that you may be justified' (Is. 43:26). Therefore, you also child, in order to disgrace sin and the devil, first say your transgressions, in order to be justified."

4. How the Spiritual Father is to listen to sins

Having said all these things, Spiritual Father, you are to keep silent and listen to the one confessing his sins, and even if they are great and many, be careful so as not to be shocked or sigh or display any other gesture or sign showing how disgusted or troubled you are, for just as when a deer is in labor, and the slightest movement of a leaf is able to prevent the deer from giving birth, as the natural philosophers say, so also it is with the sinner who is in labor, trying to say his sins, that a single gesture may cause him to have difficulty and therefore not give birth, that is, not confess, as it is written: "The children are come to the birth, and there is not strength to bring forth" (Is. 37:3). Rather, encourage him every moment, telling him

---

can say the following: You must believe, my child, that for the salvation of us men who transgressed the Commandment of God, one Person of the Holy Trinity, that is, the Son, became a perfect man as we are, but without sin, by the Holy Spirit and the Virgin Mary, being one Person and two natures, Divine and Human, that is, He is perfect God and perfect Man, Who suffered, was crucified, was buried, and rose on the third day, and ascended into the heavens and is now seated at the right hand of the Father, and will come again in order to judge all men, all of whom will be raised: and to the good who kept His commandments He will give an eternal kingdom; but to the evil who transgressed His commandments He will give everlasting hell.

not to be ashamed, and that you also, from the things you hear, are like him in every way and a sinner, and that after he confesses he will go home alleviated and joyful because he relieved his conscience from the burden of sin.

You are to examine each sin you hear, Spiritual Father, by the seven circumstances which we have mentioned, namely: who committed the sin; what kind of sin was committed;[110] why was it committed; in what manner was it committed;[111] at what time, where, and how many times was it

---

110   The divine Chrysostom says that confession of sins should be according to their specific kind, as do Metrophanes Kritopoulos (*Confession of the Eastern Church*) and St. John of the Ladder (*The Ladder*, Step 4 and *To the Shepherd*). The classes of sin are the evil deed, the evil word, and the evil thought. The specific kinds of sin derive from these three classes. For example, the kinds of evil deeds are sexual immorality, adultery, theft, murder, etc. The kinds of evil words are blasphemy, lying, perjury, etc. The kinds of evil thoughts are heresy, pride, etc. One should confess all sins according to their specific kind, including obscene sins and those of the flesh. For example, it is not sufficient for someone to merely say that they committed a sin of the flesh, but must say what kind of carnal sin it was, whether sexual immorality, or adultery, or sodomy; and whether it was committed with a layman, or someone ordained, or a monk; and whether with a stranger, or a relative. This is because there is no other way for him to be corrected appropriately by the Spiritual Father. So that which St. John of the Ladder says (*To the Shepherd*), that sins of the flesh are not to be confessed according to their specific kind, must be qualified, I say. Namely, that they are not to be confessed according to their specific kind to God, but to the Spiritual Father, as also Abba Mark says, and as we will say further ahead, so that the divine John may not be found to be speaking against himself and others, who teach that confession should be according to the specific kind of sin to the Spiritual Father.

111   The manner in which the sin was committed must be examined, as well as the place in which it was committed, because these circumstances increase or decrease the gravity of the sin and the penance given to the sinner; and also because if these are not confessed here, they will then be manifested there, according to Hosea who says: "Now their own doings have beset them about" (Hos. 7:2), and according to Basil the Great who says: "We will immediately see all our works through memory as if they are standing before us, and they will appear before our minds in the same detailed manner as they were done or said" (*In Isaiam Prophetam* 3, 120, PG 30, 312C). Therefore, it is not forbidden for one to confess his sins according to the manner in which they were committed, unto his greater shame and to alleviate his conscience even more, and especially for his soul to be further assured that on the day of judgment the manner of his confessed sin will not be displayed. For this reason, if ever such a fervent penitent appears, the Spiritual Father must be patient and listen to his sins, even if they are obscene. However, some say that sins of the flesh should not be confessed according to all of the ways in which they were committed so that the Spiritual Father not be scandalized, especially when women are confessing, and also when those confessing say them, not out of shame, but on account of their stupidity and barbarity, without showing any contrition whatsoever

committed; and also which of the Ten Commandments was transgressed. This way you also imitate the righteous Job who investigated assiduously and searched out every judgment which he did not know: "The cause which I knew not I searched out" (Job 29:16).

When you hear the penitent beginning to make excuses, how so and so was the cause and did such and such bad things, as women are especially accustomed to saying these excuses, say to him, Spiritual Father: "Child, you came here to confess your own sins to receive forgiveness and not to tell the sins of others, for by doing so you sin more, falling into judging others."

5. What people the Spiritual Father should question and how

If someone does not first say their sins, either out of ignorance or their lack of instruction or because they are ashamed, you are then compelled, Spiritual Father, to first question him about his sins and then for him to respond, as the sacred Augustine says: "The thorough researcher and fine examiner questions the penitent wisely and almost shrewdly, who may be ignorant or because of modesty chooses to hide." You should ask him, then, if he committed any of the seven mortal sins or any of the sins which are offspring of these mortal sins, if he committed any of the pardonable sins, or any of the sins which are near the mortal ones or near the pardonable ones. You should likewise ask him if he erred in any of the Ten Commandments, going over each of them, just as we examined each one previously.

Be careful however, Spiritual Father, so as not to inquire about the names of the people with which the one confessing committed the sins, because inasmuch as this is unnecessary, you also cause the sinner to mistrust you and think that you are nosy, as the aforementioned Metrophanes says. Many advise that it is of great benefit if your questions are conducted in this manner: "Child, have you perhaps committed murder? Have you stolen anything? Maybe you have committed acts of sexual immorality?

(as hard as this is to believe, but we confess it to be true). To these the Spiritual Father should say: "Enough, child, it is not necessary."

Etc." The penitent may only respond with, "Yes, Father," because in this way the sinner can expose his sins easily and without shame.

6. How the Spiritual Father is to deal with those who are ashamed

You must employ great skill and prudence, Spiritual Father, with those who out of shame do not confess all of their sins or only confess them in part and not completely. Many times, beginning with the small sin they confess, you should search little by little in order to find the larger one. For example, if someone who is ashamed only confesses to you that he saw someone and spoke with that person erotically, you should tell him, in an appropriate manner, about the obscene thoughts which follow such an encounter, about the consent which follows these thoughts, and the act which follows consent; just as God also caused Ezekiel, from a simple hole in the wall, to dig and then find a door, and from the door he was able to enter and see inside many hidden idols and abominations: "When I looked, behold a hole in the wall. Then said He unto me, Son of man, dig now in the wall: and when I had digged in the wall, behold a door. And He said unto me, Go in, and behold the wicked abominations that they do here" (Ezek. 8:7-9).[112] You must also be very careful, Spiritual Father, so as not to teach one who is pure about a sin which he did not know.

---

112   Translator's note: St. Gregory the Great applies this passage from Ezekiel in a similar fashion: "Some secret matters should, however, be closely investigated, so that from certain symptoms breaking out the ruler may discover all that lurks hidden in the minds of his subjects, and by timely reproof come to know from insignificant things what is more serious... By Ezekiel is symbolized the persons of those in authority; by the wall, the obduracy of their subjects. And what else is it to dig in the wall, but to open out the obduracy of the heart by thoroughgoing questioning? And when he dug into it, a door was discovered: that is to say, when the obduracy of the heart is penetrated by either searching inquisitions or judicious reproofs, a door, as it were, is revealed, through which every interior thought is seen... He goes in, as it were, to see the abominations, and by examining certain external symptoms, he sees into the hearts of his subjects, so that all the evil thoughts therein are disclosed to him" (*St. Gregory the Great: Pastoral Care*, ACW, New York, 1978, pp. 80-81).

7. Whom the Spiritual Father must reprove and when and how

It is not right, Spiritual Father, either for you not to reprove anyone at all or to reprove everyone, because the wise and instructed profit from reproofs: "Reprove one that hath understanding, and he will understand knowledge" (Pr. 19:25). But those who confess with audacity and hardness of heart also require reproof, according to the saying: "Rebuke them sharply" (Tit. 1:13). The uninstructed are not receptive to reproofs, for: "A scorner loveth not one that reproveth him" (Pr. 15:12); nor are the faint of heart, on account of the possibility of them falling into despair out of fear; nor are those who confess with contrition, because they do not require reproofs, but rather consolation; nor are those in authority, according to the saying: "Rebuke not an elder, but intreat him as a father" (1 Tim. 5:1). Sometimes those in authority do require reproofs, mixed together, however, with some praises, just as God does this with the bishops of the seven Churches of Asia in Revelation (Rev. 2:3).

You must, however, reprove, Spiritual Father, little by little, just as God Himself reproves, as it is written: "Thou dost reprove little by little those who trespass" (Wis. 12:2). Simply speaking, your reproofs must always be mixed together with sweetness and meekness, just as Paul commands: "In meekness instructing those that oppose themselves; if God peradventure will give them repentance to the acknowledging of the truth" (2 Tim. 2:25). The appropriate time for reproofs is after the sinner confesses, and simply, after he has cleared his head a little and become sober from sin.[113]

---

113   In the booklet, *Instructions for Spiritual Fathers*, we read that a certain leader, because he was having relations with one of his maidservants for a long time, many Spiritual Fathers tried to correct him but were unable to. Finally, an experienced Spiritual Father was found who corrected him with the following method: At first he told him: "I know that your first Spiritual Fathers were austere and did not want to forgive you, but I wish for the opposite, only if you promise to separate from the woman for only fifteen days." With great haste, the leader promised this. As he was leaving, the Spiritual Father said to him: "Remain in the village for fifteen days, and let the woman remain in the house." After the fifteen days had passed, the Spiritual Father saw the leader approaching him with such joy, as if desiring to receive the crown of chastity, and he said to him: "Because I see, child, that you are able to battle against passion, I would like to grant you forgiveness. But in order for me to

8. How the Spiritual Father is to care for those with thoughts of blasphemy and doubt

If it happens that you confess some people who have thoughts of blasphemy, or some people who always are in doubt and fear concerning their health and life, or concerning the salvation of their soul, on account of their thoughts, you should tell the first ones to disregard those blasphemous thoughts and not to think whatsoever that they are a sin, because they are not their own creations, but rather of that hater of good, the devil. Or you may tell them to rebut those blasphemous thoughts with these words: "Get thee behind me, Satan! I shall worship the Lord my God, and Him only will I adore. Your pain and your blasphemy shall return upon your own head in the present and in the age to come," just as St. John of the Ladder wisely counsels.[114] To those having incessant doubts, either caused

---

receive further evidence and proof of your repentance, let us wait another fifteen days, and so let the maidservant go to the village and you will remain in your house." After the thirty days had passed, when the Spiritual Father saw the leader approaching him, he then began to reprove him, describing to the leader with vivid words how he had scandalized the people, the fearful wrath of God which he had brought upon himself, the eternity of hell, and the long-suffering which God had endured for so long because of him. With these and other similar words he reproved him and forgave him of his sin, and he married a woman of like nobility. Do you see, Spiritual Father, how effective reproofs are at the pertinent time? Let this manner of correction be an example of what the pertinent time for reproof is and of the postponement and delay of forgiveness only, but not concerning other things. For that Spiritual Father should firstly not have granted permission to the leader to take a woman of like nobility as his wife, but to take the woman whom he had violated, even if she was a maidservant and poor, as Canon 67 of the Holy Apostles designates. And secondly, he should have given that leader a penance so as not to commune for four years on account of fornicating with and violating his wife prior to marriage, as Canons 22 and 25 of Basil the Great designate.

114   Step 23, PG 88, 977B; tr. *The Ladder*, p. 144. There are three universal medicines which you can use, Spiritual Father, to treat those who have thoughts of blasphemy: 1) tell them not to be prideful or to pry into the Mysteries of the Faith, and not to scorn and judge their brother, because both the *Gerontikon* and Anastasios of Sinai write that the thought of blasphemy is born from pride and prying, and from scorn and passing judgment. Advise them, rather, to be humble, simple, and not curious, following the faith which the Church handed down to them like a beast, as David says: "I became as a beast before Thee, and I am ever with Thee" (Ps. 72:21), and not to investigate those things which are beyond their ability. (Translator's note: St. Peter of Damaskos says the same thing: "The man of faith acts, not as one endowed with free will, but as a beast that is led by the will of God" *GrPhilokalia*, p. 614; tr. *The Philokalia*, v. 3, p. 165) 2) Tell them not to be overly sorrowful when blasphemous thoughts come to them, neither to be entirely distressed and fearful, as though they will be punished on account of

by depression and hypochondria, or by the devil, as a test or allowance of God, you should tell them: 1) to pray continuously to God; 2) not to believe

---

these. Firstly, because these thoughts are not their own creations, nor do they come to them from their own free will, but from the envy of the devil, just as St. Maximos and the above-mentioned Anastasios say. So why should they worry about an alien sin which is not their own? About a sin proceeding from the devil and not from their mind? Involuntary and not voluntary? Hated and not wanted? This is how Abba Pambo was once warred upon by the demon of blasphemy, and as he supplicated God because of these thoughts, he heard a divine voice from above saying: "Pambo, Pambo, do not be despondent on account of an alien sin, but be concerned for the actions which are your own" (*Evergetinos*, p. 722). Secondly, they should not be sorrowful because these blasphemous thoughts do not only war upon them, but they also war upon many righteous and virtuous men, as we see in the *Gerontikon*, in the *Evergetinos* (Book III, *Hypothesis 29*), and in the writings of St. Meletios the Confessor. Why do I mention only the righteous and virtuous? For Confessors and Martyrs were also warred upon by these thoughts. This is verified when the co-sufferers, the Holy Hieromartyr Peter of Alexandria and the divine Paphnoutios the Confessor, were attending to one another. When St. Peter was being disturbed by the demon of blasphemy, he told this to the divine Paphnoutios, and also related to him that during the time of his confession, when his body was being tortured by tyrants with various tortures and was being scorched by fire, the demon of blasphemy was speaking blasphemies against God inside of him: "During the time of my confession, in the torture chamber, when my body was being lacerated by various tortures and sufferings, and being scorched by fire, the demon of blasphemy was speaking against God inside of me" (*Evergetinos, ibid.*). So then, if the demon of blasphemy warred against such Saints, why should they be sorrowful who are warred upon by him, and be so afraid and despondent, as if they are the worst sinners of all? 3) They should not be sorrowful over those thoughts of blasphemy but rather rejoice, because according to St. Maximos, the devil fights with these thoughts to hinder their love for God, to quench their faith and to cut off their regular prayer to God; and when they fight back against the devil and are not hindered from virtues, they become surer and more accomplished in the faith and in their love for God, and this is how they are victorious and crowned ,and slay the devil with his own sword. Also say to those having blasphemous thoughts, Spiritual Father, to disregard them as the barking of dogs and not to consider these thoughts as sin whatsoever. For the divine Fathers and our own daily experience tells us that there is no greater and stronger weapon with which to conquer and exterminate both blasphemous thoughts and all evil and obscene thoughts, as disregard and contempt, because the devil boasts and claims as a great victory not only when he causes us to worry and distress over his bad thoughts, but also when he causes us to turn toward them with the eye of our intellect to ponder them and receive them. Thus it is written about them: "Brethren, we therefore will disregard the blasphemous enemy as having nothing to do with us, and so through this humiliation we will be able to be delivered by the grace of God Himself, for by no one else but Him will we be strengthened to prevail" (*Evergetinos, ibid.*). If you are unable to console those having thoughts of blasphemy by any of these things, Spiritual Father, and are unable to free them from their fear, try also this sensible tactic which an experienced Spiritual Father once used. Tell the one who is disturbed by the demon of blasphemy to place his hand upon the back of your neck, and then say: "Child, let this sin of yours be upon my neck, and be not anxious any longer."

in their thoughts, but rather to believe and to accept those things which you say to them; and 3) if it is possible, give them in writing the rule which you appoint for them, because as they are always in doubt, they will quickly be able to believe that which they see written.

9. For whom must confession be postponed

If it happens that someone confessing to you is not prepared to confess, either not having performed any prior examination of his sins, or when saying his many and great evil deeds he shows no remorse and contrition, but says them rather with such audacity that you would think he was recounting his virtues, or if someone did not keep the promises which he had given you and appears to be a liar once and twice, or if someone's condition and sin is complicated and difficult to correct, nor clearly addressed in the Canons, to such a person, I say, Spiritual Father, you should neither immediately read the prayer of forgiveness, nor cast them away completely, but you should postpone the time of their forgiveness, saying to them:

"Leave for now, my child, and return again on such and such a day, so that I also may consider the matter further," and give him also some rule of fasting or prostrations or almsgiving to do until the next meeting, for in this way the sinner may also come to himself better, reproved by his conscience, while you in the meantime are: 1) to resort to God through prayer, saying with King Solomon: "God and Lord of mercy, give me the wisdom that sits by Thy throne, that she may be with me and toil" (Wis. 9:1,4,10), and with King Jehoshaphat: "Neither know we what to do for them: but our eyes are upon Thee" (2 Chr. 20:12); 2) to resort to your hierarch, as say Symeon of Thessaloniki,[115] Chrysanthos,[116] and Nikephoros the Archivist to Theodosios the Recluse,[117] or resort to others who are experienced in such things and who are nearby, or by letter if they are far away (not disclosing the name of the person), in order to learn from them what you should do.

---

115   *De Sacris Ordinationibus*, ch. 249, PG 155, 468A-468B.
116   *Syntagmation*, Tyrgobist, 1715, ch. 59.
117   *Juris Graeco-romanorum*, p. 343

Know for certain, Spiritual Father, that there is nothing as advantageous and fruitful in your vocation as postponing and delaying the time of forgiveness, just as all the Spiritual Fathers commonly agree by their daily experience.

10. That the Spiritual Father is not to confess those with whom he is an accessory in sin

If (God forbid!) you commit a pardonable sin together with someone, you must not hear that person's confession, Spiritual Father, but you are to send him to another Spiritual Father. For, as the two of you are partners in the same sin, neither will he feel ashamed during confession so that he may be corrected, nor will you be able to place him under a rule and correct him appropriately. I said a pardonable sin and not a mortal one, because if you commit the latter, you will be deposed both from the priesthood and from the vocation of the Spiritual Father, as we said earlier. See also the first footnote of Chapter Eight.

11. How the Spiritual Father should examine those who will be ordained in the future

When someone comes to you seeking a *Symmartyria* (a spiritual father's witness) so that he may be ordained, open well the eyes of your soul and examine all the depths of his heart with even greater diligence than usual, for "here is wisdom" (Rev. 13:18), and here all of your skill and discretion are proved.

After you have investigated him and found no impediment to the canonical priesthood,[118] be very careful so as not to give him the *Symmartyria* immediately, but wait a little while, until you have also studied his companions

---

118   Many Canons contain the canonical impediments to the priesthood, especially Canons 25, 61, and 80 of the Apostles; Canon 17 of the First-and-Second Council; Canon 3 of Laodicaea; Canon 12 of Neocaesaria; Canon 10 of Sardica; Canon 59 of Carthage; Canon 4 of St. Cyril. Chrysostom would have that those to be ordained in the future be irreproachable (namely, not subject to serious sins), but also blameless, that is, also free from the smallest of sins (cf. *On Job*, ch. 1, PG 64,

and learned from them about the type of life he leads: "Moreover he must have a good report of them which are without" (1 Tim. 3:7).[119]

You must do this "so as not to communicate in others' sins," just as your

---

512B). Canons 9 and 19 of the First Ecumenical Council also decree that they should be blameless and unimpeachable.

Translator's note: Here is what an anonymous nineteenth century hesychast has to say about the priesthood: "The priest, then, who wishes to celebrate the Divine Liturgy blamelessly, must lead a blameless life, that is, he must be pure of all carnal thoughts and spiritually pure. His mind must be illumined by perpetual tears. His intellect must be pure, free, and noble in all things, so that, if possible, it may always be occupied with the heavenly things on high. His heart must be a dwelling place and vessel of the Holy Spirit. His thoughts must be good and beneficial. His notions must be spiritual. The meditation of God must always be nested in his heart. The fear of the Lord must be deeply rooted in him. The love of God must inhabit his soul. He must hate evil, turn from wickedness, meditate on good things, and do good. He must not be negligent in reading the divine words of Scripture. The commandments of Christ must rule him. Just as he eats the all-immaculate Body of Christ and drinks the all-pure Blood of Christ Himself with his mouth, so should he be pure with regard to the chastity of both his body and soul" (*Neptike Theoria (Neptic Contemplation)*, Hagion Oros, 1996, p. 208 (in Greek)).

119   See also Canon 7 of Timothy which says that priests must be ordained in the presence and witness of the people. And Canon 3 of the Seventh Ecumenical Council says that presbyters and deacons also vote. And Chrysostom says that the clergy should not have all of the authority of the vote, but that those who are to receive spiritual authority should be chosen by the Church and by the common multitude (*On II Corinthians*, Homily 18, 1, PG 61, 524). Cyril of Alexandria says that the people ratify the clergy (*Octateuch*, vol. I, p. 1214; *De Adoratione in Spiritu et Veritate* 11, PG 68, 780D). This is also shown by the custom which prevails to this day, that at every ordination of a presbyter and deacon the hierarch says: "The choice and examination is upon the heads of the fellow-witnesses." This is why it is called a *Symmartyria* (letter of *co*-witness), because it not only contains the witness of the Spiritual Father (for this alone is not to be believed, according to Canon 141 of Carthage), but also that of other trustworthy men. Therefore, in the *Syntagmation* of Chrysanthos (p. 58) a certain *Entalterion* also writes that the Spiritual Father must confirm those seeking ordination not only through confession, but also from learning of their manner of life and their company from those who know them. The form of the canonical *Symmartyria* is as follows: "The God-preaching Apostles and after them the Assembly of the Godbearing Fathers who established that all things be done rightly and in good order canonically decreed that no one be deemed worthy of the divine order of the priesthood without a thorough inquiry and careful examination, lest the Most Holy Mysteries be celebrated by those who are unworthy. Thus, my spiritual son (*name*), the son of (*name*), from the land of (*place*), came before me requesting to receive the great office of the priesthood. Standing him before the sacred icon of our Lord and God and Savior Jesus Christ, I searched the depths of his heart. Having also learned of him and his conduct from reliable and trustworthy men and not finding in him any impediment, I bear witness that he, being of mature age, is worthy of the office of the priesthood, as the Canons prescribe. Therefore, this letter of canonical confirmation is hereby

Entalterion writes, and because of that which Paul addresses to the hierarch who wishes to ordain someone: "Lay hands suddenly on no man, neither be partaker of other men's sins" (1 Tim. 5:22). This is also applicable to you, Spiritual Father, if you plan on giving a witness to the one seeking ordination; or may I say that it is even more applicable to you and that you have the greater responsibility, because today the hierarchs are satisfied with only the witness of the Spiritual Father (which should not be the case), and ordain as many as they ordain.

12. How the Spiritual Father is to deal with those who are excommunicated

If someone who has been excommunicated by his hierarch comes to you, know that you are not able to forgive him, as Chrysanthos says in his *Exomologetarion*.[120] Rather, you must send him to the one who excommunicated him, if that person be alive, or to that person's successor, if he has died, so that person may forgive him, just as the divine Canons[121] and many *Entalteria* decree.[122] If you are able, you must also intercede to the hierarch who excommunicated him so as to forgive him.

13. How to care for those who have made vows

If people come to you who have vowed to God that they would become a monk, or that they would go on a pilgrimage to the Holy Sepulcher, or go venerate a sacred monastery and holy relics, or that they would perform a certain amount of almsgiving, or that they would establish schools or monasteries, or that they would fast so much or perform some other good work and virtue, you must advise these people, Spiritual Father, not to only

---

given to him as evidence of this evaluation and is validated by my signature, as well as the personal testimonies of the witnesses." Then the Spiritual Father and the witnesses sign the document.

120   *Didaskalia ofelimos peri metanoias kai exomologeseos*, Venice, 1724, p. 22.

121   See Canons 12, 13, and 32 of the Holy Apostles; Canon 5 of the First Ecumenical Council; Canon 6 of Antioch; Canon 14 of Sardica; Canons 37 and 141 of Carthage; and the *Nomocanon* of Photios, Title 9, ch. 9, and Balsamon's commentary on it (PG 104, 1104A-1104B).

122   See p. 60 of the *Syntagmation* of Chrysanthos of Jerusalem.

fulfill their vows, but to fulfill them without delay, because they are sinning.[123]

If there is some great reason preventing them from fulfilling their vows, either from making a pilgrimage to the Holy Sepulcher or from establishing schools and monasteries, you must consider carefully, Spiritual Father, with great discernment, how much money and effort it would have taken to fulfill those vows, and thereby directing them to give that much money to the poor or to another similar good cause, if they have the means. If they do not have the means, you should direct them to fulfill their vows by other means, such as with fasts, prayers, prostrations, etc.

To those who vowed to become monks, but afterward married, you must say to them, Spiritual Father, that they are violators of their vow and that they must repent to God; and that they are obligated, even though married, to struggle with fasts and prayers and hardships of the body, and to be chaste, as much as they can, and try to convince their spouses with many supplications to agree to this. If their wife happens to die, they must then fulfill their promise and become monks.[124] After all this, you must counsel all of these people that they are not to make such vows and promises

---

123   God Himself says that this is true: once through the mouth of the Prophet Moses: "When thou shalt vow a vow unto the Lord thy God, thou shalt not slack to pay it: for the Lord thy God will surely require it of thee; and it would be sin in thee" (Dt. 23:21), and at another time with the mouth of the wise Sirach: "Let nothing hinder you from paying a vow promptly, and do not wait until death to be released from it" (Sir. 18:22). Therefore, Gregory Dialogos reproved the Rustician Patriciate Romaia because she had vowed to go on a pilgrimage to Jerusalem, but when she went to Constantinople in order to continue on from there, she wasted time and did not fulfill her promise quickly. When someone makes a vow they must consider if they are able to fulfill their vow, because after they make it, they are no longer able to break it, because this tempts and mocks God, according to Sirach: "Before making a vow, prepare yourself; and do not be like a man who tempts the Lord" (Sir. 18:23). See also Canon 28 of Basil the Great which by way of reproof says that it is a matter of indifference, and not only that it is allowable or permissible, if one eats pork after making a vow not to do so, and this teaches us that even those ridiculous vows one makes to God ought not to be violated, much less those vows which are correct and reasonable. This is not only applicable to someone who vows on their own accord; for when parents vow to God in a time of illness or danger that their children (who are their dependents) will become monks, then, I say, both the children and the parents must keep that vow, offering them to God as Hannah offered Samuel, and just as God commands in the thirtieth chapter of Numbers (Num. 30:1-16).

124   See Canon 19 of Ancyra and Canon 18 of Basil the Great which penance those who vow to keep their virginity but afterward violate it.

to God in the future, whenever they come upon some crisis, because they sin gravely if they are not able to keep them.

14. How the Spiritual Father is to counsel fornicators, adulterers, sodomists, those who practice bestiality, and masturbators

If you confess fornicators or adulterers or sodomists or those who practice bestiality or masturbators, Spiritual Father, you are not only to reprimand all of them, showing them that by the carnal passions they lose the nobility of reason and resemble the irrational beasts, but moreover, in order that each of them despise their sin you must demonstrate for them how damaging to the soul fornication,[125] adultery,[126] sod-

---

125   The following reasons show just how devastating of an evil fornication is: 1) Whoever fornicates, harms and corrupts his body by subjecting it to many and incurable maladies, wherefore the Apostle said: "He that committeth fornication sinneth against his own body" (1 Cor. 6:18). Therefore, whoever commits any other sin is an enemy of his soul, according to the saying: "He that loveth unrighteousness hateth his own soul" (Ps. 10:5), but whoever fornicates is also an enemy of his body; 2) Whoever fornicates loses their virginity, which is a priceless treasure, and after losing it once, there is no way of ever regaining it: "The virgin of Israel is fallen; she shall no more rise" (Am. 5:2) (concerning this, see the *Homily on Repentance* at the end of this book); 3) Fornication darkens the intellect of a person and weakens the will so much, more than any other sin, so as not to allow the unfortunate person committing this sin to return to God and repent: "They will not frame their doings to turn unto their God: for the spirit of whoredoms is in the midst of them" (Hos. 5:4). The divine Isidore, therefore, rightly said this fearful word, that: "The human race is subject to the devil more through carnal lewdness than any other sin." And 4) fornication is so abhorred by God that it was on this account alone that the cataclysmic flood was brought upon the world which no one survived except eight people, and caused God to regret having made man: "It repenteth me that I have made them" (Gen. 6:7).

126   Spiritual Father, say unto adulterers: 1) That adultery is such a great evil that God commands the man and the woman committing it to be put to death: "And the man that committeth adultery with another man's wife... the adulterer and the adulteress shall surely be put to death" (Lev. 20:10); 2) That if under the Old Law adultery was such a great transgression, then how much greater of a transgression is it now under the grace of the Gospel, where marriage has been raised to the honor of a Holy Mystery? For this reason God wrathfully said to David that he would never take away evils from his house on account of the adultery which he committed: "Now therefore the sword shall never depart from thine house; because thou hast despised me, and hast taken the wife of Uriah the Hittite to be thy wife" (2 Kg. 12:10). This He

omy,[127] bestiality,[128] and masturbation[129] are.

---

says now with even greater austerity to every adulterer; 3) Every adulterer is called a son of death, as David said by himself to Nathan: "As the Lord liveth, the man that hath done this is a son of death" (2 Kg. 12:6). And 4) that every robbery and theft, when compared to adultery, is like the Mediterranean Sea compared to the whole Ocean, or like a dwarfish man compared to a great giant; wherefore Solomon also said: "Men do not despise a thief... But whoso committeth adultery with a woman lacketh understanding: he that doeth it destroyeth his own soul. A wound and dishonour shall he get; and his reproach shall never be wiped away" (Pr. 6:30; 32-33). Tell adulterers, Spiritual Father, that even to the gentiles adultery seemed an unforgivable evil. For this reason adulterers were punished sorely, just as the so-called *Law of Julia* attests, as does one of the laws found on the Twelve Tablets of the Romans. The Egyptians cut off the nose of the adulteress and beat the adulterer with a staff one thousand times, according to Diodoros Sikeliotes (Book I). The Locrians blinded adulterers. The Krotonians burned adulterers, according to Maximus Valerius (Book VI, ch. 5). And God appointed a fearful curse for adulterers, saying: "And of them shall be taken up a curse by all the captivity of Judah which are in Babylon, saying, The Lord make thee like Zedekiah and like Ahab, whom the king of Babylon roasted in the fire; because they have committed villany in Israel, and have committed adultery with their neighbours' wives" (Jer. 29:22-23).

127   Tell sodomists, Spiritual Father: 1) that God commands in Leviticus that sodomists be put to death: "If a man also lie with males, as he lieth with a woman, both of them have committed an abomination: they shall surely be put to death" (Lev. 20:13); 2) that St. Jerome says on account of this sin of sodomy alone the incarnate Economy of Christ was delayed, and that another teacher says, on account of this sin the Second Coming will occur sooner; and how on the night that Christ was born, He sent an angel which put to death all of those committing acts of homosexuality in the world, and then He was born, so that at the time of His birth that lawless sin would not be found anywhere upon the earth. See also p. 333 of *The Trumpet*, where you will find just how severely sodomists were punished by kings.

128   Tell those that commit bestiality how God commands in Leviticus that such people be put to death, both men and women (Lev. 20:15-16). And that the political laws (Book VI of the *Basilics*, Title 37) command that the sexual organ be cut off. Worthy of note is the method employed by one experienced Spiritual Father to correct a certain callous sinner who fell into sin with a calf. He first said this to him: "You, sinner, have now become a relative of the calf, something new and unheard of, and you have become irrational and bestial like the calf. So, for one whole month, you will go every night and close yourself in your stable, fall on the ground on all fours like the animals, put the saddle of your donkey around your back, and in this manner, with tears, you will ask God for forgiveness for this fearful sin of yours." When that unfortunate man did this and came to realize the magnitude of his sin, he was reformed, whereas previously other Spiritual Fathers could not correct him with various methods. Concerning how many years those who commit bestiality are penanced, look ahead to the Canons of the Faster dealing with this.

129   On how bad masturbation is, see the footnote to Canon 8 of St. John the Faster.

15. How to care for monks

If an illiterate monk confesses to you, Spiritual Father, you are to ask him whether he attends and listens to the daily office of services designated for him. And if he does not have the means to attend and listen to them, you should instruct him to read the services with his prayer rope, that is, in the place of Orthros, he should go through the prayer rope thirty times, while standing, saying at each knot this prayer: "Lord Jesus Christ, Son of God, have mercy on me." In the place of the Hours, he should go through the prayer rope ten times. In the place of Vespers, also ten times. And in the place of Compline, another ten. This is what the *Nomocanons* found on the Holy Mountain prescribe.

You should also examine all monks as to whether they carry out their usual rule. Know that accomplished monks of the great schema are directed to do three hundred prostrations through the course of the day and night, that is, full-out prostrations, according to St. Kallistos and the Godbearing Fathers[130]; but according to the authorities on the Holy Mountain, they are to do one hundred and twenty prostrations, and twelve cycles of the prayer rope accompanied by small prostrations, that is, bowing and touching one's hand to the floor. Monks who are *staurophors* are to do one hundred and ten prostrations, and six cycles of the prayer rope with small prostrations. Novices and *rhasophors* are directed to do one hundred prostrations, and three cycles of the prayer rope, saying at each knot, as we said, the "Lord Jesus Christ, Son of God, have mercy on me," and bowing and touching their hand to the floor each time.

Know that the rule of prostrations is not to be done on Sunday, according to Canon 20 of the First Ecumenical Council, Canon 90 of the Sixth Ecumenical Council, and Canon 91 of Basil the Great,[131] nor during all of Pentecost, that is, the fifty days between Pascha and Pentecost, according to the aforementioned Canons and according to St. Epiphanios,[132] St. Irenaeos,[133] St. Augustine,[134]

---

130   See *GrPhilokalia*, p. 1053; *Writings from the Philokalia on Prayer of the Heart*, p. 213.
131   Cf. *De Spiritu Sancto* 27, SC 17[bis], pp. 484, 486.
132   *Expositio Fide* 22, PG 42, 825B.
133   *Fragmenta, deperditorum operum*, 7, PG 7[2], 1233A.
134   *Letter to Januarius*.

St. Jerome,[135] St. Ambrose, Abba Isaiah, and St. Kallistos.[136] According to the *Rubrics*, prostrations are also deferred on Saturday. Whoever prostrates on Saturday, however, does not sin, for this is not forbidden by the Canons, according to Canon 2 of Nicholas. Small prostrations or bows, however, are never forbidden in any season. See also *Subject I* which follows the Canons of the Faster.

16. How to care for clergymen who have sinned

If you confess any clergyman who committed fornication or adultery or any other hidden sin which subjects him to deposition from the priesthood, you must prohibit him, Spiritual Father, from ever liturgizing again, and from performing baptisms and marriages, from giving spiritual guidance,[137] from conducting the service of the blessing of the water, and any other sacred rite, just as the more distinguished Spiritual Fathers of the Holy Mountain prohibit such clergymen from performing all sacred rites, in accordance with the Canons.[138] If, however, they do not consent to forsake all sacred rites, you

135   *The Dialogue Against the Luciferians,* 8.

136   Translator's note: This is what St. Kallistos says: "We must practice (prostrations) on every day and night of the five weekdays. For we have been commanded to refrain from them on Saturdays and Sundays as well as on some other days and weeks established through custom for certain mysterious and secret reasons" (*Directions to Hesychasts* 39, *GrPhilokalia,* p. 1053; tr. *Writings from the Philokalia on Prayer of the Heart,* p. 213). St. Germanos also says: "We do not kneel on Sunday as a sign that our fall has been corrected through the resurrection of Christ on the third day. We do not kneel until Pentecost because we observe the seven days after Easter seven-fold; seven times seven is forty-nine, and Sunday makes fifty" (*Historia Ecclesiastica, et Mystica Contemplatio,* PG 98, 392C; tr. *St. Germanos of Constantinople: On the Divine Liturgy,* Crestwood, 1999, p. 65).

137   See the first footnote of Chapter 8.

138   If Canons 26 and 27 of the Sixth Ecumenical Council and Canon 27 of Basil the Great all agree and declare that a priest who falls into an unlawful marriage out of ignorance must stop performing the things of the priesthood and neither bless nor sanctify, how much more, then, should the priest who knowingly fornicates or commits adultery, or any other transgression entailing deposition, cease from performing these things? In addition, Canon 8 of Patriarch Nicholas declares that those who have resigned from the priesthood on account of their bad conscience can say neither "Blessed is our God" nor "May Christ our true God." Symeon of Thessaloniki says that: "On account of ordination grace operates in unworthy priests and hierarchs and all the Mysteries they celebrate are in very truth Mysteries. But woe and alas to such men, who, whether they sinned before the ordination or after the ordination, are unworthy of holy orders. And if they want to repent and to be saved, let them refrain altogether from the most holy works of the priesthood" (Notice that he

should at least, little by little, prohibit them from celebrating the Divine Liturgy. If they do not even consent to this, you cannot force them, nor can you publicize the matter, but you are to leave them to their conscience and let them realize for themselves their unworthiness.

---

says works in the plural, and not only the Liturgy) (*Responsa ad Gabrielem Pentapolitanum*, Question 13, PG 155, 860C-861A). See also p. 234 of *Salvation of Sinners*, where it is written that Abba Makarios of Alexandria did not treat an unworthy priest until he ceased from practicing any work of the priesthood any longer. (Translator's note: This account may also be found in *Historia Lausiaca*, chs. 19, 20, PG 34, 1059A-1059B; *Palladius: The Lausiac History*, ACW, New York, 1964, pp. 63-64) Canon 10 of St. John the Faster demotes a priest to the order of reader who, knowing the harm of masturbation, does this two or three times; it is evident, therefore, that such a one is prohibited from practicing all of the works of the priesthood. That those who have sinned secretly and have confessed are to resign from the priesthood and be disciplined is witnessed to by Canon 9 of the First Ecumenical Council, Canons 9 and 10 of Neocaesaria, and Canon 70 of Basil. Chrysostom says that those who commit a transgression entailing deposition from the priesthood depose themselves from the priesthood: "One ought to exercise so much caution in the matter (that is, the priesthood), as to shun the burden of the office, and when one has entered upon it, not to wait for the judgment of others should any fault be committed which warrants deposition, but to anticipate it by ejecting oneself from the dignity; for thus one might probably win mercy for himself from God: but to cling to it in defiance of propriety is to deprive oneself of all forgiveness, or rather to kindle the wrath of God, by adding a second error more offensive than the first" (*On the Priesthood*, Book III, NPNF (V1-09) p. 50). Even though Agapios, in *Salvation of Sinners* (p. 222), says that the priest who has sinned performs the blessing of the waters, Holy Unction, Confession, and the other works of the priesthood, he says it according to today's practice and not according to the strictness of the Canons.

If someone brings up Canon 9 of Neocaesaria saying that the priest who confesses a carnal sin which he committed before ordination is not to offer the Liturgy, but to remain in all other respects, let him learn, I say, that this Canon included all of the other sacred works of the priesthood together with the offering (that is, the celebration of the Liturgy), and "to remain in all other respects" does not imply to perform sacred works, but to remain seated and placed with other priests, that is, keeping the outward honor, according to Balsamon (Explanation of Canon 26 of the Sixth Ecumenical Council, PG 137, 600A-600C). Even though he may receive Communion at the holy altar, according to Balsamon and Zonaras, the unambiguous Canon 8 of Nicholas, and Symeon of Thessaloniki (*Responsa ad Gabrielem Pentapolitanum*, Question 40, PG 155, 889A) explicitly prohibit the distribution and reception of Communion at the holy altar, as does Canon 70 of Basil the Great which prohibits this for those deacons and priests who commit a sin which is greater than a passionate kiss. If such clergy are clearly and canonically deposed on account of their crimes, not only are they deprived of every sacred work, but they also lose the honor of their seat and place with the priests, and all of the outward dress of the clergy, and are transferred to the place of the laity, according to Canon 21 of the Sixth Ecumenical Council and Canon 3 of Basil. This also must we make clear to you, Spiritual Father, that you must be very careful not to give permission to those clergy who fall into fornication or adultery to commune immediately, as some have been misled to do, who do not know Canon 3 of Basil well. But besides prohibiting them from the priesthood, you also must first penance them for their sin; and after they have completed their penance, to then excuse them to commune. Also see Canon 33 of the Faster.

17. How the Spiritual Father is to deal
with those who are ill

If someone is ill, Spiritual Father, you must visit him immediately, even if it is midnight, or raining, or snowing. And after you have consoled him in his illness, telling him that this will purify him from the stain of sin, just as gold is purified with fire, urge him prior to any bodily treatment to confess with a general confession all of the sins of his life. Even if the ill person falls silent, immediately squeeze his hand or speak loudly to him, until he gives you a nod or some other sign letting you know that he wants to confess. And so, having confessed, read the prayer of forgiveness over him and have him commune in the Divine Mysteries, so that he may not die unforgiven and uncommuned.

Do not fail in visiting him frequently, in order to console him and to make him firm in the hope of the mercy of God, even until his last breath, and not to despair, for in that hour the devil fights terribly to throw him into despair.[139] Therefore, at that time he has a great need for your counsel and consolation: if he has it, he may gain an eternal profit, if not, he may lose an eternal loss.[140]

18. That the Spiritual Father
should perform confession slowly

On top of everything we have told you, Spiritual Father, you must conduct confession slowly, thoroughly, and without haste, if you want your confession to be as it should, and if you want the correction of sinners to be true and salvific, even if there are many people waiting to see you. Indeed, you should tell penitents to come days ahead of time to confess, as we would also advise them. For by conducting confession slowly you

---

139   Translator's note: For more on what St. Nikodemos has to say about assaults of the enemy at the hour of death, see *Aoratos Polemos*, pp. 256-261; cf. *Unseen Warfare*, Crestwood, 1987, pp. 252-256.

140   To learn more about visiting those who are ill, read the newly printed *Exomologetarion concerning the visitation of the sick*.

have the time to think skillfully about which fitting medicines of correction each sinner requires. For many Spiritual Fathers who often rushed and thereby did not have the time to think well, destroyed many, instead of correcting them, and at the same time destroyed themselves along with them, repenting bitterly on account of this until their death.

Know also, Spiritual Father, that it is a great help if you listen to the confessions of people, especially of women and youth, with your eyes closed, as many conduct confession this way. This is because the intellect is collected in this manner and better discerns what is said. You are also able to more easily avoid temptation by not looking upon their faces.

CHAPTER 10

How the Spiritual Father Is to Assign a Rule[141]

When you finish hearing the confession of the penitent's evil deeds and words and thoughts, Spiritual Father, then say to him: "Know, child, that the divine Canons prescribe that if a man does not first cease from his sin, his repentance is not accepted. If you, therefore, promise to abstain from evil, by the co-operation of divine grace, I will place you under a rule and you will receive forgiveness for your sins; for all the teachers of the Church commonly say that the whole of repentance is dependent upon this: that the penitent firmly resolves not to willingly sin again, and that without this resolution, his confession, the fulfillment of his rule, and simply, his repentance, will profit him little."

1. That the Spiritual Father is to assign a rule according to the Faster

And when the penitent promises, you place him under a rule according

---

141   Translator's note: In commenting upon Canon 102 of the Sixth Ecumenical Council, St. Nikodemos says the following: "After this Council had decreed concerning many different penances, lastly in the present Canon it leaves everything to the judgment of the bishops and Spiritual Fathers and

the authority to bind and to loose, saying that they ought to conjecture, or surmise, both the quality of the sinfulness, whether it be pardonable or mortal, and the disposition of the sinner with respect to repentance, and thus to offer the right treatment for his illness; lest by giving persons who are magnanimous and willing to repent lenient penances, and persons who are more unconcerned and pusillanimous on the contrary extreme penances, they fail to correct either the former or the latter, but rather wind up losing both... The whole aim both to God and to the Spiritual Father is simply this, to bring about the return of the straying sheep, the sinner, to cure the one who has been wounded or hurt by the figurative serpent commonly called the devil, and neither to drive him to despair by heavy penances, nor again to let him take the bit in his teeth, like a horse, by light penances, and hence encourage him to contemptuousness and unconcern, but in every possible way, whether with austere or with mild remedies, to endeavor to restore the sinner to health and free him from the wounds of sin, so that he may taste the fruits of repentance, and with wisdom manage to help him to ascend to the splendor of the Holy Trinity above" (*Pedalion*, pp. 312-313; tr. *The Rudder*, pp. 410-411). That the assigning of a rule and of a penance is placed in the prudent hands of the Spiritual Father, is further attested to by St. Nikodemos in his commentaries on Canon 12 of the First Ecumenical Council and Canons 3, 74, and 84 of Basil the Great. Furthermore, he not only states that a Spiritual Father must assign a penance in proportion to the repentance of the sinner, but to also consider the general spiritual state of the faithful and of the Church (*Pedalion*, p. ιθ´ [19]; *The Rudder*, p. LV). Metropolitan Anthony Khrapovitsky (1863-1936) says this about penances: "According to the Nomocanon, three-quarters of our contemporaries coming to confession are liable not just to strict penances, but to complete deprivation of Communion for ten or twenty years, or even till the hour of death. But in this same Canon Law it is explained under what conditions this excommunication can be shortened as much as two or three times. However, it does not mention the most important condition, which did not exist when the Nomocanon was compiled. By this we mean the general sinfulness of the last two centuries and the consequence of this—that it is incomparably more difficult to struggle with sin than it was in the times of ancient piety... And so, under contemporary conditions of life, which are so far removed from God's commandments, the strictness of penances has to be reduced many times. But it is regrettable that spiritual fathers no longer give penances at all, either because of their own neglect of confession or else out of false delicacy and timidity... We must fulfill the laws of our religion, even if we soften them in accordance with the lowered spiritual strength of our contemporaries. And so, first of all, people must not be admitted to Communion if they do not declare their resolve to abandon mortal sin—people carrying on an illicit liaison, for example, or the keepers of brothels or illicit gambling dens. Parishioners who have sinned by fornication, embezzlement, insulting their parents or blasphemy, but have offered repentance, can be admitted to Communion; but they should be given some rule of prayer (*canona*) and must without fail make amends for the wrong they have done and make peace with those whom they have offended... However, murderers, robbers, rapists, abortionists as well as doctors or other people who help them, sodomites, committers of bestiality, adulterers, seducers and conscious defilers of sacred objects must unfailingly be deprived of Communion for several years, and certainly no less than one year if their repentance is fervent and sincere... Concerning the imposition of prayers and prostrations, we have to reckon with the weakness and laziness of contemporary Christians: it is better to carry out a small rule than to be given a long one and not carry it out" to the Canons of St. John the Faster,[142] that is, either not to receive Communion for so many years, to fast so much, to do so many prostrations, or to do so much almsgiving.

(*Confession*, Jordanville, 1983, pp. 104-105). And St. John Chrysostom says: "But, saith one, they have been punished for a long time. How long? Tell me. A year, and two, and three years? Howbeit, I require not this, length of time, but amendment of soul. This then show, whether they have been pricked to the heart, whether they have reformed, and all is done: since if there be not this, there is no advantage in the time. For neither do we inquire whether the wound has been often bandaged, but whether the bandage has been of any service. If therefore it hath been of service, although in a short time, let it be kept on no longer: but if it hath done no service, even at the end of ten years, let it be still kept on: and let this fix the term of release, the good of him that is bound. If we are thus careful both of ourselves and of others, and regard not honor and dishonor at the hands of men; but bearing in mind the punishment and the disgrace that is there, and above all the provoking of God, apply with energy the medicines of repentance: we shall both presently arrive at the perfect health, and shall obtain the good things to come" (*On II Corinthians*, Homily 14, 3, PG 61, 502; tr. NPNF (V1-12) p. 349).

142   I said that you should place the penitent under a rule according to the directions of St. John the Faster because there is an old *Exomologetarion*, in question and answer form, of a certain Neophytos of Cyprus, also called Rhodinos, which is a heretical work on account of it prescribing many extreme accommodations and because it has the prayer of forgiveness said in the first person: "I loose you of your confessed sins." Concerning this the divine Chrysostom says that Nathan the Prophet did not say to David, "*I* forgive," but, "*The Lord* has put away thy sin" (2 Kg. 12:13) (*In Psalmum L*, Homily 1, 7, PG 55, 573). In addition, that *Exomologetarion* also claims that when the divine Canons designate penances for sins of seven or nine or ten years, they do not mean that the sinners are not to commune during those years, but they mean that during those years they are to pray or fast, that is, fulfill their rule. This is a heretical opinion and very opposed to the divine Canons and to the catholic opinion of our Eastern Church. That *Exomologetarion* of Rhodinos has recently been found by a clergyman of renown who ascribed to it his own name and published it (in Vienna, 1787) without purging it of its heretical opinions. I am truly in wonder and amazement as to how the blessed man did this without any research, on account of which he was not praised by those educated when they saw it. That this is certainly the same as that of Rhodinos, except for the variation in a few words, let whoever so desires compare the two, as we have compared them, and they will find what we say to be true. For someone to select the good and sound things, as opposed to the opposite, is not blameworthy; but they should not also borrow the rotten and heretical.

We have given you this notice, Spiritual Father, so that you may employ the Canons of the Faster to penitents, both in regard to the rule you place them under and to the reception of divine Communion, because these Canons have been accepted and are accepted commonly by the whole Church of the Orthodox. The opinions contained in the aforementioned *Exomologetaria* are not to be accepted or used, because they are impious, and throw the Holy Things to the dogs and the pearls to the swine, by allowing those committers of mortal sins to commune and by them not abstaining completely from divine Communion, and because they do not distinguish between the impure and the pure. They are opposed to the divine Canons because almost all of the Canons clearly and obviously prohibit penitents

2. How the penitent who has many sins is cared for

If the penitent has many sins, you should place him under a rule according to the greater sin mentioned, that is, the one which has a penance of the most time. As long as he is committing the sin, even if he is not communing, that time is not included as part of the time of his penance. If he refrains from the sin he confessed for awhile, and then falls into the same sin again, the time of the penance is begun again from that point. If he falls into a different sin, you must consider which has the greater amount of time, his uncompleted rule or the new sin, and thus instruct him to observe so much time.

If the penitent abstained from the sin and from divine Communion before his confession, either on his own, [143] or because of another Spiritual Father, you should take this time into account when prescribing a rule, beginning from the time when he ceased from the sin. These things are what the most accurate manuscripts of *Exomologetaria* on the Holy Mountain prescribe, which are used by the accomplished Spiritual Fathers of the Holy Mountain with much fruit.

---

from divine Communion for a certain number of years. And if the Canons of the Faster are criticized on account of their leniency and the few number of years they prescribe for a penitent to abstain from Communion, how much more should those *Exomologetaria* be criticized on account of their not prohibiting the reception of Holy Communion at all?

143   To take into consideration and include the amount of time that the penitent has already abstained from the sin and from Communion on his own in the rule you assign, without him having confessed the mortal sin, is done according to condescension and compassion and not according to strictness and righteousness. For the time after a person confesses his mortal sin and abstains from the sin and Communion is considered as part of the rule, as are all the good works which he does unto the attainment of eternal life and which free him from eternal punishment. In as much as he has an unconfessed mortal sin, however, neither abstinence from the sin and Communion nor all the good things he does profit him eternal life or free him from eternal punishment (except maybe preventing some temporary chastisement which he might receive in this life). This is evident because if he dies with that unconfessed mortal sin, he is punished. Look ahead to the third precaution of Chapter 4 in Part Three, *Counsel for the Penitent*.

3. When the one placed under a rule should receive Communion

If the penitent happens to be under a rule and is in danger of dying, he is to receive the divine Mysteries on account of necessity; and if he recovers, he is to resume his rule at the point where he was just before receiving Communion.[144]

4. That a rule is two-fold

Know, Spiritual Father, that a rule and its fulfillment generally fall into two categories: bodily and spiritual. The bodily part consists of fasting, the eating of dry foods (*xerophagia*),[145] prostrations, and the seven bodily acts of mercy, which are: to feed the hungry, to give drink to the thirsty, to take care of and take in strangers, to clothe the naked, to visit the sick, to attend to those in prison, and to bury the dead.[146]

---

144   This is prescribed by Canon 13 of the First Ecumenical Council, Canon 6 of Ancyra, and Canon 5 of St. Gregory of Nyssa. Elias of Crete says: "If someone is still breathing a little and has not outright died, or they are unconscious and cannot eat anything; or if they spit out whatever is put into their mouth, the priest should cautiously seal only his lips and his tongue by touching the Spotless Mysteries to them" (*Juris Graeco-romanorum*, p. 337).

145   Those who are under a rule of fasting must break this fast all of Bright Week and on Feast Days of the Lord, but are to fast all the other days of the year, but they are not to break the fast during the period of Pentecost as those who are not under a rule do (such as the Wednesday before the Ascension or the Wednesday and Friday after Pentecost). As many as are under a rule of prostrations are not to do them on Sunday and during the period of Pentecost; instead of full-out prostrations, let them replace these with a greater number of small prostrations or bows on these days. Refer back to the section, *How to care for monks*, to see when prostrations are to be done and when they are not to be done.

146   Some advise that almsgiving should be done with discernment: 1) to give to Christians in captivity and especially to minors and to those in spiritual and bodily danger; 2) to the poor who are in prison; 3) to the poor who are sick; 4) to poor and virtuous nuns and monks; 5) to those fallen from nobility and ashamed to ask for assistance; and 6) in general, to all who are in need. Symeon of Thessaloniki says that the Spiritual Father is not to ask for the money which is to be distributed for almsgiving from the penitent, because this gives the appearance that he will keep it for himself. He should rather tell the penitent that he is to distribute it with his own hands. If he is compelled by the penitent to distribute it, he must distribute it with the knowledge of the giver and according to his will, and not give it with partiality to his friends or relatives, but to the more pious of the poor

The spiritual part of the rule consists of contrite prayer, the reading of the sacred Scriptures, and the seven spiritual acts of mercy, which are: to motivate sinners to forsake sin and repent, to teach someone unlearned about God and the Faith, to give sound advice to someone in need of counsel, to petition God on behalf of one's brother, to console the sad, to endure one's misfortunes and sorrows without complaining, and to forgive the wrongs which others do to you.[147]

5. That an opposite rule be given

A rule must be given that is in opposition to what the malady is (because opposites treat opposites), as Canon 1 of Gregory of Nyssa prescribes. That is, a rule is to be given which is opposite of the sin and opposite to the circumstances of the sinning person's life, as the authorities say.

In the instance of someone who doubts the Faith, you should place him under a rule, Spiritual Father, that entails reading or listening piously to the sacred Gospel and the Symbol of Faith (Creed), and also that he should not investigate matters that are beyond his ability, and that he should acquaint himself with his mother, the Catholic Church, which handed down the Faith to him.

6. What rule blasphemers and perjurers are to be given

You should tell someone who blasphemes in word to glorify God, Whom he has dishonored.[148] You should also assign this same rule to a

---

(*Responsa ad Gabrielem Pentapolitanum*, Question 73, PG 155, 933A-933B). This same Symeon says that if the Spiritual Father is in need of food or clothing, he is to receive only what is necessary and nothing superfluous from the alms of the penitent, and he is to supplicate God on his behalf. He also says that the Spiritual Father is to tell the penitent that he should make offerings to have Unction services and Liturgies performed on his behalf (*ibid.*, Question 72, PG 155, 925D-933B).

147   See p. 186 of the *Orthodox Confession*.

148   Some who are experienced and authorities say that blasphemers are to be placed under a rule to drag their tongues along the ground many times and to abstain from divine Communion for a sufficient amount of time and to fast and do prostrations for a reasonable time. I found some

perjurer,[149] in addition to what Canon 31 of the Faster says about perjurers. You should place both blasphemers and perjurers under a rule to either read or listen to edifying books, especially the Psalter, which contains many doxologies to God.

---

blasphemers to be placed under a rule for seven years, and in some inscriptions to the Canons of the Faster that one who blasphemes out of the ordinary is to do one hundred prostrations and to fast for one week from meat and wine. That great one amongst the Fathers, Barsanuphios (*Letter 229*), penances the one who blasphemes against God to say three times a day for forty days, "Glory to you O God; Blessed are you O Lord unto the ages; Amen," making three prostrations each time and saying, "Forgive me the blasphemer against You, my God." Tell blasphemers, Spiritual Father, that if God commands that those who say His unutterable Name be put to death, that is, YHWH, according to the most-wise Photios (*Epistle 163 to Amphilochios Kyzikos*): "He that names the name of the Lord, let him die the death" (Lev. 24:16), how much more worthy of death are those who blaspheme Him? Tell them that blasphemy is such a fearful thing that even the devil does not venture to do it, or say it, but instead of saying 'blaspheme,' he says, 'bless,' according to Job: "Verily he will bless thee to thy face" (Job 1:11), that is, blaspheme, as Olympiodoros, Chrysostom, and Didymos all interpret it (*Series on Job*). And neither did Michael blaspheme the devil who is worthy of blasphemy, when he disputed with him over the body of Moses, but he only rebuked him according to the Apostle Jude (verse 9). And the divine Chrysostom would have blasphemers brought to reason by wounds, saying: "And should you hear any one in the public thoroughfare, or in the midst of the forum, blaspheming God; go up to him and rebuke him; and should it be necessary to inflict blows, spare not to do so. Smite him on the face; strike his mouth; sanctify thy hand with the blow" (*Ad Populum Antiochenum I*, 12, PG 49, 32; tr. NPNF (V1-09) p. 343). Tell him still the fearful examples against blasphemers contained in *Salvation of Sinners* (p. 13) and especially about how the demons snatched the body of that child who learned to blaspheme. How a person was possessed and died a terrible death because he blasphemed on account of losing a card game. Above all tell blasphemers to abstain from the causes of blasphemy, which are gambling, cards, vows, and irrational anger.

A type of blasphemy is for someone to deliver their brother to the devil and to damn him. This is penanced similarly to blasphemy against God.

Translator's note: That blasphemy against God (and any other sin, for that matter), comes back to harm the blasphemer and sinner, is attested to by St. Nikodemos: "Just as the person who throws a rock toward heaven does not harm heaven, but harms himself because the rock comes back and strikes him on the head, so whoever blasphemes against God does not harm God, but only harms himself and punishes his soul, the poor wretch" (*Chrestoetheia ton Christianon (Christian Morality)*, Thessaloniki, 1999, pp. 163-164).

149   Note that the divine Isidore Pelousiotes wrote to Zosimos and reproved him because he forgave the perjury of someone who gave him some fish. He also said to him that if the one wronged does not receive back the amount of money he lost on account of the perjury, the perjurer cannot be forgiven: "For you are not to be appeased by gifts to dismiss that crime, but in the recovery of the property by the one who was wronged by the perjury" (*Liber III, Epistola CCLX - Zosimo Presbytero*, PG 78, 940C).

7. What rule thieves and the unjust are to be given

Before placing thieves and the unjust under the rule of Canon 27 of the Faster, you should place them under a rule to return that which they took, if they have it, either to the same person from whom they took it, if they are alive, or to their relatives, if they have died. They should do this either through the Spiritual Father or through another faithful person.[150] If they do not have it, they are to return to the one they have wronged and ask forgiveness from him. If they do have it, and both the one wronged and his relatives have died, tell them to give the stolen goods to the poor. Also give thieves, Spiritual Father, that catholic advice which we mention ahead in the footnote to the section, *What rule murderers are to be given*.[151]

---

150   Therefore Gregory the Theologian also demonstrates that not even Holy Baptism is able to forgive that wrong which is able to be corrected by returning the item, but is not returned. For whoever robs something which is not their own, and afterward is baptized, it is not to be thought that that theft is forgiven if the one baptized still has the stolen item in his possession and does not return it, even though able to. In such a manner purification is fabricated, thinking that through baptism he is pure from the injustice without being so in reality: "Two sins are on your conscience, the one that you made a dishonest gain, the other that you retained the gains; you received forgiveness for the one, but in respect of the other you are still in sin, for you have still possession of what belongs to another; and your sin has not been put to an end, but only divided by the time which has elapsed. Part of it was perpetrated before your baptism, but part remains after your baptism; for baptism carries forgiveness of past, not of present sins; and its purification must not be played with, but be genuinely impressed upon you" (*Oratio* 40, 32, PG 36, 404C-405A; tr. NPNF (V2-07), pp. 371-372). Therefore they are deluded who say that that injustice is forgiven when someone becomes a monk, even if after becoming a monk that person possesses the stolen property and does not return it. And the sacred Augustine says: "When someone has a stolen item and is able to give it back, but does not, that person does not repent in truth, but falsely and in pretend." See also Canon 3 of Gregory Thaumatourgos and Canon 14 of Theophilos which excommunicate the unjust and the greedy.

151   In addition, tell thieves, Spiritual Father, that God punishes theft so severely, as to command that if a thief is unable to return the stolen item to the person, he is to sell himself and give this money to him: "If he have nothing, then he shall be sold for his theft" (Ex. 22:3), and that: "If a man shall steal an ox, or a sheep, and kill it, or sell it; he shall restore five oxen for an ox, and four sheep for a sheep" (Ex. 22:1), "If the theft be certainly found in his hand alive, whether it be ox, or ass, or sheep; he shall restore double" (Ex. 22:4). Except if someone goes and confesses on their own that they stole or wronged someone, they repay only the capital plus a fifth of the capital: "Then they shall confess their sin which they have done: and he shall recompense his trespass with the principal thereof, and add unto it the fifth part thereof, and give it unto him against whom he hath trespassed" (Num. 5:7). Why am I saying these things? God commands that it not be considered

8. What rule fornicators, adulterers, and sodomists are to be given

You are to place fornicators and sodomists under a rule of fasting, the eating of dry foods, prostrations, and, before all else, they are to leave those people with whom they sinned or make them leave their house if they are living together.[152]

9. What rule accusers and rancorous people are to be given

You are to place accusers and slanderers under a rule, Spiritual Father, to return to the same place where they made the accusation and to say that they falsely accused their brother. Or if they do not themselves go, they should send a third person to confess that they lied. Or they should send a letter, openly or in secret, retracting their slander. You are to place rancorous people and those who have animosity toward someone under a rule to make reconciliation between them.[153]

---

murder if someone kills a thief during the night (this does not apply to the daytime, however): "If a thief be found breaking in, and be smitten that he die, there shall no blood be shed for him" (Ex. 22:2).

152   Be very careful, Spiritual Father, so as not to read the prayer of forgiveness for either the unjust, if they do not return the stolen item, or for fornicators and sodomists, if they do not cast the lewd woman or the male person out of their house. Even if they promise to do these things, do not easily believe them, because most people of this type break their promises and mock you until they receive forgiveness, as experience shows. Know this also, Spiritual Father, that many times you will find callousness and have difficulties from those who have a harlot or a youth in their house, because when they plead with you with tears to allow them to have such things in their homes, do not have compassion on them, remembering that which God says: "Neither shalt thou countenance a poor man in his cause" (Ex. 23:3). And at other times when they try to intimidate you with threats, do not fear, remembering the saying of God: "That which is altogether just shalt thou follow" (Dt. 16:20), and: "Fear ye not the reproach of men, neither be ye afraid of their revilings" (Is. 51:7)

153   Be very careful, Spiritual Father, also not to read the prayer of forgiveness for those who are rancorous before they make reconciliation. And say the following so that they may be reconciled: that the Holy Spirit says of them: "The ways of those that remember injuries lead to death" (Pr. 12:28), and again: "He that remembers injuries is a transgressor" (Pr. 21:24). And John the Theologian says: "Whosoever hateth his brother is a murderer" (1 Jn. 3:15). Tell the rancorous that if they do not forgive their enemy, they cannot say the 'Our Father,' because they do not forgive those

10. What rule murderers are to be given

In addition to placing a murderer under the rule of Canon 20 of the Faster, he is also to redeem a slave, if he has the means, according to Symeon of Thessaloniki,[154] so a life may be given for a life.[155] If a woman aborted

who trespass against them, as is said in the 'Our Father.' Tell them that God demands what He is owed with torments, especially from those who have received forgiveness for their sins from Him, according to the parable of the servant who owed one thousand talents (Mt. 18:23-35). Tell them that the requirement of the commandment of love compels them not to only not seek revenge, but also not to hate their neighbor at all, not even in thought: "Thou shalt not hate thy brother in thine heart" (Lev. 19:17), and tell them that when they make peace with their enemy, their heart will be alleviated.

Relate to them, Spiritual Father, the example of the Lord, how He made supplications for His crucifiers while He was on the Cross; the example of the Protomartyr Stephen, who made supplications for those who were stoning him. Relate that fearful story of the two rancorous people who, because they did not forgive from the heart, but held onto a grudge even after death, the dead person came from Hades and snatched his living enemy out of the Church in the presence of the people; then the earth split open and both of them descended into Hades, just as the sacred preacher Prokopios tells it in his teachings (p. 78). Relate to them how St. Ambrose was giving perpetual alms to a certain thief who had tried to kill him; how a certain virtuous woman drained the pus from the breast of a wounded woman who had slandered her. Tell them how even the gentiles did not hold on to grudges, like Lykourgos, who was blinded by Alkandros, and not only did he not seek revenge, but even dined with him at the same table. Demonax, when he was struck in the face by someone with a rock, and everyone was shouting, out of their love for him, "To the judge! To the judge!" and Demonax on the contrary said, "No, men; rather, to the doctor!" Pericles, when he was being sworn at by someone all day, that night led the reviler to his home with a lantern. Finally, Spiritual Father, you should advise the one who began the strife to go and prostrate himself many times before the one whom he scandalized until he forgives him, as the divine Chrysostom says: "Let no one tell me that he has made overtures once and a second time but his enemy has not come round: if we approach this with unmixed motives, we will not give up before we prevail through intense supplication, and thus win him over and turn him from his hostility to us" (*On Genesis*, Homily 27, 8, PG 53, 251; tr. *Saint John Chrysostom: Homilies on Genesis 18-45*, Washington, D.C., 1990, p. 181).

Be careful, however, Spiritual Father, so that you do not give the appearance that, instead of judge, you have become an adjunct to the opposite, showing how you sympathize with the one who reviled and allowing him to say all of his complaints. Tell them that after they have been reconciled, they must greet one another as in the beginning; and if one of them does not agree to this, he must give alms and supplicate God on behalf of the salvation of his enemy. God may soften that person's heart in this manner, so that they may forgive one another from all of their heart and greet one another.

154   *Responsa ad Gabrielem Pentapolitanum*, Question 72, PG 155, 925D-932D.

155   Tell a murderer, Spiritual Father, that just as the most holy Patriarch Athanasios and Andronikos the Emperor order (Blastaris, verse 500, ch. 8), he must distribute his possessions to each

a child, she is to be placed under a rule to nurture and raise a poor infant, if she has the means, according to the same Symeon;[156] see also Canon 22 of the Faster concerning this.

I have said that one is to be placed under a rule according to the opposite

---

child he has and give a portion to the one killed, that is, to his wife and the fatherless children, if he has any possessions. If he does not have any, he is to perform acts of kindness and give alms on behalf of the soul of the murdered person and supplicate God with all of his soul for forgiveness, and so with these things the cry of the blood of the murdered which seeks revenge will be hushed, and the fearful punishments prepared for him, both eternal and temporal, will be prevented, for: "Whoso sheddeth man's blood, by man shall his blood be shed" (Gen. 9:6). In order to demonstrate concisely for the murderer the magnitude of his sin, tell him: 1) how among all the bad things that can happen to our neighbor, the foremost and worst is murder; 2) how the one who murders seizes the authority from God, Who is Lord of life and death; and 3) how the one who murders a person commits a greater transgression than if he had burned and destroyed all of the wide open plains, all of the fruits of the earth, all of the animals, all of the trees in the world, all of the houses in the cities and villages, because, having murdered a human being, he murdered the one ordained by God to be king of all of creation. Additionally, Spiritual Father, give this catholic advice to murderers, to grave robbers, and to every other sinner who commits sin in secret: that if someone seems eager in their repentance, it is allowable for him to go, either to the same people whom he wronged, or to their relatives, or to a foreign judge, in order to publicly confess his murder, or his theft, or his grave robbery, or any other sin committed in secret, and so agree to receive the punishment designated for that sin by the external and political laws. This should be done especially if, on account of the sin committed by him, someone innocent was arrested and punished or harmed unjustly by a judge. Who verifies this for us? 1) Basil the Great, for he says this in his explanation of Psalm 32: "Because we sinned with the body... we must confess with the body, that necessary organ, for the removal of our sins. Did you revile? Bless. Were you greedy and cheat someone? Give it back. Did you get drunk? Fast. Did you brag? Humble yourself... Did you murder? Confess it publicly, or in equivalence to this public witness, afflict your body through Confession" (*Homilia in Psalmum XXXII* 2, PG 29, 325C-328A); 2) the wise Synesios, who commanded a certain John who had committed murder to confess his murder publicly (*Epistola XLIV*, PG 66, 1365D-1373C); and 3) the following examples: we read in the *Lives of the Saints*, on April 14, that the murderer of his bride, St. Thomais, turned himself in to the ruler of the city, and was executed in turn by him; similarly, we also find in the *Evergetinos* (Book 1, *Hypothesis 3*; *The Evergetinos: A Complete Text*, vol. I, bk. 1, p. 61) that a certain holy ascetic, pierced in the soul with contrition, came down from the Mount of Olives and confessed his sins to the ruler of the city, saying to him: "Punish me, as I have broken the law;" because the ruler did not want to punish him, the ascetic himself put chains on his feet and around his neck, telling those that asked him what happened that the ruler put them on him. One day before his death, an angel of the Lord appeared to him and said: "Owing to the patience which you have shown, all of your sins are forgiven," and touching his chains they immediately fell away. The brother fell asleep shortly thereafter.

156   *Responsa ad Gabrielem Pentapolitanum*, Question 72, PG 155, 925D-932D.

circumstances of his life. For example, a rich person should be told to fast, to eat dry foods, and to do prostrations; a poor person should give alms from his deficiency; for these things seem unto them to be a rule and chastisements, especially if the rich person committed a carnal sin, and the poor person committed theft or robbery. If the rich person was placed under a rule to only give alms, and the poor person to only fast, these things would not seem to them as chastisement, but only a continuation of what they were already doing. In addition to this, the Spiritual Father is to care for them in the best manner possible and with great discernment.

Also remember, Spiritual Father, to advise sinners not to suppose or believe that they receive forgiveness from God for their sins only on account of them fulfilling their rule; God forbid! This is a heretical opinion, for according to the theologians, sin is infinite, and as an offense to the infinite God, no finite creature, especially an impure creature like a sinner, by works or by fulfilling a rule, can be loosed from it: "But we are all as an unclean thing, and all our righteousnesses are as filthy rags" (Is. 64:6). But they are to certainly believe that they receive forgiveness for their sins: 1) on account of the infinite mercy of God; 2) on account of the infinite satisfaction which the Son of God obtained on behalf of sinners through His death and through the blood shed on His Cross,[157] as Paul said: "Not by works of

---

[157]   Translator's note: St. Nicholas Cabasilas says: "He alone, then, was able to render all the honor that is due to the Father and make satisfaction for that which had been taken away. The former He achieved by His life, the latter by His death. The death which He died upon the cross to the Father's glory He brought in to outweigh the injury which we had committed; in addition, He most abundantly made amends for the debt of honor which we owed for our sins" (*De Vita in Christo* 4, PG 150, 588B-588C; tr. *The Life in Christ*, Crestwood, 1974, p. 118). In other terms: "The extent of evil can be measured by the power of its Antidote. The sick are healed by a Treatment that befits the stature of God. The Physician, instead of the patient, passes through death and inaugurates His universal healing" (Paul Evdokimov, *Ages of the Spiritual Life*, Crestwood, 2002, p. 184). And St. Symeon the New Theologian adds: "Because Adam was cursed, and the humanity descended from him sprouted every sort of sin, and because of the force of the verdict (God's sentence of the eternal punishment of death), Christ became a curse by being suspended on the tree, in order to offer Himself as the sacrificial Son to the Father, as was mentioned previously, and so overturn the verdict on account of the supreme worth of the sacrifice, for what is higher than God?... For this reason, the God Who is incomparably higher than everything, since He assumed the nature of man which is higher than every visible creature, offered it as a sacrifice to God the Father, and we can say that

righteousness which we have done, but according to His mercy He saved us" (Tit. 3:5); as John said: "And the blood of Jesus Christ His Son cleanseth us from all sin" (1 Jn. 1:7), and as Basil the Great says: "The forgiveness of sins is by the blood of Christ."[158] And finally, 3) they should consider the third reason for the forgiveness of their sins, which is all of the good works and fruits of repentance which they do after the sin.[159] These good works, however, are not to be understood as natural in and of themselves (because in thinking about them this way, they will never be able to forgive sins and gain eternal salvation), but inasmuch as they are united through faith with the supranatural grace of Jesus Christ, which brings them about and effects them and makes them worthy of divine acceptance (from Koressios). The words spoken above are verified by God Himself Who says through Isaiah: "I, even I, am He that blotteth out thy transgressions for Mine own sake" (Is. 43:25). Do you hear? He says, *I* am the one, sinner, Who blots out your sins and forgives you, and not on account of your rule and chastisement, but on account of My own mercy and compassion. "For Mine own sake."

On top of everything that we have said about placing sinners under a rule and their fulfilling it, Spiritual Father, you must also tell them to abstain from Holy Communion for as much time as St. John the Faster prescribes. If there is someone who agrees to fulfill the rule he is placed under, of fasting, of eating dry foods, of prostrations, and of giving alms, but does not agree to abstain from Communion, know that herein lies all of your knowledge and experience, to placate him in various ways so as to convince him to agree to both, saying these things:

---

the Father respected and honored it, unable to overlook it, and overturned the verdict" (*Alphabetika Kephalaia (Alphabetical Chapters)* 1, Hagion Oros, 2005, p. 46).

158   *Regulæ Brevius* 13, PG 31, 1089C. (Translator's note: Elsewhere St. Basil also says: "By the blood of Christ, through faith, we have been cleansed from all sin" (*De Baptismo I*, ch. 3,1, PG 31, 1573A).)

159   Translator's note: St. John of the Ladder says: "Repentance is reconciliation with the Lord by the practice of good deeds contrary to the sins" (Step 5, PG 88, 764B; tr. *The Ladder*, p. 54).

11. Advice to the penitent so that he also accepts the abstinence from Communion

1. "Child, know that if you wish to commune unworthily, you will become guilty of the body and blood of the Lord, as St. Paul says (1 Cor. 11:27), and you will commune unto your condemnation and perdition, becoming a second Judas and like the Jews. For just as the Jews pierced the body of the Lord then, not in order to drink His blood, but in order to spill it, as Chrysostom explains,[160] you should also consider that you are spilling the pure blood of the Lord and not that you are drinking it, on account of your unworthiness."

2. "Child, know that the divine Faster established his Canons with the discernment of the Holy Spirit, and that in almost every Canon he states with great precision and discrimination that whoever is not able to hold to both the rule designated therein and to the abstinence from Communion for the few years designated, is to hold to the many years designated by the other divine Fathers. Therefore, considering these things he says, there is no way he would allow any further condescension."

3. "Child, know that I have performed a great condescension for you and have not placed you under a rule according to the other Fathers, who designate so many years of abstinence from Communion for your particular sin (here, let the penitent know how many years the Canons of the Synods and of the Fathers designate). I have rather placed you under a rule according to the lenient Faster. I have also performed another great condescension for you in not taking into account your other sins, where for such and such a sin so many years and such and such a rule are designated, and the same for your other sins (here, let the penitent know how many years and what rule are designated for each sin he has committed). I have rather placed you under a rule on account of only one of your sins, feeling sorry for you and having compassion on your weakness. I have also performed a third condescension for you which is very great. The rule which I have placed you under on account of your sin should have been doubled or even multiplied by as many times as you committed the sin. If I had done this,

---

160   *On I Corinthians*, Homily 28, 3, PG 61, 230.

the number of years your rule would have reached could have been so great that you may not be able to complete it during your life. I had compassion on you, however, and placed you under a light rule, as if you had committed the sin only once, when in fact you have committed it many times (here, let the penitent know how many years he could have been given according to the number of times he committed the sin). Therefore, child, you should not be so hard of heart and thankless, but you should accept this small rule and the abstinence from Communion with joy."

4. "Child, know that with this abstinence from Communion your repentance will be more firm. You will be greater assured of the grace of God and you will better understand the harm which sin caused you, especially when you see others communing while you abstain, saying to yourself what that Prodigal Son said: 'How many hired servants of my father's have bread enough and to spare, and I perish with hunger!' (Lk. 15:17). And by this you will hate sin forever and in the future you will protect well the grace which you lost, so that 'your mishaps may become lessons.' 'For everything that someone builds with great labor, he is diligent to protect,' says Basil the Great.[161] And Gregory the Theologian says: 'For people cling tightly to that which they acquire with labor; but that which they acquire easily they quickly throw away, because it can be easily recovered.'"[162]

You may say these things and others, Spiritual Father, as much as the grace of the Holy Spirit would enlighten you. You may also choose not to inform him about how much time the rule entails, and say: "Go, child, for I know the proper time when you should commune, and you will come to realize it with the passage of time." Refer also to the section, *Counsel for the Penitent*, where we speak about this subject separately, so that both the rule and the abstinence from Communion be accepted.

---

161   *Constitutiones Asceticæ* 1, 6, PG 31, 1337A.
162   *Oratio* 28, 12, PG 36, 40D-41A.

12. What rule the infirm and
the elderly are to be given

If there happens to be someone who cannot carry out the bodily rule designated by the divine Faster on account of their being infirm or of old age, you may certainly, Spiritual Father, give these people another spiritual rule: of prayer, of reading edifying books, and of performing bodily or spiritual acts of mercy (see the beginning of this chapter). You may not, however, reduce the number of years designated by the Faster that they must abstain from Communion.

13. As many as do not accept their rule and the abstinence
from Communion are to be dismissed

If there is someone who is so hard of heart and unrepentant, and who is completely healthy, that does not accept the rule designated by the Faster and does not wish to abstain from Communion, and you have admonished him one, two, and three times, then you must at last, Spiritual Father, say: "Child, Basil the Great commands me in his 84th and 85th Canons to say to a disobedient and argumentative people: 'Escape for thy life' (Gen. 19:17), so that my own soul will not be condemned together with yours."[163] Tell him still, how Luke of Constantinople (in the questions he solves together with his Synod, found in manuscripts) says that a priest should not receive the offering of those who are disobedient and who do not want to receive the rule given them on account of their sin.

---

163   For it is written in the Ecclesiastical Histories that some unfortunate sinner was wrongfully forgiven by his Spiritual Father, and after he died, he appeared to his Spiritual Father and reproved him for his exceeding leniency, saying: "Because you are the cause of my damnation, come with me, so we may be damned together." After he said this, he embraced him, and then everything became black. And what wonder! The earth was rent open and swallowed the both of them. Therefore, the divine Ambrose also says that the easy forgiveness of a Spiritual Father causes the sinner to sin more: "Lest the ease of forgiveness excite the sinner."

14. How women who are married and
who have relatives are cared for

If you confess a married woman who has secretly committed adultery, be cautious, Spiritual Father, and neither allow her to Commune, nor are you to give any impression of this to her husband that he may understand what she did, for both the act, and his knowledge of it, are devastating. This caution should also be observed for other women who have parents and siblings. See also Canon 33 of the Faster.

If you come upon some sins which are not written about and addressed in the Canons, you should go to your hierarch about these and learn from him what the appropriate rule is.[164] This may be discerned either through the resemblance they have with other sins contained in the Canons, or from the writings of certain Fathers, or through the discernment of common sense. Concerning sins for which no penances can be found in the Canons, see the penances already added after the Canons of the Faster.

CHAPTER 11

Concerning the Prayer of Forgiveness

When you have also finished placing the penitent under a rule, the customary prayer of forgiveness is then read over the penitent:

"Lord Jesus Christ, the Son of the living God, shepherd and lamb, Who takes away the sin of the world, Who forgave the loan to the two debtors and granted remission of her sins to the sinful woman; do Thou, Thyself, O Lord, loose, remit, forgive the sins, the transgressions and the errors, both voluntary and involuntary, known or unknown, which have been committed through violation and disobedience by this Thy servant (*name*). And if he, being human, bearing flesh and dwelling in the world, was deceived in

---

164   Balsamon says that, as many Canons as do not contain a written penance for those who transgress them, give permission to the local hierarch on account of their silence to determine a penance for these as he deems fit (Explanation of Canon 45 of the Sixth Ecumenical Council, PG 137, 673A-673B).

anything by the devil, either in word or deed, knowingly or unknowingly, if he broke the word of a priest, or came under the curse of a priest, or fell under his own anathema, or has broken any oath, do Thou, the same good and forgiving Master, be pleased to set free this Thy servant by Thy word, granting him forgiveness of his own anathema and oath, according to Thy great mercy. Yea, Lord and Master, lover of mankind, hearken unto me as I pray to Thy goodness for this Thy servant, and, in Thy great mercy, overlook all his faults; deliver him from eternal punishment; for Thou hast said, O Master: Whatsoever ye shall bind on earth shall be bound in heaven: and whatsoever ye shall loose on earth shall be loosed in heaven. For Thou alone art without sin and unto Thee we ascribe glory, together with Thy Father which is without beginning, and Thine All-holy and good and life-creating Spirit, now and ever, and to the ages of ages. Amen."

You may also choose to read this briefer prayer while placing your hand upon the head of the penitent:

"Lord Jesus Christ our God, Who because of their tears granted forgiveness to Peter and the harlot, and justified the Publican when he acknowledged his faults, accept the confession of Thy servant (name), and if he has committed any sin, in word or in deed or in thought, knowingly or unknowingly, voluntarily or involuntarily, forgive him, for Thou alone hath the power to forgive sins. For Thou art a merciful, compassionate and man-befriending God, and unto Thee we ascribe glory, together with the Father and the Holy Spirit, unto the ages of ages. Amen."

1. Thus you make a supplication for mercy and for the forgiveness of the sins of the penitent

Then, turning to the penitent, place your hand upon his head and say this categorical word,[165] for it is the expression of the Mystery of Repentance:

"The grace of the All-holy Spirit, through my insignificance, has you

---

165   This is required by most, especially by Gabriel of Philadelphia in his *Concerning the Mysteries* and Chrysanthos of Jerusalem in his *Exomologetarion* (p. 16).

loosened and forgiven."[166]

2. That the Spiritual Father must place his hand on the penitents

Make sure, Spiritual Father, to always place your hand upon the head of the penitent, for the divine Canons require this laying on of hands as essential to the Mystery,[167] even if most Spiritual Fathers do not do this today on account of their ignorance and illiteracy.

3. Final counsel of the Spiritual Father to the penitent

Having finished everything, counsel the penitent in this fashion: "Know, my child, that you have received a second baptism today through the Mystery of Confession and Repentance, just as the Holy Church of Christ believes. Therefore, be careful so as not to soil it again by a second sin. For just as the person who touches something dirty and then washes, but again touches the same dirty thing, does not profit whatsoever from the washing which he did, likewise, the person who is washed in the bath of repentance and confession and is cleansed from his sins profits nothing

---

166   However, Chrysanthos says in his *Exomologetarion* (p. 15) that the expression of repentance is also shown through the prayer which is read over the penitents by the Spiritual Father. We have chosen to put here both the prayer of forgiveness and the categorical word. We call the categorical word the expression of repentance because both the spiritual and determinant cause of repentance clearly play a part in it, which is the grace of the Holy Spirit and the instrument of that grace, the Spiritual Father.

167   For Canon 8 of the First Ecumenical Council received those returning from the Novatians through the laying on of hands. And Canon 66 of Carthage received those returning from the Donatists through the laying on of hands. And in particular, Canon 49 of Carthage requires that repentant sinners be received through the laying on of hands. Therefore, the *Apostolic Constitutions* require these things of Spiritual Fathers: "Accept a sinner when he weeps over his sin, and after the laying on of hands, let him remain thereafter in the flock" (Book II, ch. 18; SC 320, pp. 192, 194); and again they say: "Just as you accept an unbeliever after baptizing him, so shall you restore to the spiritual pasture as purified and clean a sinner after laying hands upon him" (Book II, chs. 41 and 43), since by imposition of the hands the Holy Spirit used to be given (Acts 8:18).

when he afterwards falls into the same sins, just as Sirach says: 'If a man is baptized after touching a dead body, and touches it again, what has he gained by his washing? Such is the man who fasts for his sins, and goes again and does the same things' (Sir. 34:25-26). You must use a sword, my child, a sword. That is, you must firmly resolve in your heart that you would rather die a thousand deaths rather than sin again and disappoint God. From now on you must begin to live like a Christian and a disciple of Christ, for true repentance is not only to forsake evil, but to also do good, according to the Psalm: 'Turn away from evil, and do good' (Ps. 33:14); to take off the impure garment of sin and put on the pure garment of divine grace. Guard yourself, therefore, all the more, from taking this pure garment off and putting the old one on again, but sing the song: 'I have put off my garment; how shall I put it on? I have washed my feet; how shall I defile them?' (S. of S. 5:3) being fearful to sin again, and thereby becoming the boast of the devil and a mockery and dishonor to Christ on the day of judgment, which is worse than any other punishment, as Basil the Great says.[168] Go, therefore, in the way of peace. 'Behold, thou art made whole: sin no more, lest a worse thing come unto thee' (Jn. 5:14)."

CHAPTER 12

That the Spiritual Father Is Not to Reveal Sins

Nothing else remains after confession, Spiritual Father, except to keep the sins you hear a secret, and to never reveal them, either by word, or by letter, or by a bodily gesture, or by any other sign, even if you are in danger of death, for that which the wise Sirach says applies to you: "Have you heard a word? Let it die with you" (Sir. 19:10); and again: "With friend or foe do not report it" (Sir. 19:8); meaning, if you heard a secret word, let the word also die along with you, and do not tell it to either a friend of yours or an enemy of yours, for as long as you live. And further still, that which the Prophet Micah says: "Trust not in friends... Beware of thy wife,

---

168   *Homilia in Psalmum XXVIII*, 2, PG 29, 285C-285D.

so as not to commit anything to her" (Mic. 7:5).

For if you reveal them, firstly, you will be suspended or daresay deposed completely by the Ecclesiastical Canons, and according to political laws you will be thrown in jail for the rest of your life and have your tongue cut out.[169] Secondly, you become a reason for more Christians not to confess, being afraid that you will reveal their sins, just as it happened during the time of Nektarios of Constantinople when the Christians did not want to confess on account of a Spiritual Father who revealed the sin of a woman.[170] The divine Chrysostom both witnessed these things and suffered because of them on account of his trying to convince the people to confess. It is impossible for me to describe in words how much punishment this brings upon you, who are the cause of these things.

EPILOGUE

These few things which we have written down for you, Spiritual Father, are the most essential and necessary for your spiritual vocation. And you should never fail in studying them because they will profit you greatly. Do not stop reading the *Exomologetarion* of Chrysanthos of Jerusalem, or *Instructions for Spiritual Fathers*, or Canon 11 of the First Ecumenical Council, or Canon 102 of the Sixth Ecumenical Council, or Canons 2, 5, and 7 of Ancyra, or Canons 1 and 2 of Laodicaea, or Canons 4, 5, 7, and 8 of St. Gregory of Nyssa, or Canons 2, 3, 74, 84, and 85 of Basil the Great, for

---

169   Patriarch Luke of Constantinople disciplined the abbot of the Monastery of Xerotrophos with a penance of suspension because he revealed the sin of one of his spiritual children, as Balsamon reports (Explanation of Canon 141 (135) of Carthage, PG 138, 424D). I am resigned to say that the Spiritual Father ought not to be believed on his word alone, according to this same Canon of Carthage, and a single witness is not to be believed, but rejected, according to Leo and Constantine the Emperors (*Selections of Laws*, Title 26). Let Spiritual Fathers be reminded of this by God Himself, Who never publicly revealed the confession of any person, as John of the Ladder says: "At no time do we find God revealing the sins which have been confessed to Him lest by making these public knowledge, He should impede those who would confess and so make them incurably sick" (*To the Shepherd*, PG 88, 1196B; tr. *The Ladder*, p. 243).

170   See Socrates, *Historia Ecclesiastica* 5, 19, PG 67, 613A-620A. And Sozomen says that the Spiritual Father was chosen on account of his being secretive and discrete (*Historia Ecclesiastica* 7, 16, PG 67, 1460A).

these Canons are especially helpful to your vocation. Likewise, you should also read continuously *Counsel for the Penitent* which we have written especially for the penitent, because you should be familiar with this first, in order for you to instruct penitents with it, especially those who are illiterate and cannot read it. Besides these things, we say that if you are thorough and examine well the various matters that happen to come your way, this thoroughness and practice will, in time, cause you to learn many things and more than is written in books. For according to Sirach, he who is experienced knows much, but he who does not have experience knows little: "An educated man knows many things, and one with much experience will speak with understanding. He that is inexperienced knows few things" (Sir. 34:9-10).

Therefore, knowing that the supervision and care of souls which you will undertake is the "art of arts and science of sciences," according to Gregory the Theologian,[171] do not be negligent: "Cursed be he that doeth the work of the Lord negligently" (Jer. 48:10). Rather, imitate that shepherd who hastens to remove from the mouth of a lion, not only the entire sheep, but even if there happens to be only two legs or a piece of its ear, as Amos says: "As the shepherd taketh out of the mouth of the lion two legs, or a piece of an ear; so shall the children of Israel be taken out" (Am. 3:12). In this same manner, Spiritual Father, struggle as much as you are able, using countless ways to remove from the mouth of the noetic lion, the devil, those pitiable sinners, even if they are rotted and hopeless because of their sins,[172] just as John of the Ladder tells you: "Give heed, therefore, O

---

171   *Oratio* 2, 16, PG 35, 425A.

172   Your love must be so great for the salvation of sinners, Spiritual Father, that it must have these four things which the Apostle Paul mentions (cf. Eph. 3:17, 18): width, length, height and depth. Width, so that you receive all sinners equally: the rich as much as the poor; the nobleman as much as the peasant. Length, so that you do not grow weary when hearing their sins, even if they are many and great. Height, so that you may raise sinners from earth to heaven. Depth, so that you may descend and be lowered with them to every infirmity and weakness they have, without showing how you are nauseated from each of their wounds. An example of this kind of love is contained in a saying we found in the Patristic writings of a virtuous Spiritual Father who said: "If I had, hypothetically, one of my legs inside the door of Paradise, and then I wanted to turn back in order to confess a soul which was in need of correction, I strongly believe that when I would turn back, I would pull Paradise with me, so that I could correct that soul." Another wise man said to Spiritual

wondrous man; and towards him that is broken and gone very far astray show all your zeal, love, fervency, care, and prayer to God. For wherever there are great illnesses and wounds, there also great recompenses will undoubtedly be given."[173] In one word, Spiritual Father, Paradise and hell, life and death, the salvation and damnation of souls, lies in your hands. And if through your good corrections they are saved, you will hear: "If thou take forth the precious from the vile, thou shalt be as my mouth" (Jer. 15:19). Contrarily, if through your bad corrections and negligence one of these is condemned, you will hear: "The wicked man shall die in his iniquity; but his blood will I require at thine hand" (Ezek. 3:18).

If you desire to show true and fatherly love to your spiritual children, Spiritual Father, endeavor to be easily moved to compunction and tears, in a manner that you not only feel sorry for sinners who commit great and mortal sins, but also that you shed tears, sympathizing with their misfortune, for these tears have great power. Your tears are not only a sign of your affectionate love for the sinner,[174] but they also propitiate God for his sins,[175] and they move the most callous and insensitive sinner to have compunction on account of his transgressions, seeing you, not having committed them, weeping over them. They confirm the love which you have for him and cause him to receive your correction with ease.[176] Be

---

Fathers: "Consider, Spiritual Fathers, that when penitents confess, they call you their Fathers saying: yes Father; no Father. Therefore you also are required to show them fatherly love and to run up and down with great eagerness for their correction and their salvation."

173   *To the Shepherd*, PG 88, 1193D-1196A; tr. *The Ladder*, p. 242.

174   The Jews understood the love which Christ had for Lazaros by the tears He shed, saying: "Behold how he loved him!" (Jn. 11:36).

175   For St. Gregory of Nyssa says these things to the sinner: "Seek also the mourning of your brethren who are of the same spiritual nature, for they help you toward freedom; receive also the priest (the Spiritual Father) who partakes of your suffering as a father" (*Adhortatio ad Poenitentiam*, PG 40, 369A). (Translator's note: This *Homily on Repentance*, which St. Nikodemos attributes to St. Gregory of Nyssa, is listed in Migne's *Patrologia Graeca*, vol. 40, as *Homily 13* of Asterios, Bishop of Amaseia.)

176   St. Gregory of Nyssa in this same homily chastises those Spiritual Fathers who do not sympathize with the sin of sinners, and he calls them callous and false fathers; but he praises those who sympathize with and weep on account of the sins of their spiritual children, just as Moses was moved sympathetically toward the people of Israel when they made the calf, and just as the great Paul wept on account of the enemies of the Cross of Christ (Phil. 3:18). Thus also Basil the Great

careful, however, so as not to show any sign of sadness or of dejection or of tears while he is confessing, as we said earlier. Rather, you should be sad and weep after the confession has finished, when you counsel him and place him under a rule.

ADDENDUM

How the Spiritual Father Should Question Those Confessing About the Chief Sins, According to the Ten Commandments

We said in chapter 9 how, properly, the Spiritual Father is not to question those confessing about their sins, but that they are supposed to say them on their own accord to the Spiritual Father, and that the Spiritual Father is only to listen to them and correct them. But because most Christians today, some out of lack of education and ignorance, some out of shame, and some out of bad habit, expect to be questioned by the Spiritual Father during confession, they do not consider examining themselves and their sins before confessing; neither do they simply state their sins, as they should, but they wait for the Spiritual Father to first question them, and then they respond. And if the Spiritual Father does not question them, they do not reveal all of their sins, thus departing from the Spiritual Father unconfessed. For this reason, Spiritual Father, we have judged it necessary to include here some general information on how to question such people during confession about the more serious and grave sins based on the Ten

---

writes to the monk who had fallen to come to him, to lament over his body, dead from sin, and weep over his affliction (*Letter* 44,2). Thus Sozomen writes in his *Ecclesiastical History* that, when the Divine Liturgy finished, the sinners who did not commune in the divine Mysteries on account of their sins fell flat on the ground weeping and wailing, because they had been deprived of divine Communion, and the bishop also immediately ran out and fell on the ground facing them weeping, and all the multitude of Christians wept with bitter tears for their misfortune: "There is a place appropriated to the reception of penitents, in which spot they stand and mourn until the completion of the Liturgy of God, for it is not lawful for them to take part in the Mysteries; then they cast themselves, with groans and lamentations, prostrate on the ground. The bishop conducts the ceremony, sheds tears, and prostrates himself in like manner; and all the people burst into tears, and groan aloud" (7, 16, PG 67, 1460B-1461A).

Commandments.

So when some Christian comes to you to confess, begin by saying, "Blessed is our God," and say the *Trisagion* prayers and the 50th Psalm. Then turn and counsel the penitent in this way, holding the *Exomologetarion* in your hands:

"Behold, child, Christ (gesturing toward His icon) is invisibly present, awaiting your confession; do not therefore be ashamed, or afraid, and hide any of your sins, but from your whole heart confess them, so that you may receive forgiveness for them from Christ Himself. If you hide any, know that the unconfessed sin will not only stand marked upon your conscience, like letters printed on paper, so that it will appear on the day of judgment before all the angels and all men, but you will also bring upon yourself another sin, that of sacrilege. Therefore, because you have come to a physician, see to it that you are healed completely and not remain unhealed, because this harm will be upon yourself."

Then, having the penitent kneel before the icon of Christ, or sit on a stool, ask him who he is (if you do not know him), how long it has been since his last confession and if he is prepared to confess, having examined himself properly. Then you ask him the following:

"Do you believe, my child, absolutely and unwaveringly in all of the Dogmas of the Catholic and Eastern Church of Christ which are contained in the Symbol of Faith (Creed), and which were proclaimed by the Seven Holy and Ecumenical Councils, and by the local councils, and by the Holy Fathers? Do you likewise accept all of the Apostolic and Patristic traditions of the Church, without addition or subtraction?" And when he says that he believes these things, tell him to recite the Symbol of Faith (Creed). Then say to him:

"Know, child, that according to other criteria, whoever reveals himself to be an offender is chastised; but according to the criterion of confession, whoever first reveals his sin on his own is forgiven. For this reason the Spiritual Father has no need to question the one confessing about what he did, for then the penitent is examined rather than confessed. However, the one confessing must by himself say his sins in order to receive forgiveness for them, for so God also commands: 'A righteous man accuses himself at the beginning of his speech, until the other comes and examines him' (Pr. 18:17), and: 'First say your transgressions, that you may be justified' (Is. 43:26). Therefore, you also child, in order to disgrace sin and the devil, first say your transgressions, in order to be justified." After saying these things, Spiritual Father, be silent for a bit.

When you see that the penitent is not saying his sins, then say to him: "I see, child, that you are not speaking. Therefore, so that you do not go away unconfessed, I am compelled to ask you about your sins, and for you to respond without any shame, for I am merely human just as you are, of like nature and a sinner, and I have heard many and great sins from many other sinners. And know that after you have confessed you will go home joyful and alleviated because you relieved your conscience from the burden of sin."

If it is a person whom you know and who has previously come to you for confession, you may skip everything that was just said and immediately proceed to asking him the following important questions, which are based on the First Commandment, after beginning the service and after saying the initial word of counsel. After each question, wait for the penitent to answer yes or no, and then proceed to the next question.

1. Questions concerning the First Commandment

Perhaps, my child, you have denied God or your Faith, or have said that you would deny them?[177]

Perhaps you have willfully had thoughts of blasphemy or unbelief concerning the divine Mysteries or things of the Faith, or you have held a heretical opinion?[178]

Perhaps you have practiced magic, or cast a spell on a couple, or cast a spell on animals so that a wolf does not eat them? Or perhaps you made amulets or charms, or wore them, or have practiced some other sort of magic?[179]

---

177   See *Subject A* after the Canons of the Faster.
178   See *Rebuttal as a treatment for bad thoughts*.
179   See Canon 32 of the Faster.

Perhaps you have sought magicians or fortunetellers to help you when you were ill, or to find something for you which you had lost, or to reveal riches to you or to perform other like things?

Perhaps you committed a mortal sin and afterwards dared to commune unworthily, without receiving the necessary rule from your Spiritual Father? For this is the greatest sin of all, according to St. John the Faster.[180]

Perhaps you did not pray to God day and night as a Christian should?

Perhaps you partook of the foods and of the slaughtered animals and of the sacrifices which the impious Muslim Turks have at their weddings, at their banquets, and at their profane memorials? For, as Solomon says: "The sacrifices of the wicked are abominations to the Lord" (Pr. 21:27).

Perhaps you did not hope in the compassion of God? Or perhaps you commit sin purposefully, thinking that God is compassionate and will forgive you? Or perhaps you decided to commit a sin as much as possible, and when the opportunity to commit that sin has passed, then you will repent? Or perhaps you are obstinate towards and contravene the obvious truth? These things, my child, are mortal sins and are opposed to the first commandment of God and are blasphemies against the Holy Spirit, as the *Orthodox Confession* says.

2. Questions concerning the Second Commandment

Perhaps, my child, you have such greed and love money so much that your mind is constantly occupied with such things and your heart is affixed to them?

Perhaps you are a slave to your stomach to such an extent that you are always thinking about foods and drinks and your heart is adhered to them?

Perhaps you are a hypocrite and not a true Christian, and outwardly you appear to be pious and faithful to God, but inside you are unfaithful and impious?

Perhaps you believe in your dreams or others' dreams? For the wise Sirach says: "Dreams have deceived many, and those who put their hope

---

180   Concerning this see the penances of the Faster which follow his Canons.

in them have failed" (Sir. 34:7).

3. Questions concerning the Third Commandment

Perhaps, my child, you have sworn an oath or made someone else swear an oath?

Perhaps you violated the oath you swore?[181]

Perhaps you swear on the name of God and the Faith in every instance?[182]

Perhaps you made a vow and promise to God that you would become a monk or that you would do some other good deed and afterward you violated your vow and your promise?[183]

Perhaps you used the words of the Holy Scripture pridefully or for jokes and laughing?

Perhaps you have not given thanks while you were ill or suffering misfortunes, but complained and blamed God as unjust?

Perhaps you blasphemed God or the Faith or the Mysteries or the Saints by word? Or perhaps you cause others to blaspheme?

Perhaps you say that the divine Scripture and the words of God contain errors and contradictions, while you praise the writings of Gentiles and of the Greeks?

4. Questions concerning the Fourth Commandment

Perhaps, my child, you do not go to Church two times a day, day and night, as the divine Apostles command in the *Apostolic Constitutions*?[184] Or, at least, perhaps you do not go to Church every Sunday and Feast Day, Vespers, Orthros, and Liturgy?

If it is a monk confessing, you ask: Perhaps, my child, you do not attend and listen to your appointed daily office of services? Or perhaps you do

---

181   See Canon 31 of the Faster.
182   See Canon 31 of the Faster.
183   See *How to care for those who have made vows*.
184   Book II, ch. 59; SC 320, p. 324.

not do your designated rule?[185]

Perhaps you speak with others while in Church? Or chat and laugh impiously? Or perhaps you do not pay attention to the divine words which are spoken in Church, but willfully leave your mind to dwell on secular things?

Perhaps you have sexual relations with your wife on Sundays and Feast Days?

Perhaps you have gambling in your house or go to casinos on Sundays and Feast Days? Or perhaps you gamble yourself, or dance and sing?

Perhaps you play dice, cards, or other games on Sundays and Feast Days, or you go to watch them?

Perhaps you drink and get drunk on Sundays and Feast Days, or you vomit and cause fights and brawls?

Perhaps you do not give alms to the poor on Sundays and Feast Days, as the Apostle Paul commands (1 Cor. 16:1)?

Perhaps you do not fast on Wednesdays and Fridays and during the other fast periods which the Church of Christ has designated for Christians?[186]

5. Questions concerning the Fifth Commandment

Perhaps, my child, you swore at or struck your father or your mother? Or perhaps you are not obedient to them, or when they are sick and in need of assistance, perhaps you do not take care of them or help them?[187]

Perhaps you do not honor your teachers and the Spiritual Fathers and hierarchs and priests of God?

If it is a monk confessing, you ask: Perhaps you are disobedient to your elder and cause him much grief?

Perhaps you do not honor your mentor, or your boss, or judges, or leaders? Or perhaps you are not thankful to your benefactors?

---

185   See *How to care for monks*.

186   See *Subject G* after the Canons of the Faster.

187   See *Concerning the Fifth Commandment* for how many obligations children have toward their parents.

Perhaps you are negligent and do not put your children in school so that they may learn sacred letters or a good craft? Or perhaps you also do not instruct them to have the fear of God and good Christian morals as is required of Christians? Or perhaps you do not bother taking them to Church? Or perhaps you do not spank them when they misbehave? Or perhaps you force your children to marry against their will? Or perhaps you obstruct them from becoming monastics? Or, if they desire to marry, perhaps you beg them and force them to become monastics?

Perhaps you swear at your wife? (If a woman is confessing, you say, your husband?) Or perhaps you make her sad and strike her and do not love her as your own flesh, and you do not care for her soul and her life?

Perhaps you do not look after the salvation and the Christian life of your slave and your maidservant? But, knowing that they sin, you ignore them and do not correct them?

If a patriarch or hierarch is confessing, you say:

Perhaps, Your All-holiness (or Your Eminence, or other appropriate title), you neglect your rational flock and do not care for it in every way possible, for its correction and salvation? Or perhaps you have been a bad example and a cause of scandal to the people, by your deeds or your words? For you must give an account to God on the day of judgment.

If a Spiritual Father is confessing, you say:

Perhaps, my Father, you do not correct the souls who confess to your holiness according to the Canons as you should, and you are not vigilant and diligent in your spiritual vocation?

If a parish priest is confessing, you say:

Perhaps, my Father, you do not shepherd your parishioners and you do not teach the rational sheep of Christ with all diligence and care, and in all piety and modesty, as is proper to your priestly office?[188]

If an abbot of a monastery or an elder is confessing, you say:

Perhaps, my Father, you are prideful about being an abbot and the head, and you look down on others, considering them as slaves and not as your brethren? Perhaps you are a bad example to the brethren in word or deed? Perhaps there is disorder and bad things in your monastery, and you neglect your sanctity and do not correct things? Perhaps you do not care for and do not teach the monks of your monastery, telling them to keep the definitions and Canons of the Holy Fathers and to guard the vocation of the monastic polity?

If a teacher or mentor is confessing, you say:

Perhaps you ignore your students and they cause mischief? Or perhaps you are envious of them and do not instruct them so that they do not learn too quickly? Or perhaps you do not teach them good and Christian morals? Or perhaps you treat them like slaves, rather than like students, sending them here and there? Or perhaps you become more angry than necessary and whip them excessively, whenever they commit a small error?

If a king or ruler is confessing, you say:

Perhaps, long-time King (or Your Highness, or other appropriate title), you do not keep the royal laws which you establish for your people? Or perhaps you do not provide for the peace and for the virtue and for the salvation of the souls of all your subjects, but you leave the evil people to disturb, torment and harm the others without correcting them? Or perhaps you are a bad example and cause of scandal to your subjects by not keeping all those things which are proper to your high office?

---

188   Translator's note: St. Basil the Great says: "Shepherd, be attentive lest any of your pastoral duties as a shepherd escape your notice. And what are these? Lead back the stray, bind up the broken, heal the sick" (*Homilia in Illud, Attende tibi Ipsi* 4, PG 31, 205D-208A; tr. *St. Basil the Great: On the Human Condition*, Crestwood, 2005, p. 98).

6. Questions concerning the Sixth Commandment

Perhaps, my child, you have willfully murdered someone or have been forced to against your will? And was this carried out on your own, or with the help of other people, or because you instigated it, or did you assist in the matter or give advice?[189]

Perhaps you were envious and were saddened on account of the good things your brother has? Or perhaps you were glad on account of the bad things and misfortunes of your brother?

Perhaps you have animosity toward someone and have a grudge and desire to take revenge? Or perhaps you have not sought forgiveness from your enemy? Or perhaps your enemy sought your forgiveness and you did not forgive him?[190]

Perhaps you defamed someone and turned him in to the judges, so that they may punish him and harm him?[191]

Perhaps you gave herbs to a pregnant woman so that she would abort her child, or so that she could never have children again? Or perhaps you assigned someone else to give her the herbs?[192]

Perhaps you got mad and fought with someone and beat and wounded him? Or perhaps you caused others to fight and beat one another because of your scheming?

Perhaps you get mad at the poor and swear at them and chase them away with foul words?

Perhaps you damned yourself or damned others and blasphemed and delivered them to the devil?[193]

Perhaps you knew that you were infected and you intermingled with others, and so infected them and they died? For you are to be placed under a rule as a murderer.[194]

---

189   See Canon 20 of the Faster concerning this.
190   See *What rule accusers and rancorous people are to be given* concerning this.
191   *Ibid.*
192   See Canon 21 of the Faster concerning this.
193   See *What rule blasphemers and perjurers are to be given* concerning this.
194   See Canon 34 of the Faster.

7. Questions concerning the Seventh Commandment

Perhaps, my child, you committed adultery with a married woman?[195]

Perhaps you fornicated with an unmarried woman? And if the penitent says yes, ask again: Did you fornicate with a woman that is your relative? Is she a laywoman or a nun? Is she a Christian or a heretic?[196] And where did you fornicate, in a house or in a Church or in the narthex of a Church? And when did you fornicate, on a weekday or on a Sunday or on a Feast Day? And how many times did you fornicate? And for how long have you been doing this?[197]

(If it is an ordained person who fell into fornication, you care for him according to what is said in the section, *How to care for clergymen who have sinned*.)

Perhaps you masturbated, either by yourself or with someone else? (And here you ask with what type of person he did it, and the place and the time and how often.)[198]

Perhaps you committed colluctation with a male or a female? Or someone has done this to you? (And here, again, ask him with what type of person he did it, and the place and the time and how often.)[199]

Perhaps you committed sodomy on someone, or they on you? (And here you ask him what type of person it was and when and where and how many times.)[200]

Perhaps you fell with animals and creatures and birds? Male or female? (And here you ask him when and where and how many times.)[201]

Perhaps you fell with your wife and committed unnatural acts?[202] Or perhaps you fell with her before you were married?

Perhaps you dress yourself up and wear makeup and put on perfumes

---

195   See Canon 13 of the Faster.

196   See the penances of the Faster concerning these things which follow his Canons.

197   See Canon 12 of the Faster.

198   See Canons 8 and 9 of the Faster.

199   See Canon 9 of the Faster.

200   See Canon 18 of the Faster.

201   See also the penances of the Faster, after his Canons, and *Subject B* after the Canons of the Faster.

202   See Canon 18 of the Faster.

and colognes, which are causes of fornication?

Perhaps you gaze at the faces of women and of youth intently and with lust in your heart? For whoever gazes in this fashion, commits fornication and adultery with his heart, as the Lord said.

Perhaps you were an intermediary and matchmaker and the cause of someone to sin with a woman, delivering letters from the man to the woman, or delivering gifts and presents, or bringing erotic messages from one person to the other, or other like things?

Perhaps you are prideful and gluttonous, given to food and drink? For these things give rise to fornication and adultery and to the other carnal passions.

8. Questions concerning the Eighth Commandment

Perhaps, my child, you stole something or acquired something that was stolen from others? Or perhaps you receive thieves into your home and are friends with them?[203] Then you ask him what type of item he stole, secular or sacred, and from where did he steal it, a house or a Church or a monastery, for this is sacrilege.

Perhaps you wronged your brother by robbing something that was his?[204]

Perhaps you stole or steal from where you work?

Perhaps you cheated someone and took his money by using false scales and measures, and by telling lies, and through fraud and false oaths?[205]

Perhaps you collect interest when you lend money to someone?[206]

Perhaps you withheld pay from those who worked for you and you did not thank them?

Perhaps you take more money than your handicraft and labor is worth?

Perhaps you committed grave robbery?[207]

---

203   See Canons 27 and 30 of the Faster.
204   See *What rule thieves and the unjust are to be given.*
205   See Canon 31 of the Faster.
206   See *Subject G* after the Canons of the Faster.
207   See Canon 29 of the Faster.

Perhaps you make counterfeit money, or knowingly use counterfeit money?

Perhaps you enlarged the boundaries of your fields or your house so as to take land from your brother?

Perhaps you stole animals from your brother or cut down his trees or damaged his property?

Perhaps you found something and did not attempt to find the owner by asking around, but rather kept silent and tucked it away?

Perhaps you open others' letters and read them, or perhaps you forge others' signatures or tear them or erase them or transcribe them?

If a nobleman is confessing, you say:

Perhaps you own properties which others farm, but you treat them like slaves, overworking them with many unpaid labors? Or perhaps, when the time for harvest comes, you take all of the wheat and the wine and the oil and the other fruits, leaving those unfortunate workers with nothing?

If a judge is confessing, you say:

Perhaps you take bribes or perhaps you perform favors and are biased, violating justice and making unjust judgments?

If a patriarch or hierarch is confessing, you say:

Perhaps, Your All-holiness (or Your Eminence, or other appropriate title), you take money and ordain the unworthy, and excommunicate the guiltless and condemn the innocent, and simply, perhaps on account of favoritism or another reason, you transgress the Divine and Sacred Canons of the Holy Apostles and of the Ecumenical and Local Councils and of the Fathers?

9. Questions concerning the Ninth Commandment

Perhaps, my child, you bore false witness against your brother and spoke lies against him, or perhaps you paid others to bear false witness against him?

Perhaps you are a fake and a hypocrite, appearing one way outwardly, so that people may praise you, but you are a different person inwardly?

Perhaps you judge and speak against this and that person? Or perhaps you listen with pleasure when others are judging or speaking against someone?

Perhaps you flatter this and that person, and you praise them falsely and not in truth?

10. Questions concerning the Tenth Commandment

Perhaps you desired to have the wife of your brother, or his house or his field or his slave or his maidservant or his animal, or anything else of your brother's?

Perhaps you desire and love glory and recognitions, or the pleasures of this world or money and temporal things?

Perhaps you do not reject and war against obscene and evil thoughts which the devil hurls at you, but you enjoy them and couple with them and consent to them with your heart, so that you may also carry out the act?[208] Know, my child, that there is no greater weapon with which to fight against bad thoughts than the fearful and Holy Name of Jesus Christ, just as our Holy Fathers say. For this reason, my child, become accustomed to saying, sometimes with your mouth, and sometimes with your intellect and your heart, these words: "Lord Jesus Christ, Son of God, have mercy on me," and you should repeat this ceaselessly, even when you are working, or walking, inside and outside, and everywhere.

When you have completed all of these questions, Spiritual Father, then think about which was the greatest sin that the penitent confessed, that is, which sin calls for the most years of abstinence from Communion, and place him under a rule according to that sin. In order for you to remember the penitent's sins better, you may hold a lit candle and note next to the

---

208   See Canons 3 and 1 of the Faster.

questions which ones he answered yes to. For how you are to convince the penitent to also accept to abstain from Communion, see *Advice to the penitent so that he also accepts the abstinence from Communion*. Then place your hand upon the head of the penitent, and read the prayer of forgiveness: "Lord Jesus Christ, shepherd and lamb..." And after the prayer, make a supplication for mercy, life, etc. and then turn to the penitent and place your hand upon his head saying: "The grace of the All-holy Spirit, through my insignificance, has you loosened and forgiven." Then offer final counsel, concerning which see *Final counsel of the Spiritual Father to the penitent*.

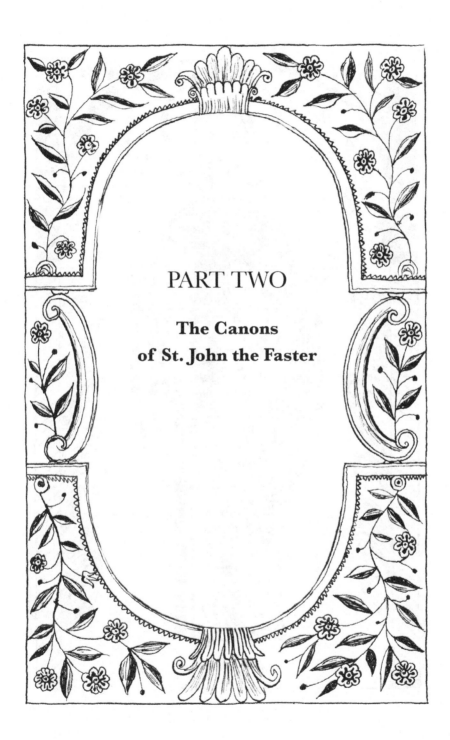

PART TWO

The Canons
of St. John the Faster

PROLOGUE

Concerning St. John the Faster

Our Father among the Saints John, who is called the Faster, flourished in the year 580 after Christ,[209] and saw the reigns of three Emperors: Justin, Tiberius and Maurice. At the suggestion of the Patriarch of Constantinople Eutychios of the Scholastics, he enrolled in the clergy and was ordained a deacon. When Eutychios died, John was compelled to be ordained, but was not persuaded. But because he saw a fearful vision in ecstasy and heard angels telling him to be silent and not to offer any resistance to this, he, against his will, ascended the Patriarchal Throne of Constantinople.[210] He of blessed memory was so partial to asceticism and fasting that for a space of six months he did not drink water and during a period of thirteen and a half years during his patriarchal reign he ate nothing else but stalks of lettuce, or a little melon, or grapes, or figs, and took exceedingly little and carefully measured sleep, on account of which the thrice-blessed man was deemed worthy by God to receive the charisma of working miracles, both in this life[211] and after death.[212] After devoutly shepherding his flock, he departed to the Lord in the year 619, leaving us the present Canons, which are more commonly called the *Kanonikon* of the Faster.[213]

---

209 Meletios of Athens, *Ecclesiastical History*, v. 3, ch. 15.

210 He is commemorated on September 2 in the Orthodox Calendar of Saints.

211 For through his prayer he both healed a blind man and enabled barren wives to have children, and freed a person from the demon which possessed him, and cured many other sick people. See also his *Life* in the *Synaxarion*.

212 For he wrought a fearful miracle after his death, when, though dead, he rose up and kissed the Eparch Neilos in return when the latter went to kiss him, in accordance with the custom, and he even spoke some words into his ear while everyone looked on with amazement.

213 The Canons of St. John the Faster are confirmed definitely by Balsamon, by Blastaris, by Armenopoulos, by Nikephoros the Archivist, by the Patriarch Nicholas, and indefinitely by the

ancient tradition of the Church, and especially by the fact that the Canons of the Faster were actually put into practice, for many people confessed and were corrected according to them, not only in the time of Balsamon (as he himself says in his interpretation of the last Canon of the Patriarch Nicholas), but also in the time of Nicholas, as is said in the aforementioned last Canon of his (PG 138, 948D-949B).

As to why the Sixth Ecumenical Council, which was after the time of the Faster, does not cite these Canons of the Faster, we reply: 1) that it is possible that these Canons were not yet available to the public at that time, just as the Council in Carthage does not cite the *Paschal Kanonion,* which was constituted at the First Ecumenical Council prior to it, because it was not yet available to many; and 2) that many other local Councils which had sound Canons and were prior to the Sixth Ecumenical Council are not mentioned by it: neither the Canons of the local Council under the Emperor Heracles which took place in the city of Antisiodoros, nor the Canons of the Council gathered in Illiberium which was even prior to the First Ecumenical Council, nor is the Council in Kavilone even mentioned, as well as others. That the Church, however, accepted these Canons, even if not ratified by the Sixth Ecumenical Council, is evident from the following: Our Church does not perform two Liturgies on the same altar table on the same day. This is a designation of the 11th Canon of the Council in Antisiodoros. Our Church has the priests place their hand upon the catechumens in the back of the narthex. This is a designation of the 39th Canon of the Council in Illiberium. The Church performs the Presanctified Liturgy during the evening. This is a designation of the Council in Kavilone.

The Righteous Nikon, who lived in asceticism on Mt. Melani of Antioch in the year 1060, during the reigns of Emperor Constantine Doukos of the East and John the Patriarch of Antioch, cites these Canons of the Faster in volume 2 of his manuscript collection.

If Nicholas the Patriarch in his Eleventh Canon, which was mentioned above, says that the *Kanonikon* of the Faster harmed many people because of its excessive tendency to accommodation, this ought not to be taken in a general sense, but only with qualification, that is to say, that it employs accommodation in regard to the years of the penances, but not also in regard to the rule which it prescribes. For if we care to examine the truth of the matter with right reason, the *Kanonikon* of the Faster, for the rule which it provides, not only is not accommodative, but (I daresay) it is even a little austere in regard to lovers of the flesh. For a lover of the flesh would prefer to abstain from the pure Mysteries for seven or ten or fifteen years, as the Canons of the rest of the Fathers prescribe, rather than abstain from Holy Communion for only three years, to eat dry foods after the ninth hour, to do two hundred or three hundred prostrations daily, and to undergo other hardships as required by the *Kanonikon* of the Faster. It would become really accommodative and could harm many persons then if Spiritual Fathers who employ it were to accommodate the years of the penances imposed upon sinners, according to the Faster, but failed to provide also the rule which it prescribes, I mean, the eating of dry foods up to the ninth hour, and so many prostrations, etc. But in exchange for money or by way of favors or for other reasons, they also accommodate these rules together with the number of years, a thing which they are doing unlawfully and contrary to the Canons, and for this they will have to answer to God for the damage they are causing to the souls confessing to them, with the wide way they open to them. Hence, for the love of God, let them take pains to correct this soul-harming evil which they are doing. For this Saint in nearly every one of his Canons asserts that whoever does not want to observe the rule which

The Canons of St. John the Faster
Together with Their Interpretation

CANON 1: The Apology

"Our reduction in the number of years of repentance will not seem illogical to those, I presume, who can reason properly. For since neither in the great Father Basil, nor in the more ancient of our glorious Fathers, has any fasting, or vigil, or number of prostrations been designated for sinners, but only abstinence from sacred Communion, we have concluded that it behooves us, in regard to those persons who are genuinely repentant and willing to subject their flesh to the infliction of hardships, and to lead a life gratefully that will offset their previous wickedness, according to the measure of their self-control, to repay them also with a reduction of the term of repentance. For instance, if someone consented not to drink wine on certain days, we decided to subtract one year from the penance fixed by the Fathers for that specific offense. Likewise if he promises temperance in respect to meat for a time, we have seen fit to deduct another year; if in respect of cheese and eggs, or of fish, or of oil, and so on in each particular case of temperance in respect of any one of these articles, to knock off a year. Nor is this all, but even if he chooses to propitiate the Deity by frequently repeated prostrations, to do likewise, and especially if he exhibits

---

he designates will not observe even the few years of abstinence from divine Communion which he prescribed, but the many years which the Fathers have prescribed. The Faster himself offers a reasonable apology in regard to such accommodativeness in his First Canon; but still more so before him does the concord to the other Canons of the Fathers provide an apology in his behalf, which are written below the Canons and take due notice of them.

We also offer readers the information that, inasmuch as many handwritten books are to be found that contain some Canons which are ascribed to the Faster, but which contain many unreasonable things and altogether in every way unlawful and uncanonical, both in regard to the ending of fasts and in regard to other matters, so that those decrees appear to be the seeds and offspring of some heretic and wrong-minded person, and not by this Saint, who owing to his excessive fasts was surnamed the Faster. For this reason we have followed two trustworthy witnesses, Matthew Blastaris and Constantine Armenopoulos, who give a summary of the genuine Canons of the Faster, especially and exceptionally so in the case of Blastaris, whose summary which he has in regard to these Canons we have employed verbatim as the very text of the Faster with but a few slight variations in point of diction only. And so it is upon the trustworthiness of these two wise men that we have based and verified the genuineness of the Canons of St. John the Faster. We rejected all the other Canons falsely ascribed to him, and we advise the rest of the brethren not to accept them, but to reject them as containing unacceptable things.

a willingness to provide generous alms without straining his power, or overtaxing his ability. If, on the other hand, even after the trespass anyone has come under the God-pleasing and solitary life, we have seen fit to shorten still further his sentence, seeing that throughout the rest of his life he is destined to suffer harsh treatment such as becomes such a course of living."

(Canon 12 of the 1st Ec. C.; Canon 102 of the 6th Ec. C.; Canons 2, 5, and 7 of Ancyra; Canons 2, 3, 74, and 84 of Basil the Great; Canons 4, 5, 7, and 8 of Gregory of Nyssa).

Interpretation

In this Canon the Saint defends himself against the criticism of those who might perhaps be disposed to blame him for reducing the term of repentance, and he says that this reduction which he has provided is not lacking in calculation and discernment in the eyes of the prudent and thoughtful.[214] This calculation is founded upon the following viewpoint:

---

214   The same apology is also given by Nikephoros the Archivist (*Juris Graeco-romanorum*, p. 343), saying: "We have received a custom of also adjusting penances in proportion to the power of each individual." Nevertheless, we say that as for those things which the Faster appears to have failed to say with reference to the strictness of the Canons, whoever is prudent and thinks thoroughly about these things will find everything in accordance with the purpose of the Fathers. For, since Basil the Great in his Seventy-Fourth Canon says that permission be given to every steward of souls to increase or to decrease the penances in accordance with the dispositions and persons concerned, and the affairs of the ones confessing their sins, and to adjust with discernment unto the benefit of the souls, it is not strange if the Faster, out of obedience to the Canon of Basil the Great, innovated in some respect, in accordance with the spiritual charisma with which he was endowed, by adjusting matters, of course unto the benefit of the penitents; rather, he did not innovate at all. Furthermore, the Saint observes most canonically in these Canons and penances both those same duties of the spiritual steward which the Sixth Ecumenical Council mentions in its 102nd Canon and which Basil the Great mentions in his Third Canon. That is to say, he observes strictness and extremeness, and form and custom, in regard to those who will not accept strictness. Strictness here means the fasts and prostrations prescribed through which the flesh is subdued and the hedonistic pleasures are subdued and abandoned, which Basil the Great mentions in his Third Canon, and says that these are true proof of the healing of the sinner. Custom and form are: 1) separation from the Mysteries, which also the Faster prescribes in these Canons, and 2) separation also from the Church, as he also prescribes in his Canons (concerning which, look to the end of these Canons). These, then, are the custom and form which almost all of the divine Canons prescribe for penitents, that is, separation from the Church and from the Mysteries. Even if today the said separation from the Church is not imposed upon penitents, what does this have to do with St. John? This practice ceased even in the time of John

since neither Basil the Great nor the other Fathers of old prescribed for penitents any rule and penance with fasting, or vigils, or prostrations, but penanced them solely with abstinence from divine Communion,[215] for this reason (says the Saint) we have deemed it reasonable to reduce the years of repentance for those who are genuinely repentant and willing to inflict hardships upon their body by means of severities and to live a virtuous life in the future, contrary to the former bad life which they had been leading: to reduce, however, these years according to the measure of the self-control they exhibit. For example, if the penitent accepts as a rule not to drink wine for so many fixed days, we have deemed it reasonable to reduce his penance by one year from the years of the penance which the Canons of the Fathers designate. Likewise, if he promises not to eat meat, we agree to deduct for him another year. Likewise, if he does not eat cheese and eggs, or fish, or oil, with respect to each one of these foods we have decided to deduct for him another year. If he wishes to propitiate God also with frequently repeated prostrations and bows, likewise in respect to these we will deduct for him a year, and especially if he wishes to be generous in handing out alms, and in proportion to the wealth he possesses, by showing a proportionate amount of readiness to give to others. If the penitent, after any transgression he may have committed, became a monk, we deemed it

Zonaras, who says the following in his commentary on Canon 19 of Laodicaea: "But now the incidents involved in repentance do not occur, and I do not know how they fell into disuse." Symeon of Thessaloniki, adding the reason, says: "But now on account of the persecutions and continual adversities, the Fathers reasoned that it was well for catechumens as well as deniers and murderers to be excluded, but for the rest, who had only obtained baptism, to be allowed, especially when their repentance was being superintended by their Spiritual Fathers" (*De Sacro Templo*, ch. 153, PG 155, 357C). That fasting and prayers, that is, the works and fruits of repentance, are called and are considered penances, see Canon 12 of the First Ecumenical Council, Canon 2 of Ancyra, Canons 1 and 3 of Peter, Canon 3 of Basil, and the penances in his Ascetical Works. So then, that we may understand everything in this footnote, the divine Faster with his Canons and penances has not only not harmed anyone, but rather has cured many and healed them completely from sin according to Canon 3 of Basil.

215   As I see it, the reason why the Fathers only prescribed abstinence from Communion as a penance for sinners is because the Christians of those times had such a desire to commune that they thought it the worst possible thing to be deprived of Communion. For this reason, then, the Fathers of those times had nothing better with which to deter them from sin than the deprivation of Communion.

reasonable to subtract even more years, since in the course of his monastic life he is going to have to pass his whole lifetime in hardship.

See also Canon 12 of the First Ecumenical Council and all of the Canons listed in the concord directly below the Canon, which vindicate this reduction of years which the Faster has decided upon. For they also say that in accordance with the disposition and repentance of those confessing, the number of years of their penances should be reduced.

CANON 2

"An assault of pleasure against the heart through thoughts is to be regarded as a sin not yet committed and not subject to the least penance."

Interpretation

An assault, according to St. John of the Ladder, is a word, that is, a simple thought, or an image of something which has happened, and which is encountered for the first time and has entered the heart.[216] So in this Canon the Faster says that this assault of pleasure upon the heart through thoughts is completely unpenanced, since no sin has yet been committed.[217]

---

216   Step 15, PG 88, 896D; tr. *The Ladder*, pp. 115-116.

217   Assault, according to Joseph Bryennios (*On the Holy Trinity*, Homily 15), is the simple effect of being reminded by the enemy or being incited by him, as, for instance, when one is told 'do this,' or 'do that.' His effect is one of the involuntary ones and not under our control, as though our will were not the cause of our thoughts assaulting us, but the devil, the wicked sower of such seeds. Note, however, that according to Basil the Great (*Ascetical Constitutions*, 17 or 18) improper thoughts assault us in two ways, either because the soul is negligent and is barren of spiritual conceptions, and drifts into improper conceptions on its own impulse, and flits from one fancy to another, or under the suggestive influence of the devil who is plotting against it and wants to evoke absurd thoughts in our mind, and thereby to prevent us from contemplating and considering the beautiful and beneficial things. Since, I say, wicked thoughts assault us in two ways, it is manifest that one assault, occurring as an effect of the devil's plotting and suggestion, leaves us altogether exempt from responsibility and is not subject to any penance; whereas the assault which occurs as a result of the soul's negligence and idleness or barrenness is not one that is not subject to any penance, not on account of the assault in and of itself, but because the soul was negligent, and, finding it thus in a state of negligence and idleness, the enemy assaulted it with the wicked thought. For this reason the same Basil (*Shorter Rules*, 21 and 306) says that the fleeting of thoughts derives from the idleness of the intellect which is not

CANON 3

"Coupling is washed away with twelve prostrations."

Interpretation

Coupling, according to the aforementioned St. John, is when a soul converses with or reflects upon what has presented itself, accompanied by passion or without passion.[218] Coupling accompanied by passion, says the Faster, is liable to a penance, and it is cleansed by twelve prostrations, since it depends upon a man's free will either to accept what has appeared as a result of the assault and to converse with it, or to reject it and not to accept it at all. John of the Ladder also places coupling under a penance.[219]

CANON 4

"Struggle is worthy of a crown or of punishment."

Interpretation

Struggle, according to the same John of the Ladder, is a power of the

---

occupied with necessary things, and that, if the intellect is in perpetual meditation and contemplation of the will and glory of God, it will not have the chance to flit to something else. Abba Mark also says that a satanic assault comes upon the intellect as a result of little faith, for the intellect received a commandment to protect the heart: "Keep thy heart with all diligence" (Pr. 4:23). When the intellect leaves the heart, it then gives room for the assault of the enemy. And note these two things: 1) that assault is mainly an initial conception and imagination, or the initial thought spoken interiorly in the heart (for through these two manners do all evil thoughts generally assault, or through the inner word of the heart, audibly stamped upon the imagination) of something not formerly conceived or thought; 2) that assault is mainly spoken about in reference to evil thoughts, and not to good thoughts. Many of the Fathers refer to assault as the first thought or movement of the intellect. See also the *Scholia* on Step 4, *On Obedience*, of John of the Ladder (PG 88, 728D-764A). Read also Chapter 6, *Concerning Thoughts*, in Part 1 of this book.

218   Step 15, PG 88, 896D; tr. *The Ladder*, pp. 115-116.

219   According to Bryennios, coupling is the acceptance of a thought suggested by the enemy, and meditation and conversation with it by our free will.

soul of equal strength to the thought which is warring upon it, according to which, if the soul wishes, it can conquer the thought, but if it does not wish to do so, it is conquered by the thought.[220] Hence John of the Ladder as well as the Faster say that this struggling becomes the cause either of the soul's receiving a crown, if, that is to say, it conquers the evil thought, or of its receiving chastisement and punishment, if the soul is conquered by the thought.[221]

CANON 5

"Consent is the cause and beginning of penances."

Interpretation

Consent, says John of the Ladder, is a pleasurable bending of the soul towards the passionate thought which is warring upon it,[222] on account of which the divine Faster says that consent becomes the beginning and cause of penances. Therefore John Zonaras, toward the end of his homily addressed against those who think that the natural seed are unclean, also says: "Those who accepted a passionate thought and conversed with it pleasurably through coupling and consent will not escape a penance, even if they did not have emissions during sleep or experience fantasies."[223]

---

220   Step 15, PG 88, 896D-897A; tr. *The Ladder*, pp. 115-116.

221   According to this same Bryennios, struggle is resistance offered either for the purpose of killing the thought which excites the passion, or unto consent to the thought.

222   Step 15, PG 88, 896D; tr. *The Ladder*, pp. 115-116.

223   *Juris Graeco-romanorum*, p. 36. According to Bryennios, consent is the yielding and assent of the thought to passion. The consent of the soul is a sin in two ways (according to the book, *Instructions for Penitents*): either on account of lust, when the soul desires to commit an evil, for example, murder, fornication, or some other sin, or on account of delight, when the soul does not desire to commit an evil, but when it hears of how someone else committed it, it takes pleasure in it and is delighted, concerning which the divine Paul said: "They not only do the same, but have pleasure in them that do them" (Rom. 1:32); this delight or "taking pleasure in" is then also sinful. On account of this, God also allowed the Israelites to be conquered twice by the Benjaminites and for 40,000 to die, even though He had told them to fight the Benjaminites, because those Israelites who were killed took pleasure and delighted in the fornication which the Benjaminites committed with the concubine of

Note that George Koressios divides consent into two types: imperfect and perfect. Perfect consent consists of a complete conquest of the intellect and a complete consent of the will, thus fixed upon committing the sin. Furthermore, note also that assault, coupling, struggle, and consent are seen in all sins, but the divine Faster offered only carnal transgressions as examples, in order to enable us to understand those subtler sins better from the grosser sins.

Concerning consent, see also Canon 4 of Neocaesaria.

CANON 6

"Anyone who has been polluted during sleep by a passionate emission shall be denied Communion for one day; but after chanting the 50th Psalm and making forty-nine prostrations, it is believed that the stain will thus be purified."

(Canon 4 of Dionysios; Letter of Athanasios to Ammoun; Letter 12 of Timothy).

---

the Levite, as many exegetes say (see ch. 20 of the book of Judges). In addition to these four evils of the soul which the Faster mentions (assault, coupling, struggle, consent), John of the Ladder adds another three which likewise act upon the soul: captivity, passion, and disturbance (Step 15, PG 88, 896C-897C; *The Ladder*, pp. 115-117). Captivity is a satanic and violent carrying away of the heart to a bad thought and a persistent conversation with it. Passion is that evil thought which infests the soul for a long time and which as a result of prolonged habit causes the soul to become addicted to it, so that on account of its addiction the soul runs to it of its own accord and of its own free choice, and not because of any compulsion. This passion, he says, is either cured here with many years of asceticism and repentance, or, if it is not cured here, it will be subjected to the future punishment. From this passion is also immediately born the act of sin. Therefore Bryennios (*On the Trinity*, Homily 15) says that: "An absurd act is the action of passion." St. Mark the Ascetic says that: "Passion is an inclination of the mind to harmful things, firmly seated in the soul and difficult to wipe out." Finally then, disturbance of the intellect is when the soul, without any passage of time, without any assault, but as the result of only the mere contemplation of a person, as the result of listening to a single song, as the result of a single touch of the hand, suddenly fornicates passionately. This disturbance mostly happens to those who have a fragile intellect. These things having been explained, whoever regards the initial assault and root of thoughts without passion, according to John of the Ladder, has at once cut off and killed all the other offshoots of sin. For this reason the first man received a commandment to keep watch over the head of the serpent: "He shall watch against thy head" (Gen. 3:15), that is, the first inkling and assault of bad thoughts, so that no consent or act occurs, according to Abba Cassian (cf. *On the Eight Vices*, *GrPhilokalia*, p. 63; *The Philokalia*, v. 1, p. 76).

Interpretation

The present Canon designates that whoever becomes polluted during the night by having an emission during sleep, must not commune that day. But after reciting the 50th Psalm of David and making forty-nine prostrations, he is purified from the pollution caused by the emission during sleep.[224]

---

224   Note that Canon 4 of St. Dionysios says that as many as suffer an involuntary emission of semen, that is, a wet dream, these are to follow their conscience, whether it convicts them or not as to whether this happened on account of some passionate thought and obscene imagination or some other passion: if it did, let them not commune; if it did not, let them commune. Canon 12 of Timothy says that if a wet dream occurred because of the lust for a woman, one should not commune; but if it occurred only on account of a temptation from the devil, one should commune. The Fathers, especially Anastasios of Sinai (*Quaestiones VIII*, PG 89, 389D-409B) and Gregory of Sinai (*On Morbid Defluxions*, GrPhilokalia, p. 906; *The Philokalia*, v. 4, pp. 254-256), say that emission during sleep occurs on account of overeating and overdrinking, from sleeping too much, from relaxation and torpor of the body, from pride, from judging others, from gossiping, from bodily illness, from extreme labor, from lust, from drinking cold liquids, from the bad habit of fornication, from the envy of the demons, and also as a natural excrement. Therefore, since it is difficult for someone to discern whether this occurred on account of himself or some other reason and envy of the demons, it is best not to commune that day, as this present Canon says plainly and not with specifics. Likewise, Basil the Great (*Regulæ Brevius* 309, PG 31, 1301D-1304A; *De Baptismo II*, Question 3, PG 31, 1584B-1585C), Symeon of Thessaloniki (*Responsa ad Gabrielem Pentapolitanum*, Questions 14 and 15, PG 155, 864D-868A), John Kitros (Question 28) and Balsamon (*Responsa ad Interrogationes Marci*, Question 10, PG 138, 961B-964A) all agree saying that priests and laypeople who have a wet dream are prohibited that day from the Mysteries.

Only if a layperson is in danger and must commune should he, or if it is a special day requiring a Liturgy should the priest liturgize, for in this case the trap of the devil must be destroyed and the power of the priesthood be lifted up.

Translator's note: See St. John of the Ladder, Step 15, PG 88, 889D-892A; *The Ladder*, p. 112.

We note this also, that of those who are polluted during sleep, some do not take *antidoron*, some do not even venerate the Holy Icons or light candles, and some do not make offerings that day. That they are not to take *antidoron* appears to be ratified by a Canon, for Canon 10 of Nicholas says that those who are prohibited from the Mysteries are also prohibited from receiving *antidoron*. Since a wet dream, then, prohibits one from the Mysteries, it also prohibits one from *antidoron*. Concerning the other things mentioned, as far as I know, no Canon or Patristic witness attest to them. Therefore, if there is some major Feast and someone has a wet dream, they should be considerately advised to first perform the rule prescribed in this Canon by the Faster, then to take *antidoron* from the priest and to venerate the Holy Icons so that no scandal is caused to the brethren. But he should not eat the *antidoron*, and either put it back or wrap it carefully in a napkin and eat it the following day. If it happens to be a Sunday, he should only say the 50th Psalm and do the forty-nine prostrations after Vespers, according to Canon

The great one amongst the Fathers, Barsanuphios, also assigns the same penance for emission during sleep.

CANON 7

"But one who has been polluted in body while awake is excluded from Communion for seven days, having also to chant the 50th Psalm and to make forty-nine prostrations."

Interpretation

But anyone who suffers an emission while he is awake is forbidden divine Communion for seven days, and is to say the 50th Psalm each of these days, and make forty-nine prostrations daily.[225]

CANON 8

"Anyone having practiced masturbation is penanced forty days, during which he must eat dry foods and make one hundred prostrations daily."

---

8 of the Sixth Ecumenical Council.

225   Note that there is found a treatise attributed to Anastasios of Antioch which makes a notable distinction concerning emission which someone suffers while awake. As for emission while awake, a person either does it to himself or to another. That which he causes himself to suffer is due either to handling with the hand, and is penanced for forty days (for this is outright masturbation), or it is caused without handling with the hand. This latter kind either occurs only because of an assault, and is penanced one day, or it occurs by coupling with the thought without consent and without titillation, and is penanced three days, or it occurs by coupling with the thought and titillation without consent, and is penanced seven days, or it occurs by coupling and consent, but without titillation, and is penanced twenty days, or it occurs by coupling, consent, and titillation, and is penanced thirty days. Emission produced on another person occurs either without colluctation or with colluctation. That which occurs without colluctation or titillation, but by touching and kissing, is penanced twenty days; if with titillation, it is penanced thirty days. If it occurs with colluctation and with another human, it is penanced eighty days; but if it occurs with an animal, it is penanced seven years. Those who suffer emission while awake on account of sickness and thus being subject to spermatorrhoea, and those who let out sperm mixed with their urine, are not subject to penance because both of these types suffer from it without an assault from, or coupling with, or consent to thoughts. For this reason the said Anastasios does not mention anything about these.

Interpretation

The present Canon designates that whoever commits masturbation is not
to commune for forty days, passing those days with the eating of dry foods,
that is, only bread and water, making one hundred prostrations daily.[226]

---

226   Masturbation is a sin so abhorrent to God that on account of it He put to death Onan,
the son of Judah, the son of Jacob, because he was the first to commit this act upon the earth, and it
is therefore also called onanism. For the Holy Scripture says in Genesis (38:10): "And the thing which
he (Onan) did appeared as evil before God: wherefore He slew him." And it is an opinion of many
teachers that God so strongly abhorred those prideful philosophers of the Greeks that he allowed
them to be ruled by this sin as a punishment for their idolatry, for having come to know God, they
failed to glorify Him as God. This is inferred from that which divine Paul says about them:
"Wherefore God also gave them up to uncleanness through the lusts of their own hearts, to dishonour
their own bodies between themselves" (Rom. 1:24), where by the expression "their own bodies
between themselves" he was referring to masturbation, during which the body both acts upon itself
and suffers an action of its own. Masturbation, says John of the Ladder (Step 15, PG 88, 885C; *The
Ladder*, p. 108), is fornication performed without another body, by which sin that great Anchorite fell,
concerning whom the divine Anthony said: "A great pillar has fallen" (*Apophthegmata Patrum* A, 14, PG
65, 80B; *The Sayings of the Desert Fathers*, Kalamazoo, 1984, p. 4). The same John calls masturbation
death and perdition (Step 15, PG 88, 885C; *The Ladder*, p. 108), which death is always present and
borne about with us, especially during the time of our youth. Therefore, it is very difficult to abstain
from it and for one to repent who has even once been caught in its snare. That is why one teacher
likens masturbation to a great net of the devil and of Hades, by means whereof he has drawn the
world to perdition, and many are caught in it, but only a few of them ever escape from it, and the
devil's heart rejoices on account of his hunting so much with this net, and he burns incense to it
because it has caught much food and many souls, as Habakkuk says (1:15-16): "He takes it (the world)
up with the hook, he catches it in his net, and gathers it in his drag: therefore his heart rejoices and
is glad, and sacrifices unto his net, and burns incense unto his drag; because by them his portion is
fat, and his meat plenteous." But why say so much? Masturbation not only causes the soul eternal
harm, but also harms the health of the body. The soul is harmed because it deprives it of the
kingdom of heaven, and condemns it to eternal hell, as Paul says: "Be not deceived: neither
fornicators, nor adulterers, nor masturbators, nor idolaters… shall inherit the kingdom of God" (I
Cor. 6:9-10). Although Chrysostom interpreted the word μαλακοί (what we interpret as *masturbators*)
to mean men who have become prostitutes, while Theophylact interprets it as those who submit to
obscenity; yet many other teachers have understood it as meaning masturbators. Masturbation
causes the soul to lose its virginity, which is the most valuable thing in the world, which if lost just
once is never regained. Never. It also causes the soul to offer a sacrifice to the devil with the seed of
its body, as St. Meletios the Confessor says (Translator's note: St. Symeon the New Theologian says:
"Just as the loathsome flow from the body and, if it may be so called, the pleasurable mingling of the
heart with any passion so to speak constitutes a sacrifice offered by us to the devil" *Catechetical*

CANON 9

"As for the mingling of men with one another, such as practicing double masturbation, it receives the stated penance of up to eighty days."

Interpretation

The Canon here says mingling, not the complete sin of sodomy, but when two men masturbate one another,[227] which act is penanced doubly by the Saint, who penances the one committing it to eat dry foods for eighty days and to make one hundred prostrations daily, because the one committing the sin is not only hurting himself, but also his brother, and this makes the sin a double one.

Discourses 4; SC 96, p. 366; tr. *Symeon the New Theologian: The Discourses*, CWS, Mahwah, 1980, p. 87). Masturbation also harms the body, as the physicians say, because masturbators: 1) grow pale; 2) their stomach becomes weak; 3) their eyesight becomes poor; 4) they lose their voice; 5) they lose the cleverness and acuity of their intellect; 6) they lose their memory; 7) they lose sleep on account of disturbing dreams; 8) their body shakes; 9) they lose all the manliness of their body and soul; 10) they are liable to apoplexy, that is, a stroke; 11) they are liable to frequent emissions in their sleep, and even while they are awake; 12) they age quickly and die badly and disgracefully. So then, this sin is like a pestilence and corruption of the human race, and causes masturbators to live here and now a disgraceful and miserable life, and to be tormented eternally in the next life in the fire of hell. The treatments for masturbation are two: 1) for them to make a firm resolve in their heart to never commit that sin again, and 2) for them not to place their hand near the hidden members or look upon them, as much as this is possible.

Therefore, my young brethren, guard yourselves for the love of God from this thrice-accursed passion, and if the lust of your flesh wars against you, do not postpone the time of your marriage (that is, as many as have not resolved to become monastics), but get married young, before falling into such an unnatural corruption of your virginity. For this is how divine Chrysostom commands children and their parents, saying: "When thy son is grown up, before he enters upon warfare, or any other course of life, consider of his marriage. And if he sees that thou wilt soon take a bride for him, and that the time intervening will be short, he will be able to endure the flame patiently. But if he perceives that thou art remiss and slow, and waitest until he shall acquire a large income, and then thou wilt contract a marriage for him, despairing at the length of the time, he will readily fall into fornication" (*On I Thessalonians*, Homily 5, 3, PG 62, 426; tr. NPNF (V1-13) p. 346).

227   Some have understood mingling to mean colluctation, which may occur between two men, or two women, or between a man and a woman, and is a lesser sin than fornication, but a graver one than masturbation.

CANON 10

"If anyone among the clergy, before being ordained, fell into the passion of masturbation without thinking perhaps that on this account alone he would be dismissed from the priesthood, let him first be sufficiently penanced, and then let him enter the priesthood. But if he was caught doing this after entering the priesthood, after being suspended for a whole year for this, and being reformed with the usual penances, let him be readmitted to the priesthood. But if after becoming aware of its sinfulness he committed it two or three times, let him cease from the priesthood and enter the order of reader."

Interpretation

The present Canon says that if perchance someone before being ordained fell into the passion of masturbation, not knowing that on this account alone he would be impeded from being ordained,[228] let this person (being, that is, distinguished and virtuous in all other respects), after first receiving a rule adequate to his sin,[229] become a priest. But if perchance after being ordained he fell into it again, let him be suspended from the priesthood for one year, and be reformed with the usual penances imposed upon masturbators, and then let him again be active in the priesthood. But if after becoming aware of its evil, he masturbated two or three times, let him cease from the priesthood and let him enter the order of reader.

CANON 11

"But also as for women, if a woman has allowed herself to be kissed and felt by a man, without, however, being violated by him, let her receive the penance of masturbation."

Interpretation

The Saint penances a woman who accepts kisses from a man and allows

---

228   Note that even masturbation alone is an impediment to the priesthood.
229   That is, to abstain from Communion for forty days, to eat dry foods, and to do one hundred prostrations every day.

herself to be touched by him with the penance of masturbation, that is, to eat dry foods for forty days and to make one hundred prostrations every day while abstaining from Communion.

CANON 12

"We instruct every monk or layman that has committed fornication not to commune for two years, provided he agrees to practice the eating of dry foods after the ninth hour and to do two hundred and fifty prostrations; but if he acts negligently, let him fulfill the whole term designated by the Fathers."

(Canon 16 of the 4th Ec. C.; Canon 44 of the 6th Ec. C.; Canons 19 and 20 of Ancyra; Canons 6, 18, 21, 22, 25, 26, and 59 of Basil the Great).

Interpretation

The present Canon designates that every monk or layman that fornicates is not to commune for two years, and every day to do two hundred and fifty prostrations, and after the ninth hour to consume only bread and water; but if he is negligent and does not want to do these things, let him abstain from Communion for as many years as the divine Fathers designated.[230]

CANON 13

"We think it good that an adulterer partake of Communion after three years, without complaining about the eating of dry foods after the ninth hour, but also doing two hundred

---

230   Canon 3 of St. Gregory of Nyssa precludes a fornicator from divine Communion for nine years. Canon 59 of Basil the Great designates seven years, according to his own penance. Those who violate their wives before they are blessed in marriage are precluded from Communion for four years, according to Canon 22 of St. Basil (that is, just as the Fathers prior to Basil penanced fornication; see Canon 20 of Ancyra), because this violating of their wives is called fornication according to Canons 25 and 26 of Basil. And Basil's 21st Canon penances greater the man who has a wife and fornicates over the man who does not have a wife. Canon 7 of Basil penances monks or nuns who fornicate or marry as adulterers, that is, fifteen years, but Canon 44 of the Sixth Ecumenical Council penances them more philanthropically, that is, the same as laymen.

and fifty prostrations daily; but if he is disposed to be slothful, let him wait for the end of the term appointed by the Fathers."

(Canon 20 of Ancyra; Canons 87, 93, and 98 of the 6th Ec. C.; Canon 8 of Neocaesaria; Canons 9, 31, 39, 58, and 77 of Basil the Great; Canon 4 of Gregory of Nyssa).

Interpretation

The present Canon designates that an adulterer be penanced not to commune for three years, eating dry foods after the ninth hour, and doing two hundred and fifty prostrations every day. But if he negligently does not want to do these things, let him abstain from Communion for as many years as the Fathers designated.[231]

CANON 14

"We order the man who has madly fallen upon his own sister to be deemed worthy of Communion after three years, if he chooses to fast until evening and to eat dry foods, and does five hundred prostrations every day."

(Canons 67 and 75 of Basil).

Interpretation

This Canon penances the man who falls with his sister not to commune for three years, if he wants to eat dry food until the evening and do five hundred prostrations every day.[232]

---

231   Canon 20 of Ancyra precludes an adulterer from Communion for seven years; Canon 58 of Basil, fifteen years; Canon 4 of Gregory of Nyssa, eighteen years. Canon 98 of the Sixth Ecumenical Council penances the man who takes a woman engaged to another man as an adulterer. Canon 8 of Neocaesaria says that, if a man's wife commits adultery, that man cannot become a priest (if, that is, after her adultery he comes together with her). If a priest's wife commits adultery, he must either cease from the priesthood, if he wants to keep her as his wife, or he can leave her and keep his priesthood (before, that is, coming together after the act of adultery).

232   Canon 67 of Basil the Great penances the man who mixes with his sister twenty years, the same as a murderer. Canon 85 of Basil penances the man who mixes with his sister, either from one father and two mothers, or from two fathers and one mother, eleven years.

CANON 15

"We banish the man who has madly fallen upon his own sister-in-law or his own daughter-in-law from Communion for two years, if he is able to eat dry foods after the ninth hour and do three hundred prostrations every day; but if he acts in negligence, let him fulfill the years appointed by the Fathers."

Interpretation

The man who falls with his sister-in-law or his daughter-in-law is penanced to abstain from Communion for two years, eating dry foods after the ninth hour and doing three hundred prostrations every day. But, if out of negligence he does not want to do these things, let him abstain from Communion for as many years as the Fathers designated.[233]

CANON 16

"The man who madly falls upon his own mother-in-law, not separating from his wife, is also liable to the same penances, according to the law which says: 'Those things which are certain from the beginning are not invalidated by later happenings.'"

Interpretation

The present Canon penances the man who falls with his mother-in-law to abstain from Communion for two years, to eat dry foods after the ninth hour, and to do three hundred prostrations every day. However, he is not to separate from his wife on account of having fallen with his mother-in-law, for there is a law which says that those things that have a certain and lawful beginning are not invalidated by unlawful things that happen later. Note, however, that if he does not have a perfectly consecrated marriage with his wife in the Church, but only a betrothal, he must, after falling with his mother-in-law, or with another female relative of his wife's, also separate

---

233   Canon 76 of Basil the Great designates a penance of eleven years.

from his wife, that is, from his betrothed, and the marriage is not to be completed, as Blastaris (verse 3, ch. 15) and others say, for it is an unlawful thing for such a mixing of blood to knowingly take place (for betrothal is not in every way equal to marriage, but lower).[234]

CANON 17

"Canon 2 of St. Dionysios, but also Canon 7 of Timothy, orders women during their menses not to touch the holy things for up to seven days. The Old Law also commands this, but neither did it permit them to mingle with men, for because of this it happens that the seeds sown become weak and prone to die. Hence the divine Moses also ordered the father to be stoned to death, because on account of his lack of self-control he did not wait for the purification of his wife. It is ordered that a woman who is disrespectful and

---

234   Note that Matthew Blastaris, who synopsized these Canons, relates how today the sacred and divine Synod penances such men not to commune for six years, and he says how they are to be managed during these six years, namely, they are not to eat any meat for six months and they are to stand outside of the Church supplicating and asking the Lord for forgiveness, neither taking *antidoron*, nor drinking any holy water, except only on the Eve or Forefeast of the Feast of Lights (Theophany) when the service of the Great Blessing of the Waters is chanted, but they are to eat a piece of the bread elevated for the Panagia, to be assured of the philanthropy of God toward them, and for the entirety of the six years they are to do one hundred prostrations every day, except on Saturday and Sunday, and they are to eat dry foods on Wednesday and Friday. They are to stand inside the Church for two years behind the chanters, and listen to the spiritual songs, and for the remaining three years they are to stand together with the faithful. And after the six years have been fulfilled, they are to commune. They are also, however, to give alms, according to their ability, send an offering once a week to the Church, not lie, not swear any oaths, and cleanse the pollution of their soul as much as they can with compunction and tears. Blastaris also relates this: that this penance is also suitable to be given to sorcerers, adulterers, and murderers, and to all who fall into grave sins, but, according to the disposition of the penitent, at times lessening the penance, if their repentance is eager and fervent, and at times increasing the penance, if their repentance is cold. Note that I found this economy and the penance of six years in old manuscripts of Canons, which said it was given to apostates from the emperors and to those who aided them, after they ceased their apostasy. This Canon and penance was written under Constantine Porphyrogennetos and was found in the Protekdikeio of the Great Church, entitled: "A Conciliar edict concerning apostasizers." It is not, however, as complete in the manuscripts as it is here, but only up to the point: "they are also, however, to give alms." Blastaris, then, receiving this, placed it in his synopsis, for which reason we also included it as a footnote and not as a writing of the Faster, for neither does Armenopoulos relate that this is the Faster's.

touches the divine Mysteries during the time of her impurity is not to commune for forty days."

Interpretation

The present Canon designates that those women who are seated in a separate place on account of their usual monthly cycle, like the Jewish women were, are not to receive Communion for up to seven days,[235] just as Canon 2 of St. Dionysios and Canon 7 of Timothy order. The same thing is commanded by the Old Law, which also does not even permit these women to mix with their husbands for as long as they have their monthly cycle, because the children that are conceived during that time consequently become weak and maimed most of the time. For this reason the Law also ordered the father of the maimed child to be stoned, because on account of his wanton lust he did not wait for his wife to be purified of her monthly cycle but slept with her while she had it, and thus did the child sown in her become maimed. If the woman who has her monthly cycle is disrespectful and receives the divine Mysteries, they order that she not commune for forty days.[236]

CANON 18

"It has seemed best to exclude the man who has madly fallen upon another man from Communion for three years, weeping and fasting, and eating dry foods toward the evening, and doing two hundred prostrations; but as for the one who for the most part practices slothfulness, let him fulfill the fifteen years."

(Canon 62 of Basil; Canon 4 of Gregory of Nyssa).

---

235   The seven days mentioned here by the Canon, although not contained in the Canons of Dionysios and of Timothy, are however expressly mentioned by the Old Law, for most women are purified within seven days.

236   This is not mentioned in the Canons of St. Dionysios and of Timothy, but is a penance and designation of St. John the Faster himself, as we found this in the manuscript of the Canons of the Faster, which Blastaris synopsized.

Interpretation

The present Canon penances the sodomist not to receive Communion for three years and to weep on account of his sin, and, fasting until the evening, to eat dry foods and to do two hundred prostrations every day. But if out of negligence he does not want to observe these, let him not commune for fifteen years, according to Canon 62 of Basil the Great.

Note that in the Canons of the Faster, from a manuscript codex which was found, sodomy has the following divisions: sodomy is of two types, either committed upon women, when men fall with them into that which is against nature, or committed upon men. Another division is that, among men, one commits the act, while the other suffers the act, while another both commits and suffers the act. The worst sin is for someone to both commit and suffer the act. And for someone to commit the act upon a woman that is not his wife is worse than committing it with men. But for someone to commit it upon his own wife is worse than committing it upon a woman who is not his wife. From these things then, we conclude that the married couple which falls into that which is against nature is penanced more heavily than a sodomist committing it upon another man or upon a woman who is not his wife. The Spiritual Father, then, should assign a penance which he deems proper. It has been found that this sin is penanced for eight years.[237] Also see the penances which follow the Canons of the Faster.

CANON 19

"A boy who has been violated in the presence of someone cannot enter the priesthood. For although on account of his immature age he did not sin himself, yet his vessel was rent and became useless in connection with sacred service. If, however, he received the emission between his thighs, after being appropriately penanced, he will not be barred from proceeding to the priesthood."

---

237   Canon 62 of Basil the Great precludes sodomists from Communion for fifteen years; Canon 4 of Gregory of Nyssa for eighteen years. The Patriarch Luke, solving various questions together with his Synod (preserved in manuscripts), says that those who fall into sodomy cannot take one another's sister as a wife.

(Canon 70 of Basil)

Interpretation

The present Canon designates that if anyone, when he was a seven year old boy, was violated by any man, although at that time, on account of his immaturity of age and knowledge, he did not sin, he cannot, however, become a priest, because the vessel of his body was broken and became useless for the service of the priesthood. But if he received the emission of sperm only between his thighs, that is to say, if he suffered colluctation, he is not impeded from becoming a priest,[238] carrying out the appropriate rule. See also the *Homily on Repentance,* at the end of this book, in order to learn that whoever loses his virginity can no longer receive the priesthood.

CANON 20

"We exclude the one who commits voluntary murder from Communion for five years, and the one who commits involuntary murder for three years, if indeed, after fasting until the evening, the murderer practices the extreme eating of dry foods, and willingly does three hundred prostrations daily; but if he is sluggishly disposed, let the rule of the Fathers be fulfilled."

(Canon 36 of the Holy Apostles; Canons 22 and 23 of Ancyra; Epistle of Athanasios to Ammoun; Canons 8, 13, 43, 55, 56, and 57 of Basil; Canon 5 of Gregory of Nyssa).

---

238   Note that, because Canon 70 of Basil the Great deposes the deacon or the priest who performs something more than a kiss, that is, performs colluctation, consequently, he who performs colluctation is impeded from the priesthood. Therefore, having found an old manuscript containing the Canons of the Faster that agrees with Basil the Great, we accepted the specifications it assigned to this present Canon, for it says that, he who received the emission of sperm between his thighs may become a priest, if however: 1) it happened to him one time, or at most two; 2) he is earnest and virtuous; 3) he weeps over that which happened to him his entire life; and 4) he was an immature child when it happened to him. But as many as performed colluctation or suffered it, being of a mature age, namely, over fourteen years old, may not become priests, in agreement with Basil the Great.

Interpretation

The present Canon penances the person who has murdered someone voluntarily not to receive Communion for five years, and the person who has murdered someone involuntary for three years. Both are to fast until the evening and practice the extreme eating of dry foods, doing three hundred prostrations every day. If they are negligent in doing these things, let the voluntary murderer not receive Communion for twenty years, and the involuntary murderer for ten years, according to Canon 56 of St. Basil.[239]

CANON 21

"We have designated that women who make it their practice to destroy embryos, and those who give or take poisons so as to abort and prematurely miscarry babies, are to be accommodated with up to five years, or for the most part, three years."

(Canon 91 of the 6th Ec. C.; Canon 21 of Ancyra; Canons 2 and 8 of Basil)

Interpretation

This Canon penances those women who deliberately kill the embryos which they have in their womb for five years, or for the most part, three.

---

239   Canon 5 of St. Gregory of Nyssa penances the voluntary murderer twenty-seven years, and Canon 22 of Ancyra penances him for his entire life. Canon 23 of Ancyra penances the involuntary murderer seven or five years, Canon 57 of St. Basil penances him for ten years, and Canon 5 of Gregory of Nyssa for nine years. See Canon 8 of Basil and Canon 5 of Gregory of Nyssa to learn who are voluntary murderers and who are involuntary murderers. Generally speaking, the difference between voluntary and involuntary murderers is deduced from two things: 1) from the disposition, the aim, and the impetus of the assaulter; and 2) from the instrument used by the assaulter. Whatever clerics or clergymen commit murder, even if it is involuntary, or even if they are attacked, are deposed, according to Canon 66 of the Apostles, Canon 5 of Gregory of Nyssa, the synodical decision of Patriarch Constantine Chliarenos, and Canon 55 of Basil the Great. Also see the epistle of St. Athanasios to Ammoun, and Canons 13 and 43 of St. Basil. Canon 14 of Timothy says that whoever kills himself and does not have a demon, nor is he out of his mind on account of sickness but out of faint-heartedness or some other suffered injury does this thing, and is of sound mind, is not to be commemorated, being a murderer of himself. Also see Chapter 10 of *Instruction to the Spiritual Father, What rule murderers are to be given.*

It designates the same penance for those women who give herbs or other prepared substances[240] to pregnant women in order that they abort the babies premature and dead.[241]

CANON 22

"A woman who has involuntarily miscarried a baby, receives a penance of one year."

Interpretation

The woman who miscarried the baby which she had in her womb, without wanting to, but on account of some involuntary circumstance, is penanced one year not to receive Communion.[242]

CANON 23

"A woman who falls asleep on her baby and smothers it is deemed worthy of

---

240   Note that in a manuscript codex containing the Canons of the Faster, we also found this according to the present Canon, that women employ these herbs in various ways. Some eat them or drink them in order to never become pregnant and have a child. Others murder the babies as soon as they are conceived or when they are close to giving birth, which is a worse sin than the first. And still others commit murder every month with these herbs, which is the worst of them all. Therefore, those who do such things are impeded from divine Communion for three years, and are to eat dry foods and do one hundred prostrations daily.

241   The Ninety-First Canon of the Sixth Ecumenical Council, and Canon 21 of Ancyra, and Canons 2 and 8 of Basil the Great number the women who do such things along with voluntary murderers. But out of philanthropy they do not penance them not to commune until the end of their life, but for ten years.

242   For this reason pregnant women must take great care not to lift anything heavy (especially when they are seven or eight months pregnant), and to keep themselves from whatever troubles them. While men, after their wives conceive, must not sleep in the same bed with them, nor have intercourse with them any longer, nor strike them, or cause them any other trouble and sorrow, for because of these things their wives miscarry the babies and the poor husbands become murderers of their children. Wherefore, if married priests, or those who plan to become priests, do any of these things and their wives miscarry their babies, those who are priests are to be deposed, and those who were going to become priests in the future are barred from the priesthood on account of the murder they committed.

Communion after three years, abstaining from meats and cheese on the specified days, and diligently fulfilling the rest of the requirements. And if this happened from the indolence or intemperance of the parents, it is next to voluntary murder; but if from a plot of the enemy, it is worthy of forgiveness. Still, even this is bound with moderate penances, for this abandonment happened on account of other errors."

Interpretation

The present Canon penances the woman who, while sleeping, rolled onto her baby and smothered it, to abstain from Communion for three years. She is not to eat meat and cheese for a designated amount of time, and she is to do other good works with grief in her heart. And if this resulted from the negligence or intemperance of the parents (for example, from eating and drinking too much, or from some other licentious appetite of theirs), it is likened to voluntary murder. But if it resulted from a diabolical plot and action, it is worthy of forgiveness but still requires moderate penances and a rule, for this abandonment of God which befell them happened on account of other past, present, or future sins of theirs.[243]

CANON 24

"When an unbaptized child dies on account of the negligence of its own parents, the parents are excluded from Communion for three years, eating dry foods during these years, and propitiating the Deity by weeping on bent knees and by giving alms according to their ability, doing forty prostrations daily."

Interpretation

This Canon penances those parents whose child died unbaptized on account of their negligence, designating that they do not receive Communion for three years, and to eat dry foods, and to weep and give alms to the poor

---

243   The same is said by Nikephoros the Archivist when answering the questions of the monk Theodosios the Recluse in Corinth.

according to their ability, and to do forty prostrations every day.[244]

CANON 25

"If a nun has knowledge that other nuns have suffered adultery or child-molestation, and does not reveal this to the abbess, she is to receive the same penance as she who did the act, according to Canon 71 of Basil the Great."

(Canon 25 of Ancyra; Canon 71 of Basil).

---

244   Note that, if the baby is healthy, parents must baptize it after forty days, according to Armenopoulos (Section 5, heading 1 of the epitome of the Canons). And if the baby gets sick and is in danger of dying, and the priest only baptizes the baby with three immersions and emersions and the epicleses of the Holy Trinity, there is no further need, if the baby lives, to read the pre-baptismal prayers over him or the exorcisms, according to Armenopoulos and Metropolitan Elias of Crete (*Juris Graeco-romanorum*, p. 340). But if a priest is not to be found in that place, and the child is in danger of dying, whoever is present must baptize it, whether it be a deacon, or a monk, according to St. Nikephoros (Canon 6, vol. 2 of the acts of the synods), or a layperson, being a Christian, however, or the child's own father. If the child dies, we must consider it as having been baptized, casting everything to the philanthropy of the all-good God, according to Gregory the Theologian who says that: "If there be any doubt let charity prevail" (*Oratio* 39, 19, PG 36, 357B; tr. NPNF (V2-07), p. 359). If, however, the child lives, a priest must baptize it from the beginning, for even though St. Nikephoros says that the child that was in danger of dying must be baptized by a Christian layperson, so that it does not die completely without hope, being cast, as we said, to the philanthropy of God, but if the child ends up living, neither does St. Nikephoros say that the child should not be baptized by a priest, nor any other Father in their Canons, nor any Synodical Canon. Indeed, the blessed Dionysios of Alexandria baptized a certain Jew from the beginning, even though he had been baptized by a layperson during a time of sickness and was nearing death, and then recovered, saying that it is not permitted for a layperson to perform any priestly service, as it is told in *Byzantis* (vol. XI, p. 188). But also Basil the Great shows in his First Canon that the baptism performed by laypeople is not accepted, and those baptized by them must be baptized.

Note also this, that in many handwritten books we also found this together with the present Canon of the Faster, that is, if the baby is seven days old and dies unbaptized, its parents are not to receive Communion for forty days and are to eat dry foods during these days, and are to do forty prostrations daily. I think that this condescension was done for them because it was the custom, as it seems, for a child not to be baptized before it was eight days old, following the reason of circumcision on the eighth day, instead of which baptism is now performed. Hence, in order to prevent the occurrence of such things, the baby must without hesitation be baptized on whatever day it may happen to become ill, according to the first Reply of Peter the Archivist. See also p. 1001 of the Minutes.

Interpretation

This Canon designates that the nun, who is living with other nuns in a monastery, finds out that any one of the nuns is being taken into adultery by someone,[245] or has been violated before coming of age,[246] and does not reveal it to the abbess so that she may correct it, but has kept it silent, is to be penanced in the same way as the nun who did it, for she could have prevented the wrong but did not, according to Canon 71 of Basil the Great.[247]

CANON 26

"The law punishes women who abandon their own babies outside of the entrances to Churches as murderesses, even if some people adopt the babies and take care of them."

Interpretation

The present Canon penances as murderesses those women who cast their babies at the doors of Churches, even if some people take them and nurture them.[248]

---

245   See that the Canon calls fornication committed by nuns adultery, in agreement with Canons 18 and 60 of Basil the Great.

246   Some interpret child-molestation in this way, that it is the violation of an immature girl, under thirteen years of age.

247   See also Canon 25 of Ancyra which assigns a penance of ten years to those family members who knew and kept silent about the fact that a man violated the sister of his betrothed and got her pregnant, and afterward took as his wife not the one whom he had violated, but his betrothed. For someone participates in the evil of another by three ways, as Basil the Great says (*De Baptismo II*, Question 9, PG 31, 1614B-1617B): either according to deed, when someone actively cooperates with the other in the wickedness; or according to knowledge, when someone consents to the disposition and way of the sinner, and takes pleasure in it; or when someone knows the evil intention of the sinner and relaxes, that is, keeps silent, and does not reprove him.

248   Canons 33 and 52 of Basil the Great also consider the woman as a murderess who neglects her child and it dies. The civil law also designates this.

CANON 27

"We bar the thief who voluntarily repents from Communion for up to forty days, but the thief who is proven guilty for up to six months, eating dry foods after the ninth hour and doing one hundred prostrations daily."

Interpretation

The present Canon penances for forty days the thief who, on his own, bears witness that he stole something. But the thief who is borne witness to by others is penanced for six months not to receive Communion, and in addition, to eat dry foods after the ninth hour and to do one hundred prostrations every day.[249]

CANON 28

"The man found guilty of state robbery, associated with so-called capital thievery, cannot enter the priesthood; but even if after entering the priesthood it happens that he falls into it, he is to be stripped of the priesthood, according to Canon 25 of the Holy Apostles."

Interpretation

This Canon impedes the man from becoming a priest who is caught having stolen capital goods, that is, those goods which bring capital punishment upon the thief. But even if someone, being a priest, steals such capital goods, he is to be deposed, according to the 25th Apostolic Canon, which should be read. Capital punishment is not only beheading, or some other death (as Theodore Balsamon interprets it, explaining the 25th

---

[249] Canon 61 of Basil the Great penances for one year the thief who voluntarily and on his own confesses the theft, and the thief that is revealed by others or caught in the act, for two years. Canon 6 of St. Gregory of Nyssa penances blatant thieves as murderers (just as Canon 78 of Basil the Great also penances them together with voluntary murderers), but he designates for secret thieves that, after their confession, they are to distribute their belongings to the poor, if they still have anything. If they don't have anything, they are to work, and from their wages they are to give to the poor. See also Chapter 10 of *Instruction to the Spiritual Father, What rule thieves and the unjust are to be given.*

chapter of the 9th Title of the *Nomocanon* of Photios),[250] but it is exile, blinding, cutting off of the hand, and other like things. See also Chapter 10 of *Instruction to the Spiritual Father, What rule thieves and the unjust are to be given*.

CANON 29

"We designate that a grave robber be uncommuned for one year, eating dry foods after the ninth hour and making two hundred prostrations every day."

(Canon 66 of Basil; Canon 7 of Gregory of Nyssa).

Interpretation

The present Canon penances the one who opens tombs in order to steal something not to receive Communion for one year, and to eat dry foods after the ninth hour, and to do two hundred prostrations every day.[251] See also Chapter 10 of *Instruction to the Spiritual Father, What rule murderers are to be given*.

CANON 30

"Sacrilege is punished for a shorter time than adultery, according to St. Gregory of Nyssa, and it is accommodated with up to three years."

(Canon 73 of the Holy Apostles; Canon 10 of the First-and-Second Council; Canon 8 of Gregory of Nyssa).

Interpretation

This Canon penances the one committing sacrilege not to receive Communion for three years, according to the customary accommodation

---

250   PG 104, 1108B-1117C.

251   Canon 66 of St. Basil impedes a grave robber from Communion for ten years, while Canon 7 of St. Gregory of Nyssa divides grave robbery into pardonable and unpardonable. He says pardonable grave robbery is when someone does not disturb the body of the deceased, but takes the stones from the area of the tomb in order to use them for building some other beneficial work of common utility. Unpardonable grave robbery is when someone takes the clothes or some other ornaments from the deceased, which person is penanced as a fornicator, that is, for nine years.

of the Faster, that is, to eat dry foods after the ninth hour and to do three hundred prostrations.[252] Note herein that, because sacrilege is penanced for less of a time than adultery, it is therefore not penanced for three years like adultery, but must be penanced less. See also Canon 13 of the Faster.

CANON 31

"We have thought it proper to deter from Communion for one year those who have out of necessity (or without necessity) committed perjury, eating dry foods after the ninth hour, and doing two hundred and fifty prostrations daily."

(Canon 25 of the Holy Apostles; Canon 94 of the 6t Ec. C.; Canons 10, 29, 63, and 82 of Basil).

Interpretation

The present Canon penances those who take a false oath, or violate their oath out of necessity, or without necessity, not to commune for one year, eating dry foods after the ninth hour and doing two hundred and fifty prostrations every day.[253]

---

252   Canon 8 of St. Gregory of Nyssa penances the sacrilegious person less than the adulterer. Canon 10 of the First-and-Second Council completely deposes those clergymen who either steal the sacred vessels and vestments which are within the sanctuary or use them for profane or unholy purposes. It excommunicates those who use the sacred vessels and vestments which are without the sanctuary for profane or unholy reasons, as does Canon 73 of the Apostles.

253   Although it is necessary that the penance be different for the one who commits perjury out of necessity than the one who committed it without necessity, we, however, seeing how Blastaris cites the Canon of the Faster indeterminately, stating: "Those who have out of necessity *and* without necessity committed perjury," wrote it this way. But the hierarchs and the Spiritual Fathers should assign them penances with discernment. Canon 64 of Basil the Great simply and without differentiation penances perjurers for ten years. But Canon 82 of Basil does differentiate, penancing the one who committed perjury out of pressure and necessity for six years, and the one who committed it without necessity and pressure for seven years. Canon 94 of the Sixth Ecumenical Council excommunicates those Christians who swear oaths according to the custom of the Greeks, saying, for example, "upon the sun!" "upon heaven!" and other like things. Whatever ordained clergymen take false oaths are deposed, according to the 25th Apostolic Canon. That oaths should never be taken is attested to by the divine Chrysostom, who says the following: "'But what,' says one, 'if it be necessary to take an oath?' Where there is a transgression of the law, there is no such thing as necessity. 'Is it possible then,' it is replied, 'not to swear at all?' What sayest thou? Hath God commanded, and darest thou to ask if it be possible for His law to be kept? Why, truly it is a thing impossible that His law should not be kept; and I am desirous to persuade you from present

CANON 32

"We have shortened the accommodation of repentance to three years for those professing sorcery or magic, if indeed they eagerly fast to the greatest extent every day, and eat hard and dry food after the ninth hour, and live as simply as possible, and also do two hundred and fifty prostrations, reverently placing their forehead upon the ground. Together with these we also censure those women who make amulets or charms and practice fortunetelling."

(Canon 61 of the 6th Ec. C.; Canon 24 of Ancyra; Canon 36 of Laodicaea; Canons 65, 72, and 83 of Basil; Canon 3 of Gregory of Nyssa).

Interpretation

Sorcerers and magicians, and also women who make amulets or charms and tell fortunes, are penanced for three years not to receive Communion, and to eat dry foods after the ninth hour, eating only as much as is necessary to live, and to do two hundred and fifty prostrations every day.[254]

---

circumstances of this; that so far from its being impossible not to swear, it is impossible to swear" (*Ad Populum Antiochenum V*, 7, PG 49, 80; tr. NPNF (V1-09), p. 399). And again he says: "But, someone says, So-and-so is a good man and a priest and lives a life of temperance and piety. Yet he swears oaths... Let it be, if you wish, Peter or Paul or even an angel who has come down from heaven. Not even in such cases do I regard the dignity of persons. I do not recognize the law of any servant in the matter of oaths, but only the King's law" (*Ad Illuminandos I*, 5, PG 49, 229-230; tr. *St. John Chrysostom: Baptismal Instructions*, ACW, New York, 1963, p. 144). See also Homilies 5, 14, and 15, *On the Statues* (*Ad Populum Antiochenum*). Wherefore also Basil the Great says in his Twenty-Nineth Canon that an oath is completely forbidden; also see his penances. Even the civil laws do not want credible witnesses to take oaths, according to Armenopoulos (*Basilicae*, Book I, Title 1). But why say so much? Our Lord emphatically says: "But I say unto you, Swear not at all" (Mt. 5:34), neither for good, nor for bad, neither out of necessity, nor without necessity. And James the Brother of God says: "Swear not, neither by heaven, neither by the earth, neither by any other oath" (Jas. 5:12).

254   Canon 65 of St. Basil penances those who have confessed their sorcery or magic with the penance given to a voluntary murderer. His Seventy-Second Canon likewise sentences those who deliver themselves over to fortunetellers with the same penance. Canon 61 of the Sixth Ecumenical Council penances such people for six years and Canon 24 of Ancyra for five years. Canon 3 of St. Gregory of Nyssa penances those who go to fortunetellers out of disregard and spurn for the faith of Christ as those who have voluntarily denied Christ, that is, not to receive Communion for the rest of their life. But those who went to magicians because they became fainthearted out of some necessity or pressure, he penances like those who denied Christ on account of tortures and sufferings, that is, for eleven years. Canon 36 of Laodicaea says that ordained clergy and clerics cannot be

CANON 33

"Neither a laywoman, nor a nun, is to be separated from the Church, no matter what the offense, except only from Communion. For the Canon says that we do this on account of them taking their own lives because of their great shame. Likewise, neither a presbyter, nor a deacon, on account of the command: 'Thou shalt not take vengeance twice for the same thing' (Nahum 1:9)."

(Canon 25 of the Holy Apostles; Canon 34 of Basil).

Interpretation

The present Canon designates that no woman, neither a laywoman, nor a nun, is to be separated from the Church and the gathering of the faithful, on account of a sin she commits, but only from divine Communion. For the Canon says (Canon 34 of Basil the Great) for us not to do this, in order that they do not kill themselves on account of their great shame, just as neither a priest nor a deacon who sins is to be put out of the Church, but only from the Communion of the Mysteries, so they do not receive two chastisements at the same time, according to Canon 25 of the Apostles and Canon 3 of Basil the Great. But Balsamon adds (in his explanation of the 34th Canon of Basil) that, if the sin of an adulterous woman is made public, separation from the Church must also be charged to her.[255] It is concluded from the present Canon by contradistinction that the divine Faster follows the Canons of both the divine Synods and the Fathers, for if it says here that women who have mortally sinned are to remain in the Church, it is obvious from its silence that it designates that men who have mortally sinned are to go out of the Church, as he says this clearly in his *Kanonikon*, even if this penance is not in force today. See the footnote to the Faster's 1st Canon and the end of these Canons and penances.

---

magicians, or enchanters, or numerologists, or astrologists, or make amulets or charms. Whatever ordained clergy utilize these things are to be deposed and put out of the Church, according to Balsamon and Zonaras.

255   PG 138, 697D-700C.

CANON 34

"If something unclean falls into a well, or into oil, or into wine, let whoever has tasted of it not touch meat and cheese for three days, and let him not commune for seven days."

(Canon 63 of the Holy Apostles; Canon 63 of the 6th Ec. C.; Canon 2 of Ancyra).

Interpretation

This Canon designates that if any of the so-called unclean things (like a mouse, or something else) falls into a well, or into oil, or into wine, and someone eats, or drinks from it,[256] he is to be penanced for three days not to eat meat and cheese, and not to commune for seven days.

CANON 35

"Anyone who vomited after receiving divine Communion is to keep away from divine Communion for forty days, singing the 50th Psalm daily, and doing fifty prostrations, howsoever this may have happened. For even though he may think that, up until that point, he did not himself give rise to such an occasion, yet however, on account of some other errors of his own, this certainly was allowed."

Interpretation

Whosoever vomits, in whatever way it may be, after having received Communion, is penanced for forty days not to receive Communion, saying the 50th Psalm every day, that is, the "Have mercy on me, O God," and doing fifty prostrations every day. For although the person who had this happen to him did not, on his part, give any reason for it, yet on account

---

256   Perhaps the person who tasted of it is penanced because before the particular liquid was sanctified with holy water, he tasted it, while being condemned by his conscience: "He that doubteth," according to the Apostle, "is damned if he eat, because he eateth not of faith: for whatsoever is not of faith is sin" (Rom. 14:23), or because he tasted of it after the impure thing that fell in had rotted inside and it became manifest that he was partaking of something strangled and dead, and simply, the blood of an animal, which things are forbidden. Also see the 63rd Apostolic Canon, the 67th of the Sixth Ecumenical Council, and Canon 2 of Gangra.

of his other sins it was allowed by God that this should happen to him.[257]

Note that, in some manuscripts of the Canons of St. John the Faster, we also found the following three Canons written, and correctly so.

CANON A

One is not to receive Communion from any priest that does not fast from fish and oil on Wednesdays and Fridays, even if he is Orthodox.[258]

CANON B

Any man or woman who slanders others is to do forty prostrations, and is to say with each prostrations: "Lord have mercy."

CANON C

If two people have animosity toward one another and one of the two dies, the living person must go to the tomb of the deceased and weep and ask for forgiveness from him as if he were alive. The living person is also to eat dry foods on Wednesdays and Fridays (that is, also when there happens to be a relaxation of the fast on those days because of some Feast), he is to do twenty prostrations every morning and evening, and he is to supplicate God on behalf of his deceased enemy and give offerings to the Church and have liturgies celebrated in order that the deceased may be commemorated.

With these three Canons is also included the Canon against blasphemers. See Chapter 10, *What rule blasphemers and perjurers are to be given*, in *Instruction to the Spiritual Father*.

---

257   Balsamon says, if someone vomited on account of eating or drinking too much, that person ought to receive a more severe penance, but if it happened because of an upset stomach or some illness, that person is penanced more lightly, for this is due to divine abandonment (*Responsa ad Interrogationes Marci*, Question 12, PG 138, 964C-964D). Wherefore, that person who is disturbed by the sea should not board a ship in order to sail the same day he plans to commune, for many have vomited from this and therefore come under a rule.

258   This penance was given to the priest more as a threat, for, as it seems, he scornfully breaks the fast, and so that he may be ashamed and correct himself, just as Canon 22 of St. Nikephoros likewise commands that one is not to commune from a young hieromonk who serves nuns. I said more as a threat because we are obliged to receive Communion indiscriminately, even from the priest whom we see committing mortal sin, because the unworthiness of the priest does not harm us at all, as the divine Isidore Pelousiotes says.

Note that in an old manuscript codex there was found a *Kanonikon* of the Faster also containing the following penances, outside, that is, of the Canons already written above and mentioned by Blastaris.[259]

1.   If someone falls with his step-mother, he is penanced for three years, fasting until the evening, eating fry foods, and doing five hundred prostrations daily.[260]

2.   If someone falls with a mother and daughter together, he is penanced for four years, eating dry foods after the ninth hour, and doing three hundred prostrations daily.

3.   If someone commits sodomy with two brothers, he is penanced for four years, eating dry foods after the ninth hour, and doing three hundred prostrations daily.

4.   If someone commits sodomy with his brother-in-law, he is penanced for four years, eating dry foods after the ninth hour, and doing two hundred prostrations daily.

5.   If someone falls with his daughter one time, he is penanced for five years; if more than one time, six and seven years, eating dry foods after the ninth hour, and doing five hundred prostrations daily.

6.   If someone (i.e. a sponsor/godfather) falls with his spiritual daughter (goddaughter) by Holy Baptism one time, he is penanced for eight years; if more than one time, for ten years, eating dry foods after the ninth hour, and doing five hundred prostrations.

7.   If someone (i.e. a sponsor/godfather) falls with the mother of his spiritual daughter (goddaughter), he is likewise penanced for eight years, eating dry foods after the ninth hour, and doing three hundred prostrations daily.

8.   If someone commits sodomy with his brother, he is penanced for

---

259   Let no one blame us for writing here the penances for the most impious and most unnatural sins, for we did not do this undiscerningly and needlessly, because we know that the corrupter of the human race, the devil, does not let much time pass before casting those unfortunate people into these sins, even if infrequently. And the Spiritual Fathers, hearing these sins from the penitents, and unable to find penances for them in all of the other Canons, are at a loss, not knowing how to correct such people. Therefore, we wrote them here as needful.

260   Basil the Great, in his Seventy-Ninth Canon, penances for twenty years the man who falls with his mother-in-law. He likewise penances the man who falls with his sister.

eight years, eating dry foods after the ninth hour, and doing four hundred prostrations.

9.   If a younger brother is sodomized by his older brother, without he himself committing sodomy, he is penanced for three years, eating dry foods after the ninth hour, and doing one hundred prostrations daily.

10.   If someone falls with his mother one time, he is penanced for seven years; if many times, for twelve years, eating dry foods after the ninth hour, and doing five hundred prostrations.

11.   If someone falls with a beast many times, and he has a wife, he is penanced for eight years, eating dry foods after the ninth hour, and doing three hundred prostrations. If he does not have a wife, and he fell once with a beast, or two or three times at most, he is penanced for three years, eating dry foods after the ninth hour, and doing three hundred prostrations. A woman who falls with a beast is to receive the same penances as these.

12.   If someone falls with his female first cousin, he is penanced for two years, eating dry foods after the ninth hour, and doing five hundred prostrations daily.

13.   If someone falls with a gentile woman, namely, a Jew, or a Turk, or a heretic, and if he does not have a lawful wife, he is penanced for three years to abstain from Communion, eating dry foods after the ninth hour, and doing two hundred prostrations daily. A woman who does not have a lawful husband and who falls with a Jew, or a Turk, or a heretic, is likewise penanced. But if the man has a wife, and the woman has a husband, and they fall with the aforementioned gentiles and heretics, they are penanced for four or five years, eating dry foods daily, and doing two hundred and fifty prostrations.[261]

14.   If the wife of a presbyter or a deacon commits adultery, she is penanced for three years, eating dry foods after the ninth hour, and doing three hundred prostrations daily.[262]

---

261   Note that such people are not to be anointed with the Holy Myron, as some who are unlearned do unlawfully, for these people did not deny Christ. But they are only to be penanced more severely than fornicators, as they are here, according to the 31st reply of Kitros, and Balsamon (*Responsa ad Interrogationes Marci*, Question 47, PG 138, 996B-996C).

262   That is, they are penanced more severely than other adulteresses, because they virtually murder their ordained husbands, their adultery being a reason for them to be deposed from their

15. If a woman falls with two brothers, she is penanced for three years, eating dry foods after the ninth hour, and doing two hundred prostrations daily.[263]

16. If a woman falls with a eunuch, she is penanced for three years, eating dry foods daily, and doing three hundred prostrations.[264]

17. If someone commits sodomy upon his wife, he is penanced for eight years, eating dry foods after the ninth hour, and doing two hundred prostrations daily.

The divine Faster also mentions the following general penances in the aforementioned *Kanonikon*: 1) All who are under a rule and are not receiving Communion are to drink holy water from the Great Blessing on Holy Thursday, Pascha, Christmas, and the Feast of the Holy Apostles. 2) Those who commit mortal sins and then disdainfully receive the divine Mysteries unworthily, sin worse than all. Therefore, it is necessary that they be penanced for a greater time not to receive Communion than those who sin and, fearfully, do not receive Communion. 3) Those who sin and are under thirty years old are penanced more condescendingly than those who sin and are over thirty years old. 4) Those who are under a rule and are not receiving Communion must depart from the Church at the point of the Divine Liturgy where the priest says: "As many as are catechumens depart," and stand in the narthex. But during Vespers and Orthros, they are to stand in the Church.

The end of both the Canons and the Penances of the Faster.

---

priesthood. If the priests wish to retain their priesthood, they are to separate from their wives before coming together with them after their adultery, according to Canon 8 of Neocaesaria.

263   Concerning this, see also Canons 23 and 87 of Basil, in which the Saint designates that, if the woman is the wife of one of these brothers, they must separate, or not be received to repentance.

264   Concerning eunuchs, see the *Homily on Virginity* by Basil the Great.

Some Pertinent Subjects
Outside of the Canons of the Faster

A

Concerning Those Who Have Denied Christ

Canon 73 of Basil the Great penances those who have voluntarily denied Christ not to commune for the rest of their life, but only at the time of their death. Canon 2 of St. Gregory of Nyssa likewise forbids those who have denied Christ from the Mysteries for the rest of their life. But those who through constraint and tortures involuntarily denied Christ are penanced like harlots, that is, for nine years. See also Canon 81 of Basil, Canon 11 of the First Ecumenical Council, Canon 6 of Ancyra, and Canon 3 of Peter of Alexandria.

The present practice of the Church is for the most part, to use economy for those who deny Christ, according to the formulation of Methodios of Constantinople. That is, if someone was taken as a slave when he was a child, and out of fear or ignorance denied the Faith, after returning to the Faith he is to listen to the usual expiatory prayers for seven days, and on the eighth day he is washed and anointed with the Holy Myron and then communes, remaining after these things in the Church for eight days and listening daily to the Sacred Services and the Divine Office. If someone was a mature adult and denied the Faith on account of tortures, he is to first fast for eighty days, abstaining from meat, cheese, and eggs (and on three days of the week, Monday, Wednesday, and Friday, he is to abstain also from oil and wine),[265] he is to listen to the expiatory prayers for seven days, and when he is washed and anointed with the Holy Myron, he then communes.

If someone voluntarily denied Christ, he is to fast for two years according

---

265   Note that all Christians are obligated to fast on Wednesday and Friday, and that this rule is given to deniers of the Faith out of the philanthropy and condescension of the Church. It may also mean that these people must also fast on Wednesday and Friday even when a Feast falls on these days, while those not under a rule do not keep the fast on these days.

to the fast we just mentioned, and he is to do one hundred or two hundred prostrations daily, depending on his ability, and then he is to listen to the expiatory prayers and be washed after seven days, and being anointed with the Holy Myron he then communes, as those above.[266]

B

Concerning Those Who Have Committed Bestiality

Canon 16 of Ancyra divides those who fall with animals into three categories. If they are twenty years old or younger and fall with animals a few times, they are penanced for twenty years to abstain from Communion. If they fall many times with animals, they are penanced for twenty-five years. If they are over twenty years of age and have wives, they are to commune after thirty years. If they are over fifty years old and have wives, they are to commune only at the time of their death.

Canon 4 of St. Gregory of Nyssa penances those who have committed bestiality nineteen years. Canon 7 of Basil the Great penances those who have committed bestiality as sodomists and murderers, that is, for twenty years. In his 63rd Canon he penances them as adulterers, that is, fifteen years.[267]

C

Concerning Those Who Marry
a Second and Third Time

Someone who enters into a second marriage, according to Canon 4 of Basil the Great, is impeded from the divine Mysteries for one or two years. According to Canon 2 of St. Nikephoros and the first response of Niketas

---

266   Blastaris in the Synopsis of the Canons of the Faster and Armenopoulos, Section 5, Paragraph 4 of the Compendium of the Canons. See also the aforementioned formulation and prayers in the *Euchologion*.

267   Counted as bestiality are also acts committed with fowl, whether male or female in gender. See also the penances of the Faster concerning this.

Herakleias, they are neither to be crowned during their second wedding ceremony, and according to Canon 5 of Neocaesaria and the aforementioned Niketas, neither is the priest who blessed them to eat at their table. A third marriage is called a transgression by Gregory the Theologian.[268] Canon 4 of Basil the Great calls it polygamy, his 80th Canon calls it worse than fornication, and his 50th Canon calls it the shame and defilement of the Church. Canon 4 of St. Basil excommunicates those who marry for a third time for five years from Communion.[269] Joseph Bryennios says that those being married for the first time are engaged, blessed, and crowned; those being married for a second time are only engaged, and blessed, and not crowned; those getting married a third time are only engaged, and this by allowance, but they are neither blessed nor crowned.[270]

D

Concerning Marriage Between an Orthodox and a Heretic

Canon 14 of the Fourth Ecumenical Council, Canons 10 and 31 of

---

268   "The first (marriage) is the law. The second is done out of forgiveness. The third is a transgression" (*Oratio* 37, 8, PG 36, 292B).

269   Note that in the year 922, under Constantine Porphyrogennetos, a Synodical Tome was published, the so-called Tome of Union, which declared that those who had married a second time, forty years of age and without children, were allowed to take a third wife on account of their childlessness. But they were to be penanced for five years not to receive Communion, without exception, and after the five years they were to commune but once a year, on Pascha. But if they had children, they were never allowed a third marriage. Those who were thirty years of age and without children were also allowed, on account of their youth and proneness to fall, to marry a third time, but they could not commune for four years, and after the four years they could commune but three times a year, on Pascha, Christmas, and the Dormition of the Theotokos. If they had children, they were penanced five years (see p. 976 of the second volume of the Synodicals). Those above forty-five years of age are never allowed to marry a third time, even if they do not have children. If they insist to get married a third time by pressing the issue, they are to be penanced, according to the Synodical analysis of the Archivist Manuel of Constantinople (*Juris Graeco-romanorum*, p. 239). And the priest conducting that third marriage is to be deposed, because he disregarded a significant law, according to Balsamon (*Responsa ad Interrogationes Marci*, Question 62, PG 138, 1009D-1012A).

270   Volume III, p. 108.

Laodicaea, and Canon 29 of Carthage forbid Orthodox Christians from marrying heretics. Canon 72 of the Sixth Ecumenical Council dissolves the marriage between an Orthodox Christian man or woman and a heretic and renders it invalid. Balsamon says that an Orthodox person who married a non-Orthodox or heretic is not permitted to commune in the divine Mysteries, unless they first separate and are penanced.[271] Symeon of Thessaloniki says the same thing,[272] adding that the person is not to receive Communion until the end of their life, having the Service of Unction first read over them (if they repent, that is). The priest is neither to remove a portion of the Lamb and commemorate that person at the *prothesis*, nor accept that person's offerings to the Church, but only sometimes to accept candles and incense, and sometimes (not always) give that person holy water and *antidoron*, in order that he may not fall into despair and to direct him to give alms. The *Codex* (of Justinian), Book I, Title 5, Ordinance 12, says that if there is a dispute between the parents (who managed in some way to get married), the parent who desires to make the children Orthodox is to prevail. Ordinance 18 of this same Title says the same thing.[273]

E

Whose Offerings are Not Accepted

The *Apostolic Constitutions* (Book IV, chs. 6, 7, and 9) say that clergy are not to accept offerings and gifts from the following types of people: from those who are indicted of a crime, from those who do not repent of their sins but rather persist in them, from those who do not bring offerings to God out of just labors and earnings but out of unjust means, and from those who demand interest upon their loans to others. Canon 1 of St. Nikephoros and the 5th response of Peter the Archivist and deacon of the Great Church designate that priests are not to accept the offerings, or even incense, from those who wrongfully have mistresses, and they are not to

---

271   *Responsa ad Interrogationes Marci*, Question 33, PG 138, 985C-985D.
272   *Responsa ad Gabrielem Pentapolitanum*, Question 47, PG 155, 893A-893C.
273   From Photios, *Nomocanon*, Title 12, ch. 13.

bless this or allow this at all. Elias of Crete[274] says that offerings are not to be accepted from a father who allows his dependent children to fornicate because, being able to prevent this sin by lawfully marrying them, he does not, and allows them to sin.

The aforementioned Peter says that offerings and incense are also not to be accepted from harlots, because they are under penance. And Symeon of Thessaloniki[275] says that the offerings of those who sin publicly and visibly and do not refrain from sin are not to be accepted.[276]

F

Concerning Fasting on Wednesday and Friday

Canon 69 of the Holy Apostles designates that any hierarch or priest or deacon or subdeacon or reader or chanter who does not fast during Great Lent and Wednesday and Friday is to be deposed. If a layperson does not fast during these times (unless he cannot fast on account of bodily illness), he is to be excommunicated. Do you see how the Apostles numbered the Wednesday and Friday fast together with the fast of Great Lent? Therefore, just as the fast of Great Lent consists in the eating of dry foods, namely, to eat but once a day, at the ninth hour, without consuming oil or wine, likewise, the fast of Wednesday and Friday is to be conducted in the exact same manner. St. Epiphanios also says: "We fast on Wednesday and Friday until the ninth hour."[277] Likewise, Philostorgios says that the fast of Wednesday and Friday does not consist in the abstention from meat, but it designates that one is not to eat any food until the evening.[278] St. Benedict (Canon 41) also designates that the fast of Wednesday and Friday

---

274   *Juris Graeco-romanorum*, p. 337.

275   *Responsa ad Gabrielem Pentapolitanum*, Question 47, PG 155, 893A-893C.

276   See also the abovementioned sixth chapter of the fourth book of the *Apostolic Constitutions* which lists by name those people from whom offerings are not to be accepted. See also *Instruction to the Spiritual Father*, where it says that offerings are not accepted from those people who do not accept the rule or penance they are given for their sins (p.184).

277   *Expositio Fide* 22, PG 42, 825B.

278   *Ecclesiasticae Historiae* 10, 12, PG 65, 592C.

is until the ninth hour. And Balsamon forbids the consumption of shellfish on Wednesday and Friday just as during Great Lent. Let us therefore stop insensibly thinking that the fast of Wednesday and Friday is not an Apostolic directive, for behold, the Apostles in their Canons number this fast together with that of Great Lent, and in the *Apostolic Constitutions* they number it together with the fast of Holy Week, saying:

"One must fast during Holy Week and Wednesday and Friday."[279] But why should I say that this regulation is only of the Apostles? It is a regulation of Christ Himself, for this is what the Apostles say in Book V, ch. 14 of the *Constitutions*:

"He (that is, Christ) commanded us to fast on Wednesday and Friday."[280]We therefore fast on these days according to the Holy Hieromartyr Peter (Canon 15): "On Wednesday because on this day the council of the Jews was gathered to betray our Lord; on Friday because on this day He suffered death for our salvation." The divine Jerome says the same thing.

Therefore, because the fast of Great Lent is equal to the fast of Wednesday and Friday it follows that, for those who are sick or weak, the relaxation of the fast is also to be equal during these fasts. For this reason, as Canons 8 and 10 of Timothy allow a woman who is pregnant during the Great Fast to consume as much wine and food as is necessary for her condition, this also applies to the fast of Wednesday and Friday. The same holds for those who have become weak from excessive sickness, that is, they are allowed to consume oil and wine during these fasting periods. So says the divine Jerome: "The fast of Wednesday and Friday is not to be broken unless there is great necessity." The divine Augustine says the same.[281]

But because those who are lovers of the flesh desire to eat and break the fasts of Great Lent, Wednesday, and Friday, or pretend that they are sick (without actually being so), or if they are indeed sick they say that oil

---

279   Cf. *Apostolic Constitutions*, Book V, ch. 20; SC 329, p. 284.

280   SC 329, p. 258.

281   Note however that the divine Apostles in Book V, ch. 20, of the *Constitutions* also command the following: "We order you to fast on every Wednesday and Friday, and out of the surplus of your fast to give to the poor" (SC 329, p. 284). The same is said by Ignatios the Godbearer (Theophoros) in his Epistle, *To the Philippians* (ch. 13), namely, that those who fast on Wednesday and Friday are at the same time to distribute alms out of their abundance to the poor (PG 5, 937A).

and wine are not sufficient to carry them through their illness, because of these pretenses a Spiritual Father or hierarch should not believe only the words of those claiming these things, but should ask an experienced and God-fearing physician about their condition, and according to his recommendation allow the sick to break the fast.

We must also note the following, that just as there must be a fast from food on Wednesday, Friday, and Great Lent, there must also be a fast from pleasures of the flesh. For this reason weddings cannot take place on these days, because the divine Paul commands that married couples are not to come together during a time of prayer and fasting: "Defraud ye not one the other, except it be with consent for a time, that ye may give yourselves to fasting and prayer" (1 Cor. 7:5). And the divine Chrysostom, bringing the saying of Joel as a witness: "Sanctify a fast... Let the bridegroom go forth of his chamber, and the bride out of her closet" (Jl. 2:15-16), says that even newlyweds, who have strong desire, vigorous youthfulness, and unfettered urges, are not to come together during a period of fasting and prayer.[282] How much, then, are other married couples, who do not have such impulsiveness of the flesh, not to come together? Therefore, Balsamon says that married couples who do not exercise self-control during the Great Fast are not to commune on Pascha and are also to be penanced.[283] Likewise, married couples who come together on Wednesday and Friday must be corrected through penances.

Concerning the fast of Monday, even though designated in the Rubrics for monastics, many people in the world however, and especially women, observe this fast. Worthy of mention and trustworthy is the saying which some wise men put forward concerning fasting on Monday: "Our Lord commands that if our righteousness does not exceed that of the Scribes and the Pharisees (cf. Mt. 5:20), we will not be able to enter the kingdom of heaven. And because the Pharisees fasted two days of the week, as the Pharisee said: 'I fast twice in the week' (Lk. 18:12), we Christians, then, are obligated to fast three days of the week, in order for our righteousness to exceed the righteousness of the Pharisees." That the Pharisees fasted on

---

282   *De Virginitate* 30, PG 48, 554.

283   *Responsa ad Interrogationes Marci*, Question 50, PG 138, 997B-997C.

Wednesday and Friday is clearly stated by the divine Chrysostom, explaining the words of the Pharisee: "Twice in the week."[284] Although Theophylact when explaining the Gospel passage about the Publican and the Pharisee says, along with others, that the Pharisees fasted on Monday and Thursday, not on account of some commandment, but according to tradition, believing that Moses ascended the mountain on Thursday and descended on Monday. St. Meletios the Confessor says that we should fast on Monday in order to always begin the week with fasting.[285]

G

That One Should Not Demand Usury, That Is, Interest

Canon 44 of the Holy Apostles says that whatever hierarch or priest or deacon who loans money to someone and then demands interest, must cease from this exploitation or be deposed. The same thing is commanded by Canon 10 of the Sixth Ecumenical Council and Canon 4 of Laodicaea, prohibiting anyone ordained from demanding 1% or even 0.5% a year on their loan. Canon 17 of the First Ecumenical Council forbids not only ordained clergy but all clergy as well, such as readers, chanters, etc. from taking interest. Canon 5 of Carthage goes further still, saying that clergy cannot take interest on anything, whether it be money or any other item they might loan. Canon 20 of this same council says that a clergyman should receive back exactly what he loaned. Canon 14 of St. Basil says that whoever demands interest and wishes to become a priest must first distribute the money he received as interest to the poor, and then be ordained.

Laypeople as well must not demand interest, for as the divine Chrysostom says, if the Jews did not take interest from other Jews, according to Deuteronomy: "Thou shalt not lend upon usury to thy brother; usury of money, usury of victuals, usury of any thing that is lent upon usury" (Dt. 23:19), what excuse do we Christians have who take interest, becoming

---

284   *In Publicanum et Pharisaeum*, PG 62, 727.
285   *Alphabetalphabetos*, Degree 35.

more savage than the Jews even after the grace of the Gospel and the Incarnate Economy of Christ?[286] And Basil the Great, explaining the passage: "He hath not lent his money on usury" (Ps. 14:5), says that it is truly inhuman for a poor man to borrow from a rich man simply to comfort himself in his misfortune, and for a rich man not to be content with his assets and seek to gather profit and interest from the misfortune of the poor man.[287] Interest is called *tokos*,[288] that is, procreation or reproduction, on account of the great proliferation and increase of evil, because the money which usurers loan at one time and which gives birth to more money is immediately prepared to give birth again. Or it may be that interest is called reproduction because it naturally causes grief and stomachaches to those who owe money, and just as the birth pangs of a pregnant woman are grievous, so is it a grievous thing for the one who owes money when the time for him to pay interest comes around.

For this reason the *Novel* of Emperor Leo decrees that: "Even though our former Emperors allowed the taking of interest on account of the hardheartedness of the lenders, we, however, have deemed it just for this thing to be forever absent amongst the Christian polity, as unbecoming to such a life and forbidden by the divine Laws. Therefore Our Gentleness orders that no one for any reason has permission to take interest, lest in keeping the law of man we transgress the Law of God, but as much as a lender has taken from someone, let him estimate the amount of his debt."[289] Let the seal upon what has been said be Canon 29 of St. Nikephoros the Confessor, which prescribes that priests not commune those clergy and laity who do not cease from taking interest, and that no one eats with such persons. And the divine Apostles in their *Constitutions* (Book IV, ch. 6) order that the offerings of those people who demand interest are not to be accepted. For if Christians are not to loan with the hope of receiving back any of their capital, as the Lord says: "And if ye lend to them of whom ye hope to receive, what thank have ye?" and again:

---

286   *On Genesis*, Homily 41, 2, PG 53, 377.

287   *Homilia II in Psalmum XIV*, 6, PG 29, 261C-264C.

288   Translator's note: τόκος = *a bringing forth, childbirth; the offspring; the produce of money lent out, interest* (*Greek-English Lexicon*, Oxford, 1997, p. 811).

289   Constantine Armenopoulos, *Basilicae*, Book III, Title 7.

"Lend, hoping for nothing again" (Lk. 6:34-35), if, I say, Christians are required not even to receive back what they loaned, how much more are they required not to take any interest? Why do I say Christians? For even the Jews were sometimes commanded to forgive the debts of those who owed them. God commands them that if the seventh year is approaching (whether it be ten months or five months away, or even closer), in which year all debts were forgiven, and a needy poor man comes seeking to borrow money from them, He commands them saying not to plot wickedly on account of the seventh year of forgiveness by not giving their poor brother what he needs. They should rather give and not be sad over the fact that they are actually granting him it all on account of the seventh year. "Beware that there be not a thought in thy wicked heart, saying, The seventh year, the year of release, is at hand; and thine eye be evil against thy poor brother, and thou givest him nought; and he cry unto the Lord against thee, and it be a great sin unto thee. Thou shalt surely give him and thou shalt lend him as much as he wants, according as he is in need... because that for this thing the Lord thy God shall bless thee in all thy works" (Dt. 15:9-10).

If then the laity clearly cannot take interest, how much more then are monastics not to, those who have promised to have no possessions, and are required to live a higher and holier life, and who are to be examples to the laity of every virtue and good? So then, monks who take interest and do not cease from this exploitation must be penanced by Spiritual Fathers not to receive the divine Mysteries, as being unworthy, until they are corrected.

H

Concerning Clergy Who Marry After Ordination and Monks and Nuns Who Marry After Taking the Monastic Schema

Canon 26 of the Holy Apostles designates that only readers and chanters have permission to marry after ordination. All the rest, that is, presbyters, deacons, and subdeacons, do not have permission to marry after ordination. Canon 6 of the Sixth Ecumenical Council, confirming Canon 26 of the Apostles, says that whatever presbyter or deacon or subdeacon is so bold as to marry after ordination, will be deposed. The same is said by Canon 1 of Neocaesaria. Canon 15 of the Fourth Ecumenical Council designates that if there is a deaconess who disdains the grace of God by marrying, she is to be anathematized together with the man who took her as his wife.

This is also decreed by both the 2nd Ordinance of Title 1 of the *Novels* (of Justinian), and the 6th *Novel* of Leo, which says that whatever hierarch grants permission to a subdeacon or a deacon to marry after ordination, is to be deposed and put out of the Diocese.[290] The 44th Ordinance of Title 3 decrees that the children which are born to priests, deacons, and subdeacons, after they have married after ordination, are not to be considered either as natural children or as illegitimate, nor are they to receive anything from their lawless fathers, either as an inheritance, or as a gift, or in the form of a loan, or any other pledge, and the same applies to their mothers. But all these things are to be received by their Church. Those who marry after ordination, after they are stripped of their priesthood, are not to be promoted within the ranks of the laity or the military, but they are to pass

---

290   From Photios, *Nomocanon*, Title 9, ch. 28. I cannot be silent here about the wise method used by a certain prudent hierarch, of one of the Orthodox islands which used to be subject to Venice, to prevent a certain worldly priest with much money and possessions, who had lost his wife and was seeking to marry a second time, from doing this. For this truly knowledgeable hierarch, disturbed many times by the above priest to receive permission to marry a second time, and who often counseled the priest to forsake this notion and disobedience, finally said to him: "Are you asking to marry a second time? Let thy will be done. But against my will, just as I bestowed the priesthood upon you in the presence of everyone, so will I take it in the presence of everyone." So calling for a Liturgy, and liturgizing together with other priests, including the one mentioned above, when the time of the Liturgy came during which ordinations are performed, the hierarch told the head chanter of the right choir to chant the following troparion: "Today Judas forsakes the Master and takes to himself the devil; he is blinded by the passion of avarice, and in his darkness falls from the light..." and the rest. He then told the head chanter of the left choir to chant the following troparion: "Today Judas simulates piety and estranges himself from grace. He is a disciple and he becomes a betrayer..." and the rest. When that priest heard these hymns being chanted, out of shame he came to his senses about that wrong which he was considering to do. His heart was pricked and he began to weep and shed bitter tears. And when the hierarch approached him in order to take off his priestly vestments one by one, and at each for "Ἀνάξιος," "Unworthy," to be proclaimed, the priest fell at the hierarch's feet trembling and in agony, and with his eyes full of tears, saying: "Do not do this, my Holy Master, do not. I repent and do not any longer wish to marry, nor would I even accept an entire kingdom if it meant losing the grace of my priesthood." In this way he was forgiven, and he passed the rest of his life in prudence and chastity.

their entire life as ordinary civilians.

These penances are always to be given to those ordained clergymen who marry after their ordination, if they have not yet become monks. If they have also become monks, in addition to the abovementioned penances of the Sacred Canons and Civil Laws, the penances mentioned below concerning monks who marry should also be added to them.

Even if someone brought up Canon 10 of Ancyra which states that a deacon who marries after ordination is to retain his diaconate, we would reply that the Council in Ancyra did not say this simply and without specification, but it added that he should retain his diaconate if, when he was ordained plainly stated that he plans to get married after his ordination as one unable to keep chaste, and if the ordaining bishop upon hearing this said nothing, and proceeded to ordain him. The deacons who are ordained today do not state that they are unable to remain chaste, but are silent, and their silence declares their consent, according to Gregory the Theologian.[291] It then follows that, by their silence, they plainly accepted celibacy, just like monks who were silent during their tonsuring accepted the unmarried state, according to Canon 19 of Basil. This we must also know that according to Canon 6 of Basil the Great and the canonical collections, immoral relations (whether of monks and nuns, or clergy and those ordained, according to Balsamon and Zonaras),[292] are not to be considered as marriage, but must be discontinued in every way. Therefore hieromonks and deacons who married after their ordination, whether they were monks or not, must separate without fail from their wives, whom they illegally married. And the separation of such an unlawful union is to the advantage of the Church, according to the abovementioned 6th Canon of Basil. One such advantage is that someone else will not do the same thing. Another is so that the priesthood not be disdained. And a third is so that the heretics not find an occasion to reproach us on account of this. When they have separated, they must then receive the penance and the rule appointed for fornicators (if not for adulterers) and then commune. For their marriage is fornication and not marriage at all, according to the

---

291   *Oratio* 23, 6, PG 35, 1157B.
292   Explanation of Canon 6 of St. Basil, PG 138, 604C-605D.

aforementioned Canon 6 of Basil. And furthermore, when they have separated from the illicit marriage and repented, they are also to don the appropriate clerical garb, according to Canon 21 of the Sixth Ecumenical Council, and not be dressed like the laity. And even if they do not want to wear it, they must, according to the 7th and 8th *Novel* of Leo. These things concern the ordained clergy.

If a monk or a nun marries, Canon 16 of the Fourth Ecumenical Council dictates that they be excommunicated. Canon 44 of the Sixth Ecumenical Council penances monks who marry as fornicators. Likewise does Canon 19 of Basil. Canon 19 of Ancyra penances those who have violated their vow of chastity as those who have married a second time, that is, they are prohibited from Communion for one year. Basil the Great, however, in his 18th Canon, quoting the Fathers of the Council in Ancyra, says that those Fathers condescendingly appointed this Canon for those virgins who reneged on their promise of chastity (and note that, that which the Fathers of Ancyra appointed concerning men, Basil says is the same as that appointed for women), because, according to his opinion, the breaking of the promise of chastity subjects her to the penance of an adulteress (and not only of a fornicator), as being a bride of the heavenly Bridegroom Christ. And whoever takes her is indisputably called an adulterer, just as we call an adulterer he who takes the wife of another man. Basil the Great himself, in Canon 60, also places monks and virgins who break their vows under the penance of adultery. And the divine Chrysostom, in his second letter to the fallen Theodore, says that the monk who marries commits a much worse sin than adultery, inasmuch as God is far above man.[293]

These penances are always given to those monks who marry and afterward separate from their illicit and adulterous marriage, according to the often mentioned Canon 6 of Basil. But if they persist in their wickedness

---

[293]   "'Marriage is good,' you say; I also agree to this. For 'marriage,' we read, 'is honorable and the bed undefiled; but fornicators and adulterers God will judge'; but it is no longer possible for you to observe the right conditions of marriage. For if he who has been joined to a heavenly Bridegroom deserts Him, and joins himself to a wife, the act is adultery, even if you call it marriage ten thousand times over; or rather, it is worse than adultery, in proportion as God is greater than man" (*An Exhortation to Theodore After His Fall*; SC 117, p. 60).

and do not wish to separate and be corrected, Basil the Great orders that
no one open the door of their home to receive such people, even if it is
cold outside and they are seeking to come inside for warmth and shelter.[294]
But this is to be done, not out of hatred, but that they may be shamed and
corrected, as Paul says. And in his letter to a fallen monk, he says not to
even greet them. The same things are said by St. Nikephoros in his 24th
Canon, and in his 33rd Canon he further adds that a monk who marries
and does not repent is to be anathematized and forced to wear his schema
and be shut up within a monastery. The Imperial Laws are also in agreement
with St. Nikephoros. Therefore the 7th and 8th *Novel* of the Emperor Leo
orders that those monks who remove their schema and become like laymen
are to be forced to wear their former schema.

The same penances which we have said are given to monks who marry
are also given to nuns who marry. Whatever men violate them and take
them as their wives are disciplined by the sacred Canons and the Imperial
Laws. For Canon 4 of the Sixth Ecumenical Council deposes those clergy,
and excommunicates those laymen, who violate a woman consecrated to
God. And Ordinance 2 of Title 1 of the *Novels* orders that those who violate
a hermitess or a nun, and those who assisted in the offense, are to be
penalized with fines, and all of their possessions are to be taken by the ruler
and given to the monastery of the violated nun.[295] Likewise, anyone who
takes or attempts to take a nun for his wife is also penalized with fines, as
is ordered by Book I of the *Codex*, Title 3, Ordinance 5, and the nun who
goes with him is put into a monastery, along with her belongings, and shut
in securely. Book IV, Title 3, of Armenopoulos further says that those who
fornicate with nuns, and also the nuns themselves, are to have their noses
cut off.

---

294   *Regulæ Fusius* 14, PG 31, 949C-952A.
295   From Photios, *Nomocanon*, Title 9, ch. 30.

I

Concerning the Monastic Schema and Monastic Apparel

The monastic schema or habit, from above and from the beginning, was only one, the great schema, and as many as became monks after the customary novitiate were made monks but once, and not two or three times, and monks of the great schema at that.[296] For this reason St. Theodore the Studite, being of the same mind as the Canons, commands the abbot in his *Testament* saying: "You are not to give someone the so-called small schema (that is, *staurophoros*) and then the great one, for the schema is one, just as baptism is one, and just as the Holy Fathers practiced."[297] Even if some bring forth the prayer which is found printed together with the *Catecheses* of St. Theodore which says that the composer of that prayer received the small schema and then the great one, and insist that it is a composition of St. Theodore, we reply that they wrongly deduce this, for it is not a work of St. Theodore, but of a certain Theodosios, as is apparent from the prayer having been put together from many sources. And the great illuminator of Thessaloniki, Gregory Palamas, writing a letter to the hieromonk Paul of Asanes also says: "This is the great and only schema, for the Fathers did not know of a small schema, but some newer people thought that the schema was divided into two. But through investigating the questions and answers in the services of both the small and great schema, one schema has again been reestablished."

The sacred Symeon of Thessaloniki in agreement with them says that: "Just as baptism is only one, so is the monastic schema one, for the small schema is the promise (engagement) and precursor of the great schema, and it was invented by some later Fathers on account of the weakness (or

---

296   Canon 15 of the so-called First-and-Second Council designates that whoever wishes to become a monk must be a novice for three years, with the exception of one who is ill or in the case of someone who lived in the world as a solitary and led a virtuous life. In such cases, the novitiate may only be six months.
297   PG 99, 1820C.

ignorance) of man."[298] And both the *Euchologion* (Priest's Service Book) and Balsamon[299] also call the small schema an engagement and the promise of the great schema. And Job, called the Sinner, also sets forth a third schema, saying: "The monastic schema progresses from lowest to highest: from the small schema (called *rasoforos*) to the holy schema of tonsure, and from this to the angelic or great schema."[300] Note here that he is the only one who calls the small schema *rasophoros*, for all the others call the small schema *staurophoros*. Also, the *Euchologion* has three services of the monastic schema: for the *rasophoros*, for the small schema, and for the great schema.

Having said these things, as many as become *rasophoroi* are no longer able to cast off their robes and get married. God forbid! How can they dare such a thing, having been tonsured, which tonsure declares that they have removed from their head every worldly thought and consecrated their life to God? How? When they have by a blessing donned monastic robes and put on the monastic hat, and had their name changed, and had two prayers read over them by the priest, in which prayers the priest thanks God for having redeemed them from the secular life and called them to the solitary vocation of monasticism, and in which prayers God is asked to receive them into His salvific yoke? And if the person who merely promised to become a monk, without even having donned the monastic robe through a blessing, must not break his promise (as we said in Chapter 9 of Part 1), how much more is the person who wears the monastic robes by a blessing not to break his promise? For this reason Balsamon also says that the one wearing the monastic robe cannot any longer be a layman, but must be encouraged to fulfill his initial goal and become a perfect monk.[301] And if he does not want to, he is subject to discipline, as the laws decree in Title 1 of Book IV (of the *Basilics*).

As many as are of the small schema, that is, *staurophoroi*, are also found between a rock and a hard place, for on the one hand they are required to keep the lifestyle and strictness of those of the great schema because they

---

298   *Dialogus Contra Hæreses*, ch. 20, PG 155, 104C-104D.

299   Explanation of Canon 2 of the Council in Hagia Sophia, PG 137, 1090D-1092B.

300   In *On the Mysteries*, from the *Syntagmation* of Chrysanthos of Jerusalem.

301   Explanation of Canon 5 of the First-and-Second Council, PG 137, 1032A-1032C.

made the same exact vows to God as did those of the great schema,[302] as Gregory Palamas said above, and because they also were adorned with the same monastic vestments (minus a few) by God, and they were also deemed worthy of the same prayers (except three). Therefore they must not "make excuse with excuses in sins" (Ps. 140:4) saying that they are not of the great schema and for this reason they are not required to live the strict life of monks. This is a deception of the devil. On the other hand, they are also required to strive for the great and perfect schema, that is, to become great-schema monks, and not to be negligent in this by putting it off. They should rather be fearful that death may soon come to them, and then they would be found incomplete, and not perfect, monks before God. For just as engagement is incomplete when compared to marriage, so the small schema of *staurophoroi*, being a promise, is incomplete when compared to the great schema. Therefore it follows that those of the small schema are incomplete monks. For this reason the sacred Symeon of Thessaloniki also declares that: "As many as are incomplete with regard to the schema must become complete so that they do not die imperfect, not having undergone the perfecting rite of the schema... and just as the person who is not baptized is not a Christian, so the one who has not been perfected with regard to the schema (that is, not having become a great-schema monk) is not a monk."

So then, what kind of ignorance is this, when small-schema monks are required to keep the strict lifestyle and perform the works of a great-schema monk through the vows they make to God, and then not to become great-schema monks? Are they merely to endure such labors and be deprived of that grace? Are they to grow old in their monastic life never having become monks? Are they to fight in this arena and in this struggle and then be unworthy to receive the crown? Is there any greater harm to be found than

---

302   Translator's note: The vows of obedience, chastity, and poverty. For a detailed discussion of the questions, answers, and vows taken during the service of the monastic tonsure, both of the small and great schema, see Archimandrite Sophrony, "Principles of Orthodox Asceticism," *The Orthodox Ethos*, vol. 1, Oxford, 1964, pp. 259-286 (this is an abridged treatment of Part 1 (pp. 13-106) of Elder Sophrony's book, *Askesis kai Theoria (Ascesis and Contemplation)*, Essex, 1996 (in Greek)).

this? Or is there anything more ridiculous than for someone to pass thirty-
five years as a small-schema monk, and then, when about to receive the
great schema, for him to be asked: "Why have you come, brother?" and
then for him to reply: "Out of desire for the ascetical life, honorable Father,"
that is, for him to be dressed as a layman, to be questioned as a layman,
and for him to reply as a layman? If someone were to ask today's small-
schema monks why they are not great-schema monks, some would reply,
because the great schema is fearful and angelic; some would reply that they
are waiting for their later years to come in order to take the great schema,
while still others, finding another excuse on account of their negligence,
abdicate and never take the great schema. On account of these foolish
reasons, therefore, out of the thousands of monks to be found in the world,
few die as great-schema monks, and these received the great schema either
because they had aged greatly, or because they were severely ill and in
danger of dying, or because they were compelled on account of some other
circumstance. Rarely have healthy and young monks received the great
schema with all of their will and without some necessary circumstance.
The rest die as small-schema monks, that is, as incomplete monks only
"engaged" to Christ, and not married. Because of this they resemble those
Christians of old who found excuses and postponed their baptism, on
account of which many of them died still as catechumens and unbaptized.
This is why Basil the Great, Gregory the Theologian, Gregory of Nyssa,
and the rest of the divine Fathers spoke so much about baptism, exhorting
and encouraging them not to postpone their baptism, but to be baptized
when young and healthy, in order to be strengthened by and cultivate the
grace which they received.

These exhortative words are also necessary for someone to say today,
in order to encourage today's monks to receive the second baptism, which
is the great and perfect schema. We, however, will not expend too many
words, but will say only these few and general words to them. As many as
have renounced the world and have entered the solitary life, even if under
compulsion, must sooner or later and without fail receive the great and
perfect schema, because if they do not, they are not monks, as was proven
above, for the schema is one, as baptism is one, and this oneness determines

and constitutes and completes the great schema, the true schema, as this also has been proven. Therefore it is more exact and more correct and better for monks to become great-schema monks one time, without first becoming small-schema monks, even if the authorities do this. Once because, by this one and only time, the schema of monks is shown in fact to be one and singular, just as the Tradition of the Holy Fathers intends. And also because when the young and healthy receive the schema, they are to cultivate the grace they received and multiply and increase the talent of their Lord, namely, the spiritual strength which the divine schema mystically granted their soul,[303] through struggles against the demons, through conquering the passions, and through the charismata which they will receive from the Holy Spirit. Even if someone brings up that Athanasios of Athos and Dounale the Confessor and others first received the small schema and then the great one at different times, we reply that exceptions are not to become a law of the Church, according to Gregory the Theologian,[304] and that which is contrary to the Canons cannot be taken as a standard. For, those who later become great-schema monks repeat the questions and answers, and the prayers, and the putting-on of the schema, and they appear to duplicate the singular monastic schema, which is nearly as absurd as someone repeating the One Holy Baptism.

The garments of the schema are as follows. Those of the small schema, that is, of the *staurophoroi*, are four. The tunic, also called the *zostikon rason* or inner cassock (*esorason*), represents the tunic of gladness and righteousness which the monk puts on, according to Symeon of Thessaloniki[305] and the *Euchologion*. The leather belt, or girdle, which girds the torso and the loins,

---

303   See Book I of the *Evergetinos, Hypothesis 31*, p. 184, for there you will find that a great and clairvoyant elder declared and said "that the power of Grace which he saw, during a Baptism, near at hand to the person being Baptized, he *also* saw at the time that a monk was receiving the angelic *schema*" (tr. *The Evergetinos: A Complete Text*, Etna, 1998, vol. III, book 1, p. 105). Further, see also in this same *Hypothesis, From the Life of St. Alypios*, that, according to the vision of the mother of St. Alypios, the one who does not desire the monastic schema (especially the great one) is not worthy to be in the company of monks in the heavenly glory, even if they struggle in the same fashion as monks (*ibid.*, pp. 103-105).

304   "That which is rare is not the law of the Church" (*Oratio* 39, 14, PG 36, 352B).

305   *De Poenitentia*, ch. 273, PG 155, 497B.

where the appetitive aspect of the person is, represents the mortification
of the carnal lusts, and chastity, and self-control, and that the monk is ready
to perform his service, according to the *Euchologion*, Symeon of Thessaloniki,[306]
Cyril of Jerusalem,[307] Dorotheos,[308] and Sozomen.[309] The pallium, which
is a Latin word meaning garment or cloak, as Symeon of Thessaloniki and
Abba Isaac[310] call it, and Skrevellios, in his lexicon, interprets pallium to
mean cloak or upper-garment. Today, this is the so-called upper or outer
cassock (*exorason*): 1) because the pallium is a garment, as we said, and the
outer cassock or *exorason* is also a garment, specifically, a monastic outer
garment; 2) because the outer cassock can also be called a mantle, and
therefore the schema of the *staurophoros* is also called the schema of the
mantle in the *Euchologion*, and many call the outer cassock a *mandorason*; and
3) because the *exorason* is worn like a smaller and second mantle by the
staurophoroi and the great-schema monks (under their larger mantle), it is
more appropriate to call it a paramantle (note: that undersized square cloth
which is today called a paramantle by the unlearned and which is worn
over both shoulders, for which reason I truly wonder what person invented
this and placed it among the monastic garments fixed by the Fathers. This
garment, I say, is not only not a paramantle according to its name, but

---

306   *Ibid.*, 497D.

307   This explanation and the following concerning the garments of monks were found in a
manuscript collection ascribed to Cyril of Jerusalem.

308   "Our schema consists of a *kolovion* (a sleeveless garment), a leather belt, a scapular, and a
cowl. Each one of these is a symbol, and it will profit us to learn what they symbolize... We also have
a belt, and why do we wear it? The belt which we wear is a symbol first of all that we are ready for
work... Again, as the belt is made from a dead body, so should we be dead to our lusts. The belt is
worn around the loins, in which area it is said the appetitive aspect of the soul lies" (*Doctrina I, De
Renuntiatione*, 12; 13, PG 88, 1632C; 1633B).

309   "It is said that the peculiar vestments of these Egyptian monks had reference to some
secret connected with their philosophy, and did not differ from those of others without some
adequate cause. They wore their tunics without sleeves, in order to teach that the hands ought not to
be ready to do presumptuous evil. They wore a covering on their heads called a cowl, to show that
they ought to live with the same innocence and purity as infants who are nourished with milk, and
who wear a covering of the same form. Their girdle, and a species of scarf, which they wear across
the loins, shoulders, and arms, admonish them that they ought to be always ready in the service and
work of God" (*Historia Ecclesiastica* 3, 14, PG 67, 1069C-1072A; tr. NPNF (V2-02) p. 292).

310   "Wrap your head in your cloak" (*Ascetical Homilies*, Homily 50, p. 241).

neither is it a garment at all). So, the priests, having learned this information, when they tonsure a monk, they are to bless the outer cassock, the *exorason*, instead of that undersized square cloth, and give the *exorason* to the monk to wear as a pallium, in order that when the *exorason* is given to the monk it is not ridiculously given without a blessing. If, however, someone out of habit also wishes to wear that undersized square cloth over their inner cassock, as a symbol of his carrying the Cross, let him wear it without it being blessed, just as he wears the monastic hat and the hat cover, which are also not blessed, and this does not seem to me improper. The pallium or *exorason* represents the garment of incorruption, and modesty, and the divine protection and covering, according to the *Euchologion* and Symeon of Thessaloniki.[311] There are also the sandals or shoes worn by the monk which represent that the monk is to be prepared to tread the way of the Gospel of peace without stumbling, and that, just as the shoes are subject to and below the rest of the body, so also the body of the monk is to be subject to the soul, according to the *Euchologion*, Symeon of Thessaloniki,[312] and Cyril of Jerusalem.

Such are the garments of the *staurophoros*. The great-schema monk, in addition to the garments already mentioned, has three more: the cowl, or hood, the scapular, and the mantle.[313] The cowl represents the helmet of salvation, according to the *Euchologion*; the overshadowing of divine grace and the putting off of worldly cares, according to Symeon of Thessaloniki[314]

---

311   *De Poenitentia*, ch. 273, PG 155, 497B.

312   *Ibid.*, 497D-500A.

313   The garments of monks are always black in color for two reasons: 1) so that, seeing these black garments, they may weep and mourn like those who wear black when they mourn the dead. For which reason John of the Ladder says the following to every monk: "Let your very dress urge you to the work of mourning, because all who lament the dead are dressed in black" (Step 7, PG 88, 805B-805C; tr. *The Ladder*, p. 73). 2) So that they may live solitarily and have their senses and their intellect gathered into themselves, just as black gathers light into itself, as Pachymeres said in his paraphrase of St. Dionysios the Areopagite: "The monastic order lives solitarily, for this is what the black vesture represents" (PG 3, 548A). Not only black garments are appropriate to monks, but any dark or dusky colored ones as well, which are neither very dark, nor very light, but a composite of the two, like light brown for example, as the divine Chrysostom said: "Chastity is not found in darkly colored robes" (*De Virginitate* 7, PG 48, 537). Zosimos the Historian also says the same thing.

314   *De Poenitentia*, ch. 273, PG 155, 497B-497C.

and Cyril of Jerusalem; and innocence and humility, according to Sozomen and Abba Dorotheos.[315] The scapular, called "a species of scarf" by Sozomen, and which is to be made of leather, according to Symeon of Thessaloniki, is today called a *polystaurion*, which represents that the monk takes up the Cross of the Lord and follows Him, according to the *Euchologion*, Symeon,[316] and Dorotheos,[317] because it also has a cross on the front and the back, representing, according to Cyril of Jerusalem, that the world is crucified to the monk through his withdrawal from it, and that the monk is crucified to the world through his detachment from it, according to the saying of St. Paul: "The world is crucified unto me, and I unto the world" (Gal. 6:14). The mantle (which Sozomen calls a sleeveless tunic and which Dorotheos calls a *kolovion*), because it envelops all of the other garments, represents, according to Symeon of Thessaloniki, that the monk is wrapped up in his mantle as if in a grave.[318] According to Sozomen and Abba Dorotheos,[319] the mantle, not having sleeves, represents that the monk is not to raise his hand against anyone or practice anything of the old man. The length of the mantle, according to Cyril of Jerusalem, represents the wings of the angels, the monastic schema also being called the angelic schema. The mantle also had a red or purple marking, as Abba Dorotheos

---

315   "We also wear a cowl or hood: this is a symbol of humility. For little babies who are innocent, not full-grown men, wear a cowl. We wear it for this reason: that we may be as little ones in malice" (*Doctrina I, De Renuntiatione* 13, PG 88, 1633C-1633D).

316   *De Poenitentia*, ch. 273, PG 155, 497C-497D.

317   "We also have a scapular, and the scapular is placed over our shoulders crosswise: this signifies a cross on our shoulders... What is the cross, but the perfect mortification set up through our faith in Christ... It means that one is to die to all the things of this world. He has given up parents, possessions, riches, all that a man can give up to take up the contest; let him also renounce self-will and the desire for these things. This is what we mean by perfect renunciation" (*Doctrina I, De Renuntiatione* 13, PG 88, 1633B-1633C).

318   *Responsa ad Gabrielem Pentapolitanum*, Question, 60, PG 155, 916A.

319   "Why do we wear a *kolovion* which does not have sleeves, while others wear sleeves? Sleeves symbolize hands. Hands are given to do things with. When the thought occurs to do something suited to the 'old' man—for example, to steal, or to strike someone—or simply to commit anything sinful with our hands, we ought to pay attention to our schema and learn that we have no sleeves, that is, we have no hands to do something of the 'old' man" (*Doctrina I, De Renuntiatione* 12, PG 88, 1632C).

says,[320] by which mark monks understood that they were soldiers of the heavenly King. Such are the true and designated garments of monks, which are also worn by virgins and hermits. The monastic hat (*kamilaukion*) and hat covering (*epanokamilaukion*) do not have separate prayers designated for them, so some recite the prayer and blessing of the cowl for them, because these have been devised to replace the cowl by more recent people. Those great-schema monks from among us Grecians should wear the mantle, if not always, then at least during the *synaxis*, or Church gatherings, and during the Divine Liturgy, just as it is worn by the great-schema monks from among the pious Russians and Romanians, being that the mantle is the most characteristic garment of great-schema monks. But we (barring a few) have changed the order, being satisfied with just the outer cassock or *exorason*, as we have said, which should not have been done and is incorrect.

Having said these things, we also add as an afterthought that every Christian has the permission to choose the monastic life and to wear the monastic schema, no matter what sin they may have committed and no matter if they live in the world, and no one can prevent them from this choice, as Canon 43 of the Sixth Ecumenical Council orders. We added this on account of some unlearned Spiritual Fathers who prevent those people who have committed murders and performed magic and other grave sins from becoming monks. Furthermore, such sinners, and indeed everyone, in order to become monks, must undergo the three year canonical novitiate and be supervised by a sponsor and a virtuous and godly elder, according to Canons 2 and 5 of the First-and-Second Council.

---

320   "Our *kolovion* also has a purple mark, and what does this mark signify? Anyone fighting for a king has purple in his mantle. For because a king wears purple, all those who fight for him put purple on their mantle; this is the royal garment which shows they are the king's men and that they fight for him. So we put the purple mark on our *kolovion*, showing that we fight for Christ, and that we are obliged to endure for Him all the sufferings He endured for us. For when our Master was suffering for us He wore a purple garment; first as king, for He is King of kings and Lord of lords, and then because He was mocked by impious soldiers. Therefore, also having purple for a sign, we promise, as I said, to endure all that He suffered... So also we ought to contend, neglecting worldly affairs, and to be occupied with God alone" (*ibid.*, 1632D-1633A).

J

Monks and Hieromonks Are to Reside in Their Monasteries and They Should Not Be in the World Involved in Ecclesiastical and Political Affairs

Canon 4 of the Holy Fourth Ecumenical Council states the following: "Let them who truly and without any hypocrisy enter upon monastic life be accorded due honor. But inasmuch as some use the monastic schema as a pretext and lure to get themselves honored and to disturb ecclesiastical and civil affairs by wanting to meddle in them, and by carelessly going about the cities neglecting their duties and even undertaking to build themselves monasteries, it has seemed reasonable that no monk, either in a village, or in a city, or in the desert, or in any other place, shall be allowed to build and establish a monastery or a prayer house without the approval of the local bishop; and that monks in every city and country be subject to the local bishop, and that they are to practice stillness, and pay heed only to fasting and prayer, remaining in the monasteries wherein they were tonsured, without leaving them and meddling in ecclesiastical and political affairs, unless as a matter of need and necessity they be appointed to do so by the bishop, after he has judged them to be fit for such an undertaking... Anyone that violates this Canon shall be excommunicated, in order that the monastic order be not blasphemed, and on their account the name of God also be blasphemed."[321]

Therefore, Peter the Archivist, following this sacred Canon, says that monks should not be sponsors for children undergoing Holy Baptism (except in the case of great need, such as if an infant is in danger of dying and no other sponsor is available), nor should they become adopted brothers, nor should they be sponsors for weddings, for these are against the Canons.[322] And Nikephoros the Archivist says that the Church authoritatively commands

---

321   Translator's note: St. Nikodemos does not quote the original wording of the Canon here, but for the sake of the reader of his day, he quotes his Modern Greek *Interpretation* of the Canon from the *Pedalion* (pp. 188-189; *The Rudder*, pp. 248-250).

322   *Juris Graeco-romanorum*, p. 416.

the abbots and exarchs of monasteries not to allow monks to take part in co-parentage or to enter into any compact of brotherhood, for the law, at any rate, does not allow these brotherhoods at all.[323]

So it follows, according to the above mentioned Canon, that so-called hieromonks should not be ordained in or be assigned to parishes in the world, for they are also monks according to their name and have professed to be chaste, as we said before in *Subject I*, and so they should be ordained in monasteries and practice their priesthood there, and not in the world in the Church parishes. This is also confirmed by Michael of Constantinople, called the Sovereign of Philosophers, who decreed, together with the entire Synod of holy hierarchs about him, that all of the sacred rites which are celebrated in the world must be performed by married priests in the world, and not by hieromonks, and that hieromonks are to remain in their monasteries, as Balsamon says.[324]

Peter the Archivist of the Great Church also says that a hieromonk cannot even bless a marriage, even within a monastery.[325]

Therefore, those hierarchs who ordain hieromonks in the cities are acting contrary to the Canons, and so they should correct this impropriety. For, as many bad things and sins which these hieromonks do on account of being in the world, and partaking of the desires of the world, those hierarchs who ordain them will be punished for all these things and will have to give an account, for this is what the divine Chrysostom says: "Do not say to me, 'the presbyter sinned,' or 'the deacon sinned.' The guilt of all these comes perforce upon the head of those who ordained them."[326]

But, if there is a need and a necessity, a hierarch has the permission, according to the summary of the above divine Canon, to choose the more virtuous and prudent hieromonks from the monasteries and assign them as Spiritual Fathers to the Church parishes, or assign them as teachers in the schools, or also have them as part of the synod and family of his Metropolis, unto the profit and benefit of the people.

---

323   *Ibid.*, p. 366.
324   Commentary on ch. 3 of Title 1 of the *Nomocanon* of Photios.
325   *Juris Graeco-romanorum*, p. 419.
326   *On Acts*, Homily 3, 4, PG 60, 40.

St. Nicodemos
the Hagiorite

Let the
Jesus
Prayer
be your
breath

PART THREE

Counsel for the Penitent

Repent ye: for the kingdom of heaven is at hand

Matthew 3:2

TO THE BRETHREN IN CHRIST: GREETING

Just as God, on the level of nature, not only provided that we be born into life healthy, but also further provided that we receive again our health when we become physically ill through baths and various treatments, so likewise on the level of grace, God not only provided that we be spiritually reborn healthy through Holy Baptism, but also provided that we reclaim again our spiritual health when we become spiritually ill with a cathartic bath and a wondrous treatment, and this is nothing other than the Mystery of Sacred Confession.

For on the one hand, confession is truly a bath through which, as many souls as are washed, immediately come out relieved from the weight of sin which they bear, which souls Solomon mystically alludes to in the Song of Songs: "As flocks of shorn sheep, that have gone up from the washing" (S. of S. 4:2). Therefore, in explaining this passage, Theodoret says: "One must see in the flock of sheep those who approach repentance from sin;"[327] and Michael Psellos says: "They are those whose conscience has been cleansed by washing."[328] It is a bath in which all the stains of our trespasses are washed away and disappear, according to the divine Chrysostom: "The confession of those who have sinned brings about the disappearance of their trespasses."[329] And it is a bath which is a second baptism for penitents, more laborious than the first baptism, and just as necessary for salvation as the first baptism, according to Gregory the Theologian: "Yes, and I know of a fifth (baptism) also, which is that of tears, and is much more laborious."[330]

---

327   *In Canticum Canticorum* 2, 4, PG 81, 129A.

328   *In Canticum Canticorum*, PG 122, 609D.

329   *On Genesis*, Homily 20, 2, PG 53, 170.

330   *Oratio* 39, 17, PG 36, 356A; tr. NPNF (V2-07), p. 358.

Translator's note: St. John of the Ladder says: "Repentance is the renewal of baptism" (Step 5, PG 88, 764B; tr. *The Ladder*, p. 54). And elsewhere he says: "Greater than baptism itself is the fountain of

But on the other hand, confession is such a potent treatment that it immediately neutralizes every poison of pardonable and mortal sin, which is an infinite evil, and causes every invisible illness to disappear, restoring to the soul its initial health and grace. It is such a wondrous treatment that it instantly changes the sinner into a beautiful angel from that which it was before, having been transformed through sin into an ox, like Nebuchadnezzar (Dan. 4:33), or into a pig, like Tiridates,[331] or into a devil, like Judas: "And one of you is a devil" (Jn. 6:70). In brief, it is a treatment which changes the sinner from convicted to free, from carnal to spiritual, from a slave of the devil to a son of God, and from liable to eternal hell to an inheritor of the heavenly kingdom. And it is a treatment which, on account of the supranatural results that it brings about, surpasses all of the works of nature, because the justification which it grants to the soul of the sinner so many times over is incomparably greater than if God wanted to create another new universe. For Sirach also hinted at this saying: "No balance can weigh the value of a chaste soul" (Sir. 26:15).

But, O what grief! This cathartic bath and this wondrous treatment, I mean, confession which is most profitable to the soul, has become today to Christians most unprofitable, thinking that they are cleansed in this bath, even if they have not bathed, according to Solomon: "There is a generation that are pure in their own eyes, and yet is not washed from their filthiness" (Pr. 30:12).

For some of them either do not confess at all, or confess very rarely, those wretched ones preferring rather to roll around in the muck of their sin like the animals than to run to the bath of confession and be cleansed. And still others do not confess as they should, neither performing the necessary examination of their conscience and of their sins, nor confessing with the necessary contrition and compunction, nor with the resolve not

---

tears after baptism, even though it is somewhat audacious to say so. For baptism is the washing away of evils that were in us before, but sins committed after baptism are washed away by tears. As baptism is received in infancy, we have all defiled it, but we cleanse it anew with tears. And if God in His love for mankind had not given us tears, those being saved would be few indeed and hard to find" (Step 7, PG 88, 804A-804B; tr. *The Ladder*, p. 71).

331   Translator's note: Tiridates III, King of Armenia (286-344 A.D.). See the *Life* of St. Gregory the Wonderworker, November 17.

to sin again, nor having fulfilled their rule, all of which are elements of a confession pleasing to God. Rather, they confess unexamined and unprepared, with no compunction, with no resolve, not having fulfilled their rule, and simply, they confess out of routine only, when it happens that Pascha, or Christmas, or Theophany is approaching. Therefore, in this fashion those unfortunate Christians confess wrongly and they think that they have confessed well, mocking the truth and being greatly harmed.

We then, being greatly saddened on account of the great harm and delusion of our brother Christians, took great pains to gather together from various teachers the present concise counsel for the penitent, and with it to motivate unconfessed sinners to confess frequently; to explain to those who confess wrongly how they should confess, so that their confession may be God-pleasing and beneficial, and in turn, that the forgiveness of their sins from God through the Spiritual Father may be certain and without question.

So then, my fellow sinners, I ask that you receive this counsel with joy, and as many of you as have stained your souls like I have through the various pollutions of sin, run to the cathartic bath of Sacred Confession in order to be cleansed: "Wash you, make you clean," God commands you through the Prophet Isaiah, "put away the evil of your doings from your souls" (Is. 1:16). As many of you who have spiritual wounds in your soul and "your wounds stink and are corrupt because of your foolishness" (cf. Ps. 37:5) according to David, run to that wondrous treatment in order to be healed. And as many of you who have confessed wrongly up until now, attend to your soul for the love of God, and confess from now on and forevermore correctly and properly.

Receiving this beneficial counsel, I fervently ask you to make a small supplication to God for those souls which labored and worked together for this, and also for that soul which published and printed this counsel, unto your common benefit.

Farewell!

ὁ ἅγιος Ἰωάννης ὁ
πρόδρομος βαπτίζων τῶ
ἐβραίνε :—

EPIGRAM

For The

PRESENT COUNSEL

Naaman having washed seven times in the streams of Jordan,
Was cleansed of his grievous leprosy.

One is washed anew of every evil in the depth of repentance,
And thus is cleansed from the defilements of diabolic assaults.

Therefore the purpose of the Jordan was repentance,
In which John washed the offenses of the crowds.

The return of the prodigal son

The compassionate father

Confess your faults to one another (Jas. 5:16)

CHAPTER 1

How Everyone Should
Prepare Before Confession

1. What is repentance?

My brother sinner, this is the preparation you must undergo before you repent and go to confession. Know firstly that repentance, according to St. John of Damaskos, is a returning from the devil to God, which comes about through pain and ascesis.[332] So you also, my beloved, if you wish to repent properly, must depart from the devil and from diabolical works and return to God and to the life proper to God. You must forsake sin, which is against nature, and return to virtue, which is according to nature. You must hate wickedness so much, that you say along with David: "Unrighteousness have I hated and abhorred" (Ps. 118:163), and instead, you must love the good and the commandments of the Lord so much, that you also say along with David: "But Thy law have I loved" (ibid.), and again: "Therefore have I loved Thy commandments more than gold and topaz" (Ps. 118:127). In brief, the Holy Spirit informs you through the wise Sirach what in fact true repentance is, saying: "Turn to the Lord and forsake your sins... Return to the Most High, and turn away from iniquity, and hate abominations intensely" (Sir. 17:25-26).[333]

---

332   "Repentance is the returning from that which is against nature to that which is according to nature, from the devil to God, through ascesis and agony" (*De Fide Orthodoxa* 2, 30, PG 94, 976A).

333   Concerning true repentance, see the *Homily on Repentance* at the end of this book.

2. The aspects of repentance

Know secondly that the aspects of repentance are three: contrition, confession, and satisfaction.[334]

3. Contrition

Contrition is sorrow and perfect pain of heart,[335] which comes about in a person who, on account of the sins committed, disappointed God and transgressed His divine Law. This contrition comes only to the perfect and those who are sons of God, because it only proceeds from the love for God, just as a son repents simply because he disappointed his father, and not because he was deprived of his inheritance or because he will be ousted from his father's house. Concerning this the divine Chrysostom says: "Groan after you have sinned, not because you are to be punished (for this is nothing), but because you have offended your Master, one so gentle, one so kind, one Who loves you so much and longs for your salvation as to have given even His Son for you. On account of this, groan."[336]

4. Affliction

Related to contrition is affliction, which is also a sorrow and imperfect pain of heart, which comes about, not because a person disappointed God

---

334   George Koressios, writing about the Mysteries, adds a fourth aspect of repentance, the loosing of sin (also called "keys"), which happens by the grace of the Holy Spirit through the mediation of the Spiritual Father, and which, he says, especially defines the Mystery of Repentance (from his *Theology*).

335   This grief does not only consist of its sensible manifestations, like groans and tears, but it mainly consists of the interior will of man hating sin and in wishing that sin never occurred, and the resolve to never commit sin again. And note this also, that this grief and contrition of the heart, according to Koressios, is an element of repentance and, as long as it is found in the heart, a person is in the state of repentance. But as soon as grief leaves the heart, so also does a person leave from the state of repentance, which means that grief and contrition must be present in the heart of the penitent perpetually, for in this way is his repentance true. Concerning this grief, see more on it in the *Homily on Repentance* at the end of this book.

336   *On II Corinthians*, Homily 4, 6, PG 61, 426.

by his sins, but because that person was deprived of divine grace, lost Paradise, and gained hell. This affliction belongs to the imperfect, that is, to the hired hands and slaves, because it proceeds not out of love for God, but out of fear and out of love for themselves, just as a hired hand repents on account of losing his wage and a slave repents because he fears the disciplines of his master.[337]

So you also, my brother sinner, if you wish to acquire this contrition and affliction in your heart, and through these for your repentance to be pleasing to God, you must do the following.

5. Confess to an experienced Spiritual Father

First, search around and learn who is the most experienced Spiritual Father, because Basil the Great says, just as people do not show their maladies and bodily wounds to just any physician, but to experienced physicians who know how to treat them, so also sins must be revealed, not to just anyone, but to those who are able to heal them: "The same fashion should be observed in the confession of sins as in the showing of bodily diseases. As then men reveal the diseases of the body not to all or to chance comers but to those who are experienced in their treatment; so also the confession of sins ought to take place in the presence of those who are able to treat them, as it is written: 'Ye that are strong bear the infirmities of the weak' (Rom. 15:1)—that is, take them away by your care."[338]

6. How one is to examine his conscience

Second, just as you would sit down and count your money after a certain business transaction, in like manner go to a particular place, my brother, and two or three weeks before going to the Spiritual Father you found,

---

337   Some teachers divide the sorrow and the grief which a sinner has on account of his sins into three parts: the grief he has before confession, which they call infliction, or reproach (προσ-τριβή); the grief he has during confession, which they call contrition (συν-τριβή); and the grief which he has after confession, which they call affliction (ἐπι-τριβή).

338   *Regulæ Brevius* 229, PG 31, 1236A; tr. *Ascetic Works of Saint Basil*, pp. 313-314.

especially at the beginning of the four fast periods of the year,[339] sit down in that place of quietude and, bowing your head, examine your conscience, which Philo the Jew calls: "The testing of the conscience," and become: "Not a defender, but a judge of your sins," according to the divine Augustine. Consider, like Hezekiah, the whole span of your life in sorrow and bitterness of soul: "I will ponder all my years in the bitterness of my soul" (Is. 38:15). Consider also how many sins you committed in deed, word, and by coupling with thoughts[340] after you last confessed, counting the months, weeks, and days. Remember the people with whom you sinned and the places where you sinned, and diligently reflect upon these things in order to find every one of your sins. This is how the wise Sirach counsels you from one side saying: "Before judgment, examine yourself" (Sir. 18:20), and from the other, Gregory the Theologian says: "Examine yourself more than your neighbor. Account of actions is superior to an account of money. For money is subject to corruption, but actions remain."[341]

---

339   My Christian brethren, do not wait until the last moment to confess and go to your Spiritual Father when the days you wish to commune are very near, but go many days in advance. And certainly during the four fast periods of the year, as soon as they begin, go to confession with leisure and when you have time, so you may be properly corrected. One or two days before you are to commune, go to your Spiritual Father so that he may read a prayer of forgiveness over you on account of the pardonable sins which you committed between the time of your confession and your reception of Communion, and so receive in this manner, according to this good custom which is followed by the monks of the Holy Mountain.

340   Because the people of today either find it burdensome to carry out this light examination of their conscience, or on account of forgetfulness they are unable to remember their sins, see the pertinent areas of Part 1 of this book, *Instruction to the Spiritual Father*, which we have prepared for you, brother, in particular, Chapter 3, *Concerning Mortal Sins, Pardonable Sins, and Sins of Omission*, and Chapter 4, *Concerning the Ten Commandments*, where we explain who errs in these commandments, in order to lighten your conscience by helping you easily remember your sins. So, look there and examine your conscience and bring to mind the sins you have committed according to what is said there in order to confess them. Read also Chapter 6, *Concerning Thoughts*, in order to learn from there that you must also confess your bad thoughts, if not all of your thoughts, and certainly those thoughts which disturb you and assault you the most, because just as the eggs of birds when they are hidden in dung are enlivened and hatch chicks, so also bad thoughts, when they are not revealed to a Spiritual Father, are vivified and become deeds, according to John of the Ladder: "As hens' eggs that are warmed in dung hatch out, so thoughts that are not confessed hatch out and proceed to action" (Step 26, PG 88, 1085C; tr. *The Ladder*, p. 193).

341   *Carmina Moralia* 33, PG 37, 932A.

And just as hunters are not satisfied with merely finding a beast in the forest, but attempt through every means to also kill it, likewise, my brother sinner, you should also not be satisfied with merely examining your conscience and with finding your sins, for this profits you little, but struggle by every means to kill your sins through the grief in your heart, namely, through contrition and affliction. And in order to acquire contrition, consider how much you have wronged God through your sins. In order to also acquire affliction, consider how much you have wronged yourself through your sins.

7. Sin wrongs God in three ways

Consider first how your sins have wronged God. 1) By your sins you offended and dishonored the Most High and Great God – you who are but a worm have offended and dishonored the Almighty One; you who are but clay have offended and dishonored the Maker of all; you who are nothing have offended and dishonored the Infinite Being – because you transgressed His law: "Through breaking the law thou dishonourest God" (Rom. 2:23).

2) By your sins you have shown yourself to be a thankless slave and son to such an all-good Master and to your most-affectionate Father, Who loved you before the ages, not on account of some worthiness of your own, but only on account of His goodness did He decide in His divine mind to create you, when He could have created others instead of you. You have wronged Him because you have shown yourself to be thankless to the God Who granted you being, Who formed you in His image and likeness, Who gave you a body containing all of the senses and a soul with all of the faculties, Who made you king of all earthly creatures, Who has provided you with sustenance, clothing, and shelter, Who commanded all of His sensible creatures to serve you, Who has saved you from so many dangers, illnesses, and poverty that so many others suffer from, Who gave you an angel to stand by you always and protect you.

You wrong God because you have shown yourself to be thankless to your great Benefactor, Who ordained it that you be born from Christian parents, Who received you so many times at His Mysteries, Who made you His son through Holy Baptism, Who redeemed you from the hands of demons, Who became a man for your sake, Who shed His blood to the last drop in order to make you an heir of His kingdom, Who so many times waited for you to repent after you sinned, while condemning many others who had committed lesser sins than your own, Who followed you when you fled from Him, Who knocked on your heart when you did not want Him, Who spoke to you, loved you, pleaded with you, desiring your salvation.

In brief, you wrong God because you have shown yourself to be thankless to such a Master, Who bestowed upon you so many blessings of nature and of grace, in part and in whole, hidden and manifest, and the worst thing of all is that, at the same time that you received all of these graces before your eyes, you, the ungrateful creature, dared to repay Him with your wicked acts.

O my sinful brother! If someone were to give you only a single one of all these blessings, you would not know how to thank him. But, when not a man, but the Most High God, the Creator of all the angels, has bestowed so many graces upon you, how is it that you, on the contrary, show yourself to be so thankless toward Him? Wonder, my brother, wonder at how the earth has carried you and has not yet split asunder to swallow you alive. Wonder at how the sky has not yet hurled lightning bolts in order to scorch you; how the air, which you have polluted by your sins, has not yet blown noxious winds in order to poison you, and how all of the elements have not yet risen against you like beasts in order to swallow you alive, unable to endure seeing you, the apostate and insidious one, to display such thanklessness by your sins toward their Creator and your utmost Benefactor: "Perverse and crooked generation, do ye thus requite the Lord?" (Dt. 32:5).

3) You wronged God, because by your sins you committed an unheard of injustice and mockery against the redemption which the Son of God accomplished for you, for you placed Him on the Cross a second time, you stomped on His love, you profaned His All-holy Blood, you insulted the grace of His Spirit, you opened His wounds, you renewed the spittings, the slappings, the crown of thorns, the scourgings, the nails, the spear, and all of the sufferings and humiliations, because you committed sin, which

was the cause of His Crucifixion: "They crucify to themselves the Son of God afresh, and put Him to an open shame" (Heb. 6:6), says the divine Paul.[342]

O my brother, if you carefully consider these three spears by which you wounded God through sinning, I am certain you will roar and growl like a lion on account of your sighs: "I have roared from the groaning of my heart" (Ps. 37:8), and you will hate and be disgusted with sin, and your heart will be broken into a thousand pieces, even if it was calloused and hard as a rock, and you will cause it to shed tears of blood. Therefore, as much as possible, concentrate and meditate upon these three points in order to acquire holy contrition, which is the noblest and most precious part of repentance, being sad for no other reason than because you sinned against God and grieved the Holy Spirit, according to the Apostle: "And grieve not the Holy Spirit of God" (Eph. 4:30).

This is why David was not grieved on account of the other injuries which sin brought upon him, but only grieved because sin caused him to wrong God, even considering all of the harm he brought to himself and to others, wherefore he said: "Against Thee only have I sinned and done this evil before Thee" (Ps. 50:4). Likewise, Manasseh was grieved only because he wronged God, and his heart never found rest, wherefore he said: "I have no relief, for I have provoked Thy wrath and have done what is evil in Thy sight, not doing Thy will, and not keeping Thy commands" (Manasseh 1:10).[343]

8. Sin wrongs the sinner in three ways

Then, in order for you to also acquire affliction brother, consider also how many bad things sins have brought upon you.

1) Consider how they have caused you to lose the supranatural graces

---

342   For a fuller explanation of these three points, look ahead to Precaution 5.

343   The Prayer of Manasseh is confirmed as genuine by St. Ephraim, who brings forth evidence from the prayer. You also, brother, should read it, especially when preparing for Confession, for it brings much compunction. The divine Scripture also refers to this prayer, saying: "Now the rest of the acts of Manasseh, and his prayer unto his God" (2 Chr. 33:18).

which God granted to you in this life: the grace of justification, the grace of sonship, of being His dwelling place, and all the rest, any one of which is more precious than all the nobilities, than all the wisdoms, than all the beauties, and than all the powers. In brief, even one degree of any of these graces is more precious than all of the endowments of nature and of all the most valuable goods in the world, as Solomon says: "All gold is but a little sand in her sight" (Wis. 7:9).

2) Consider how sins have caused you to lose the eternal blessedness of Paradise, the delight and vision of God, the vision of the most-sweet Theotokos, the Mother of God and Mother of all Christians, the fellowship with the angels, the company of the Saints, inexpressible joy, the heavenly kingdom, everlasting rest, eternal light, and simply all of the good things which no eye has seen, nor ear heard, nor can the mind of man comprehend (cf. 1 Cor. 2:9). Sins caused you to trade all of these good things for a small, bitter, and confounded pleasure. Sins caused you to disregard all of these good things as nothing, just as those Jews disregarded Jerusalem, the antitype of Paradise: "And they set at nought the desirable land" (Ps. 105:24).

3) Consider how sins have brought you eternal hell, the unquenchable fire, the gnashing of teeth, the sleepless worm, the tormenting of all the members of your body and all the powers of your soul, and where there are always those things which are abhorred and not things desirable. There you will never enjoy a single pleasure, you will never see a friend, you will never converse with a relative, you will never sleep, and you will never find rest, even for a single moment, from those torturous demons that will torment you. Simply speaking, consider how sins caused you to gain an eternity of the infinite torments of hell, in which one single moment is, even after thousands of years, like the sand of the sea, or like the stars of heaven, or like the drops of rain, or like the leaves of the trees, or like the atoms in the air, and that moment will never, ever pass: "And he shall be tormented with fire and brimstone... And the smoke of their torment ascendeth up for ever and ever" (Rev. 14:10-11).

Considering these things for a second reason, beloved, your heart will certainly be pricked with compunction and you will acquire the aforementioned affliction, being grieved for no other reason than that, because of your sins, you suffered an infinite loss, an injury which not even all the kingdoms of the world are worthy of recompensing in the slightest measure.

Alas! Is it but a small loss and slight grief for you to lose God, you poor sinner, Who is complete delight, complete joy, complete desire, and complete insatiable satiety? Who is complete light and the origin of light, complete life and the origin of life, complete wisdom and the origin of wisdom? Is it but slight grief to lose God, Whose beauty surpasses every beauty, Whose wisdom surpasses every wisdom, Whose sweetness surpasses every sweetness, a single ray of Whose glory, if it shone in Hades, would immediately change Hades into Paradise?

Is it but slight grief to lose the beginningless Father, the co-beginningless Son, and the All-holy Spirit, the One Trihypostatic God, from Whom everything beautiful derives its beauty, from Whom everything bright derives its brightness, from Whom every living thing derives life, from Whom everything rational derives its rationality, and from Whom every being derives its principle of being?

In a single word, is it but slight grief to lose your God, you poor soul, Who is absolute good, Who is your beginning, your middle, and your end? "Know therefore and see (God Himself cries out to you), know and see that it is an evil thing and bitter, that thou hast forsaken the Lord thy God" (Jer. 2:19). For this reason Basil the Great said that even if someone is not punished, even if someone is not tormented, but they are only deprived of God, this is more intolerable than all of the future punishments: "Separation and estrangement from God are more unbearable than the punishment reserved for hell and more oppressive to the sufferer than the being deprived of light is to the eye, even if there be no pain in addition, or than the loss of its life is to an animal."[344] And if Esau, on account of losing his birthright and his father's blessing, was so greatly distressed that he bellowed such a bitter and fearful cry: "And when Esau heard the words of his father, he cried with a great and exceeding bitter cry" (Gen. 27:34), how will you, the thrice-wretched, not cry out to heaven? How will you, the poor soul, not groan from the depths of your heart on account of losing

---

344   *Regulæ Fusius* 2, 2, PG 31, 912B; tr. *Saint Basil: Ascetical Works*, pp. 235-236.

so many supranatural blessings and graces of your heavenly Father? Or because you are deprived of beholding the sweetest face of the Mother of God, the vision of which, after God, is like a second blessedness in Paradise, and because you lost forever the most-compassionate Mother of Christians, in whose Churches you worshipped, and whose icons you venerated, and whose name you called upon in all of your troubles and who immediately heard you? Or because you are deprived of the blissful company of all the angels and the Saints, whose Feasts you celebrated and whose sacred books you listened to and read every day? Or because, on the contrary, instead of all these good things, you inherited unending evils and torments? In brief, how will you not lament, sinner, on account of losing your God, together with Whom you lost everything, everything?

O infinite loss! O immeasurable loss! I am certain, brother, that if you saw but once this great loss which you caused by your sins, you would cry out like that king who said at the time of his death that he had lost everything, for by losing God, he also lost body and soul, earth and heaven, temporal things and eternal things, and indeed, everything: "All is lost! I am deprived of everything!" I am certain that if you saw at once before your eyes all of the things which you lost, you would promise yourself a thousand times over that you would never sin again, and that you would be reformed and live a holy life, just like that young man was reformed who was losing a lot of money playing cards because he did not see the future consequences. For when one day he lost twelve thousand ducats[345] and saw all of the money gathered before him and then placed into twenty-four sacks by his father, that poor soul became terrified by this great loss and from then on he decided to never play cards again.

9. Sorrow over temporal goods is futile

Know this also, brother, that you should not grieve if, on account of your sins, you lose some natural or temporal good, whether it be your children, or your wife, or even all of the kingdoms of the world, or even

---

345   Translator's note: The Venetian golden ducat was coined from the 1200s through the 1700s. One ducat is worth approximately $3791.00 today (twelve thousand ducats = $45,492,000).

your own life, for this sorrow is not considered as repentance, but it is rather vain and futile and unacceptable to God. For Saul also grieved when he heard from Samuel that he would lose his kingdom and his very life, so much that, out of his fear, he fell to the ground: "Then Saul fell straightway all along on the earth" (1 Kg. 28:20), but in vain. Antiochus also came to realize the evils he had committed when he saw that he would lose both his kingdom and his life by a painful death, but in vain, as the Scripture says: "Then the abominable fellow made a vow to the Lord" (2 Macc. 9:13). I leave to say that sorrow over worldly and temporal goods is not only futile for the sinner, but also brings him death: "The sorrow of the world worketh death" (2 Cor. 7:10).

CHAPTER 2

How the Sinner Should Confess

When you have considered your sins in this way, my fellow sinner,[346] and have prepared yourself through contrition and affliction, then go to an experienced Spiritual Father, as we said, and even if he is far away, do not be lazy, just as you are not lazy to go to a far off experienced physician for your bodily illnesses, but say like the Prodigal Son: "I will arise and go to my father" (Lk. 15:18).

Coming to him, when he tells you to confess your sins before the Master Christ, then kneel before His sacred icon, saying: "'Father, I have sinned against heaven, and before thee, and am no more worthy to be called thy son (Lk. 15:18-19),' but behold, today, through this my Spiritual Father 'I will confess to Thee with uprightness of heart (Ps. 118:7).'" In this way begin your confession.

---

346   If you know letters, brother, write down your sins on a piece of paper so that you do not forget any. You also must know this, that if you do not do the proper examination of your sins before you confess, as many sins as you forget and do not confess remain unforgiven. For this forgetfulness occurred voluntarily when you would have been able to remember them through proper preparation. If, however, you do conduct the proper self-examination, and it happens that you forget some sin, forgetful human being that you are, this sin, some say, is forgiven with the rest that are confessed, because this forgetfulness is not voluntary, but involuntary. But if after confession you remember it, you must go again to the Spiritual Father and confess it.

1. The meaning of confession

Before you begin, know that confession is a voluntary vocal articulation of one's evil deeds, words, and thoughts. It is compunctionate, accusatory, honest, done without shame, and resolute, taking place before a legitimate Spiritual Father.

2. Confession must be voluntary

So then, my brother, you must confess with your own mouth[347] all of your evil deeds, all of your evil words, and all of your evil thoughts, not out of any compulsion or necessity, but voluntarily and by your own free will, saying with David: "Out of my desire will I confess to Him" (Ps. 27:7). You should not wait for the Spiritual Father to question you, but you should be the first to begin confessing.[348] Do not imitate King Nebuchadnezzar who did not reveal his dream to the magicians for them to interpret it, but they rather inquired from him about the dream and its interpretation: "Therefore shew me the dream, and the interpretation thereof" (Dan. 2:6), but you should rather first reveal your dream, that is, your sins, and then the Spiritual Father will listen to them and correct them.

3. Confession must be compunctionate

You must confess compunctionately, with much humility and a broken heart, in the same manner as the harlot confessed her sins, and the Canaanite

---

347   I said that you are to say your sins with your own mouth because, even if you have them written down in order not to forget them, you yourself must still read them to your Spiritual Father. Hence, those who write their sins down and then give them to the Spiritual Father while they themselves depart, do this wrongly and erroneously, and their confession is incomplete. Let them cease from this improper habit and let them themselves read their sins aloud.

348   Therefore, the divine Chrysostom, when interpreting the verse: "Do thou first confess thy transgressions" (Is. 43:26), says: "Do not wait for someone to accuse you, and do not let the prosecutor anticipate you - beat him to the punch by having the first say" (*On Genesis*, Homily 20, 3, PG 53, 171).

woman, and just as the Publican prayed, in order for God to accept your confession and grant you the forgiveness of your sins: "A heart that is broken and humbled God will not despise" (Ps. 50:17). You should continue to exhibit this compunction and humility when the Spiritual Father is reproving you for some transgression, remaining silent and not angry, nor interrupting his words, but receiving the reproof with joy, as if God Himself were reproving you. What am I saying, to receive it with joy? If it is possible, you should fall to the ground like a convict and wet his feet with your tears, as St. John of the Ladder advises you: "At confession, be like a condemned criminal in disposition and in outward appearance and in thought. Cast your eyes to the earth, and, if possible, sprinkle the feet of your judge and physician, as the feet of Christ, with your tears."[349]

4. Confession must be accusatory

You must not accuse one and the other when you confess, making excuses that they were the cause for you to sin, like Adam accused Eve and Eve accused the serpent. No. You must only accuse yourself, and yourself alone, and your evil will. "If you wish to accuse," says the divine Chrysostom to you, "accuse yourself."[350] And Solomon says: "A righteous man accuses himself" (Pr. 18:17). Himself, it says, and not others, so that you do not, while seeking to belittle your sins by your confession, actually increase them by adding the sin of passing judgment to them. John of the Ladder advises us as to what you should say to the Spiritual Father: "Without being ashamed, say: 'It is my wound, Father, it is my plague, caused by my own negligence, and not by anything else. No one is to blame for this, no man, no spirit, no body, nothing but my own carelessness.'"[351]

5. Confession must be honest

You must confess truthfully and honestly from your heart, revealing all

---

349   Step 4, PG 88, 708D-709A; tr. *The Ladder*, p. 41.

350   *On Matthew*, Homily 51, 6, PG 58, 517.

351   Step 4, PG 88, 708D; tr. *The Ladder*, p. 41.

of your sins just as you committed them, including all of the circumstances, such as the place, the time, with what person, the reason, how many times, and the manner,[352] without adding or subtracting anything, without telling half of your sins to one Spiritual Father and the other half to another, as some cunning people do, and without saying them in a cryptic manner, by which at the same time you both reveal and conceal your sin, in order to lessen your shame. But you should confess simply and straightforwardly, with a guileless and true heart, for if you merely confess deceptively and superficially, know that, not only will your confession be abhorrent to God, Who always loves truth: "Thou hast loved truth" (Ps. 50:6), but the sins which you confessed will once again crop up within you after a short while, just as the white hairs of the elderly appear after a short time because they do not pluck them out, but simply superficially shave them. In this way you resemble what David says: "Like a sharpened razor hast thou wrought deceit" (Ps. 51:2).[353]

6. Confession must be done without shame

You must confess without shame, for the shame which you feel when you confess brings you glory and grace from God, according to Sirach: "For there is a shame which brings sin, and there is a shame which is glory and grace" (Sir. 4:21). This shame liberates you from the future shame of the fearful day of judgment, according to John of the Ladder: "You cannot escape shame except by shame,"[354] and according to Gregory the Theologian: "Do not disdain to confess your sins, that by present shame you may escape from future shame (for this too is a part of the future punishment); and prove that you really hate sin by making a shew of it openly, and triumphing

---

352   See Chapter 5 of Part 1, *Instruction to the Spiritual Father*, concerning these circumstances. However, the names of the people with whom you sinned must not be revealed.

353   The divine Chrysostom, explaining the verse: "I will confess to Thee with uprightness of heart" (Ps. 118:7), says: "Judas also confessed, saying: 'I have sinned in that I have betrayed the innocent blood, (Mt. 27:4)' but not with uprightness of heart, for love of money had consumed him" (*In Psalmum CXVIII*, 2, PG 55, 677). Do you see how confession is in vain when it is not done with uprightness of heart?

354   Step 4, PG 88, 708D; tr. *The Ladder*, p. 41.

over it as worthy of contempt."[355] Why are you ashamed, sinner? When you committed the sin you were not ashamed, and now when you ask that it be taken away, are you ashamed? O madness! Do you not know that this shame which you now experience during confession is of the devil who, when you sin, gives you courage and shamelessness, but when you are to confess, he gives you fear and shame? This is what Chrysostom attests: "These are two things, sin and repentance. There is contempt and derision in sin. There is praise and boldness in repentance. But Satan overturns the order and gives those who trust in him boldness in sin, but shame in repentance. Therefore, do not trust him."[356]

For this reason, we read in the writings of the Fathers that a certain virtuous Father saw the devil with his own eyes frequently visiting the confessionals of Spiritual Fathers in order to cause the sinners who were going to confess to feel shame. God has not given you as a Spiritual Father any angel or archangel so that you should feel shame, but a human being who suffers the same things as you do so that you may not be ashamed; so why are you ashamed? Either you learned this from others or you suspect that your Spiritual Father reveals your sins to everyone. Let this not, my brother, keep you from confession, for it is a deception of the devil, by which means he wishes to destroy your soul. And if a Spiritual Father does reveal them (which is extremely unlikely, if not impossible, for him to do), he will have to give an account to God for this evil thing which he has done, but you, having confessed, are completely innocent and forgiven for your sins. This is how St. Meletios the Confessor proves this to you:

---

355   *Oratio* 40, 26, PG 36, 397A; tr. NPNF (V2-07), p. 369.

356   *De Poenitentia XIII*, 2, PG 49, 338. For know, brother, that the shame that you will experience on the day of judgment, if you are ashamed now, is more fearful than the eternal darkness and fire. Basil the Great confirms this in this way: "For they who practice evil will resurrect to reproach and to shame, beholding in themselves the ugliness and the marks of their sins. And, perhaps, that shame with which the sinners are going to live forever will be more fearful than the darkness and the eternal fire, since they have always in their eyes the traces of sin in their flesh like certain indelible stains, which remain perpetually in the memory of their soul" (*Homilia in Psalmum XXXIII*, 4, PG 29, 360D-361A).

"If someone reveals and disparages your confession,
He will have to give account to God at the judgment.
But the one who confessed is altogether innocent,
And he is delivered in every way from his errors."[357]

The penitents of old would stand in the entrance of the Church and confess their sins before the entire congregation, as Sozomen says: "It seemed best from the beginning that sins would be confessed to the priests, as a public witness, before the whole assembly of the Church."[358] And Canons 56 and 75 of Basil the Great attest to this as well.

The Righteous Job was not ashamed to confess before a multitude, as he himself proclaims: "For I was not dissuaded by a great multitude, so as not to confess boldly before them" (Job 31:34). And you, my brother, being a sinner and coming before only one human being to confess, why should you be ashamed?[359]

---

357   *Alphabetalphabetos*, Degree 171.
358   *Historia Ecclesiastica* 7, 16, PG 67, 1460A
359   But know, beloved, that it is still also now permitted for someone to confess their sins openly, if they are found to be eager in their repentance. And whoever does this will more quickly receive God's philanthropy and forgiveness on account of the greater shame and humiliation they will experience in this public confession. Besides the example of Job, whom we mentioned above, and the ancient custom of the Church of Christ of public confession, we also find in the histories that the Emperor Romanos, called the Elder and Lekapenos, also did this. For when he repented on account of the oaths that he had broken, which he had made with his son-in-law, Constantine Porphyrogennetos, and for his other sins, he sent for and gathered three hundred monks from Rome and Jerusalem and, during the Divine Liturgy, at the time of Communion when the priest said: "With the fear of God, with faith...," he stood in the midst of the Church, and the good Romanos, shunning all humiliation, openly confessed his sins and asked for forgiveness. He then wrote his sins on a piece of paper and sent it to the monks who did not come and then to the monks on Mt. Olympus, asking them to supplicate God on his behalf for the remission of his sins. Now listen to the philanthropy and mercy which God showed towards him. A certain virtuous monk residing on Olympus, named Dermokaitos, was supplicating God on the Emperor's behalf, when a divine voice from above said to him: "The philanthropy of God has conquered." Then the monk unfolded the piece of paper and, O what wonder! he found the sins erased and removed (from Dositheos, *Dodekabiblos*, Book VII, p. 743).
John of the Ladder narrates a similar story, saying that a man who was a thief and a murderer and a magician and licentious happened to come to a certain coenobitic monastery seeking to become a monk. The abbot of the monastery told him to confess openly in the presence of everyone his sins.

7. Sins will be made manifest either now or then

One or the other, brother: either you will reveal your sins now before one Spiritual Father, or then at the fearful judgment. If you hide them now, know that then they will without fail be exhibited by the fearful Judge to all of the angels and to all mankind as a great reproof unto you: "I will reprove thee, and bring thy sins before thy face" (Ps. 49:22). What am I saying, the Judge? Your very unconfessed sins themselves will reprove you then and will make a spectacle of you in that universal court: "Thine own apostasy shall correct thee, and thy wickedness shall reprove thee" (Jer. 2:19).[360] St. John Chrysostom also advises you saying: "You are a sinner. Enter the Church, fall on your face, weep. You sinned, so confess your sins to God. Say them at that time so that there, before myriads of angels and

---

With joy he accepted to do this, and if he wished, he could even do this in the midst of the city of Alexandria. So on a Sunday, when there was Liturgy taking place, after the reading of the Gospel, the thief entered the Church looking like one condemned, dragged by the brethren, being struck, his hands bound behind his back, dressed in a hair shirt and with ashes on his head. As soon as he neared the door of the Church the abbot shouted: "Stop!" Stop, for you are not worthy to enter here. Thinking that he had heard thunder and not the voice of a man, the thief instantly fell on his face, trembling and shaking and wetting the ground with his tears. The abbot then exhorted him to confess in detail all of his sins. The thief began and confessed them one by one. Now see the mercy of God. During his confession, one of the brethren present saw a terrible looking man holding a piece of paper with writing on it and a pencil, and as soon as the thief confessed each of his sins, that fearful man would cross the sin out with the pencil, and rightly, for God said through the Prophet David: "I said: I will confess mine iniquities before the Lord against myself. And Thou forgavest the ungodliness of my heart" (Ps. 31:5). Immediately after the confession, the abbot tonsured the thief a monk and numbered him among the rest of the monks (Step 4, PG 88, 681C-684D; *The Ladder*, pp. 23-25). Look ahead to the story about the Hierarch Potamon who confessed before an entire Synod. So let us also imitate them and so many others like them, and let us not be ashamed when we confess, so that we may more quickly receive the mercy of God. (Translator's note: The wise Sirach counsels: "Do not be ashamed to confess your sins" (Sir. 4:26), and St. John Chrysostom tells us: "Be ashamed when you sin; be not ashamed when you repent" (*De Poenitentia XIII*, 2, PG 49, 338).)

360   And the divine Chrysostom says: "There they (our faults) will be seen plainly before our eyes and hung around our necks, and we will there lament in vain." (*Non Esse ad Gratiam Concionandum* 2, PG 50, 657). Note also the testimony of Basil the Great, which states that we will then see every one of our sins and how they were enacted: "We will immediately see all our works through memory as if they are standing before us, and they will appear before our minds in the same detailed manner as they were done or said" (*In Isaiam Prophetam* 3, 120, PG 30, 312C).

men, you may not be reproved unto your humiliation. Tell me what is better, to confess here in the Church before only God and your Spiritual Father, or to be publicly displayed there before thousands."[361]

8. If a single sin is unconfessed, the other sins also remain unforgiven

If you confess all of your sins but conceal just one of them out of shame, know that, not only do the sins which you confessed remain unforgiven,[362] but you also add another sin to yourself, that of sacrilege, on account of this concealment, as Chrysanthos of Jerusalem says in his *Exomologetarion*. Therefore a certain teacher wisely advises you that if you wish to conquer the devil who causes you to feel shame, say right at the beginning of your confession the sin that makes you feel the most ashamed.

9. Confession must be resolute

Finally, you must confess resolutely, namely, you should make a firm and certain resolution in the presence of the Spiritual Father that you would rather die a thousand deaths than ever voluntarily sin again, through the co-operation of divine grace. For if you do not make this resolution in your heart, contrition will profit you little, and your confession and repentance

---

361   *De Oratione*, PG 62, 738.

362   See p. 208 of *Salvation of Sinners*, where it is reported that a certain woman confessed all of her sins to a certain pious Spiritual Father, but concealed one great sin and did not confess it. While she was confessing, the disciple of that Spiritual Father saw a snake coming out of her mouth as she confessed each sin, but again and again he saw a great snake which three times appeared to be coming out of her mouth but which finally went back inside of her and did not come out. On account of this all of the other snakes which had left her returned and entered back into her through her mouth. After that poor woman's death, she appeared to her Spiritual Father and to his disciple sitting upon a fearful dragon and said that she had been damned on account of not confessing that great sin. John of the Ladder says that one cannot receive forgiveness for their sins if they do not confess them: "Without this (confession), no one will obtain forgiveness" (Step 4, PG 88, 684D; tr. *The Ladder*, p. 25).

will profit you little, as all of the teachers in common say.[363]

For this reason, as many as do not make this resolution have one foot with their Spiritual Father and the other foot with sin, confessing with their mouth while planning in their heart to sin again. In this way they resemble the dog that, after vomiting, returns to its own vomit. They also resemble the pig that, after being washed, goes back and rolls around in its former mud, as St. Peter says: "But it is happened unto them according to the true proverb: The dog is turned to his own vomit again; and the sow that was washed to her wallowing in the mire" (2 Pet. 2:22).

They, as the divine Augustine says, do not cease from sin, but put it off for another time, and only out of habit do they confess, and not in truth, as when Pascha or Christmas approaches, or because they are nearing death.

We read in the lives of the Fathers that a certain Abba saw souls descending into Hades like snow falling to the earth during the winter. And why is this? It is not because Christians do not confess (for rarely does someone die unconfessed), but because they do not confess correctly with the resolve that they will not sin again; because they do not tear their hearts with the genuine grief of resolute amendment, but only tear their outer garments, according to the Prophet, with a false and superficial grief: "Rend your heart, and not your garments" (Jl. 2:13).

And what does it profit you, brother, if you only say: "I have sinned; I repent"? Saul also said this (1 Kg. 15:24), as did Judas (Mt. 27:4), but it did not profit them. Therefore Basil the Great says that the one who simply says "I sinned," but does not hate his sin, even though he completely confesses, does not profit from his confession but rather remains in his sin, and that he does not profit from the forgiveness he receives from the Spiritual Father for his iniquities if he again commits those same iniquities: "So, not

---

363   On p. 307 of *Salvation of Sinners* we read that a certain priest assigned to the Church of the Theotokos, even though he confessed all of his sins while on his death bed with compunction and tears, because he did not make a firm resolution not to sin again, but rather was decided that if he lived he would return to those same sins, was on this account damned. He appeared after his death to the priest of that Church where he was formerly assigned and told all this to him.

even the one who says, 'I sinned,' and then persists in sin truly confesses. But, according to the Psalm, he who finds his sin should hate it (Ps. 35:2). For what profit does a sick man receive from the diligence of a physician when he pursues the destructive things of life? Such a person profits nothing from the forgiveness he receives for his iniquities when he again goes and does wrong."[364]

All of your repentance depends on this resolution to amend your life.[365] Do not say: "If I am able, I will change," or: "I did not want to sin." Such is not the proper way. You must say: "I resolve to change, I do not wish to sin again, just as I never wish to drink a glass of poison, just as I never want to be thrown off of a cliff, just as I never want to be put to death," with a firm, adamant, and resolute will.[366]

And because the will of man cannot remain steadfast without divine help, we have written a prayer that asks such help from God and have placed it at the end of this section, after Precaution 6.[367]

---

364   *Comment. in Isaiam Prophetam* 1, 34, PG 30, 185C-188A. (Translator's note: St. Nikodemos said that he found this reference in the unpublished series of Niketas on the Psalms, Psalm 35.)

365   We see such an example of this in the Ninevites who not only fasted and wore hair shirts, from the youngest to the oldest of them, even the king himself, and wailed and cried out to God with tears and moans, but also had earlier amended their life and completely abstained from evil. For this reason God accepted their repentance as genuine and true, and did not destroy them as He had said He would through Jonah: "And God saw their works, that they turned from their evil way; and God repented of the evil, that He had said that He would do unto them; and He did it not" (Jon. 3:10). But because the Ninevites returned to their former wickedness and sins, God destroyed them and obliterated their city, so much that hedgehogs and chameleons and crows and all beasts took up their abode there, as the Prophet Nahum reports (ch. 2) and also the Prophet Zephaniah (2:13).

366   Translator's note: St. Dionysios the Areopagite says: "It is not enough merely to withdraw from all wrongdoing. Rather, one must be bravely resolute. One must fearlessly confront any disastrous backsliding. There must never be any decline in the sacred love of truth. Indeed one must ceaselessly and prayerfully be raised up as much as one can toward it and strive always to be uplifted in a sacred fashion toward the ultimate perfection of the Deity" (*De Ecclesiastica Hierarchia* 2, 5, PG 3, 401C; tr. *Pseudo-Dionysius: The Complete Works*, p. 207).

367   We must note here that there are three reasons to confess the same sins a second time: 1) if someone confesses his sins without saying their circumstances, without the necessary preparation, without compunction, without resolution, and without keeping his rule; 2) if he was not corrected or penanced properly by a Spiritual Father, as some say; and, 3) according to Symeon of Thessaloniki, if someone falls again into the same sins and into others, as a result of the former (confessed) sins, he should say both the latter and the former sins, being that the former sins are the roots of the latter

CHAPTER 3

The Sinner Is to Accept His Rule With Joy

1. The meaning of satisfaction

After confession comes the third aspect of repentance, namely, satisfaction, which is the actual completion or fulfillment of the rule assigned by the Spiritual Father,[368] as defined by Gabriel of Philadelphia in his work *On the Mysteries*.[369] So, my fellow sinner, you must accept the rule assigned to you by your Spiritual Father with great joy, whether it be fasting, or prostrations, or to give alms, or anything else. And above all, you must wholeheartedly accept to abstain from Communion for as many years as prescribed by your Spiritual Father, for by this light chastisement you pacify the great wrath of God. By this temporal penance, you escape the eternal penance of hell.

(*Responsa ad Gabrielem Pentapolitanum*, Question 34, PG 155, 884A-884B). One should confess sins a second time also unto the greater contrition of their heart and humility. It is written in *Instruction for Penitents* that it is a most profitable thing for someone to make a general and complete confession of all the sins of his life (as those who are going to be ordained do and those who are approaching death do) even once a year, and certainly when one begins to go to a new Spiritual Father. For through this general confession, all of one's sins are gathered together like many rivers into a sea, or like many mountains stacked upon other mountains, looking as if they reach to heaven, as Esdras says: "Our trespasses have increased even unto heaven" (2 Esd. 9:6). The penitent, seeing this great number of sins gathered together in a single glance, experiences greater shame, greater grief, greater humility, and as a result, he fears even greater divine righteousness, which he outraged so much. Furthermore, he receives greater peace in his conscience and proof of the forgiveness of his sins. And above all, he receives great restraint and an obstacle to keep him from falling again. The Spiritual Father also profits from this, for learning from this general confession about the condition of life in which the penitent lives, he is better equipped to correct him.

368   Translator's note: See the *Introduction* to this book by Fr. George Metallinos. And Fr. Athanasios Gikas writes: "St. Nikodemos transcends this opinion (that of satisfying an insulted divine righteousness through good works) and gives a new meaning to the term *satisfaction*... This term is here employed with the meaning of reconciliation between the penitent and God. The penitent undertakes to fulfill his rule, not with the scope to satisfy divine righteousness, but as beneficial to his soul, in order to shake off the burden of sin and to proceed toward purification and deliverance from the passions" (*He metanoia kata ton hagio Nikodemo Hagiorite (Repentance According to St. Nikodemos the Hagiorite)*, Thessaloniki, 2000, pp. 23-24 (in Greek)).

369   *Syntagmation peri ton hagion kai hieron mysterion*, Venice, 1591, p. 98.

2. Examples of people placed
under a rule for their sins

If the sister of Moses was not shut out of the camp for seven days, she would not have been cleansed from leprosy (Num. 12:14). If the fornicator in Corinth was not given over to Satan, his soul could not be saved (1 Cor. 5:5).

So my brother, if you do not accept the small chastisement of your rule, neither will you be completely cleansed from the leprosy of sin, nor will your soul be saved. This is a most profitable and great transaction, beloved, for those who are prudent. You give one, and you escape a million. You receive something temporal, and escape the eternal.

King David, on account of the satisfaction he had to make for his sins, was chased from his kingdom by his own son Absalom. He walked through the mountains and valleys with bare feet. He was cursed at and stoned by Shimei. And he was scorned by all. And you wish to propitiate God without any rule? How foolish you are! Emperor Theodosios the Great made satisfaction of great renown in Milan, as he was ordered to do by St. Ambrose. Emperor Romanos, called the Elder and Lekapenos, in order to make satisfaction on account of the oaths which he broke, repented and became a monk, and when he wished to eat some bread, he had a boy strike him on the legs with a whip, saying: "Enter, you wretched monk, into the refectory."[370] And another Emperor, because of a murder which he committed, ascended a high mountain with bare feet and remained there, stripped of his royal stole, for a period of forty days, consuming only bread and water, and passing the time in unceasing prayer and silence, sleeping on the hard earth. And many other Emperors made even more austere satisfactions on account of their sins. And you, sinner, are you greater than them? Or do you have a more delicate and tender body, so that you do not accept such a light rule from your Spiritual Father for your sins? Do not let the thought deceive you that says you can give money and pay off your rule. Those Emperors had more money than you and could have given

---

370   Dositheos of Jerusalem, *Dodekabiblos*, Book VII, p. 743.

millions to try and pay off their rule. But this is impossible, even if one were to give his entire kingdom. For the impartial righteousness of God is not pleased by any other means than by the very person who sinned, and for that person to be chastised.[371]

If you find some money-loving Spiritual Father who tells you to give him money and he will forgive you, be careful so as not to believe him. For you cannot receive forgiveness this way, and all you do is lose your money and remain unforgiven.[372] St. Isidore Pelousiotes writes to one such Spiritual

---

371   Translator's note: Concerning the chastisement of God, elsewhere St. Nikodemos says: "Do not think that God scourges and chastises someone out of revenge or hatred; God forbid! But because people do not listen to or heed the words of God's counsels and admonishments, God is compelled to counsel and admonish them in deed, that is, with chastisements and scourges, as the wise Judith said: 'The Lord has not taken revenge upon us, but He scourges in order to admonish' (Judith 8:27)" (*Pneumatika Gymnasmata* (*Spiritual Exercises*), Thessaloniki, 1999, p. 239). Again in the same book, St. Nikodemos says: "O sinners, the righteousness of God is not some hate which God has towards His creatures, as you think it is. No. But it is a love which God has for equality and righteousness… Therefore, the righteousness of God is most lovely and worthy of every love, just as are His other energies" (p. 440). And in his book, *Kepos Chariton* (*Garden of Graces*), he writes: "Even if God is long-suffering and slow to anger towards sinners, and even though He does not immediately recompense them for their sins, so that they are given time to repent, He does not, however, forget their sins or let them go completely undisciplined, but when someone sins, God then disciplines him. First, through the unceasing reproof of the conscience, which is the torment of torments, and a hell before hell, as Chrysostom said: 'He who lives in wickedness is punished before hell, being pierced by the conscience' (*Ad populum Antiochenum XVI*, 6, PG 49, 170). Second, He disciplines the sinner through fearful dreams, according to Job: 'A second time sending a dream, or in the meditation of the night (as when a dreadful alarm happens to fall upon men…), then opens He (God) the understanding of men: He scares them with such fearful visions to turn a man from unrighteousness' (Job 33:14-17). Third, God disciplines man when he sins with various bodily illnesses, with afflictions, with misfortunes, with disasters, and through many other temporal trials. However, even with all these things, if the person still does not repent or does not amend himself, He finally disciplines him with the torments of Hades and with the punishment of hell. Wherefore Sirach said: 'The Lord will not delay, neither will He be slow to anger towards them, till He crushes the loins of the unmerciful… till He takes away the multitude of the insolent… till He repays the man according to his deeds' (Sir. 35:19-22)" (Thessaloniki, 1992, pp. 73-74).

372   I say to you again brother, be careful, and do not believe such a Spiritual Father, so that you may not suffer (God forbid!) that which a great leader suffered, as we read in the histories. Let this terrible and fearful example be deeply etched in your memory. This leader, when nearing the end of his life, called for a lawyer of the city to come and assist him to write his will. After telling him a number of things and the lawyer having written them down, he also said the following: "I want my body buried in the ground from where it was formed, and my soul to be given over to the devil

Father that Spiritual Fathers cannot forgive the rich by their payments, and that they who take bribes are not the masters and lords of forgiveness or heirs of the divine altar, just like the ungodly: "Come, let us inherit the sanctuary of God for ourselves, for those who offer sacrifices on behalf of their own sins, as the Apostle says, clearly do not have authority over the unrepentant, even if they are rich, and they cannot forgive sins."[373]

3. Whoever keeps their rule is a genuine child of the Church

If you keep the rule of your Spiritual Father, you show that you are truly repenting and that you are a genuine child of God and of the Holy Church, which designated this chastisement. If, on the contrary, you violate the rule of your Spiritual Father, it is a sign that your repentance is not true, but false. It is a sign that you are not a genuine child of God and of the Church, as Paul says: "If ye endure chastening, God dealeth with you as with sons; for what son is he whom the father chasteneth not? But if ye be without chastisement, whereof all are partakers, then are ye bastards, and not sons" (Heb. 12:7-8).[374]

---

because it is his." When the lawyer heard these things he trembled with fear and could not believe what he heard, and he did not desire to write any more. The sick leader, full of anger and rage, said to him again: "Yes, my soul must be received by the demons, and the soul of my wife, and the souls of my children, and the soul of my Spiritual Father. My own soul, because I unjustly stole others' belongings and kept them. The soul of my wife, because she urged me to do this thing. The souls of my children, because they wanted me to make them rich, and I did many injustices for their sake. And the demons must receive the soul of my Spiritual Father because he unlawfully forgave me, and never examined me, and never admonished me." As he was saying these things, that wretched man gave up his spirit. (From *The Political Theatre*, p. 353, ch. 25).

373   *Liber III, Epistola CCLX - Zosimo Presbytero*, PG 78, 941C. See also the beginning of Chapter 9, Part 1.

374   That the satisfaction and the rule which the penitent receives from the Spiritual Father is not chastisement as punishment but, rather, salvation, is attested to by the divine Chrysostom who says: "These laws, then, of philanthropy let us learn also (which law of love Paul used on the fornicator). For if thou seest a horse hurrying down a precipice, thou appliest a bit and holdest him in with violence and lashest him frequently; although this is punishment, yet the punishment itself is the mother of safety. Thus act also in the case of those that sin. Bind him that hath transgressed until he have propitiated God; let him not go loose, that he be not bound the faster by the anger of God.

4. The penitent should of his own accord seek even a greater rule

I am resigned to say that if your Spiritual Father assigns you a small rule, you should, of your own accord, ask him to give you a greater one, as many others do who repent fervently, in order to greater propitiate divine righteousness by this temporary rule and to be more assured that God loosed you from eternal punishment, which you were liable to on account of sin.[375]

5. The sinner will receive either a temporary rule now or an eternal rule then

In brief, we say to you that you must choose one of two things, brother: either to receive now a temporary rule for your sins, or an eternal one then. If you accept it now, you avoid the one then. If you do not accept it now, you most certainly will receive an eternal one then, as Gabriel of Philadelphia writes: "Whoever is not convinced to accept their rule will necessarily be sent to the tribunals then, and will have to give account for committing

---

If I bind, God doth not chain; if I bind not, the indissoluble chains await him. 'For if we judged ourselves, we should not be judged' (1 Cor. 11:31). Think not, then, that thus to act cometh of cruelty and inhumanity; nay, but of the highest gentleness and the most skillful leechcraft and of much tender care" (*On II Corinthians*, Homily 14, 3, PG 61, 502; tr. NPNF (V1-12) p. 349). (Translator's note: And in his *Letter On Confession*, St. Symeon the New Theologian says: "Let us receive the penances he (the spiritual physician) assigns as an antidote, and always strive to fulfill them with a warm faith and in the fear of God" (*On the Mystical Life*, vol. 3, Crestwood, 1997, p. 192).)

375   We read in Step 5, *On Repentance* (PG 88, 776C-777A; *The Ladder*, pp. 62-63), that a certain zealous and virtuous brother of a coenobitic monastery, when he sinned one time went to confess his sin to the abbot. Seeing that he was not penanced austerely, he fell at the feet of the abbot and wet them with his tears, asking him to heavily penance him and send him to the monastery of the penitents, which, on account of the severity of its location and its other unutterable hardships which the sinful penitents there suffered, was called the Prison. So that good penitent persuaded the philanthropy of the physician and convinced him in this manner, who allowed him to go. And he went to the Prison, that blessed one, weeping so much and pricked so greatly by compunction that within eight days he fell asleep in the Lord. He asked many not to bury his body but to cast it aside unburied. The abbot, however, sent for the body and buried it worthily together with the other Fathers in the cemetery.

impious acts, as the laws of the Holy Church have set forth."[376] Furthermore, if you do not agree with the counsel of the Spiritual Father and you do not accept the just rule given to you, know that the Spiritual Father does not have the authority to forgive you, as Basil the Great says: "Authority to forgive sins has not been given unconditionally, but is dependent on the obedience of the penitent and his agreement with the man who is entrusted with the care of his soul. For it is written concerning such: 'If two of you shall agree upon earth as touching anything that they shall ask, it shall be done for them of my Father which is in heaven.'"[377]

6. The penitent must maintain the abstention from Communion

Above all that we have said to you, brother, is that you must exactly maintain the abstention from Communion for as many years as designated by your Spiritual Father, for this abstention is the satisfaction of satisfactions, necessary and essential to your true repentance. For if you dare to commune during those years, you become a second Judas, and if you constrain your Spiritual Father to allow you to commune, you are no longer a penitent, but a dictator and a tyrant who violates the divine laws and the Canons of the Holy Synods and of the Fathers. You then receive divine Communion, not unto the remission of sins, but unto greater condemnation and punishment. For you to understand this better, read the following example.

Just as someone who has wounds on his body goes and shows these to a physician and then receives instructions from him to apply a certain salve to the wounds, and then is further instructed not to drink wine and not to eat certain foods on account of the wounds not healing, in like manner, my brother, you had spiritual wounds on your soul, your sins, and you went and showed them to a Spiritual Father, that is, you confessed them. The Spiritual Father prescribed that you apply a salve to them, that is, he prescribed for you a rule of fasting, of eating dry foods, of prostrations, of giving alms, or of prayer. Furthermore, he instructed you not to drink

---

376   *On the Mysteries.*
377   *Regulæ Brevius* 15, PG 31, 1092B-1092C; tr. *The Ascetic Works of Saint Basil*, p. 236.

certain drinks or eat certain foods, that is, not to commune in the divine Mysteries. So if you disobey him and eat, what happens? Your wounds and your sins do not heal, but, rather, they become worse and larger. What am I saying, they do not heal? Spiritual and bodily death results, as the divine Paul says: "For this cause many are weak and sickly among you, and many sleep" (1 Cor. 11:30), that is, because some were unworthily communing, they became sick and weak and died, even many of them.[378] In agreement with Paul, his disciple, St. Dionysios the Areopagite, says: "The rest of the orders of those who are being purified (those in penitence, that is) have already been initiated into the sacred tradition. True, they continue to be foolishly drawn to sin instead of being uplifted toward a higher perfection, and that is why they are rightly dismissed from the divine visions and communions manifested by the sacred symbols. If they were to participate unworthily in these Divine Mysteries they would be the first victims of their own folly and would decrease their respect for divine realities and for themselves."[379]

Finally we say to you, brother, that you must carry out the rule which your Spiritual Father gives you (even if you try a little, the grace of God will be with you), and that you cannot put it off for another time, for you do not know what the next day will bring: "Boast not thyself of tomorrow; for thou knowest not what a day may bring forth" (Pr. 27:1).

---

378   If someone wonderingly poses this question—"If the sins of the penitent are forgiven through the prayer of forgiveness of the Spiritual Father, why is he not permitted to receive Communion as already forgiven and justified?"—we reply in three ways. 1) Yes, the sins of the sinner are forgiven, but not simply, but under the presumption that he will keep his rule and the abstention from Communion (for this reason the Spiritual Father assigns the rule and the abstention from the Mysteries *before* the prayer of forgiveness is read). 2) The sins are forgiven, but not their consequences and chastisement, which is the assigned rule and the abstention from Communion. For yes, David's sin was forgiven by God when Nathan said to him: "The Lord has put away thy sin" (2 Kg. 12:13), but the chastisement for his sin was not forgiven, for after the forgiveness, he was cast out of his kingdom by his son Absalom, he did not even take a sword with him from his house, and he suffered many other evils, as Nathan himself had prophesied to him. 3) The sins of the sinner are forgiven, yes, but it is necessary that he also be tested and strengthened by time in the grace of God. [Translator's note: The same is stated by and expounded upon by Elder Joseph the Hesychast in his Twenty-first Letter (Monastic Wisdom, Florence, 1998, pp. 123-124).]

379   *De Ecclesiastica Hierarchia* 7, 3, PG 3, 557C-557D; tr. *Pseudo-Dionysius*, p. 253.

And we advise you above all, beloved, to never believe that your sins are loosed and forgiven on account of your rule, even if it be hard and a large one. No. But believe that your sins are forgiven on account of the mercy of God and the satisfaction of Jesus Christ.[380]

CHAPTER 4

Precautions After Confession

After you have confessed and received your rule from your Spiritual Father, in order to take precaution and not fall into the same sins again, or others, use the following six precautions as preventative medicines.

Precaution 1:
Remembrance of sins

The first precaution is for you not to forget, but to always remember, the sins you committed. This is what God commands you through Isaiah: "I, even I, am He that blotteth out thy transgressions for Mine own sake, and will not remember thy sins. But do thou remember, and let us plead together" (Is. 43:25-26). You should do this, that is, remember your sins, not in order to torture yourself, but in order to discipline your soul not to run after the passions and not fall again into the same sins, as the divine Chrysostom says to you,[381] and in order for you to know by your memory

---

380   See Chapter 10 of Section 1, *What rule murderers are to be given.*

381   "For thus is the custom of God to deal with us. When we sin, He does not straightway visit the transgression, but lets it pass, giving us space for repentance, in order that we may be amended and converted. But if, because we have not paid the penalty, we suppose that the offense too is blotted out, and make light of it; then somewhere, where we think not of it, we are sure afterwards to be punished. And this takes place in order that, when we sin and are not punished, we may not be free from fear, unless we amend, knowing that we shall certainly fall into punishment where we do not expect it. So that if thou sinnest, beloved, and art not punished, do not grow presumptuous, but for this very cause be the more alarmed, knowing that it is an easy matter with God to recompense again when He pleases. For this reason then He hath not punished thee, that thou mightest receive space for repentance... If our minds are thus disposed, we shall never forget

the great grace you received from God when He forgave you so many sins. Paul also always remembered how he persecuted the Church in order to show the magnitude of the grace of God, according to the same Chrysostom.[382] Remember your sins for your heart to become contrite and for your soul to be pricked with compunction, according to Chrysostom: "Remember your sins exactly and by type, for this is no small torment for the soul. When you see compunction in someone's soul, know that their soul is always suffering. When you see someone remembering their sins, know that their pain arises from there."[383] And finally, remember your sins to be humbled and so that you consider yourself unworthy even of this life, as the golden Orator of the Church says: "It is no small thing for correction to always recollect your sins in detail, continuously recalling them and considering them. For by doing this, one is pricked to the heart with compunction, thinking yourself as unworthy of this life. Thinking this, one becomes softer than wax."[384] When someone barely escapes a great danger and then later recalls it, he trembles and becomes fearful, and this fear causes him to avoid the same danger the next time. Thus David, even after the forgiveness of his sins, always remembered them and had them continually before his eyes, saying: "For I know mine iniquity, and my sin is ever before me" (Ps. 50:3).

If you want God to turn His face away from your sins, says the divine Augustine, you must have them before you for you to see them and lament them. If you record your sins and remember them, the divine Chrysostom assures you that God will erase them and forget them. But if you erase them and forget them, God will record them and remember them: "Recall

---

our own sins, but, always fearful and trembling lest we should have to pay the penalty, we shall readily recollect them. For nothing is so apt to bring sin to remembrance as punishment and chastisement" (*Ad Populum Antiochenum III*, PG 49, 58; tr. NPNF (V1-09), pp. 362-363).

382   "On this account therefore neither does he simply, as I said, declare himself to be the last and unworthy of the appellation of an Apostle, but also states the reason, saying: 'Because I persecuted the Church.' And yet all those things were forgiven, but nevertheless he himself never forgot them, desiring to signify the greatness of God's grace" (*On I Corinthians*, Homily 38, 5, PG 61, 328; tr. NPNF (V1-12) p. 230).

383   *On Matthew*, Homily 41, 4, PG 57, 450.

384   *Ibid.*

all of your sins as if they are written in a book. If you record them, God will erase them. If you do not record them, God will record them and will call for a trial. It is much better that we record them and have them erased above, than for us to forget them and for them to come before the eyes of God on that day."[385] And again he says: "For there is no better medicine to repudiate sins than the continual remembrance of them and to incessantly condemn them."[386]

St. Mark the Ascetic advises you, however, that when you confess your sins to God, you should not recall them in detail, imagining the manner in which you sinned and visualizing the people with whom you sinned, because, being that you are still passionate and a lover of pleasure, desire will arise in you and you will be darkened,[387] or because, recalling them in such detail, you experience such remorse that you become despondent.[388] You must especially be aware of this when it comes to your carnal sins and to be careful so as not to recall the manner of these sins and the people with whom you sinned, for your mind will be polluted. You should simply remember that you are a sinner who has committed many sins, by which you have angered God.[389]

---

385   *De Confessione Peccatorum*, PG 63, 893.

386   *De Prophetiarum Obscuritate II*, 9, PG 56, 189.

387   "When the intellect through rejection of the passions attains to unwavering hope, then the enemy makes it visualize its past sins on the pretext of confessing them to God. Thus he tries to rekindle passions which by God's grace have been forgotten, and so secretly to inflict injury. Then, even though someone is illumined and hates the passions, he will inevitably be filled with darkness and confusion at the memory of what he has done. But if he is still befogged and self-indulgent, he will certainly dally with the enemy's provocations and entertain them under the influence of passion, so that this recollection will prove to be a prepossession and not a confession" (*No Righteousness by Works* 152). And: "If you wish to make a blameless confession to God, do not go over your failings in detail, but firmly resist their renewed attacks" (*ibid.*, 153). (*GrPhilokalia*, p. 108; tr. *The Philokalia*, v. 1, p. 138).

388   "To recall past sins in detail inflicts injury on the man who hopes in God. For when such recollection brings remorse it deprives him of hope; but if he pictures the sins to himself without remorse, they pollute him again with the old defilement" (*ibid.* 151).

389   St. John of the Ladder, in agreement with St. Mark, says that one should not think in detail about their carnal and obscene sins (*To the Shepherd*). And in Step 28, *On Prayer*, he says: "Do not go into detail in confessing carnal acts (to God that is), lest you become a traitor to yourself" (PG 88, 1140A; tr. *The Ladder*, p. 219). But one should think about all of the others in detail, night and day. And the divine Chrysostom says: "It does not suffice for someone to say, 'I am a sinner,' but he must

Precaution 2:
Avoidance of the causes of sin

The second precaution is for you to avoid the causes of sins,[390] for

remember his offenses in detail" (*Non esse ad Gratiam Concionandum* 5, PG 50, 662). He brings as an example the Apostle Paul who, after baptism, confessed that he was a blasphemer and persecutor before baptism: "If he (Paul) remembered his forgiven sins, we must much more remember the sins we committed after baptism" (*De Prophetiarum Obscuritate II*, 9, PG 56, 189). And in Homily 12, *On the Statues*, he says: "For if the memory of these terrors abide with us, we shall never be overtaken by the actual experience of such terrors. For what need have we of the experience, whilst our memory acts the part of a monitor?" (*Ad Populum Antiochenum XII*, 1, PG 49, 127; tr. NPNF (V1-09) p. 418). If someone wonders why Chrysostom says that we should remember our sins in detail, but the aforementioned Mark says that we should not remember them in detail, let the above-quoted saying of John of the Ladder be the solution. For Mark is speaking about carnal sins, while Chrysostom is speaking of all the rest which, if someone recalls them in detail, they do no harm to themselves. Note however, that when someone is being warred upon by prideful thoughts, it is then beneficial to also remember and confess the carnal sins in detail, as this brings humility. Therefore that saintly and most-experienced elder said: "When the thought of pride comes to you and says, 'Remember your virtues,' say in return, 'Look at your fornication.'" And Symeon Metaphrastes remembers such sins in detail in his sacred Communion Prayer which begins: "In the presence of Thy fearful...," unto greater contrition of heart and humility (*Precationes*, PG 114, 220C-224B). Even then one should not remember the manner of the sin or the persons with whom he committed them, but only the specific type of sin, that is, whether it was fornication, adultery, etc. And to remember the number of times each sin was committed also causes humility. See Chapter 3 of Part 1 of *Instruction to the Spiritual Father* (in the footnotes) for a detailed account of the classes and specific kinds of sins.

390   There are two causes for someone to sin. One is called extended, and the other is called brief. For example, a man associates one on one with a woman or a youth for an entire year, and in that year he falls one time into sin with the other person. That year-long association is called an extended cause, for the sinner fell only one time over an extended period of time. But if he fell into sin every time he associated with that person, this is called a brief cause. So when you decide not to fall into sin again, you must avoid both of these causes, because after you sin just once, you are prone to fall into it again, and the extended cause becomes a brief cause, as we have come to learn through our daily experience. So when your Spiritual Father tells you that which Sarah said to Abraham, that you must expel the woman or youth from your house: "Cast out this bondwoman and her son" (Gen. 21:10), do not object, but remember what God said to Abraham concerning this: "Let it not be grievous in thy sight because of the lad, and because of thy bondwoman; in all that Sarah hath said unto thee, hearken unto her voice" (Gen. 21:12). Remembering this, obey with joy this command of your Spiritual Father, for it is not from himself, but from God. "What are you saying?" you say, "I need that woman or that youth in my house because they are faithful servants, prudent, diligent, and they take care of my needs." O my brother, these are all excuses, underneath which you seek to hide your passion, like a viper hiding underneath soft grass. Tell me, if these servants were thieves, would

according to the rules of philosophy, causes always produce the same effects and results, wherefore Basil the Great said: "That he who has once repented commits again the same sin is a proof that he has not purged away the prime cause of that sin, so that from it as from a root the same growth comes again necessarily."[391] Avoid then, my brother, evil sights, evil conversations, unruly company, and especially avoid conversing with and keeping company with those persons with whom you sinned carnally. One of two things must happen: either you must avoid them, or you must distance them from you and send them away if they live in your home, whether a maidservant or a slave, or even a close friend. For the Lord said concerning such: "And if thy right eye offend thee, pluck it out, and cast it from thee: for it is profitable for thee that one of thy members should perish, and not that thy whole body should be cast into hell" (Mt. 5:29).

And never trust yourself, saying: "I am able to keep company with those harmful persons and not be harmed." This is a most deceitful thought, for it is written: "Never trust your enemy" (Sir. 12:10). And it is the opinion of some teachers that if the most prudent Joseph had not fled from the house of his lord's wife, he would certainly have fallen into sin.[392] Whoever

---

you not immediately cast them out and find other servants to assist you? Alas! And now that they are thieves, not of your home, but of your soul, you wait and do not cast them out? You resolved not to fall into sin again, so how is it that you do not avoid the causes, which can easily cast you into sin again? So if you want your resolve to remain firm, you must avoid the causes which provoke you to sin. And know also this, that as long as you openly keep that lewd woman or child in your home, you not only cannot receive forgiveness from any Spiritual Father, but your offerings to God are not even acceptable. See the Canons of St. John the Faster which verify this. If it is not in your own power, however, to cast out these people or for you to distance yourself from them, do not look upon them, and do not let your mind be pleased with the memory of their faces, and ask God fervently from the start to help you, and do other like things to remove your passion for them from your heart.

391   *Regulæ Brevius* 289, PG 31, 1285A; tr. *The Ascetic Works of Saint Basil*, p. 340.

392   In order for you to learn to avoid the causes of sin, brother, let the following fearful example told by St. Makarios frighten you. During a time of persecution, a certain pious Christian who was at a place of torture, hanging and being beaten and wounded all over his body by the tyrants, was then thrown into the jail and was there cared for by a certain nun. But as he became accustomed to her company, he fell into fornication with her in the jail. O most pitiable and lamentable fall! So if not even the blood which that martyr spilt for Christ, nor his wounds, nor the jail, nor the piety of the nun, were able to help them not fall into sin, because they did not avoid the cause, how can your own courage or resolve help you not to fall if you do not avoid the causes of

fears danger does not want to fall into it; but whoever loves it desires to fall: "Whoever loves danger will fall into it" (Sir. 3:26). Wherefore the divine Chrysostom also says: "So also he who does not avoid sins from afar, but walks near them, will live in fear, and will often fall into them."[393]

Precaution 3:
Frequent confession

The third precaution is to confess frequently, but not in a fashion that every time you commit a mortal and grave sin you immediately run to your Spiritual Father, but also when you commit any small and pardonable sin, if it is possible. For just as wounds, when shown to a physician, do not get worse, so also when sins are confessed, they do not increase, according to John of the Ladder: "Wounds displayed in public will not grow worse, but will be healed."[394] Storks have a custom of never returning to their nests if they are somehow destroyed. The demons, too, depart from those who frequently confess, for by frequent confession, one destroys their nest and

sin? Therefore, the Apostle Paul, when speaking about carnal sins, did not say "stand and fight," but purposefully said: "Flee fornication" (1 Cor. 6:18).

393   Translator's note: The whole passage reads as follows: "Therefore, let us not only avoid sins, but those things too which seem to be indifferent, yet by degrees lead us into these misdeeds. He, indeed, who walks by the side of a precipice, even though he may not fall over, trembles; and very often he is overset by this same trembling, and falls to the bottom. So also he who does not avoid sins from afar, but walks near them, will live in fear, and will often fall into them. Besides, he who eagerly looks at strange beauties, although he may not commit adultery, hath in so doing entertained lust; and hath become already an adulterer according to the declaration of Christ (Mt. 5:28); and often by this very lust he is carried on to the actual sin. Let us then withdraw ourselves far from sins. Dost thou wish to live soberly? Avoid not only adultery, but also the licentious glance! Dost thou wish to be far removed from foul words? Avoid not only foul words, but also inordinate laughter, and every kind of lust. Dost thou wish to keep far from committing murders? Avoid railing too. Dost thou wish to keep aloof from drunkenness? Avoid luxury and sumptuous tables, and pluck up the vice by the roots" (*Ad Populum Antiochenum XV*, 4, PG 49, 159; tr. NPNF (V1-09) pp. 442-443).

Elsewhere, St. Nikodemos also says to especially avoid small sins: "And I must say something rather astounding. Brethren, you must take even greater care to keep yourselves from small sins, even more so than large ones. For a man can easily keep himself from large sins, because he does not ignore them. But he falls into small sins more easily, because he ignores them. And then, the small sins become large sins, on account of ignoring them" (*Chrestoetheia ton Christianon*, p. 144).

394   Step 4, PG 88, 681B; tr. *The Ladder*, p. 23.

their web, and they have no place in nor authority over someone who confesses frequently, as one virtuous man was told by the demons themselves. Furthermore, they also said that when a person is unconfessed, his members are all bound in sin and cannot move to do good, but when he confesses, his members are immediately loosed.

And why didn't Naaman the Syrian wash only one time in the Jordan, but seven? (2 Kg. 5:14). For no other reason than to teach us all, small and great, patriarchs and hierarchs, Spiritual Fathers and priests,[395] to confess seven times, that is, frequently and many times (for the number seven means many, according to the divine Scripture), and to wash in the waters of repentance, of which the Jordan was a type, for which reason the Forerunner was baptizing in it: "A baptism of repentance for the people" (Mk. 1:4). In addition to vexing the power of the demons, frequent confession also brings five additional benefits to the one who frequently confesses.

---

395   I said that the eminent patriarchs, hierarchs, spiritual fathers, and priests should frequently confess, in order so that I may overturn that most awful custom which prevails in many places: that the aforementioned sacred persons do not confess at all. I truly wonder how this originated. If they think that they do not sin, such a thought is wrong, for John the Theologian cries out: "If we say that we have no sin, we deceive ourselves" (1 Jn. 1:8). And if they think that because they are ordained they do not need to confess frequently like the laity do, this thought is also not correct, for when the divine James said: "Confess your faults one to another" (Jas. 5:16), he did not distinguish between the ordained and the laity, but simply and indiscriminately said that both the ordained and the laity should confess. For even physicians need other physicians when they get sick, and prophets need other prophets when they sin, according to the divine Chrysostom: "Then Nathan approached David; a prophet goes to a prophet. How is it that, being a prophet, David does not treat himself? Indeed, when physicians are ill, they have need of other physicians, for the illness overruns the skill. Such also is the case here" (*In Psalmum L*, Homily 1, 6, PG 55, 572). If they are ashamed, let them imitate the Hierarch Potamon who confessed, not in front of just one Spiritual Father, but in front of an entire Synod. If John the Theologian confesses: "If we confess our sins, the Lord is faithful and just to forgive us our sins, and to cleanse us from all unrighteousness" (1 Jn. 1:9), why do not those sacred leaders confess? For this reason, most-holy Fathers, I fall before you and implore you for the love of God to frequently confess and for you not to be a bad example to the laity so that they also do not confess. But just as you are a type and example to them of all that is good, so become a good example of frequent confession. For even Symeon of Thessaloniki says that both hierarchs and priests must perform the sacred rites and receive Communion with care, compunction, and confession (*De Ordine Sepulture*, ch. 360, PG 155, 672B-673D).

Benefit 1

First, just as trees that are frequently transplanted cannot become deeply rooted in the earth, so also frequent confession does not allow the bad habits and addictions of sin to become deeply rooted in the heart of the one who frequently confesses. Or rather, just as an old and large tree cannot be cut by just one chop, so also an old bad habit or addiction of sin cannot be uprooted or removed completely by the penitent having just one experience of pain of heart during a confession, and that probably incomplete, even if his sin is forgiven through the prayer of forgiveness of the Spiritual Father.

Benefit 2

Second, whoever confesses frequently has great ease examining his conscience precisely and determining the number of his sins. For by continually being relieved of the burden of the multitude of his sins through frequent confession, there are always fewer and fewer that remain. On this account it becomes easier for him to find them and remember them. But the one who does not confess frequently, on account of the multitude of sins which accumulate in him, neither with precision is he able to find them, nor can he remember them, but very often he forgets many and grave sins which, remaining unconfessed, remain unforgiven. Wherefore the devil has him remember his unconfessed sins at the hour of his death, which upsets him so much that the poor wretch sweats violently and wails, but to no avail, for then it is too late and impossible to confess them.

Benefit 3

Third, whoever confesses frequently, even if he is to commit a mortal sin, immediately enters into the grace of God when he confesses, and as many good works as he does become for him worthy of eternal life. But the one who does not confess frequently, if he happens to commit a mortal sin and does not immediately run to confess it, for as much time as he remains unconfessed, he is not only deprived of the grace of God, but as many good works as he does, whether fasts, or vigils, or prostrations, and the like, are not worthy of any reward or eternal life, for they are bereft of the grace of God, which is the beginning and the foundation of all works unto salvation.

Benefit 4

Fourth, the one who confesses frequently is more assured that death will find him while in the grace of God and thus be saved. And the devil, who is always accustomed to visiting the dying, not only sinners, but Saints as well, as Basil the Great says,[396] and even the Lord Himself: "The prince of this world cometh, and hath nothing in Me" (Jn. 14:30), and who is present at people's deaths in order to see if he can find anything, will visit the one who frequently confesses but will find nothing, because he made time to confess, and cleared his debts and balanced his register through frequent confession. But the one who does not frequently confess will most likely die unconfessed and thus be eternally damned, because he easily and repeatedly falls into sin and does not confess, and because of the uncertain time of death.

Benefit 5

The fifth and final benefit of frequent confession is that it deters and restrains people from sin. For when the person who frequently confesses remembers that in just a few days he will confess, and the notion to sin arises, he is deterred from doing it, thinking about the shame he will experience when he confesses it and the rebuke he will receive from his Spiritual Father. Therefore St. John of the Ladder wrote: "Nothing gives the demons and thoughts more power against us than the unconfessed sins

---

396   "I think that the noble athletes of God, who have wrestled considerably with the invisible enemies during the whole of their lives, after they have escaped all of their persecutions and reached the end of life, are examined by the prince of the world in order that, if they are found to have wounds from the wrestling or any stains or effects of sin, they may be detained; but, if they are found unwounded and stainless, they may be brought by Christ into their rest as being unconquered and free" (*Homilia in Psalmum VII*, 2, PG 29, 232C; tr. *Saint Basil: Exegetic Works*, Washington D.C., 1963, pp. 167-168).

in our heart upon which they feed." And again: "By resolving to make one's confession, the soul is therefore held from sinning as by a bridle. For what we do not confess, that we do fearlessly as though in the dark."[397] Wherefore St. John speaks about those brethren of that wondrous monastery who had a tablet of paper hanging on their belts, and upon these tablets they would daily write their thoughts, in order to confess them to that great abbot.[398]

So my brother sinner, having learned these things, go frequently to Holy Confession, for as often as you frequent that bath, the more will you be cleansed. Do not postpone the time, saying, "Let me do this first, and then I will go confess," because even if God is slow to anger and tolerant many times over, He always catches up: "Do not say, 'I sinned, and what happened to me?' for the Lord is slow to anger. For both mercy and wrath are with Him, and His anger rests on sinners" (Sir. 5:4, 6).

Always remember Samson who, even though enabled to break the enemy's bonds three times, was unable to break them a fourth time and escape: "'I will go out as at other times before, and shake myself free.' And he knew not that the Lord was departed from him" (Jg. 16:20). You too, brother, even if you have sinned one, two, and three times and put off correction and confession, and then were deemed worthy to make it to be corrected and to confess, you may not make it a fourth time if you sin and postpone the time of your confession, and die unconfessed and uncorrected. May this never happen to any Christian.

Precaution 4:
Remembrance of the last things

The fourth precaution, brother, is for you to remember the last things, that is, to always contemplate your death, the fearful judgment of God, eternal hell, and the eternal delight of Paradise, for the remembrance and fear of these four things will be for you like a strong bridle which does not allow you to sin, just as the Holy Spirit says through Sirach: "Remember

---

397   Step, 4, PG 88, 705C; tr. *The Ladder*, p. 39.
398   Step 4, PG 88, 701C-701D; tr. *The Ladder*, p. 37.

the end of your life, and then you will never sin" (Sir. 7:36).

So when evil thoughts, the devil, and the passions war against you and urge you to sin, think upon your death and consider how your body, which is about to fornicate, or murder, or steal, or commit some other sin, will die and lose its beauty, its health, its mass, and all of its abilities, and will become a corpse, formless, without shape, without beauty, without breath. Consider how it will be buried in a most dark tomb and will decompose there, becoming food for the worms, dirt, repulsive, decayed, and dust. Remember how much fear, how much pain, how much agony you will experience when your soul separates from your body, and when the fearful demons stand about you ready to snatch you, with no one there to help you.

Remember also how these same things will happen to the person with whom you desire to sin, for that body which you now so desire and long for, will after but a short while be accompanied by death, becoming a corpse, cold, repulsive, food for the worms, and foul.

And above all, remember how death is a sudden thief, and you do not know when it will come to you. It may come this day, this hour, this moment, and you who woke up so well may not even make it until the evening, or you who have come to the end of the day may not wake up,[399] as the Lord said: "Watch therefore, for ye know neither the day nor the hour wherein the Son of Man cometh" (Mt. 25:13).

Therefore be informed, my brother, from what has been said, and thus say to yourself: "If I am going to die, and possibly a sudden death, what will happen to me, the wretch? What will it profit me then, if I delight in all of the hedonistic pleasures in the world? What will I gain, if I commit this sin? What will I have left, if I commit this wicked act? Get thee behind me, Satan, and evil thought, I will not listen to you and sin."[400]

---

[399]   Translator's note: This is how St. Isaac the Syrian advises one to approach his bed each night: "When you approach your bed, say to it, 'This very night, perchance, you will be my tomb, O bed; for I know not whether tonight instead of a transient sleep, the eternal sleep of death will be mine'" (*Ascetical Homilies*, Homily 64, pp. 314-315).

[400]   We read in the *Evergetinos*, p. 24, that many Fathers meditated upon death, and in this way they were not ruled by the passions, nor did they fall into sins. Wherefore Abba Evagrios says: "Do not forget that you will one day die, being thereby certain that you will not sin" (*Evergetinos*, p. 28; tr.

If you do not want to sin, place the fearful day of judgment before you and remember all of the things that will then take place, namely, how the sky will fold up like paper, how the stars will fall from the sky, how the luminous objects will become dark, how the mountains and the hills will melt like wax, how the sea will shudder and draw back, how the elements will burn, how the earth will quake, how the tombs will open and all people from Adam to the end will resurrect in order to stand before the fearful Judge, how the heavenly angels themselves will tremble from fear, how the books will be opened, and how each will be judged, giving an exact account of their wicked deeds, their wicked words, and their wicked thoughts.

Therefore, sinner, say this in your mind: "If I sin now, what will I do in that fearful day and hour? What defense do I have to give for my sin to that just and impartial Judge? O, how much fear and dread I, the wretch, will experience! Alas! Alas! How will it be for me when I hear that frightful decision: 'Depart from Me, ye cursed, into everlasting fire, prepared for the devil and his angels' (Mt. 25:41)? Alas! Alas! What shame I will experience then, standing naked, exposed before that universal gathering of angels, Saints, righteous, sinners, and all of humanity. Knowing for certain that I will not be able to endure that incomprehensible dishonor and shame, I will tell the mountains and the hills to fall on me and bury me, to hide me from the eyes of men, indeed, to escape the anger of that fearful Judge: 'And they said to the mountains and rocks, Fall on us, and hide us from the face of Him that sitteth on the throne, and from the wrath of the Lamb'

The Evergetinos: A Complete Text, vol. I, book. 1, p. 77), and Abba Isaiah says: "He who each day thinks of death and says to himself that, 'I have only today in this vain world,' will never sin before God" (*Evergetinos*, p. 27; tr. *The Evergetinos: A Complete Text*, vol. I, book. 1, p. 76). And Clement of Alexandria says: "The remembrance of death protects against sins," and Basil the Great says: "The remembrance of death is the most necessary food for the penitent." Worthy of remembrance is the custom which our divine Father Athanasios of Athos practiced in his monastery of Great Lavra. In order for his disciples to always remember death, during Great Lent, at the third hour, he purposefully designated a prudent brother to go around to all of the workshops and other places of duty of the monastery, and say the following words in each place: "Brethren and Fathers, let us mind ourselves, for we will die, we will die, we will die. Let us also remember the eternal hell." When the brethren heard these things, they immediately stood up to pray and chanted the Trisagion, and then sat back down (from the *Ordinances* of St. Athanasios).

(Rev. 6:16). So in order to avoid all these things, I will never commit sin."[401]

If you do not want to sin, my brother, place before you all of the forms of punishment which the righteousness of God devised in order to castigate sin, namely, the eternal deprivation and absence of God, the outer darkness, the unquenchable fire, the unsleeping worm, the frigid netherworld, the inconsolable weeping, the gnashing of teeth, and the other innumerable and various torments. And above all, remember that you will forever be in the company of the very enemies you hate so much, the demons, because they caused you all of these torments, something which is worse than all of the other forms of punishment, according to St. Maximos who, in his admonition to George the Eparch of Africa, says: "And the worst of all, or to state it more harshly, the truest of all, is that we will be in pain and suffer from (have mercy, O Christ, and save us from such pain): the separation from God and His holy angels, and the close company we will have with the devil and the evil demons… And this is the hell of hells and most terrible of punishments, the eternal coexistence of haters with the hated."[402] Then remember how all of these torments will punish sinners, not for a hundred thousand years, not for a thousand millenniums, but unto the ages of ages, without any hope of any end. Never. Never.

So say thus to yourself: "If I cannot endure the pain of a broken bone, how will I, the wretch, endure to be eternally separated from God, Who is the center of my being? If I cannot endure to be in an oven for even an hour, even if I had enjoyed all of the hedonistic pleasures of the world beforehand, how will I endure to be in that furnace of unquenchable fire for eternity?[403] May you be accursed, sin, always pestering me. No. I will not practice you and, for just a bit of your hedonistic pleasure, gain an eternity of torments, and weep as an inconsolable fool like Jonathan: 'I did

---

401   We also read in the aforementioned *Evergetinos* that many Fathers, by remembering the judgment of God, were kept from sin. Evagrios says: "Remember always the eternal judgment… being thereby certain that you will not sin" (*Evergetinos*, p. 28; tr. *The Evergetinos: A Complete Text*, vol. I, book. 1, p. 77).

402   *Sermo Hortatorius*, PG 91, 389A-389B.

403   We read in the *Life* of St. Martin that, on account of the fear of the eternal fire of hell, he was delivered from the sin of fornication, thinking about the impossibility of enduring the heat of that blazing sensible fire.

but taste a little honey with the end of the rod that was in mine hand, and, lo, I must die' (1 Kg. 14:43)."

If you do not want to sin, brother, remember all of the eternal and ineffable good things that God has prepared for you in the heavens in order for you to delight in them after death. Imprint on your imagination well the delight of that most-sweet Paradise, the unspeakable glory of heaven, the eternal joy, the never-setting light that knows no night, and the blessed vision and knowledge of God, which is the absolute subject and principle delight of all beatitudes. Remember the inseparable company you will have with the angels unto the ages of ages, the friendship and converse you will have in the kingdom of heaven with the Forefathers, with the Prophets, with the Apostles, with the Martyrs, with the Hierarchs, with the Ascetic Fathers and Mothers, and simply with all of the Righteous and the Saints. Consider that the joy there is only joy, without sadness. The life there is only life, without death. There the light is without darkness, health is without sickness, peace is without turmoil, and simply, there is to be found all of the good things, and only good things, without a single bad thing. And how can I describe for you, brother, one by one, the future good things of Paradise in which you will delight? They are not only beyond any words and description, but are also incomprehensible to the mind.[404]

In all of these things will you delight, beloved, not only with your mind and your soul, but also with your senses and with your body. So when a wicked thought suggests for you to sin, turn around and look up into the heavens with all of their beauty and splendor. After looking at them, say this to yourself: "Behold your most-sweet Fatherland. Behold your eternal dwelling place. Here I am to enjoy an eternal Paradise, so why should I deprive myself of it for a single temporary hedonistic pleasure? Here I am to become a son and heir of God and fellow heir with Christ, as Paul says: 'And if children, then heirs; heirs of God, and joint-heirs with Christ' (Rom. 8:17). Here I am to reign in an eternal kingdom: 'And they shall reign for ever and ever' (Rev. 22:5). So why should I sin and become a son of the devil and the heir of an

---

404   For this reason a certain wise and pious teacher was accustomed to always saying the following memorable maxim: "O Paradise, we will be able to delight in thee, but we will be unable to comprehend thee."

eternal hell? The soul which I have is a bride of the heavenly King and is to shine here like the sun with the glory of its immortal Father, as it is written: 'Then shall the righteous shine forth as the sun in the kingdom of their Father' (Mt. 13:43), so how can I corrupt it with sin and make it a darkened torch of gehenna? My body is to be glorified together with my soul and be conformed to the glorified body of Christ, as Paul says: 'Who shall change our vile body, that it may be fashioned like unto His glorious body' (Phil. 3:21). So how can I dare pollute it with the filth and mire of sin? Each of my senses is to eternally delight in the content of the beauty and of the blessedness of Paradise which is proper to its nature. My eyes are here to look upon the light and the glory of the Tri-luminous Godhead: 'I shall be filled when Thy glory is made manifest to me' (Ps. 16:16). My ears are here to eternally listen to the sweetest psalmody of the angels and of the Saints: 'And I heard a great voice of much people in heaven, saying, Alleluia' (Rev. 19:1). My mouth and my tongue are here to glorify God forever: 'Blessed are they that dwell in Thy house; unto ages of ages shall they praise Thee' (Ps. 83:5). My hands are here to be always uplifted to God, and my feet are to walk upon the golden plains of the upper Jerusalem. And simply, all of my members are here to be glorified eternally. Therefore, how can I pollute my eyes with obscene sights, and my ears with satanic words? How can I pollute my mouth with profanities and jeers? How can I pollute my hands with thievery and injustices, and my feet by walking the paths of sin? Or how can I make the holy members of my body, members of a harlot? 'Shall I then take the members of Christ, and make them the members of a harlot? God forbid' (1 Cor. 6:15). So get thee behind me, Satan, and wicked thought, I will not obey you and sin."

Precaution 5:
Knowledge of sin[405]

Use the fifth precaution, brother, to learn what a bad thing sin is, especially mortal sin, for all people commit sin for this reason: that they do

---

[405]   We have expanded this precaution for you, beloved, so that you not only read it after confession, but also before confession, so that by reading it your heart might become contrite, as it is very compunctionate.

not know and understand what a great evil it is.[406] Therefore, in many places of divine Scripture sinners are called foolish and ignorant.[407] So in order for you to understand the wickedness of sin, we have explained it here, not perfectly however, but only inasmuch as it is possible, for no mind is able to understand it completely: "As for transgressions, who will understand them?" (Ps. 18:13). We have explained the knowledge of sin according to: sin in and of itself, the circumstances of sin, and the punishment which sin received from God.

1. Knowledge of sin according to sin in and of itself

Sin in and of itself is an infinite evil because it is an offense against the infinite God and a complete disregard for His infinite majesty. For when, let us suppose, you commit murder, or fornicate, or steal, or commit some other sin, consider how God is standing on one side of you, and the devil on the other. God says to you: "O man, do not commit this sin, for it is something which is contrary to My law, and if you do not do it, you will gain an eternal Paradise, but if you do commit it, you will gain an eternal hell." And the devil says to you: "Commit this sin, and do not even consider the offense it is to God, nor the chastisement you will receive for it."

So if you listen to the devil and commit the sin, what do you do? You offend God, disregard His law, dishonor His majesty, and, if not in word, certainly in deed, it seems as if you are saying to Him: "'Lord, depart from me; I desire not the knowledge of Thy ways' (Job 21:14); I do not care about You; I do not want Your Paradise; I do not regard hell; I do not fear

---

406   Translator's note: Elder Sophrony says: "Sin is committed first of all in the secret depths of the human spirit but its consequences involve the individual as a whole. A sin will reflect on a man's psychological and physical condition, on his outward appearance, on his personal destiny. Sin will, inevitably, pass beyond the boundaries of the sinner's individual life, to burden all humanity and thus affect the fate of the whole world. The sin of our forefather Adam was not the only sin of cosmic significance. Every sin, manifest or secret, committed by each one of us affects the rest of the universe" (*Saint Silouan the Athonite*, p. 31).

407   The wise Solomon says: "It is as sport to a fool to do wickedness" (Pr. 10:23). And Sirach says: "A senseless and misguided man thinks foolishly" (Sir. 16:23). And David calls sin foolishness: "My bruises are become noisome and corrupt in the face of my folly" (Ps. 37:5).

Your wrath; I do not consider You as my Master. Therefore, I will not listen to Your voice or Your command." And so you resemble stiff-necked Pharaoh, who said: "Who is He, that I should obey His voice? I know not the Lord" (Ex. 5:2).

Thus do you offend and disregard God, sinning in all things, as it is written in the Song of the Three Youths: "We have sinned in all things" (Song of the Three Youths verse 6), for you disregard Him as the Lawgiver, not wanting to keep His law. You disregard Him as Master, not obeying His authority. You disregard Him as Creator, turning your being against Him, your mind, your free will, and everything else you received from Him. You sin in everything, for you disregard Him as the ultimate end, not caring about the blessedness which He promised you. You disregard Him as Redeemer, not thinking about the blood which He shed and the excruciating death He experienced for you. You disregard Him as Judge, not fearing His frightful judgment, nor His anger, nor His punishments. You disregard Him as Friend, not wanting His friendship, nor His grace. You disregard Him as Father, rejecting the inheritance and the dignity of your sonship.

You sin in everything, for you disregard His compassion, using it as an instrument for you to sin uncontrollably. You disregard His goodness, making it endure your apostasy and making it a servant of the very acts which it prohibits. You disregard His righteousness, not taking into consideration the universal chastisements it has given to so many lawless people like you. You disregard His providence, upsetting the role and the end for which you were ordained. You disregard His eternity, committing sin, which, if it were possible to corrupt the being of God and all of His majesty, and glory, and life, and kingdom, your sin would corrupt everything.

In brief, you sin in everything, for you disregard all of the other perfect, all-beautiful, and infinite characteristics of God, and you use all of the good things of nature and all of the good things of His divine grace which He gave to you as weapons to fight against God Himself. O incomprehensible offense! O infinite disregard!

Therefore, as infinite as the energies and attributes of God are, and as many as the natural, supranatural, common, unique, hidden, and manifest charismata which God granted to man are, this is how infinite the wickedness of your sin is, O man, which disregards and offends all of these things.

That these things are not mere speculations, but true certainties, God Himself attests, sometimes complaining and saying that sinners transgressed His law and disregarded Him: "But they like men have transgressed the covenant: there have they disregarded Me" (Hos. 6:7); sometimes complaining that He gave birth to and nurtured His offenders: "I have nourished and brought up children, and they have rebelled against Me" (Is. 1:2); sometimes complaining that He loves them like a lover, but they disregard Him and reject Him: "As a wife treacherously departeth from her husband, so have ye treacherously departed from Me, O house of Israel" (Jer. 3:20); and sometimes complaining that their anger and their pride resist Him: "Thy wrath wherewith thou hast been enraged, and thy bitterness has come up to Me" (Is. 37:29).

The divine Paul also attests to these things, crying out that sinners disregard the goodness and longsuffering of God: "Thou despisest the riches of His goodness and forbearance and longsuffering" (Rom. 2:4), that they step on the Son of God, that they defile His blood, and that they offend His grace: "Who hath trodden under foot the Son of God, and hath counted the blood of the covenant, wherewith he was sanctified, an unholy thing, and hath offended the Spirit of grace" (Heb. 10:29).

All of these, my brother, are living and true words which show how much God is wronged and offended by sin, especially mortal sin, and just how true that saying is which a certain virgin said, namely, that if, hypothetically speaking, there was a sea of fire in front of her, and in its harbor there was a mortal sin, she would rather fall into the sea of fire than fall into the hands of sin.[408]

Do you wish to understand, sinner, the infinite offense that sin is against God? Understand it by the infinite payment that the Son of God made because of it, with so many sufferings and such a disgraceful death. For if,

---

408   A certain bishop said that if he saw on one side the door of hell open, and on the other side a mortal sin, he would prefer to be cast into hell rather than fall into that sin. Some say that when Mary Magdalene merely heard the name of a mortal sin, she would tremble from head to toe and fall to the ground as dead, saying that she could never understand how man could dare to mortally sin and grieve God so much.

let's say, you place mortal sin on one side of a scale, and on the other side you place all of the love of the angels, all of the worth of the Queen of angels and Theotokos, all of the blood of the martyrs, all of the tears and the labors and the fasts of the ascetics, and simply, all of the good works of the Saints, all of these gathered together do not weigh as much as one mortal sin.

What am I saying? If God were to create as many other worlds as the stars of heaven, and were to fill them all with holy people who, in a thousand years of their lives, did nothing other than weep and supplicate God, all of these good works of theirs would not be able to counterbalance the smallest mortal sin, but it would seem like you placed a grain of sand on one side of the scale and a great mountain on the other side. And all of the treasures of the world are insufficient not to only make recompense, but they could not even buy a single drop of water which the rich will long for in Hades.

The only payment for the infinite debt of sin is the infinitely precious blood of God, and only His Cross, and the nails, and the sufferings, which only were able to counterbalance the weight of sin.

Are you bewildered, brother, hearing such things? But I am bewildered even more than you, at how you, a Christian, dare to sin, believing in these truths. Wherefore, either you must lead a Christian life, or not be called a Christian.[409]

---

409   For according to Athanasios the Great: "A Christian is a true rational house of Christ, consisting of good works and correct dogmas" (*Liber de Definitionibus*, PG 28, 549C). And Cyril of Alexandria, explaining the passage of Isaiah: "He shall call His servants by a new name, which shall be blessed on the earth; for they shall bless the true God" (Is. 65:15-16), says: "Let us come to Christ in the newness of the evangelical life, living in every respect below heaven according to His call, indeed, as if having been delivered some crown, having that famous and blessed name of *Christians*" (*Commentarius in Isaiam Prophetam*, PG 70, 1417B-1417C). And Theodoret of Cyr, explaining the same passage of Isaiah, says: "After the epiphany of the Master Christ, those who believed were designated the name 'Christians.' For this reason they offer every praise, and when they wish to be uplifted, they offer every glory to God. This is a true Christian. And again, they continually bless and supplicate God. This is what you must do as a Christian. Do whatever is befitting to a Christian, so that you may be called a Christian, and this name will be praised and glorified" (*In Isaiam Prophetam*, PG 81, 485B-485C). Ignatios the Godbearer writes the following: "Let us therefore prove ourselves worthy of that name which we have received... This was first fulfilled in Syria; for 'the disciples were called

2. Knowledge of sin according to its circumstances

We have faintly described the wickedness of sin, contemplating it in and of itself. Now we will also describe its wickedness according to the circumstances which accompany sin.

Circumstance 1:
The sinner

The first circumstance of sin is you yourself, the one who commits the sin. And who are you to challenge the great majesty of your Creator? You are but a lowly worm of the earth, a lump of clay, as Isaiah says: "Thou art our Father, we are the clay" (Is. 64:8). You are a person who not only comes from the dirt, but will return to the dirt and decompose there, but also a person extremely blessed by God, created by His infinite power and wisdom, sustained by His infinite providence, redeemed by His innumerable torments and sufferings, adopted as a son through His baptism, a communicant in His Mysteries, nursed by His blood, nurtured by His body. How can such a person sin? O most abominable sight!

For a Scythian, or a Muslim, or an idolater to sin, is tolerable: "For if mine enemy had reviled me, I might have endured it" (Ps. 54:12). But for a Christian to sin, who has been intoxicated with the Holy Spirit, who serves under the flag and protection of Jesus Christ, who is of His household, who so many times enjoyed His graces, who owes his entire being to Him,[410] this is intolerable: "But thou it was, O man of like soul with me, my guide

---

Christians at Antioch' (Acts 11:26)" (*Ad Magnesios* 10, PG 5, 769B-772A). And in another epistle he says: "May I not merely be called a Christian, but really be found to be one. For if I be truly found one, I may also be called one" (*Ad Romanos* 3, PG 5, 805A-805B). Gregory of Nyssa, in his Letter to Arrmonios, teaches what the Christian name and profession is, saying: "Christianity is imitating the Divine Nature" (*De Professione Christiana*, PG 46, 244C). And in his letter to Olympios the monk he says: "Three things characterize the life of a Christian: praxis, word, and conscience" (*De Perfectione*, PG 46, 284A).

410   A certain teacher, deducing from the formation and reformation of man how much man owes God, was accustomed to saying these memorable words: "I owe my whole being to Thee, because Thou hast created me. What more can I add, because Thou hast renewed me?" (from *Sure Guidance*).

and my familiar friend, thou who together with me didst sweeten my repasts" (Ps. 54:14-15).

For this reason the sacred Augustine was justified to say that when an unbeliever sins, he is worthy of punishment, but when a Christians sins, he is not only worthy of the punishment of Hades, but there needs to be added a second Hades for him, and that great furnace of fire which will embrace him must have, like Babylon (Dan. 3:19), seven more times the flames, and demons that are seven times more severe, and other diabolical torments which are seven times more fearful and greater in number than those of the unbelievers.

Circumstance 2:
The cause

The second circumstance of sin is the cause or reason why you sin, sinner. Do you dare to sin because of some great need, or to save your life, or to acquire glory or riches and a kingdom? No. You commit sin for some lentils, like Esau (Gen. 25:34), or to eat a little honey, like Jonathan (1 Kg. 14:43), or to acquire a little barley or a piece of bread: "Ye pollute Me among My people for handfuls of barley and for pieces of bread" (Ezek. 13:19). This is how God complains through Ezekiel.

You many times cast away His grace, stomp on His Law, and disregard His blessings. Why? For one confounded hedonistic pleasure; for a negligible profit; for a single vain fantasy of yours; for nothing. Behold to what an extreme the wickedness of your sins reaches, O man, for which reason Jesus complainingly cries out: "They hated Me without a cause" (Jn. 15:25). Alas! And because of such disregard, should not the sky again rain fire and brimstone upon you, as in Sodom (Gen. 19:24), in order to scorch you? Should not the earth suddenly open beneath your feet and swallow you alive, as it did Dathan and Abiram (Num. 16:27-33)?

Circumstance 3:
The place

The third circumstance of sin, brother, is the place where you commit it.

Alas! If you were to offend God in some place where He would not see the offense, that would be tolerable. But if God inhabits all places, as being everywhere present, and beyond everywhere, how could such a place ever be found? Therefore, you sin before His face, right in front of His face, sinner, before His very eyes, and it seems as if you are saying to Him:

"Even if You are present, even if You see and hear every one of my thoughts, words, and deeds, even if Your most-luminous eyes angrily see my wickedness, I will still do it. If You see it and do not like it, I don't care; it is enough for me that the eyes of men do not see me. And if Your own eyes see me, it does not bother me." O unheard of audacity! O inexpressible disrespect!

What culprit ever dares to commit a crime before his own judge? What rebel ever conspires before the eyes of his own master? You and you alone, poor sinner, dare to do such a thing. Only you, who, compared to the infinity of God, are infinitely smaller than the smallest worm of the earth, dare to lift your neck against the highest majesty and seek to take the crown from its head and corrupt it, something which is more audacious than an ant trying to rise up against the sun and extinguish it: "He has hardened his neck against the Lord Almighty; and he has run against Him with insolence" (Job 15:25-26).

Circumstance 4:
The time

The fourth circumstance of sin is the time during which you commit the sin, by which circumstance the great wickedness of sin is surely demonstrated. For you do not commit sin only when God is disciplining you and chastising you, but always and continually. This is how God Himself complains: "A people that provoketh Me to anger continually to My face"

(Is. 65:3). You sin continually, even when He provides for your needs, even when He sustains your being, even when He grants you your nourishment and clothing. You sin continually, even when He protects you from thousands of fearful dangers, even when He gives you strength, health, beauty, friends, possessions, and every other good thing you have.

But the worst thing of all is that, at the same time that you are receiving these things from God, you use them as weapons to ceaselessly war upon the very One Who gave them to you in the first place, something that, if you were to do against an earthly king, would make you a lawless and thankless monster. All of the histories of the world would speak of your ingratitude, and every person would be ashamed that they shared a common nature with you.

Circumstance 5:
The evil results

The fifth circumstance of mortal sin is the terrible evils and results which sin brings upon you. There are seven, like the seven heads of the venomous dragon (Rev. 12:3).

Evil 1

The first evil is the deprivation of the grace of God, that is, the initial, dynamic, and justifying grace, and simply, the general grace of Christ which comes through faith, which is such a precious pearl that the Lord expended all of His blood in order to purchase it for you, and which you, the unfortunate sinner, exchange for nothing, acting more foolishly than a child who exchanges a diamond for a single walnut.

Without this grace, brother, your soul is so repulsive that someone cannot look upon it as it is and not perish. And from where is this known? Listen. According to the Ecclesiastical Histories, a certain virgin saw a demon that was so hideous, that she swore she would prefer to walk upon a road full of lighted coals and flaming irons with her bare feet until the end of the world, rather than see that unbearable sight one more time. And even considering all this, God told her that she did not see all of the hideousness of the demon as it truly is, but only an image of it.

Alas! If a single mortal sin brought upon the demon such monstrous hideousness, and from a bright star of heaven transformed it into a torch of Hades, how hideous, then, has your own soul become, brother, from so many countless sins? Who can understand how repulsive it is in the eyes of God? And how much filth has come out of its wounds? And if that virgin sensed the filth of sinners and could not endure it, suppose how filthy you appear, decayed and rotted by sins, before God?

For certain, no creature, no dragon, no beast, is as detestable to you, sinner, as you are detestable to God because of sin. But even considering all this, you the poor wretch still do not see your filthy soul and grieve over it, but like a peacock you strut around and take joy in either the stylish clothes you wear, or in your beautiful face, or in your other superficial externals. Therefore, with every right the Lord called you and your kind whitewashed tombs, which outwardly are made of beautiful marble or have an attractive inscription, but inside they are full of filthy bones: "Woe unto you... for ye are like unto whited sepulchres, which indeed appear beautiful outward, but are within full of dead men's bones, and of all uncleanness" (Mt. 23:27).

Evil 2

The second evil of mortal sin is that it deprives your soul, sinner, of divine sonship, which is a special and unique gift, and is such a high charisma that it causes the Holy Spirit to dwell within you (as opposed to all the other places) with an especial and unique presence and energy. This divine sonship makes you a son of God and an heir of His kingdom, and it renders your works worthy of such a great reward that the smallest of your deeds is worth as much as all of Paradise. But as soon as you lose this grace, what do you become? Alas! You become a son of the devil and like the devil on account of sin, just as a son resembles his father according to nature: "Ye are of your father the devil" (Jn. 8:44).

Evil 3

The third evil of sin is that it deprives you, brother, of the eternal inheritance of Paradise, as we have said, which your heavenly Father has prepared to give you. And who is able to describe how much a firstborn son and heir is preferred over everyone else by a king, and how much he is envied by the others, and how much he is praised? Certainly no one. On the contrary, no one is able to describe how foolish and how ridiculous the person is who would sell his birthright and his inheritance for a small amount, as Esau sold his for a small amount of lentils (Gen. 25:34). Compare now, sinner, heaven with earth, the inheritance of the incorruptible kingdom which you lost, with the birthright of Esau and with the earthly inheritance of a corruptible kingdom, and you will understand much more how ridiculous and foolish you are. For this reason the Apostle wrote: "Lest there be any fornicator, or profane person, as Esau, who for one morsel of meat sold his birthright. For ye know how that afterward, when he would have inherited the blessing, he was rejected: for he found no place of repentance, though he sought it carefully with tears" (Heb. 12:16).

Evil 4

The fourth evil caused by sin is that it deprives you, beloved, of all the rewards for all of the good works which you performed before you sinned. For example: if you were to pass sixty entire years harshly, remaining completely naked, being chafed by the heat of the sun in the summer, and frozen by the cold in the winter, like Onouphrios and Peter the Athonite, if you carried an iron chain around your neck for twenty years, like St. Eusevios, if you dwelled in a tomb for fourteen years, like the Righteous Iakovos, if you stood upon a column for forty years, like St. Symeon the Stylite, if you turned more gentiles to the Faith than the Apostles, if you received more revelations than the Prophets, if you shed more blood than all the Martyrs, and then after all these things you committed a single mortal sin, all of your prior good works and rewards would straightway disappear because of it, and if you died in sin, you would profit nothing from them. This is what God Himself judges concerning the righteous person who sins, that his former righteousnesses will not be remembered: "All his righteousnesses shall not be remembered" (Ezek. 33:13),[411] for according to the divine Gregory of Nyssa: "The divine eye always looks at the present, and does not consider that which is passed."[412]

Can a greater disaster be found in the whole world? Most certainly, brother, someone would be speechless seeing this great loss of yours, not knowing what to say, just as those friends of Job, seeing the great tragedy and misfortune he suffered, sat silently for seven days in his presence, unable to offer a single word: "So they sat down with him upon the ground seven days and seven nights, and none spake a word unto him: for they saw that his grief was very great" (Job. 2:13).

Evil 5

The fifth evil caused by sin is that it deprives you, brother, of the exceptional assistances of God, for just as a loving mother always loves and provides for her child from her heart, so does God provide for your soul when it is without mortal sin: "As one whom his mother comforteth, so will I comfort you" (Is. 66:13). He assists it, governs it, holds it in His arms, gladdens its heart, illumines its intellect, encourages its will, and gives it

---

411   In agreement, Basil the Great says: "For he who labored in good works and then returned again to his old ways does not only damage the wages he received for his labors, but is also worthy of even greater condemnation, because having tasted the good words of God and having been deemed worthy of the knowledge of the Mysteries, he betrayed everything by being seduced by a brief hedonistic pleasure" (*In ebriosos* 1, PG 31, 445A). And Gregory the Theologian, in his tetrastich Iambic Poetry, said: "Those who walk low we call evil, for they have abruptly fallen from their heights" (*Carmina Moralia* 33, PG 37, 931A). And Solomon said: "Severe judgment falls on those in high places, for the lowliest man may be pardoned in mercy, but mighty men will be mightily tested" (Wis. 6:5-6). Concerning this, see also Homily 91 of St. Symeon the New Theologian (*Tou Hosiou Symeon tou Neou Theologou ta Heuriskomena*, Venice, 1790; see *Thanksgiving Prayers* 2, SC 113, pp. 330-356). (Translator's note: This work contains 92 homilies, 181 practical and theological chapters, and 55 hymns of St. Symeon the New Theologian which were gathered together out of the libraries of Mt. Athos, translated into the Modern Greek of the day by the monk Dionysios Zagoraios, and then introduced and edited by St. Nikodemos.)
412   *In Psalmorum Inscriptiones I*, 7, PG 44, 460C.

potent strength in order to easily work out its salvation.

But when you mortally sin, even if God does not completely withdraw from you, He does not, however, pour out on your soul the former streams and assistances of His grace. Wherefore, being deprived of these assistances, your salvation becomes more difficult. For the higher part of your soul becomes weak, and the lower and passionate part strengthens and takes over, thereby falling again and again into one sin after another, finally ending up in an abyss of evils.

Evil 6

The sixth evil which sin causes you, brother, is that it makes you liable to eternal hell, for as soon as you mortally sin, your name is erased from the book of life, and you are sentenced to the frightful torments of Hades to be punished eternally.

Evil 7

The seventh evil of sin is the final one, which comes after death, for if you do not destroy sin before your death with a truthful and complete repentance and correction, your soul really descends into the prisons of Hades, into a painful place, into a dark place, waiting until the general resurrection for your body to resurrect, in order to receive the fullness of hell.

Meditate upon and consider at all times all of these infinite evils and tragedies which sin causes you, my fellow sinner, in order that you come to hate sin from the depths of your heart as your most deadly and greatest enemy, and so you do not commit it another time.

3. Knowledge of sin according to
the three punishments it received

It now remains, brother, to demonstrate to you the evil[413] of sin according to the severe punishment with which God punished it: in the angels, in men, and in the Person of Jesus Christ.

Punishment of sin in the angels

God punished sin in the angels because of their single prideful and rebellious thought, and cast an innumerable multitude of angels into Hades. It did not matter to Him that they were immaterial spirits according to nature, immortal in their being, wiser than all men, and more powerful than all of the lower creatures. Their nobility did not matter to Him, nor their fine intellect, nor their spiritual knowledge, but He condemned them to be eternally punished by the worst torments of Hades, in order to teach us how much He hates and punishes sin: "And the angels which kept not their first estate, but left their own habitation, He hath reserved in everlasting chains under darkness unto the judgment of the great day" (Jude 6). And the Apostle Peter said: "God spared not the angels that sinned, but cast them down to Tartaros, and delivered them into chains of darkness, to be reserved unto judgment" (2 Pet. 2:4).[414]

---

413   Note that sin is in and of itself mainly called evil, that is, it is caused from a malevolent and malicious will. Unduly, then, is the punishment and chastisement of sin called evil, because it is for the mortification of sinners, that is, punishment is unto their benefit and for the correction of their faults, according to the ensuing will of God, concerning which Amos says: "There is no evil in the city which the Lord did not make" (Am. 3:6). (See St. Basil the Great, *Quod Deus non est Auctor Malorum* (*That God is not the Author of Evils*), PG 31, 329A-353A; *St. Basil the Great: On the Human Condition*, pp. 65-80.)

414   Translator's note: And we read in the *Euchologion*: "God, the holy, the fearful, the glorious, Who is incomprehensible and inscrutable in all His works and all His might, Who foreordained for you, O devil, the punishment of eternal hell" (Second Exorcism of the Service for the making of a catechumen).

Punishment of sin in men

God punished sin in men, for as soon as the first man, Adam, disobeyed His commandment, He cast him out of Paradise and condemned him, and us, all of his descendants, to live upon this accursed earth in poverty, with sicknesses, pains, worries, misfortunes, and finally, to experience a painful death, which is against nature. He punished sin, for the sinful men during the time of Noah drowned in the universal cataclysmic flood, and Sodom and Gomorrah burned in another new cataclysm of brimstone and fire. And finally, He condemned unrepentant sinners to eternally burn in the fire of hell, who will never have reprieve from the torments of the demons, and God will never feel for their calamity, never hear their wailings, but will rather oppose and despise them eternally, for those are the pitiful people mentioned by Malachi: "The people against whom the Lord hath indignation forever" (Mal. 1:4).

Do these punishments seem great to you, my brother? But know that each sin is never punished by God as it deserves, but always with compassion. And even if a sinner is eternally punished, he is punished less severely than he should, and he can say with Job: "He has not punished me according to the full amount of my sins" (Job 33:27).[415]

Punishment of sin in the Person of Jesus Christ

God also punished sin in the Person of Jesus Christ with such a severe

---

415   Translator's note: St. Nikodemos also has this to say about God's punishment: "In truth, God of Himself does not discipline and punish anyone, but we are punished because of our own doing, becoming subject, on account of our own sins, to the wrath and punishment of God, which we bring upon ourselves according to righteousness. Wherefore Tertullian said this brief but dogmatic word: 'God is supremely good out of His own character, and righteous on account of ours' (*On the Resurrection of the Flesh*, ch. 14). Solomon also attests to this saying: 'God did not make death, and He does not delight in the death of the living. For He created all things that they might exist' (Wis. 1:13-14). And James the Brother of God says: 'God tempteth no man. But every man is tempted, when he is drawn away of his own lust, and enticed' (Jas. 1:13-14)" (*Kepos Chariton*, pp. 118-119). Read also Clement of Alexandria's *Paedagogus* (*The Instructor*), Book I, chs. 8-10 (SC 70, pp. 222-278; ANF (V2), pp. 225-233).

punishment that all of the abovementioned punishments seem as but a shadow in comparison to it. For only a single light wound in the Person of Jesus Christ, a single thorn from His crown, a single one of His scourges, is a greater punishment than if God destroyed the whole world and cast men, angels, archangels, and every other creature into the fire of hell. For what has the punishment of all creatures to do with the smallest torment of the Creator, the most innocent One, the Most-holy One, the only-begotten Son?

However, in order to destroy sin, His heavenly Father was not pleased that His Son should suffer a light torment, but extreme torments. Do you wish to understand this, sinner? Turn and see how Jesus suffers because of your sin![416] He is betrayed, slandered, mocked, and dragged to the courts like a criminal. See how His eyes are wounded from the buffets and the blows! How His face is full of spittings! How His cheeks are bruised from the slaps! How His throat is dried up from thirst! See how His lips are embittered from the gall! How His head is pierced from the rigid thorns! How His arms and wrists are bound with strong ropes! How His shoulders are weighed down from the weight of the Cross! How His hands and His feet are nailed with sharp nails![417] Look, sinner, and see how all His veins

---

416   Translator's note: St. Peter of Damaskos says: "Thus one ought to constrain the intellect as much as possible within the bounds of some meditation acceptable to God. For as there are seven forms of bodily discipline, so there are eight types of contemplation, or types of spiritual knowledge, that pertain to the intellect. Three of these, which have already been mentioned, are connected with the holy sufferings of the Lord and we should always of our own accord meditate on them, so as to grieve over our own soul and over those of our fellow men" (*Twenty-Four Discourses* IX, *GrPhilokalia*, p. 662; tr. *The Philokalia*, v. 3, p. 236).

417   A certain pious teacher, seeing the Lord nailed to the Cross, burning with love said: "I do not want to be unwounded, seeing Thee wounded" (from *Sure Guidance*). And Ignatios the Godbearer wrote the following longing words of love in his Twelveth Epistle to the Romans: "I long after the Lord, the Son of the true God and Father, even Jesus Christ. Him I seek, Who died for us and rose again... Permit me to be an imitator of the passion of Christ, my God... My eros has been crucified, and there is no fire in me that loves anything; but there is living water springing up in me, and which says to me inwardly, Come to the Father. I have no delight in corruptible food, nor in the pleasures of this life. I desire the bread of God, the heavenly bread, the bread of life, which is the flesh of God, Jesus Christ... and I desire the drink of God, namely His blood, which is incorruptible love and eternal life; I no longer wish to live as men... Believe me that I love Jesus, who was delivered for my sake... Do not hinder me in attaining to life; for Jesus is the life of believers. Do not wish to

are emptied of blood! How His side is pieced with a spear! How all His joints are distended from the extreme tension of the Cross! And how He gave up His spirit hanging upon the rigid nails! See how all His body became a great wound, without form, without human beauty! "We saw Him, but He had no form nor beauty" (Is. 53:2).

Now pass your mind, brother, to the internal part of His soul, in order to see there how much incomparably more His soul suffered than His body, being exceedingly sad on account of so many sins, so many offenses, and on account of the great disregard the very sinners He suffered for and came to save will have for His majesty and for His sufferings. In brief, the interior suffering which Jesus endured for men is so extreme, that it is impossible for someone to understand it in this present life. Only on the day of judgment, according to some teachers, will every single person completely understand it. For the Lord will reveal it then, for all men to see, unto the shame of the reprobate sinners.[418]

What have you to say about sin now, beloved? Do you understand how infinite its evil is from the incomprehensible punishment which sweetest Jesus suffered in order to destroy sin?[419] So now that you have learned the evil of sin, according to sin in and of itself, according to the circumstances

---

keep me in a state of death, for life without Christ is death… Though I am alive while I write to you, yet I am eager to die for the sake of Christ" (chs. 6-8, PG 5, 812A-816B). And Paul, being possessed with eros for the Crucified, enthusiastically said: "I am crucified with Christ: nevertheless I live; yet not I, but Christ liveth in me: and the life which I now live in the flesh I live by the faith of the Son of God, Who loved me, and gave Himself for me" (Gal. 2:20). And elsewhere, showing how much love all Christians should have for the crucified Jesus, Paul said: "They which live should not henceforth live unto themselves, but unto Him which died for them, and rose again" (2 Cor. 5:15).

418   Translator's note: Elsewhere St. Nikodemos says: "The torments which He suffers is like an ocean of pains and sufferings, but not only externally from His enemies, but also internally from His love" (*Pneumatika Gymnasmata*, p. 38).

419   Concerning this, a certain teacher said: "From this remedy (the Passion of Christ), I understand the severity of my wounds" (*Instruction for Penitents*, p. 202). And Ignatios the Godbearer said that the wounds of sinners were so great that the Lord needed to be wounded in order to heal them. (Translator's note: St. Symeon the New Theologian also says: "So in order for there to be a fearful and great mystery, so that instead of Adam who fell into sin, He who did not fall into sin would be punished, and he who did fall would become worthy of mercy. For this reason instead of the tree, the Cross, instead of the feet walking toward the forbidden tree and instead of the outstretched hands which took the forbidden fruit, large iron nails driven into His divine hands and into His immaculate

of sin, and according to the punishment it received from God, grieve your soul, crush your heart, come to yourself, and firmly resolve that you would rather die a thousand deaths than commit a single mortal sin ever again.

Precaution 6:
Prayer

The divine Augustine says that a person must do whatever he is able, and should ask God for whatever he is unable to do: "Do what you are able, and ask for whatever you are unable to do." For this reason, brother, after giving you the above five precautions so that you do not again fall into sin, and which you are able to do on your own with your own strength and will, we lastly also give you a sixth precaution, which is divine prayer. Do not cease, therefore, from dedicating yourself to God, and fervently asking Him to strengthen your weakness and to make your will firm in the resolution you made with His grace and assistance from on high, hoping that He will hear you out of His great mercy, as He Himself promised: "If then he shall cry to Me, I will hearken to him, for I am merciful" (Ex. 22:27).

You do not have strength of your own? You do not have resoluteness in your will? The reason is because you do not ask for these things from God: "Ye have not, because ye ask not," says the divine James (4:2). Are you afraid of danger? Are you frightened of the temptation of sin? Keep vigil and pray, so that you do not fall into it: "Watch and pray, that ye enter not into temptation" (Mt. 26:41). For your convenience, see the following prayer which we have composed for you.

A Prayer

Most merciful Lord Jesus Christ my God, I thank Thee for deeming me, the sinner, worthy to receive forgiveness from Thee, through the Mystery of Confession to my Spiritual Father. So then, imitating David who said: "I have sworn and resolved that I will keep the judgments of Thy righteousness" (Ps. 118:106), I promise Thee, with the resolute

---

feet, instead of the tasting of the fruit, He tasted of gall and vinegar, instead of death, death" (*Alphabetika Kephalaia* 1, p. 44).)

will of my soul, that I would rather die a thousand deaths than ever commit a single mortal sin again, and grieve Thine infinite goodness. But because mine own will is weak on its own without Thy help, I fervently ask Thee to strengthen me with Thy grace, and establish me with Thy mighty help, so that I may remain steadfast in my holy resolution until the end. Yea, my most-loving Jesus, enable me to pass the rest of my life in repentance, in order to receive Thy grace here below, and Thy blessed glory in heaven above. Through the intercessions of Thy supremely blessed Mother and of all Thy Saints. Amen.

Epilogue

I conclude and seal this counsel with the following words. The Father, He Who sent John the Forerunner to baptize, preached through the Baptist's mouth to sinners: "Repent" (Mt. 3:2). The Son, when He appeared to the world, made this word the beginning and foundation of His preaching: "Repent" (Mt. 4:17). The Holy Spirit, when He descended in the form of tongues of fire, spoke this word through the Apostle Peter: "Repent" (Acts 2:38). There are Three that bear witness, and the witness of the Three is true,[420] rather, truth itself. So my fellow sinners: repent, repent, repent, "for the kingdom of heaven is at hand" (Mt. 3:2).[421]

---

420   cf. 1 Jn. 5:7-8

421   Let it be known to you that, as Job the Sinner says in his work, *On the Mysteries*, the person who repents is said to be found according to nature (for it is proper to human nature to repent whenever it errs in something). But the person who errs and does not repent, nor is corrected, rightly and correctly is and is called against nature, because he is found to be outside of the parameters of human nature and is likened unto the irrational beasts, or rather, with the demons, who never repent. Therefore, God complainingly says: "No man repented him of his wickedness, saying, What have I done?" (Jer. 8:6). And let this also be known to you, that repentance, because it is a secondary good effect, coming after the primary evil effect, as designated by St. Maximos, makes the sin which was committed knowingly as if it were committed in ignorance. And because repentance is voluntary, it makes the sin committed voluntarily as if it happened involuntarily, according to Gregory Palamas of Thessaloniki. And because repentance overthrows the eternal, that is, the infinite punishment of hell, sin, which is an infinite (or endless) evil, is brought to an end, according to George Koressios. Therefore, whoever repents shows that he sinned in ignorance, that he sinned involuntarily, and furthermore, brings his infinite sin to an end. And whoever does not repent, in addition to showing that he knowingly and voluntarily sinned, causes his sin to remain infinite forever, because he did not bring it to an end with repentance and confession.

HOMILY ON REPENTANCE[422]

Concerning the Audacity of Those Who Intentionally Sin With the Hope That They Can Confess and Repent

INTRODUCTION

For what reason, I ask, does man tend more to fear than to hope when it comes to matters of the body, while, when it comes to matters of the soul, he tends more to hope than to fear? This certainly occurs for no other reason than that man cares little for and does not love his salvation. And therefore he does not fear, because he does not love. There are many and perhaps countless Christians who, according to Job (15:6), drink wickedness like water, for each one of these, before he sins, thinks and says to himself: "Let me sin, and then I will confess and repent." And when he has sinned and confessed, he no longer concerns himself with his sin, for he says: "I have confessed; I have repented." "O evil imagination!" says Sirach, "why were you formed to cover the land with deceit?" (Sir. 37:3). O most lawless delusion and presumption which covers the earth with sins, from which depth did you arise? Certainly from none other than Hades. Should you not then return again to Hades and no longer deceive Christians? We, therefore, wish to speak in this present homily about the audacity of the people who say such things.

---

422   This homily, my brother, is very needful and most profitable to the soul, because it shows what true repentance is, and what its results are, and the signs of forgiveness of sins from God. To say it simply, this homily breaks bones (cf. Ps. 50:8, 17). Therefore, if you read it frequently, you will be greatly edified.

Translator's note: The majority of this homily is also included in St. Nikodemos' book, *Pneumatika Gymnasmata* (first published in Venice, 1800). It is the Second Reading (pp. 355-379) of the eight Readings included in the book. This homily was not included in the first edition of the *Exomologetarion* of 1794, but was added by St. Nikodemos to the expanded edition of 1804.

PART 1

There has most certainly never been found any merchant so ignorant that, without reason, he would throw his merchandise into the sea with the hope of getting it back. There do exist, however, Christians who are so ignorant that they willfully throw away the purity of their soul and the grace of God, which is the greatest gift in the world that the Lord could give us, with the hope that they will regain that purity and those heavenly gifts through confession and repentance. These wretched people become chained slaves of Hades on account of this boldness, because they think that they can cut their chains whenever they want. And they present themselves before Lucifer holding out the keys to their soul in their hands, thinking that they will be able to take them back from him whenever they so desire. On the one hand, this is not so surprising, since this error is not something new to the human race. In fact, this was the first temptation in the world, with which the devil enticed Eve to transgress the commandment of God by showing her the compassion and goodness of God saying: "Ye shall not surely die" (Gen. 3:4). That is, do whatever you want, and nothing bad will happen to you, because God is very compassionate and good. And Adam himself, who, according to the Apostle, was not deceived like the woman: "And Adam was not deceived" (1 Tim. 2:14), in spite of this, became an accomplice of Eve by eating the forbidden fruit, for he thought his offense, even though very grave, would nevertheless be easily forgiven by his Fashioner, as the sacred Augustine says in his eleventh Book, and as another theologian of the Church says: "Adam sinned counting on divine mercy," that is, Adam fell thinking that the compassion of God would not punish him, as God had threatened.

And what further proof than this do you want, my brother, when you see how audacious the devil was when he went out to fight against our Lord Jesus Christ with great boldness, thinking to conquer Him with this same weapon of hoping in God's compassion, the same weapon which the devil had successfully used on others so many times before? Thus the wicked one urged the Lord to cast Himself down from the pinnacle of the Temple, in the hope that the angels would come straightway to catch Him and so

He would suffer no harm, according to the commandment which God gave His servants to observe: "Cast thyself down: for it is written, He shall give his angels charge concerning thee: and in their hands they shall bear thee up, lest at any time thou dash thy foot against a stone" (Mt. 4:6).

Therefore, no one should wonder that the enemy continuously tempts Christians with this deceptive thought, urging them to cast themselves down and to fall into every act of lawlessness and for thousands more to join in that first sin, with the expectation and hope that they will confess and that the Spiritual Fathers will forgive them, scurrying like angels of peace in order to keep them from falling into Hades.

That at which someone should wonder is the fact that Christians do not recognize such a blatant and obvious deception of the devil, and how they show such thanklessness to God, for they use confession and repentance as an excuse for sins, and the compassion and goodness of God, which is the cause of their salvation, they make into an excuse for their fall and their perdition! And just as the poisonous plant called wolfsbane increases its poison with the sweet dew of heaven, likewise do those unfortunate Christians increase their poison and their death with the most sweet and salvific blood of Jesus Christ, because this blood which helps drown every one of their sins in the bath of repentance and confession, they rather, in a manner of speaking, use to water and increase their sins.[423] Alas! Is there still to be found greater lawlessness than this? And what is it? Is it not that we use our treatment as a triumph and victory of the devil? Thus does the divine Ambrose lament over this: "Our medicine has become a triumph of the devil himself."[424]

---

[423] Translator's note: As St. John of Damaskos says in one of his pre-Communion Prayers: "Account me worthy to receive without condemnation Thy divine, glorious, immaculate, and life-creating Mysteries, not unto punishment, nor unto an increase of sins" (*Deprecationes*, PG 96, 816D; tr. *A Prayer Book for Orthodox Christians*, Boston, 2000, p. 344).

[424] *On Repentance*, Book II.

PART 2

The Harm Caused to the Salvation of Those Who Sin With the Hope of Confessing and Repenting

But who is able to sufficiently show the harm which those who sin with the hope of repenting bring upon themselves? I believe that the greater portion of Christians will be punished on account of this evil and deceptive hope which, little by little, steers them toward the fearful precipice of Hades, because, although they believe that an eternal fire has been prepared for those who sin, in spite of this, they still sin, as if believing that hell is just a myth. And why is this? It is because they consider the treatment for their sins so easy, and that all they have to do is confess the sins they committed to their Spiritual Father and receive a light penance. And immediately after they do this they are at peace and carefree, thinking that they have paid every debt.

1. An excessive amount of sins

The first harm which those who sin with the hope of repentance bring upon themselves is the amount and great number of sins which they commit. For, finding it easy to confess their sins with some slight compunction and thinking that upon this alone stands all of their repentance, on account of this ease and this false hope, I say, these wretched people fall again into the passions. And after they fall once, they forsake the restraint of reason and caution and run like mindless animals down the road of perdition. Therefore, who is able to number the transgressions they commit? As often as they find the opportune manner and place, they immediately fall into sin; as often as their foul appetite desires, they immediately fall; as often as a bad thought comes to them, they also immediately fall into the act. Out of curiosity, then, let us take an accurate count to see just how many sins they commit.

Many of these sinners, who think it easy to receive forgiveness for their sins through confession, may commit ten sins every single day, either by their evil deeds, or by their wicked lusts, or by their imprudent conversations, or by their inappropriate indulgences, especially, however, and above all, by the scandals they cause others, thereby killing those people's souls. Therefore, according to this count, the total sins they commit in one month is three hundred sins, and in one year they will commit over three thousand sins, so that each one of them will have knocked more than three thousand times on the gates of Hades. Why is it so difficult for us to believe that the righteousness of God will open the gates of Hades one time to one of these sinners, allowing him to fall into that abyss? This is exactly what the righteousness of God threatens to do by the mouth of Jeremiah: "Thou hast been painfully treated for healing, there is no help for thee… for I have smitten thee with the stroke of an enemy, even severe correction, for the multitude of thine iniquity: thy sins have multiplied" (Jer. 37:13, 14). Weigh these words carefully, my brother. God does not say that you are not treated, but that you do not benefit from the treatment: "Thou hast been painfully treated for healing, there is no help for thee." Indeed, with many treatments, for not only once, but many, many times have you confessed, and in spite of this confession, which is supposed to heal and kill sins, on account of your own wickedness it has served to increase them. This is because you say to yourself: "If I sin, it is enough that I confess; and if I sinned one time, I can sin again and again, because, whether I commit many sins or a few sins, I am able to confess and repent." Therefore, yes, you were treated, but you did not benefit whatsoever from that treatment, for the benefit you received from so many confessions is an innumerable multitude of sins, without you even knowing that this multitude of sins plunges you into Hades. It makes you liable to God's harsh chastisement, without compassion, and for God to punish you as one of His enemies who is at fault with God to such a degree that it is equal to the amount of compassion which God has shown toward him: "I have smitten thee with the stroke of an enemy… for thy sins have multiplied." For this reason, the Prophet Jeremiah speaks elsewhere allegorically about the soul which confesses and is treated for its sins, but afterward sins again and becomes untreatable and liable to be severed completely from God and to be punished: "We would have healed Babylon, but she is not healed: forsake her… for her judgment reacheth unto heaven" (Jer. 28:9).

2. The excessive gravity of sins

The second harm they bring upon themselves, that is, those who sin with the hope of confessing and repenting, is the gravity and excess of sins they commit. For these people who say: "I will confess," under this false presumption, sin without any fear, I say, and without any limitation, and plunge into the depths and the most impure mud of sin by practicing such shameless acts of wickedness, that not even the godless do those things, and they roll around in the muck of sin and in filth, in which not even the mindless animals themselves roll around. But what does God do to them? He does not forget this wickedness, but when the time comes, He punishes it, as He says with the mouth of Hosea: "They have corrupted themselves according to the days of the hill[425]"; behold the sins of these evil people. "He will remember their iniquities, He will take vengeance on their sins" (Hos. 9:9); behold also the punishment with which God chastises them.

3. Disregard, boasting, unrepentance, and denial

The third harm that those who sin with the hope of repentance bring upon themselves is the deliberate disregard for their salvation, and the deliberate disregard for the Lord's commandments, for according to Solomon: "When an ungodly man comes into a depth of evils, he despises everything" (Pr. 18:3). Concerning these, when they reach the uttermost of evil, their intellect becomes calloused, their heart hardens, and they have no reckoning of sin whatsoever. Some of them go further still, for they not only have disregard for everything, but they also take pleasure in their sins and rejoice in them, boasting as if they have made some great accomplishments as Solomon says: "O who rejoice in evils, and delight in wicked perverseness!" (Pr. 2:12). And as Isaiah says: "They have proclaimed their sin as Sodom, and made it manifest" (Is. 3:9). And those who at first said, "Let me go ahead and sin now, and I will confess and repent later," degenerate to such a level that, when they reach the depth of evils, they do not wish to confess

---

425   Namely, they have been corrupted by such grave and excessive wickedness, as in the days of the godless and idol worshippers, when they would sacrifice to the idols upon the hills.

or repent any longer. And if it happens that at some point they wish to confess and repent, they will not be able to, for their habitual sin will have become an addiction, and their addiction will have become as part of their nature and will have hardened their heart like stone, making it numb and insusceptible to repentance and correction.[426] And this is how these wretched souls die, uncorrected and unrepentant.

And it is a great miracle how these Christians who reach the uttermost of evil hold on to their faith and do not deny it. For many of them—alas!—even let go of the anchor of the Faith, for an evil way of life gives birth to evil dogmas, as the divine Chrysostom says.[427]

Do you see, brother, how much harm and what awful destruction those who sin with the false hope that they will confess and repent bring upon themselves? Therefore, Abba Isaac most wisely said that, whoever falls into a second transgression with the hope of repentance deals deceitfully with God and will die without hope, not having time to repent as he had hoped: "The man who slips a second time, hoping that one day he will repent, walks craftily before God; death falls upon him unexpectedly, and he does not reach the time when he hoped to accomplish the works of virtue."[428] Basil the Great says something very similar: "He who perpetrates sin with the hope of repentance has the way of evil and does not have repentance."[429] And that which St. Ambrose says is in agreement with this: "The ease of forgiveness provides the occasion for sin."

---

426   Translator's note: Concerning the vicious cycle sin creates, St. Nicholas Cabasilas says: "The habit of sin arises from evil actions, like a disease introduced by tainted food. It is permanent and chains souls with unbreakable fetters. It enslaves the mind and brings about the worst effects of all by inciting its captives to commit the most wicked actions. It is produced by them and constantly engenders them; it is born and similarly gives birth in a vicious cycle. Accordingly sin has no end, since the habit gives rise to the actions and the accumulation of actions aggravates the habit. Thus the evils are mutually reinforced and constantly progress" (*De Vita in Christo* 2, PG 150, 536A-536B; tr. *The Life in Christ*, p. 76).

427   *On I Corinthians*, Homily 40, 3, PG 61, 351.

428   *Ascetical Homilies*, Homily 51, p. 250.

429   *Homilia de Poenitentia* 6, PG 31, 1488B.

PART 3

Concerning the Treatment of Those Who Sin With the Hope That They Will Confess and Repent

1. Prayer as a treatment

"Thou art good, O Lord, and in Thy goodness teach me Thy statutes" (Ps. 118:68). The Prophet David made this prayer, and you, brother, must also make this prayer to God with all of your heart. For prayer is the primary treatment of that evil presumption and false hope which we have been criticizing up till now. O Lord, Thou art good, Thou art goodness itself according to essence: "Thou art good, O Lord." Show me the way, then, by which Thy very goodness will teach me how to keep Thy law: "In Thy goodness teach me Thy statutes." This is what the Lord seeks from you, being good towards you, waiting for your confession and to forgive your sins. That is, you should also learn from Him to be good. How then are you not fearful of infuriating Him by distorting His intent? Why do you wish to be so bad and lawless toward God, when God is so good and gentle towards you? "Shall evil be recompensed for good?" (Jer. 18:20). Is that how you reciprocate the blessings of your God? Is that how you manipulate the goodness of God and the grace of confession, making it into an instrument of sin and an insult to God?

One of two things occur, sinner, even if you do not believe it. Because there exists between the goodness of God and evil an infinite antithesis, essential and irreconcilable, by confusing evil with goodness, you do not believe correctly in God as one should believe in God. But if you do believe in Him correctly, you then turn the goodness of God into an occasion for you to sin, which is a great enemy of the goodness of God. Know that this is nothing other than setting God against God, and like making His mercy and His righteousness to fight against one another.[430]

---

430   Translator's note: St. Basil the Great says: "These qualities are joined to each other, mercy and judgment, lest either mercy alone should produce presumption, or judgment alone cause despair" (*Homilia in Psalmum XXXII* 3, PG 29, 332A), as the Psalmist sings: "Of mercy and judgment

Therefore my brother, always supplicate God to remove from your heart this false and deceptive hope, concerning which it is written: "We have made falsehood our hope, and by falsehood shall we be protected" (Is. 28:15), and to enlighten you by His grace to understand that this hope is a deception and trap of the devil, with which he deceived our forefathers in Paradise, as we mentioned earlier, and which continues to deceive innumerable miserable sinners, plunging them into Hades. And in order for you to be saved from this deception, say that Psalm of David to the Lord: "Keep me from the snare which they have laid for me" (Ps. 140:10).

2. Knowledge of true repentance and its fruit as a treatment

The second treatment, my brother, is to fight against the root of this false hope, which arises from two forms of ignorance: 1) from not knowing what true confession and repentance is, and 2) from not knowing what

---

will I sing unto Thee" (Ps. 100:1). And the wise Sirach says: "Do not say, 'I sinned, and what happened to me?' for the Lord is slow to anger. Do not be so confident of atonement that you add sin to sin. Do not say, 'His mercy is great, He will forgive the multitude of my sins,' for both mercy and wrath are with Him, and His anger rests on sinners. Do not delay to turn to the Lord, nor postpone it from day to day; for suddenly the wrath of the Lord will go forth, and at the time of punishment you will perish" (Sir. 5:4-7). Again, St. Basil says: "God is good, but He is also righteous, and those who are righteous reward in proportion to merit, as it is written: 'Do good, O Lord, unto them that are good and unto the upright of heart. But them that turn aside unto crooked ways shall the Lord lead away with the workers of iniquity' (Ps. 124:4-5). He is merciful, but He is also a judge, for: 'The Lord loveth mercy and judgment' (Ps. 32:5) And: 'Blessed are the merciful,' says the Lord, 'for they shall obtain mercy' (Mt. 5:7). Do you see with what discernment He bestows mercy, neither being merciful without judgment, nor judging without mercy? For: 'Merciful is the Lord and righteous' (Ps. 114:5). Let us not, therefore, know God only in part, nor make His philanthropy an excuse for our sloth; for this, thunders, for this, lightnings—that His goodness may not be held in despite. He Who causes the sun to rise (Mt. 5:45) also strikes men with blindness (4 Kg. 6:18). He Who sends the rain (Zech. 10:1) also causes the rain of fire (Gen. 19:24). By the one He manifests His goodness; by the other, His severity. For the one let us love Him, for the other let us fear" (*Regulæ Fusius*, PG 31, 897C-900A). Also note what St. Nikodemos has to say about Scripture attributing wrath to God: "But the wrath of God is not passion and inner agitation, as it is in men, for God is dispassionate; but what is called the wrath of God in a manner befitting man is the prudent (κατ' οἰκονομίαν, according to economy) punishment of the sins of men" (*Kepos Chariton*, p. 56).

kinds of results and fruit true repentance and confession produce. Therefore, when someone removes these two forms of ignorance from his intellect, it will most certainly be healed.

Those then that sin with the confidence of confession do not know what confession is. They think that confession is nothing more than thoroughly telling their sins to their Spiritual Father and that, once they have carefully revealed them, they have done everything. On this account all of their diligent preparation for confession is focused on remembering the sins they have committed, and right after their confession they are preoccupied with nothing else than to make sure that they did not forget a single sin. But if this diligent recollection of and preoccupation with sin is alone sufficient to reconcile them with God, the way to heaven would not be narrow, as the Gospel tells us: "Narrow and difficult is the way, which leadeth unto life" (Mt. 7:14), but it would be wider than the city streets. And what great effort is it to tell our sins to some Spiritual Father, since we have become accustomed to doing this since we were children? And if everything depends solely upon this (simply to say our sins), those unabashed and shameless sinners, who boast about their sins and speak about them in their get-togethers with their friends as if it is just a game, would be most prepared to confess thoroughly, I say, for they confess all of their sins shamelessly. Confession would then be something accomplished only with the mouth, and would be more an unloading of the memory rather than of the heart. But this is not the truth, for confession in a distinct manner means for the sinner to turn away from sin and to return again to God.

A. Confession must entail grief

Therefore, even if this outward revealing of sins by the mouth of the sinner is necessary, so that the Spiritual Father may hear them and correct the sinner and forgive him, it is not alone sufficient, for it is necessary that the sinner also has an interior pain of heart on account of his sins. This grief must have these three elements: 1) that it is drastic, 2) that it is extreme, and 3) that it is supranatural. If then during your own confession, brother, one of these elements is missing, your confession will be like that of Saul, and like that of Antiochus, and like that of Judas, because the repentance of these men was with the mouth alone, and not with the heart.[431]

But because these three elements of the grief of the heart are required, so also is it required for us to receive forgiveness from God for our sins. Therefore it is necessary that I clearly explain to you here, brother, or at least remind you, about each of these one by one.

B. The grief must be drastic

So then, the grief of repentance must be drastic, which means that it is not to be slight and faint, having no drastic and remarkable effect. But it should be so drastic that it rules the heart, and that it does not allow the heart to be conquered by (not to say, to be completely numb to) the appetite of the flesh and the pleasure of sin, which enters through the assaults of the enemy. And it should be so resolute that it makes the penitent never again want to wrong God through sins: neither at any time, nor for any reason, nor on account of the desire for some created thing, nor out of fear of some evil, just as an esteemed woman is determined to keep the honor of her husband and is absolutely never unfaithful, even if innumerable evils were to pursue her.

C. The grief must be great and extreme

This grief must not be made-up, or small and minimal, but great and extreme. And that grief which prompts us to abstain from and to hate sins out of love for God, because we saddened God with these sins, is called contrition. And that grief which prompts us to turn away from sins out of love for ourselves, because on their account we are deprived of Paradise

---

431   For Saul said to Samuel: "I have sinned: for I have transgressed the commandment of the Lord, and thy words" (1 Kg. 15:24). And Antiochus, in anguish from that God-sent plague of worms, and from the decay of his body, said in repentance: "It is right to be subject to God, and no mortal should pridefully think that he is equal to God. Then the abominable fellow made a vow to the Lord, who would no longer have mercy on him" (2 Macc. 9:12-13). And Judas said: "I have sinned in that I have betrayed the innocent blood" (Mt. 27:4).

and condemned to Hades, is called affliction.[432] These two griefs, I say, must be so extreme and complete that they cause the penitent to turn away from and hate sin with all of his soul, more than any other evil. That is, to hate it with so much force that the soul would rather choose any other harm that could come to it over committing sin, whether it be the deprivation of goods, or the deprivation of honor, or even the deprivation of this present life.[433] Therefore it is mandatory for the person who repents in truth to show God, Who sees the depth of the heart, that his heart is in such pain that, when there is a conflict between his love for God and his love for things, he prefers the love for God over everything created. And these griefs must be so extreme that they not only forever remain with the penitent and afflict his heart, and not only cause the heart to groan and shed tears, as it is written of sinners: "Ye shall cry out for pain of heart, and shall howl for vexation of spirit" (Is. 65:14), but furthermore cause the heart to hate sin from within and to turn away from it, wishing that the sin had never occurred, nor ever occur again.

D. The grief must be supranatural

This pain of heart must also be supranatural, both according to the principle from which it arises, and according to the end for which it exists. For the principle and cause of this grief is not nature, or some other natural cause, but the supranatural grace of God which afflicts and pricks the heart with this grief of repentance. For this reason Basil the Great said: "Such

---

432   Concerning contrition and affliction, see the beginning of Part Three, *Counsel for the Penitent.*

433   Translator's note: St. Tikhon of Zadonsk on sin: "There is nothing more harmful to man than sin, but man is not so inclined to anything else as much as to sin" (p. 62). "Sin is an evil more evil than any other evil. O it is truly better to go about naked than to sin. It is better to be captive and imprisoned than to sin. It is better to be wounded and have every disease than to sin. It is better never to see the light and to sit in darkness than to sin. It is better to endure curses, mockery, reproach, abuse, beatings and wounds than to sin. Finally, it is better to endure every evil that can possibly be in this world than to sin" (pp. 64-65). "Sin harms more than any poison. Sin is more venomous than any serpent. Sin strips us bare more than any robber, and deprives us of temporal and eternal blessings, and kills the body and the soul" (p. 65). "Sin is more evil than the very devil since sin made the devil" (p. 66) (*Journey to Heaven*, Jordanville, 1994).

spontaneous compunction is God's gift... that the soul having tasted the sweetness of such sorrow may strive to cultivate it."[434] Some have even taken that which the Apostle says: "God hath mercy on whom He will have mercy" (Rom. 9:18), to mean that God afflicts the heart, for the Apostle continues: "And whom He will he hardeneth," hardness and compunction being complete opposites. Likewise, the end and purpose of this grief should not be anything natural or on account of some natural and temporal goods which we lost (for if someone is saddened over such things and grieves, this sorrow and grief does not count as repentance, but is futile). We should rather grieve over the supranatural goods which we were deprived of on account of sin and the supranatural tribulations which we received, which also supranatural faith revealed to us. But the main reason that this grief should be supranatural is this: that through this supranatural grief we are to receive reconciliation and union with God and thereby blessedness, which exceed the laws of nature. So whoever confesses and does not have in his heart this drastic, extreme, and supranatural grief, straightway after confession returns again to his home together with all of his sins.

Therefore, the self-examination of the conscience which someone conducts in order to be able to discover all the sins he committed in deed, word, and by consenting to thoughts, is good and beneficial. It is good that someone confesses to their Spiritual Father all of their sins, without leaving a single one unconfessed, for this complete confession brings great relief to the soul. Accompanying self-examination and confession, however, must also be contrition and the interior pain of heart, about which we are presently speaking. This is because part of the rule which the penitent receives from the Spiritual Father, whether it be fasting, or prostrations, or some other hardship, afflicts and disciplines only the body and the exterior person, and one could even say, it cuts only the outer branches of the tree. But grief afflicts and wounds the interior person and the heart itself, which is the primary and main cause and root of all the sins. When the heart is afflicted, so also are sins afflicted and wounded, that is to say, the devil himself, that dragon and head of all evils, is afflicted and wounded, who,

---

434   *Regulæ Brevius* 16, PG 31, 1092D; tr. *The Ascetic Works of Saint Basil*, p.236.

having nested in the heart, from there assaults and speaks all the obscene and evil and blasphemous thoughts and sins: "For out of the heart proceed evil thoughts, murders, adulteries, fornications, thefts, false witness, blasphemies" (Mt. 15:19).

E. Pain of heart is an element of repentance

For this reason it is a dogma of our Orthodox Church (as George Koressios theologizes in his work, *On the Mysteries*), that this grief and inner sorrow of the heart is one of the necessary and constituent and essential elements of the Mystery of Confession and Repentance. So for example, just as a necessary and essential element of the Mystery of Repentance is the verbal confession of sins by the penitent, and the loosing and binding of sins by the Spiritual Father, and just as water and three-fold immersion and emersion while exclaiming the Name of the Holy Trinity is essential to the Mystery of Baptism, in the same manner the interior pain of heart is also necessary and essential to the Mystery of Repentance. And if this grief is absent from the heart of the penitent, it is obvious that he is unrepentant and unconfessed, even if he repents and confesses, just as whoever does not confess their sins and is not loosed or bound by a Spiritual Father is unrepentant; or just as someone who is baptized without water or without the exclamation of the Name of the Holy Trinity is unbaptized. For this reason the Lord emphatically said: "Except ye repent, ye shall all likewise perish" (Lk. 13:5), namely, if you do not repent with this drastic, extreme, and supranatural pain of heart, you will all be punished. Therefore, the Holy Spirit also wishing to show how necessary this pain of heart is to repentance, *first* seeks this grief from penitents, saying through the Prophet Joel: "Rend your hearts, and not your garments" (Jl. 2:13), and *then* seeks their repentance, for He continues: "And turn unto the Lord your God" (ibid.). Do you see, brother, what proper and rightful confession is? Do you see what true repentance is?

I now ask you to consider, brother, whether the person who audaciously sins saying: "I will confess; I have time to confess," is able in such a manner to grieve for his sins, and to grieve according to the manner about which we have spoken. It seems to me most assuredly that he is unable to have this grief, because by the things he says it is apparent that he does not know that it is necessary to repent rightly and properly. If, however, he does know this and still says these things and sins with the hope of repentance, it is apparent that he is completely without reason, for the things he says are equivalent to saying: "I wish to commit this particular evil, and immediately after I commit it, that very evil will seem hideous to me. I wish to stain my soul now, and afterwards I will want to be able to wash away that pollution with all of my blood. I will love this sin, and afterwards I will hate that I loved it." Do you see how these words are of a foolish person? And when you wish to prevent someone from some evil deed, you say to him: "Be very careful, brother, because you will straightway want to repent." And if that brother is prudent and believes that he will need to repent of it, he will without fail not do it.

Now, brother, consider if you are one of these foolish and ignorant people who say such words. And from now on forsake such nonsense and deception, because inasmuch as you say these things and continue in this deception, sinning with the hope of repentance, it is impossible to attain true repentance and for you to return to God with all of your heart; it is impossible for you to attain pain of heart, the inseparable companion of true repentance, as we said earlier. And it should be so drastic and so extreme that this grief of yours, in comparison with every other grief, would be like the sea compared to a river: "The cup of thy contrition is enlarged like the sea" (Lam. 2:13).

F. Grief and contrition are primarily a charisma of God

It is impossible for you to attain this supranatural grief on your own because, as you heard above, such grief must come from the grace of God, and it is a charisma of God. Since then it is a charisma of God, it is granted to just a few and not to all souls (otherwise it would not be a charisma), and therefore this grief is one of the more precious charismata which the Lord could give you. It is one of the more sublime benefactions of his goodness.

It is one of the greatest works of His omnipotence so that, if God created
a new world completely made of gold, and a new heaven completely made
of sapphire and diamond, and then made you the ruler of this world, this
would certainly be an infinitely smaller charisma than if He gave you one
instant of true grief and true contrition.

Do you now believe that God will at once grant to you whenever you
want this most precious charisma of contrition? This charisma which He
does not bestow upon so many others, whom He leaves in their callousness:
"And whom He will he hardeneth" (Rom. 9:18)? This charisma which, in
order for the Saints to receive it, endured so much, shed so much sweat,
and prepared themselves to receive it with such diligence? If you believe
this, you believe wrongly; so remove this idea from your imagination. For
this reason Basil the Great also says that many times the soul constrains
itself to have compunction, but is not able to, and that for someone to
attain compunction, much diligence and frequent practice is required: "But
to constrain oneself and yet not be able is at once a proof of our neglect
at other times—for it is not possible for a man having come to a thing
suddenly to master it without much a frequent practice in company with
others—and it shows that our soul is dominated by other passions and
allowed by them to be free in the directions in which it desires."[435]

A certain virtuous man made a general confession every year, that is,
he confessed all of the sins which he had committed during his entire life,
and for no other reason than to receive in his heart true grief on account
of his sins. Therefore he prepared many weeks beforehand in silence and
by studying the spiritual exercises, and on the day that he was to confess,
he would spend eight hours trying to cultivate contrition and seeking this
great charisma from God. And you who most likely were stained recently
by new sins—without even considering the gravity of sin, without considering
at all the majesty and goodness of God, without reading any book which
contains these edifying subjects, but only recollecting your bad actions and
confessing to your Spiritual Father—you think in this way you attain true
repentance and that drastic and extreme pain of heart which is inseparable

---

435   *Regulæ Brevius* 16, PG 31, 1093A; tr. *The Ascetic Works of Saint Basil*, p. 236.

from true repentance? Far, my brother, far are you from true repentance
with such confessions, for you are like those whom David speaks about,
who tear their garments and appear outwardly to be in anguish, but interiorly
in their heart they have no compunction: "They were rent asunder, yet not
pricked at heart" (Ps. 34:19). And by confessing in this manner, you wash
only the exterior vessel and the periphery of your heart, but the heart's
internal depth is full of uncleanliness: "Cleanse first that which is within
the cup and platter, that the outside of them may be clean also" (Mt. 23:26).

Let us suppose, however, that you commit a sin and do not consider its
gravity, but when you confess it, you realize its gravity and are disgusted at
it more than any other wrong, and you are saddened and pricked in the
heart with grief because of it during your confession (which is something
which rarely occurs). By this alone, however, you cannot attain true repentance
and true pain of heart.

In order for you to understand this, we must show you what the results
and fruit of repentance and confession are, so that you may have these as
indications. For you think that, since you confessed your sins with compunction
to a Spiritual Father, and since he read the prayer of forgiveness over you,
you think, I say, that you are clean, as if you had never committed any sin,
and that you leave the Spiritual Father as if you had never been polluted.
But this thought is not true because, although baptism removes ancestral
sin and every other voluntary sin, it does not, however, remove the ignorance
of the intellect, lust, the implanted inclination of the heart toward sin, and
the other effects which that ancestral sin brought about in human nature,
for these things remain as a consequence even after baptism in order to
test our free will and for us to struggle and conquer, and for the baptized
to receive their crowns.

G. Confession does not remove
the evil inclinations of the heart

Therefore, even the confession which is performed well and proper,
even though it removes sins, does not however also remove all the harm
which the sins did to the soul, namely, the blinding and darkening of the

intellect, the evil inclinations and dispositions of the will, the habits and addictions of the heart, the corruption and vileness of the powers and energies of our nature, and the distortion of the image and likeness of God in us. This is because confession does not procure on our behalf all of the consequences and penance which we should receive on account of our sins, nor does it take away all of the strength of the bad addictions and habits we developed because of sin, although they may diminish for someone. These things are rather left up to us to correct and to remove from ourselves by the ceaseless pain of heart and with the labors and toils and struggles of repentance which we are required to carry out throughout our life after sin.

H. What one needs to do after confession

Know then, my brother, that right after a good and compunctionate confession you must: 1) fulfill the rule and the discipline which the Spiritual Father gives you on account of your sins, whether it be fasting, or prostrations, or prayer, or something else; 2) you must fulfill the rule and the discipline which God gives you with thanksgiving and with uncomplaining patience in order for your sins to be treated, whether it be illnesses, or injustices, or the loss of your possessions, or premature death (your own or of a relative or of someone you love), or insults and defamations, or other temptations coming from the demons or from people or from our corrupt nature. For these things, especially the insults and defamations, always give rise to grief and compunction in the heart, and it is for this reason that God allows these things to happen to you, as one Father said: "When you suffer insult and defamation, and grieve exceedingly, know that you benefit greatly."[436] And another Father, when grief afflicted him, was accustomed to saying: "It is a cautery of Jesus." Such disciplines were also sent to David by God after forgiving him his adultery and murder, for God is the most-wise Spiritual Father of them all, and He knows how to correct sinners better than any other Spiritual Father with a sound rule. And because the

---

436   *Scholion* on Step 25.

righteousness of God, even if it forgives both the sin and eternal punishment, does not simply forgive by chance, but it forgives with some reference to the fitting rule and discipline. I said some reference because, even if the rule of the sinner co-operates in the forgiveness of his sins, at the same time all of the forgiveness of sins lies with the infinite mercy of God and the infinitely precious satisfaction which the Son of God made through His sufferings and His death, as the sacred theologians say. Indeed, God is accustomed to disciplining sinners, at times through the rebuke of the conscience, when they are awake, by melting them away and drying them out like a spider's web, as David says: "With reprovings for iniquity hast Thou chastened man, and hast made his life to melt away like a spider's web" (Ps. 38:14), and at times He scares them in their sleep through fearful dreams, as Elihu says to Job: "For when the Lord speaks once, or a second time sending a dream, or in the meditation of the night (as when a dreadful alarm happens to fall upon men, in slumberings on the bed), then opens He the understanding of men: He scares them with such fearful visions" (Job 33:14-16). And the reason is because, if God does not discipline the sinner in this life with a rule and a fitting chastisement for his sins, He will most certainly chastise him in the other life with eternal punishment. This is what the righteous Job said out of fear for all of his works: "I quake in all my limbs," for he knew that God does not forgive the debt of the sinner without chastisement, "for I know that Thou wilt not leave me alone as innocent" (Job 9:28).

I. True repentance requires four things

Know that the person who wishes to plant a garden in a wild place requires four things: 1) to cut the shoots and the branches of the wild trees; 2) to remove all of the roots of those wild trees, for if the roots remain, wild shoots sprout again; 3) to plant in that place of wild trees other cultivated and fruit-bearing trees; and 4) to protect the new trees from every animal and every adversity so they may take root and become great trees and bear fruit. In like manner, my brother, in order for you to attain true repentance, four things are required of you. You are required to cut the shoots and the branches of sin, namely, to make a firm resolution with all of your will and your heart not to sin again, but to avoid every practice and act of sin, just as you would avoid death and hell itself, because the branches and shoots are the recent acts of sin. This avoidance of sin will cause you to constantly supplicate God to protect you by His grace. You will be mindful of death, the judgment of God, and of hell. It will cause you to confess your sins frequently and to commune in the divine Mysteries often (if you do not have any impediment). It will help you, most certainly, to avoid all the causes of sin. And it will especially help you to avoid harmful sights and conversations and companionships with those persons with whom you sinned. And in general, it will help you to avoid the bad company which harms your soul.[437] You are required not only to cut the branches of sin through the avoidance of sinful acts, but to also remove the roots of sin. For the roots of sin are the evil inclinations, attachments, addictions, passions, appetites, and lusts of sin which remain rooted in the depth of your heart. And immediately after you practice the avoidance of sinful deeds and do not actively sin, you must struggle, brother, to remove and uproot those inclinations and attachments and roots and bad habits and addictions and passions and lusts of sin completely from your heart, because, if you do not remove them, there is a danger that they will sprout again and give birth to the act of sin, as Basil the Great says: "For just as, if a man should wish to cut off the branches of a treew while leaving the root, the root remaining produces the same results once more in no less degree, so since certain sins have not their beginning in themselves but grow out of others it is altogether necessary that he who wishes to be clean from them should remove the first causes of those sins."[438]

It is for this reason that we see many penitents who, although they had resolved not to practice sin again and although they had cut the branches of sin and completely abstained from evil, left the roots alone and therefore incline with their heart again toward sin and desire it and think about it often with their mind. And just as the Israelites departed from Egypt in deed and with their bodies, but their souls and inclinations of their heart

---

437   We spoke about this subject in Chapter 4 of Part 3, *Counsel for the Penitent*.
438   *Regulæ Brevius* 289, PG 31, 1285A-1285B; tr. *The Ascetic Works of Saint Basil*, p. 340.

remained in Egypt, remembering and desiring the garlic, and the onions, and the meats of Egypt: "Who shall give us flesh to eat? We remember the fish, which we did eat in Egypt freely; the cucumbers, and the melons, and the leeks, and the onions, and the garlic" (Num. 11:4-5), so are those who truly forsake sin according to deed, but do not also forsake the inclination toward sin and its memory and their lust. They also forgive their enemy and bring them to repentance and do not seek revenge, but they do this in word alone and in outward appearance only. For in their heart, they continue to hold a grudge and have malice, not loving their enemy perfectly. For this reason, when their enemy comes upon some misfortune, they immediately are pleased. And when their enemy comes upon some good fortune, they are immediately disappointed. And they have the firm resolve no longer to sin with that person with whom they previously sinned, but they think about that person always, and are secretly attached and inclined toward that person. For this reason with the eyes of their intellect they also frequently fantasize and speak sweetly with that person, while awake and asleep. For this reason they also frequently turn their physical eyes to see that person and desire to speak with that person whenever they are present, or speak about them when they are absent, just as the wife of Lot, having departed from Sodom in the body, did not however also depart according to her heart, and for this reason turned back to look: "But his wife looked back from behind him, and she became a pillar of salt" (Gen. 19:26). Or they are like sick people who abstain from melon and other foods that may harm their health, and do not eat them out of fear of dying. But they continue to ask about those foods, unable to eat them and satisfy their appetite for them. And they desire to at least hold them with their hands and feel them and smell them, and who think that those who are able to eat such foods are most fortunate and blessed.

J. How the Scripture reveals the evil inclinations of the heart

Therefore the Holy Spirit, also wishing to reveal to us the evil roots and inclinations and habits and addictions which remain in the heart after the

committal and act of sin, says to us with the mouth of Sirach: "The father
may die, and yet he is not dead, for he has left behind him one like himself"
(Sir. 30:4). The preceding words can be taken to mean sin which, although
having died after confession and after abstaining from it, nevertheless
appears almost not to have died, for it leaves the bad habit and inclination
to sin alive in the heart, which habit we can justly call a daughter or a
mother of sin, because if it is not uprooted, it can give birth again and
again to more and more sins. And the Holy Spirit, again wishing to reveal
to us that this evil disposition and bad habit which sin leaves in the heart,
little by little, and according to the extent that it increases sins, places the
salvation of the soul in greater danger, says to us through Solomon that
the sinner follows after forbidden hedonistic pleasures like an ox, that is,
slowly and with delay and with resistance and difficulty: "As an ox goeth
to the slaughter" (Pr. 7:22). The Holy Spirit then says to us that the sinner
seeks sins like a deer, that is, leaping after them and desiring them: "Or as
a deer shot in the liver with an arrow" (ibid.). And finally, the Holy Spirit
adds that the sinner goes flying like a bird in pursuit of sin: "And he hastens
as a bird into a snare, not knowing that he is running for his life" (Pr. 7:23).
Likewise, He also says to us through David that the sinner dresses himself
with accursed sin as his own clothes: "And he put on cursing like a garment"
(Ps. 108:17), and then says that the bad habit of sin and the sinful practices
which the sinner returns to is like the water we drink which passes through
our inward bowels: "And it went in like water into his bowels" (ibid.). And
finally, the Holy Spirit adds that sin, like oil, even penetrates bones, even
to the inner marrow of the sinner's bones: "And like oil into his bones"
(ibid.). In another place the Holy Spirit says that sin initially pursues us like
an enemy: "Let the enemy pursue my soul" (Ps. 7:5), and after it catches
us, it throws us to the ground and tramples on us: "And take it, and let it
tread down my life into the earth" (ibid.), and then it reduces us to a small
piece of dust, in order for the wind to carry us away and for us to disappear
completely: "And my glory let it bring down into the dust" (ibid.). Through
these and other like sayings from the Scripture the Holy Spirit informs us,
as we said earlier, that as much as the soul continues to sin, so much more
strongly do the evil inclinations and habits and addictions and passions

take root in the heart and in the intellect, and hence so much more does the soul distance itself from its salvation. And the Holy Spirit further informs us that sin is not easily removed from the sinner, like a dirty shirt is easily taken off and thrown away. No. Rather, sin is like a tree which has its roots deeply rooted in the heart with its branches penetrating through to the bones, even to the marrow of the bones. But sinners, being fools and mindless, think that it is an easy thing for someone to break free from sin. They believe that if one commits a single sin, or a hundred sins, it is the same thing, without those unfortunate sinners considering that when they add sin to sin, they continuously place their salvation in a worse state, because their intellect becomes more and more blind, and their heart grows more and more hard. Additionally, the weight of sin increases, while the assistance of God is not there to sustain them. The war which the devil wages upon them grows fiercer, while their strength to conquer the enemy grows weaker.

K. Those who have recently repented are like the sick when they just recover from an illness

Hence, one teacher most wisely likens those sinful penitents who recently came out of the stagnancy of sin and resolved to abstain from evil to the sick who have just recovered from their illness, because these people, even though they are no longer ill, are nevertheless still pale and unsightly; they eat, but without an appetite; they sleep, but not restfully; they laugh, but without joy; they walk, but it appears as though they are hobbling rather than walking. And in short, in whatever they do, they experience great encumbrance, great difficulty, and great impotence. In like manner, the sinners who have recently departed from sin, when they happen to want to do some good, they do not do it with the proper desire and diligence, but they do it grudgingly, and with great impotence and difficulty, because the remains and roots of sin are still in their heart and has not been completely cured.

These roots and evil inclinations and passions of sin which remain in your heart, brother, how can you remove them? Listen. Those who wish to remove the root of some large tree use hoes, shovels, axes, and other tools. In like manner, you must also use many tools to remove those evil roots of sin, namely, self-control and moderation in regards to food and sleep, prostrations, sleeping on the floor, and every other exterior hardship of the body, because all of these not only remove the dirt which surrounds the roots, and shake and move the roots, but they also strike and cut those roots, because such bodily hardships afflict the heart where those roots are implanted, as St. Mark the Ascetic says: "Without contrition of the heart it is altogether impossible to rid ourselves of evil. Now the heart is made contrite by threefold self-control: in sleep, in food, and in bodily relaxation."[439]

L. What gives rise to grief and contrition

The sharpest axe of all axes and tools which is able to cut and to remove those evil roots of sin is pain of heart, which we spoke about above, and contrition and grief of the soul. The aforementioned pain of heart will help you remember the following seven things, about which we have already spoken: 1) how by your sins you wronged God and His natural energies; 2) how you appeared thankless for the innumerable blessings which God bestowed upon you; 3) how you committed an unheard-of injustice and had complete disregard for the redemption which the Son of God accomplished with so many sufferings and His own blood; 4) how you harmed yourself, both temporally and eternally, by the sins which you committed; 5) how you lost God and the divine grace of sonship and righteousness which you had; 6) how you lost the eternal blessedness of Paradise; and 7) how you inherited eternal punishment and eternal torment by your sins.

And further, this pain of heart must be so drastic and so extreme and great, as we said above, like the grief of a mother who has lost her only-begotten son or her beloved husband; like the pain of being stabbed or pierced in the leg by a large needle or thorn, concerning which David said: "I was reduced to misery whilst the thorn stuck fast in me" (Ps. 31:4), in

---

439   *No Righteousness by Works* 210, *GrPhilokalia*, p. 111; tr. *The Philokalia*, v. 1, p. 143.

such a way that this grief and sorrow weighs upon the heart like a heavy stone slab, and afflicts it, and overwhelms it, and causes the heart to groan and to weep. For this reason Abba Isaac said that: "Repentance is a contrite and humble heart,"[440] and again: "What is repentance? It is the abandoning of former deeds and grieving over them."[441] And John of the Ladder said: "Repentance is a mighty persecution of the stomach, and a striking of the soul into vigorous awareness."[442]

M. Pain of heart must be perpetual

This sorrow and pain of heart must be perpetual, just as repentance is perpetual. Therefore, brother, you also must perpetually have this pain of heart, because as long as you have this, you also have repentance. And as soon as this grief departs from your heart, you also immediately depart from repentance, as George Koressios and the rest of the theologians say. For this reason the divine Isaac said that: "No virtue is more pre-eminent than repentance, for a man can never complete the work of repentance."[443]

N. Why this grief must be perpetual

There are three reasons why pain of heart and repentance must be perpetual. First, because sin is called mortal for this reason, for after someone commits it he is liable to be put to death by God and be deprived of this life (just like the old law punished mortal sins with death), and be thrown into eternal hell. God, however, on account of his philanthropy does not put him to death, but allows him to live so that he may repent of his sin for the rest of his life, as St. Mark the Ascetic says: "He who but one time commits something worthy of death is to be put to death according to the

---

440   *Ascetical Homilies,* Homily 71, p. 344.

441   *Ibid.*

442   Step 5, PG 88, 764C; tr. *The Ladder,* p. 54.

443   *Ascetical Homilies,* Homily 32, p. 153. And St. Mark the Ascetic says: "The Lord therefore designated repentance up until death. Whoever says they have completed repentance before death breaks the commandment which takes away death. Therefore, repentance is unending until death for both young and old" (*De Poenitentia* 10-11, PG 65, 980D).

law. But if he lives, he lives by faith, for the sake of repentance."[444] Therefore, the person who falls into sin once, and a mortal one at that, is no longer able to forget that sin for the rest of his life, but is obligated to grieve daily, to ache, to repent and to be sorry for his sin, even if he received forgiveness from his Spiritual Father. For just as the Prophet David, even though forgiven by God through the Prophet Nathan for the two sins he committed, and even though he fulfilled a sufficient rule for his sins through the apostasy of his son Absalom and his being thrown out of his kingdom, did not cease to be sorry for them and repent and weep on account of his sins for the rest of his life, saying: "For I will declare mine iniquity, and I will take heed concerning my sin" (Ps. 37:18). And again he says in another place: "Every night I will wash my bed, with tears will I water my couch" (Ps. 6:5). David calls the place where he committed adultery "bed," and the place where he gave the command to murder the innocent Uriah he calls "couch," according to the interpretation of some teachers. For this reason too the Apostle Peter, as often as he heard the cock crow, remembered his denial and repented and wept, as his disciple St. Clement says. Therefore the divine Chrysostom also says: "Groan when you have sinned... and do this continually, for this is confession. Be not today cheerful, tomorrow of a sad countenance, then again cheerful; but continue ever in mourning and self-contrition. For, 'Blessed,' He says, 'are they that mourn,' that is, that do this perpetually. Continue then to do this perpetually, and to take heed to yourself, and to afflict your heart; as one who had lost a beloved son might mourn."[445]

O. Repentance does not erase the scars and marks of sin

The second reason why pain of heart and repentance must be perpetual is because every sin is like a wound, and if the wound is treated, the scar, the mark, and the print of the wound yet remain in the soul, for it is impossible to completely erase these in this present life, as most, if not all,

---

444   *De Poenitentia* 12, PG 65, 981C.
445   *On II Corinthians*, Homily 4, 6, PG 61, 426.

of the theologians say. For someone who stole one time, or fornicated or murdered, cannot become as innocent and as pure through repentance as if he had never stolen at all or fornicated or murdered. Therefore, as often as the sinner remembers the sins which he committed and sees the prints and the marks of his wounds, it is impossible for him not to grieve because of them and not weep and not repent, even if we suppose that these wounds are cured. The scars and marks, then, of all sins remain indelibly in the soul, as we said before, especially those of carnal sins. For this reason Basil the Great, in his homily, *On Virginity*, also says that repentance is able to forgive the sin of a man and of a woman who ruined one another's virginity through fornication, but it is not able, however, to change someone corrupted into one who has not been corrupted or into a virgin. This is why, even if the sin is forgiven, it brings remorse to fornicators for the rest of their life: "Repentance is for the remission of sins, but to make her who has been violated as if she had never been violated is impossible, lamenting for this through her life. For how can the corrupted become uncorrupted? How can something wounded by lust and hedonistic pleasure and passion, once and for all, become something unwounded, and the signs of corruption in the soul and in the body not remain at all?"[446] And at the end of his homily, *On Repentance*, he says: "There is healing after a wound, but the scar remains."[447] And the divine Gregory says: "There is no second regeneration, or re-creation, or restoration to our former state, even though we seek it with all our might, and with many sighs and tears, by which it is scarred over (with great difficulty in my opinion, though we all believe that it may be scarred over). Yet if we might wipe away even the scars I should be glad, since I too have need of mercy."[448] Scarring over means the closing and healing of the wound, concerning which God promises through Jeremiah: "Behold, I will scar it over and cure it" (Jer. 40:6). And Athanasios the Great says: "He who repents ceases from sinning, but he still has the scars from the injuries of sin."[449] And Cyril of Jerusalem says the same thing: "And

---

446   *De Virginitate* 59, PG 30, 789A.
447   *De Poenitentia* 6, PG 31, 1488B.
448   *Oratio* 40, 7, PG 36, 368C.
449   *Epistola IV ad Serapionem* 13, PG 26, 656B.

the stains of sin also remain in the body; for as when a wound has gone deep into the body, even if there has been a healing, the scar remains, so sin wounds both soul and body, and the marks of its scars remain in all."[450] Isidore Pelousiotes is also in agreement with this, saying: "Just because you know about repentance does not mean you should proceed to sin without fear and in the hope that you will be treated. You should know, however, that even if many had the time to repent, they were punished at the moment of their sin. Afterward repentance treats the passions with the passing of much time, because much toil, and fasting, and vigil, and almsgiving, and prayer, is required as well, in order for the previous injuries to be treated. Thirdly, you should know that, even if they are treated, the scar of sin which remains attests to the passion. For the body which has been treated is no longer the same as the previously unimpaired body, just as a tattered and patched garment is not the same as a brand new one, even if by means of some technique it appears to have been restored to its previous condition."[451] And even if the divine Chrysostom says the following: "When God erases sins, He does not even leave a scar, not even allowing a mark to remain, for together with the healing He grants also beauty,"[452] he says this on account of the infinite philanthropy of God, and not in reference to repentance, that is, repentance in and of itself is unable to do this. For he says in the same place the following, as if to explain what he just said: "Not because repentance by itself can erase sin, but because the ineffable philanthropy of God and His immeasurable goodness is united to repentance."[453] In agreement with these things, St. John the Faster says in his 19th Canon: "A boy who has been violated in the presence of someone cannot enter the priesthood. For although on account of his immature age he did not sin himself, yet his vessel was rent and became useless in connection with sacred service." God also wishes to show this through the word which He spoke through the Prophet Amos: "The virgin of Israel is fallen; she

---

450   *Catechesis XVIII*, 20, PG 33, 1041A.

451   *Liber III, Epistola CLVII—Casio Magistratum Gerenti*, PG 78, 852C-853A.

452   *De Poenitentia VIII*, 2, PG 49, 340.

453   *Ibid.*, 1, PG 49, 337. Byssarion Makres in the *Orthodox Confession*, together with others, says that Chrysostom does not mean that a scar will not remain in this life, but that one will not remain in the future life.

shall no more rise" (Am. 5:2). For this reason we also read in the *Gerontikon* that Makarios the Great was always grieving and weeping because, when he was a small child, he stole some cucumbers from a garden.

The third reason for perpetual grief and perpetual repentance is because every person, whether righteous or sinner, is unable to remain sinless and free from either mortal or pardonable sin: "Who will boast that he has a pure heart? Or who will boldly say that he is pure from sins?" (Pr. 20:9). For almost every day and every hour all people sin, at one time in word, at another time with evil, blasphemous, and obscene thoughts, and infuriate God. Therefore it follows that we all must have pain of heart and repent daily on account of these sins, and to ask forgiveness from God, not only because of our past sins, but also because of our present and daily sins. St. Isaac also verifies this: "The concise sense of this chapter is the following: at every moment we should know that we stand in need of repentance throughout the twenty-four hours of the night and day."[454]

P. How many good things pain of heart brings

If you then have this pain of heart, brother, as strongly and as perpetually

---

454   *Ascetical Homilies*, Homily 70, p. 340. Going further, St. Mark says that even if we suppose that we have never erred voluntarily (which is impossible), we must however repent to God simply on account of the ancestral sin: "He who but one time commits something worthy of death, is to be put to death according to the law. But if he lives, he lives by faith, for the sake of repentance, even if it is not on account of his own sin that he repents, but because of the sin of the fall" (*De Poenitentia* 12, PG 65, 981C). The great Gregory Palamas of Thessaloniki, in agreement with this, says: "Repentance is the beginning, the middle and the end of the Christian life, for it is both asked and required before Holy Baptism, during Holy Baptism, and after Holy Baptism" (*Homily on the Eve of the Feast of Lights*). Therefore you also, brother, must always supplicate God, saying together with David to the Lord: "Heal my soul, for I have sinned against Thee" (Ps. 40:4). You should, however, supplicate Him with grief in your heart, because according to St. Mark: "The remembrance of God is pain of heart endured in a spirit of devotion" (*No Righteousness by Works* 131, *GrPhilokalia*, p. 106; tr. *The Philokalia*, v. 1, p. 136).

Translator's note: In agreement with the above mentioned statement of St. Mark, St. Maximos also says: "As man I deliberately transgressed the divine commandment, when the devil, enticing me with the hope of divinity (cf. Gen. 3:5), dragged me down from my natural stability into the realm of sensual pleasure" (*Third Century on Various Texts of Theology* 11, *GrPhilokalia*, pp. 363-364; tr. *First Century of Various Texts*, *The Philokalia*, v. 2, p. 167).

as we have said, know that this grief will bring many good things to your soul, because this grief will cause your intellect to be gathered into your heart, not allowing it to think about evil things and sins. For according to nature, in whatever part of the body a person is hurting, there also will the intellect be drawn. This grief will cause your heart to vomit out the poison and the hook of sin which it swallowed. It will soften the heart, it will humble it and it will quickly detach it from the passions and inclinations which it acquired through sin. For the heart of a sinner is hard, stone-like, and haughty; and being without grief, it is impossible to be humbled and softened, as it is written: "A hard heart will be annoyed by grief" (Sir. 3:27). This grief will ascend before the Lord of Hosts and will virtually compel Him to forgive your sins, as it is written: "My judgment is with the Lord, and my grief is before my God" (Is. 49:4).

Q. The lifestyle and diet of those who are penitents and culpable must be different from that of those who are blameless

And David says: "Behold my lowliness and my toil, and forgive all my sins" (Ps. 24:18), and again: "A heart that is broken and humbled God will not despise" (Ps. 50:17). The grief which we have been speaking about will also cause you to change what foods you eat, what you drink, your clothes, your sleeping habits, and the whole previous lifestyle you had as a sinner. For this is the appropriate life of penitents: humble, solemn, simple, and poor: 1) because those who are ill do not have the same lifestyle as those who are healthy, as Gregory of Nyssa says: "He who says that someone ill should live like someone healthy is not correct. For the lifestyle of someone ill is different than that of someone who is in good health"[455]; and again: "He who is ill in body is like this: he is badly disposed toward the soul, he goes around as if to invisible physicians pretending to confess and show his illness, he is forsaken to wander, and passion consumes him, so that the whole tumor spreads; but be wise, and know thyself"[456]; and again: "The

---

455   *Adhortatio ad Poenitentiam*, PG 40, 368A.
456   *Ibid.*, 368B-368C.

promise we make to God says that we will repent and change, while our actions do not show any effort on our part, and we rather exhibit the same manner of life as we had before our sin. For we act cheerfully, eat cheerfully, have a bountiful and delectable table, long sleep and are always satiated. We have constant preoccupations and cares, bringing about the willful destruction to the soul. We therefore repent only in name, without any fruit and without any action."[457] 2) Because those who are placed under a rule on account of a mortal sin are not to rejoice and lead the same type of cheerful life as those who are not in their same condition, as the Prophet Hosea says: "Rejoice not, O Israel, for joy, as other people: for thou hast gone a whoring from thy God" (Hos. 9:1). John of the Ladder says this very same thing: "One kind of abstinence is suitable for those who behave irreproachably, and another for those subject to weaknesses. For the former, a movement in the body is a signal for restraint; but the latter are affected by such movements without relief or reconciliation till their very death and end."[458] And in general, this grief will cause you to become a monk, or at least to live a monastic-type life while being in the world. This grief and sorrow is not bitter, so as to bring about despair (for you must reject that grief and sorrow which brings about hopelessness, for it is from the evil one), but it is sweet and joy-producing because it is mixed with the hope of salvation, with most-sweet compunction, with tears, and with the easing of the conscience. For this reason John of the Ladder says: "When I consider the actual nature of compunction, I am amazed at how that which is called mourning and grief should contain joy and gladness interwoven within it, like honey in the comb. What then are we to learn from this? That such compunction is, in a special sense, a gift of the Lord. There is, then, in the soul no pleasureless pleasure, for God consoles those who are contrite in heart in a secret way."[459] And in short, this grief will uproot from your heart the bad habits and addictions of sin, and will cause you to attain true repentance which is, according to the divine Gregory of Nyssa, the disappearance of not only the works and acts of sin, but also the disappearance

---

457   *Ibid.*, 365C-365D.
458   Step 14, PG 88, 865C; tr. *The Ladder*, p. 99.
459   Step 7, PG 88, 812A; tr. *The Ladder*, p. 76.

of the dispositions and inclinations of the heart and of the effects and assaults on the intellect: "This is repentance: the release from and disappearance of past things, either those things which were practiced or those things which were thought about."[460] O most-sweet grief which brings about true repentance through divine grace! O joy-producing grief which causes a person to be unmoved or difficultly moved toward evil! O blessed grief which brings painless blessedness!

You have learned, brother, how to cut the shoots and the branches of sin through the resolute abstinence from the committal of sin. You also learned how to uproot from your heart the roots of sin through drastic and perpetual pain of heart. Now also learn how you must plant in your heart, in place of the previous wild trees, cultivated and fruitful trees, that is, instead of vices, virtues; instead of pride, humility; instead of gluttony, self-control; instead of avarice, generosity and almsgiving; instead of callousness, meekness; instead of carnal passions, chastity and modesty; instead of injustice and thievery, righteousness and to give from yourself; instead of envy and hate, love and friendship; and instead of the initial transgression of the commandments of God, the keeping and practice of the commandments. This is necessary for your salvation or for you to attain true repentance, brother, because it is not sufficient only to remove the roots of sin from the heart, and then to leave the place of your heart barren, and not plant it with the plants and trees of the virtues. For if you leave your heart to be barren, it will again produce wild thorns and trees, namely, passions and sins. For this reason the Holy Spirit also counsels you through David the Psalmist to flee evil and to do good: "Turn away from evil, and do good" (Ps. 33:14).[461]

And finally, after you have planted these virtues in your heart, you must

---

460   *Adhortatio ad Poenitentiam*, PG 40, 368D.

461   Therefore Gregory of Nyssa the illuminator, in his *Homily on Repentance*, says: "Have you sinned on account of food? Treat this indulgence through fasting. Did you harm the soul through debauchery? Let modesty be the medicine for this illness. Did greedy materialism cause a spiritual fever? Relieve it through abundant almsgiving; for the purification of those who have in abundance lies in giving. Have we harmed ourselves through robbing others? Let us return the stolen item to its owner. Have we lied and brought someone near perdition? Let us practice truth and put a stop to the danger" (*Ibid.*, 368C).

protect them as much as you are able so that they may take root, namely, so that they may become to you through habit like second nature, just as previously passions and sins became to you like second nature, and so that they may blossom and yield the fruit of salvation and true repentance and the forgiveness of your sins. For if you do not protect them and care for them, that sower of tares, the devil, will come at a time when you are sleeping and neglectful and uproot them, and plant again his own tares and vices, according to the parable of the Gospel: "The kingdom of heaven is likened unto a man which sowed good seed in his field. But while men slept, his enemy came and sowed tares among the wheat, and went his way" (Mt. 13:24-25). And because if you do not carefully protect these virtues, the passions return again to your heart. For this reason the Fathers called the passions recrudescent (φιλεπίστροφα), because they love to return to the place of the heart and find it cultivated and worked over, thereby rooting themselves even deeper than before, hence: "Your last state is worse than the first" (cf. Mt. 12:45). May this never happen to you, my beloved.

These are the four elements of true repentance, brother. With these you can attain true repentance within yourself, the grace of which the Church supplicates the Lord to give us in some of her prayers: "That Thou may be pleased to lead us to true repentance."

These are the fruits and results of true repentance: with these you will be assured that God has truly forgiven your sins and that He has been reconciled with you.

R. The signs of forgiveness of sins from God

This most certain and true forgiveness of sins has four signs, each sign surer and higher than the next. The first sign is that a person hates sin from the bottom of his heart whenever it is recollected, being afraid that he might again fall into sin, and that a person also does not desire or incline toward sin. The second sign, higher than the first, is when a person remembers his sins dispassionately, that is, without pleasure or grief and hate. The third and even higher sign is when someone remembers his sins and rejoices and glorifies God on account of the many virtues he acquired on account of his sins through divine grace and repentance. And the fourth and highest sign of all is when a person completely removes all of the passionate effects of sin from his heart, and forgets them to such an extent that they no longer assault him.

The first sign is confirmed by Basil the Great. For when the Saint was asked how the soul is assured that God has forgiven its sins, he answered that this is how it is assured: "When it sees in itself the state of mind of him who said: I hate and abhor iniquity."[462] When Abba Isaac was asked the same thing, he answered in the same way saying that someone will know that he has received forgiveness for his sins: "When in his soul he becomes conscious that he has completely hated them with his whole heart."[463]

The second sign is confirmed by Niketas Herakleias of Serres. For when he was commenting upon the following words from the *Second Paschal Oration* of Gregory the Theologian: "And if, like a Thomas, you were left out when the disciples were assembled to whom Christ shows Himself, when you do see Him be not faithless; and if you do not believe, then believe those who tell you; and if you cannot believe them either, then have confidence in the print of the nails."[464] Niketas commented: "If you are not, however, convinced by these, then be convinced by the print of the dispassionate memory of your old sins upon your intellect (that the word of virtue has resurrected within you). A dispassionate memory is recollecting, without pleasure and grief, the print of past events, and without harm occurring from the remembrance of past injuries, which is possible on account of the acquired dispassion, and whoever does not have dispassion will not believe anyone, just like Thomas. The prints are the memories of sins, and

---

462   *Regulæ Brevius* 12, PG 31, 1089B; tr. *The Ascetic Works of Saint Basil*, p. 234.

463   *Ascetical Homilies*, Homily 28, p. 141. This same divine Isaac said this memorable word: "We are not only sinners when we commit sin, but also when we do not hate sin and when we do not regret our sin" (*Epistle 4*).

Translator's note: St. Silouan also says: "Every soul that has lost peace should repent and the Lord will forgive her her sins, and there will be joy and peace in the soul. We have no need of other witnesses, for the Spirit Himself testifies that our sins are forgiven. Here is a token of forgiveness: if you now detest sin, it means the Lord has forgiven you your sins" (*Saint Silouan the Athonite*, p. 347).

464   *Oratio* 45, 24, PG 36, 657A; tr. NPNF (V2-07) p. 432.

these sins are the nails which pierce those who fall upon them. When you are therefore able to remember them dispassionately, then you will know that the dispassionate word has resurrected within you."

We find the third sign in the *Lausiac History*, in the life of Makarios the Younger.[465] For when he was asked if he grieved when he recalled the murder which he once committed as a young man, he answered that he does not grieve but rather rejoices, not because of the sin of murder in itself, but because it became the cause of his repentance and the cause of his acquiring many virtues, and that he glorifies and gives thanks for the goodness of God, for it even changes those things which are bad by nature into causes of good. In this manner God changed the murder which Moses committed in Egypt into the cause of something good, for on account of this murder Moses withdrew to the desert and was deemed worthy to see God. Therefore the Apostle said: "All things work together for good to them that love God" (Rom. 8:28). Explaining this passage the divine Augustine said that for those who love God, oftentimes even bad things and sins assist toward virtue: "Those who are written in the book of life cannot perish. For such people, all things work for the good, even sins."[466]

The fourth sign is confirmed by St. Theodore of Edessa, for he says in the eleventh chapter: "Memories of all the impassioned actions we have performed exert an impassioned tyranny over the soul. But when impassioned thoughts have been completely erased from our heart, so that they no longer affect it even as provocations, this is a sign that our former sinful acts have been forgiven."[467] St. Maximos also says roughly the same thing: "False prophets are also those thoughts which cause sins to appear as insignificant and which foretell that they have already been forgiven. These thoughts are ravenous wolves in sheep's clothing which we can recognize by their fruit. For as long as our intellect is disturbed by the passions, it is evident that we have not yet received perfect forgiveness, and that we have not yet shown fruit worthy of repentance. A fruit of repentance is the dispassion of the soul, and dispassion is the disappearance of sin. Accordingly, those

---

465   PG 1041A-1041B; *Palladius: The Lausiac History*, pp. 51-52.
466   *Prayer XXVIII.*
467   *A Century of Spiritual Texts* 11, *GrPhilokalia*, p. 266; tr. *The Philokalia*, v. 2, p. 16.

who are sometimes disturbed by the passions, and sometimes not disturbed by them, do not have perfect dispassion, those thoughts not ceasing which predict forgiveness for us."[468]

Do you see, brother, how true repentance is attained? Do you see with what labors and toils and blood true forgiveness of sins is gained?[469] How

---

468   From the series on Matthew, ch. 7; (cf. *Liber Asceticus* 44, PG 90, 953D-956A).

469   If you desire, brother, to receive in your soul and in your memory an image and example of true repentance, open the book of St. John of the Ladder, find Step 5, *On Repentance* (PG 88, 764C-777B; *The Ladder*, pp. 54-63), and read therein concerning the penitents condemned to stay in the Monastery called "The Prison," on account of the inconsolable place where it is found. There you will see: 1) the lifestyle of true penitents, for the penitent brethren there did not consume oil, they did not drink wine, they did not eat cooked food, but only bread and raw vegetables. Many of them were parched from thirst, and had their tongues hanging out like dogs. Others took only a little bread, the remains which had already been thrown away, thinking themselves unworthy to eat rational food, because they committed acts like the irrational animals. They did not have mattresses, nor clean clothes to wear, but all of their clothes were torn, filthy and full of lice. There you will see: 2) works and traits of true penitents, because of those blessed penitents, some would stand erect until the morning and pray the whole night without sleeping at all, others had their hands bound behind their backs like condemned criminals, others, seated upon sackcloth and ash, would strike their foreheads upon the earth, others watered the earth with their tears, while others, unable to shed tears, struck themselves, lacerating their flesh and their members, so that they would be in pain. They tormented themselves with the heat of summer and punished their bodies with the cold of winter, and when their life was at an end, they commanded that their bodies not be buried in the earth, as unworthy of burial, but they had their bodies either thrown into the flowing river or off some cliff. There you will hear: 3) words and cries of true penitents, because out of the mouths of those blessed ones nothing else was heard except these words: "Woe is me, woe is me! Alas, alas! It is just, it is just! Have compassion, have compassion, Master! Have mercy, Lord, have mercy! Forgive, Master, forgive, if it is possible." And others, striking their breasts violently, and as if they were before the gate of heaven cried out: "Open unto us, Judge, open the gate of Thy mercy, for on account of our sins we have been shut out." Others, bowed down to the earth, said: "Yea, we know, we know that we are worthy of every chastisement and punishment. And we have nothing with which to defend ourselves compared to the great debts of our sins, even if we called the whole world to weep on our behalf. But only this we ask of Thee, that Thou not chastise us with Thine anger and Thy wrath, nor punish us as we deserve, according to Thy just judgment, but that Thou chastise us somewhat more lightly, for it is sufficient that we only be liberated from those unspoken and hidden torments, and not be completely liberated from them all." Finally, you will also see there, beloved, the appearance and form of true penitents, for the knees of those thrice-blessed men were calloused from the multitude of their prostrations, their eyes were dried out and hollow, their cheeks looked as if they had been burned by their hot tears, their faces were withered and pale, looking like corpses, their chests were wounded and their spit was full of blood from the constant beating of their breast, their appearance was pensive, sullen, grievous and like that of convicts. Why mince words? There you will see the

is it, then, that you say: "Let me sin, for I will confess, I will repent," as if true repentance is something easy? Therefore, from now on be on your guard, for the love of God, and when the devil provokes you to fall into some sin, instead of falling easily by saying: "I will confess, I will repent," establish in your soul this invincible fortress and say: "Who knows if I will be able to confess? Who knows whether this sin I am considering to commit will be my last, and which God will not tolerate or forgive, but will cut the rope of His patience and allow me to fall into perdition? Who knows whether or not God will give me the charisma of true repentance, which He did not give to other sinners like myself, who are now consumed by flames in Hades? Who knows whether I, who have become accustomed to not fearing God, will be given over little by little to a reprobate life and to ultimate despair?" "The heart of the intelligent man will ponder a parable," says Sirach (Sir. 3:29), and you, brother, if you are prudent and wise in heart, do not place the matter of your salvation in such obvious danger, placing your hope in some fruitless confession and some false repentance, and while you are able to hang your salvation on a strong rope in order to be saved, you rather hang it on a rotten string which, after it breaks, will plunge you into a sea of infinite and everlasting fire. The strong rope is to abstain from committing sin; to fight to uproot from your heart the evil

---

forms and diets and works and words and appearances of those who truly are penitents, which are able to constrain God Who is unconstrainable and at the same time convince His philanthropy to forgive them. Seeing these things, I am certain that you will receive courage in your soul, my brother, to imitate much of what you have just read in your own repentance. I am certain that you will feel for those blessed ones and have your heart afflicted so much that you will finish and close the book full of tears.

Translator's note: A contemporary example of true repentance is to be found in the person of St. Silouan, as described by Elder Sophrony: "When repenting of sin he did not merely seek pardon which God is swift to grant—for a single sigh of regret, maybe. He looked for a forgiveness so complete that his soul might really know the grace of God within him again. He prayed for strength if possible never to repeat his sin. He prayed to be delivered from 'the law of sin which is in our members' (Rom. 7:23). The consequences of sin—the loss of grace—he felt so intensely, so painfully, that he dreaded any repetition. Worst of all for him was the feeling that Divine love and the peace of Christ were gone from his soul. Knowing that he had grieved God—God so meek and humble—was unbearable. He suffered the most acute misery when he sinned against Christ's holy love" (*Saint Silouan the Athonite*, p. 32).

inclinations with drastic grief, and to attain true repentance and the forgiveness of your sins through the practice of the virtues and by executing the commandments of God. For if someone does not abstain from sins, it is as if he is swallowing wickedness whole and without chewing, which shows that he is a complete fool, because he willfully commits an infinite wrong, being presumptuous of that which is only in the hand of God, namely, presuming upon the fact that he will have time to repent and have the help of God to repent worthily, as if God was a friend of sinners and not their greatest and most fearful enemy and the most powerful of all to punish them, and as if He did not have infinite hate for every sin.

3. How the saying "Fall and rise" is explained

Let not this thought deceive you, brother, which says to you: "Look at what the Fathers say, 'Fall and rise,' that is, as many times as you fall, get up and be saved." Is this then repentance, for someone to fall and then get up, and when he gets up to fall again? This is an erroneous and bad interpretation of this saying, brother, for the Fathers said this to remove the fear of despair from people; they did not say it so that they would sin with the hope of confession and repentance. God forbid! Therefore, St. Isaac says: "The encouragement which the Fathers give in their divine writings [concerning] repentance… must not be employed by us as an aid for sinning and for breaking the Lord's inviolable decrees… But the fact that repentance furnishes hope should not be taken by us as a means to rob ourselves of the feeling of fear, so that one might more freely and fearlessly commit sin."[470] The Fathers said, "Fall and rise," not, "Rise and fall," as you backwardly interpret it, for the one greatly differs from the other, so that if someone falls and gets up, and then, after getting up falls again, this is neither in truth nor even called repentance, as you call it, but is in fact and is called by the Apostle Peter a dog which returns to its own vomit, and a pig that rolls around in its previous mud: "The dog is turned to his own vomit again; and the sow that was washed to her wallowing in

---

470   *Ascetical Homilies,* Homily 10, p. 74.

the mire" (2 Pet. 2:22). The correct meaning of, "Fall and rise," is that a person must, with all his strength, abstain from sin and be careful so as not to fall. If, however, out of human weakness he happens to fall, and not with his complete will, he must not despair but immediately get up and confess and repent without losing any time. For according to St. John of the Ladder: "It is the property of angels not to fall… and it is quite impossible for them to fall. It is the property of men to fall, and to rise again as often as this may happen."[471] For this reason, brother, even if you fell on account of great adversity or weakness, do not laugh and say to yourself: "I have fallen, let me then fall again and commit the sin again and again, for I have already fallen into the mud once, and I will afterward confess and repent for everything and then sin no more." Do not, brother, for the sake of the Lord, do not listen to this thought, for it is blatantly, blatantly from the devil, who desires your destruction. Rather, as soon as you sin once, do not sin a second time, do not delay, do not hang around waiting to return again to the mud: "Do not delay to turn to the Lord, nor postpone it from day to day" (Sir. 5:7), but arise and go to your Spiritual Father and confess. For, the newer the wound is, the more easily it is treated; the older the wound is, the more difficult it is to treat, according to John of the Ladder: "While a wound is still fresh and warm, it is easy to heal; but old, neglected and festering ones are hard to cure."[472] If you do not immediately have the time to go and confess, repent to God then and there, and do not wait for the time of confession to come, and seek reconciliation and peace with God through many acts of grief, contrition, and repentance, according to your ability. And do not let a single night go by without falling before and repenting to God until the time you go to confess to your Spiritual Father, for this is insufferable audacity for you to be liable each hour to death, for you to remain for even a single moment in a mortal sin and for your life to be hanging by a thread over Hades, the abyss of all evils. Alas! But you, the wretch, not only remain unrepentant in sin for a moment, but for months and seasons, and for you to depart from such a danger you wait until the day of Pascha, or of the Apostles, or of Christmas to confess, and

---

471   Step 4, PG 696D; tr. *The Ladder*, p. 33.
472   Step 5, PG 88, 777D; tr. *The Ladder*, p. 64.

you play and laugh and sleep without care as if you damaged, not your rational and immortal soul, but some unfeeling piece of wood which cannot even feel the damage you do to it, nor can it take revenge. So, listen to this fearful example which we have read.

4. A fearful story

A certain young man's heart was fettered by his love-affair and relations with a harlot. Having been exceedingly reproved by his parents, his relatives, and his Spiritual Father, he decided to break off these relations and be delivered from this sin by making a general and complete confession of all of his sins. Compiling all of his sins, he wrote them down on a piece of paper. During this self-examination of his sins however, he did not have the proper grief and contrition in his heart that those who recall their sins in preparation for confession should have. Rather, his sins grieved him so little that on his way to confession he happened to pass the door of that accursed harlot's house, and as if he were some stranger, he was roused to enter therein again, and when he entered, he decided to fall into sin and add to his old sins another new sin, with the hope that he would confess all of his sins. But what followed? Just as he was contemplating this evil thought as an excuse to fornicate, another young lover of the harlot came in and saw the other young man and, becoming angry, struck him with such a blow that he killed him. And when the people were taking his body to burial, they found the paper upon which he had listed his sins in preparation for confession. O miserable death! O false hopes! O most deceitful thought of that young man!

Now brother, if you are so audacious like that thrice-wretched young man so as to wrong God and intentionally sin with the hope of forgiveness, come to your senses, I beg you, so that it may not happen that you also suffer punishment and perdition like him.

Conclusion

Hell is such a great and fearful evil that the mere fact that it exists and that this story happened should cause you to shudder greatly and deter you from all sin: "Smite a scorner, and the simple will beware" (Pr. 19:25). Forget such audacity, then, and its false boldness which causes you to sin with the hope of confession and repentance, and always having the example of that pitiful young man in your mind, never take liberties, but "work out your own salvation with fear and trembling" (Phil. 2:12), as the Apostle commands you. For true repentance is born from fear, and repentance is like a ship which brings you to the harbor of divine love, while fear is the captain of that ship, as Abba Isaac says: "Repentance is the second grace and is begotten in the heart by faith and fear."[473] And again: "Repentance is the ship and fear is the pilot; love is the divine haven."[474] For this reason, my beloved brethren in Christ (I change here from the singular manner of the homily to the plural), to repentance, I call all to repentance with the present homily, small and great, clergy and laity. Let us run to repentance, brethren, men and women, young and old. Let us all, every one of us, seek shelter in the embrace of repentance, without exception, for no other virtue can reconcile all of us who have sinned with God except repentance. Let us also cry out with David: "O come, let us worship and fall down before Him, and let us weep before the Lord Who made us. For He is our God, and we are the people of His pasture and the sheep of His hand" (Ps. 94:6-7). Let us cry out with the three holy youths unto God: "We have sinfully and lawlessly departed from Thee, and have sinned in all things and have not obeyed Thy commandments; we have not observed them or done them, as Thou hast commanded us that it might go well with us" (Song of the Three Youths verses 6-7). Let each of us turn from this evil road, as also the Ninevites of old turned, and then let us also call out to God, as they called out: "Who can tell if God will turn and repent, and turn away from His fierce anger, that we perish not?" (Jon. 3:9). And whoever of us disappointed God after Holy Baptism, let him not cease, night and

---

473   *Ascetical Homilies*, Homily 46, p. 223.

474   *Ibid.*, p. 224.

day, to shout those compunctionate words which were taught to him by that herald of repentance, John of the golden tongue and golden heart: "Whoever received heavenly baptism and then sinned, sinned in heaven. For he who sinned prior to baptism, sinned on earth: 'For earth thou art and to earth thou shalt return' (Gen. 3:19), it was said to Adam. But, whoever through baptism put on Christ is no longer earth, but heaven: 'As is the earthy, such are they also that are earthy: and as is the heavenly, such are they also that are heavenly' (1 Cor. 15:48). So whoever sinned after baptism, sinned in heaven. Let him therefore come forth and say: 'Father, I have sinned against heaven, and before Thee' (Lk. 15:18). Why? State the reason. 'Because my heart which was sprinkled with the blood of Jesus and had blossomed like a rose, I have soiled by hedonistic pleasures. I have infuriated Thee. I have grieved Thy Holy Spirit. I have smeared the resplendent garment of Faith through sin. I have subjugated my soul, liberated through baptism and whitened like snow by illumination, to the darkness of sin. Make me as one of Thy hired servants' (Lk. 15:19)."[475]

Let us take care, brethren, to acquire within our soul true repentance and the signs of true repentance, as we have demonstrated at length in the present homily. Let us struggle to always have in our heart also the necessary grief of repentance on account of our sins, which grief generally comes from two causes, one voluntary and the other involuntary. The voluntary one also comes from two causes, one interior (of the soul), and the other external (of the body). The voluntary interior cause which gives birth to pain of heart and afflicts it is firstly a grievous and sorrowful thought, united with self-reproach and self-chastisement on account of our sins, and on account of how we saddened and grieved God, how we lost His grace and His kingdom, and how we inherited an eternity of infinite punishments and torments. For this thought, just as a rock presses grapes and produces wine, presses down on our heart and does not allow it to leap to the passions and to the hedonistic pleasures of the flesh, but troubles the heart, afflicts it and causes it to grieve and to produce tears. The great Gregory Palamas of Thessaloniki confirms this for us, saying: "Indeed, self-reproach on its

---

475   *In Drachmam, et in illud, Homo Quidam Habebat Duos Filios*, PG 61, 782.

own, when lying for a protracted time upon the soul's thoughts like some intellectual weight, crushes and presses and squeezes out the saving wine that gladdens the heart of man, that is to say, our inner self. This wine is compunction. Together with grief, compunction crushes the passions and, having freed the soul from the weight that oppresses it, fills it with blessed joy. That is the reason why Christ says: 'Blessed are they that mourn, for they shall be comforted' (Mt. 5:4)."[476] This interior sorrow of the soul brings about true repentance, as the Apostle said: "For godly sorrow worketh repentance to salvation not to be repented of" (2 Cor. 7:10).

The voluntary interior cause which gives birth to pain of heart and afflicts it is secondly the remembrance of sins, a humble disposition, and ceaseless entreaty and prayer from our heart to God for our sins, at times saying: "Lord Jesus Christ, Son of God, have mercy on me," and: "My sweet Jesus, I have greatly saddened Thee"; and other times saying: "I have sinned, Lord, I have sinned," and: "Father, I have sinned against heaven, and before Thee, and am no more worthy to be called Thy son," and other like things which afflict the heart and cause it to grieve and shed tears. Therefore Abba Mark said: "When the intellect prays without distraction it afflicts the heart; and 'a heart that is broken and humbled God will not despise' (Ps. 50:17)."[477] And elsewhere he said: "The remembrance of God is pain of heart endured in a spirit of devotion."[478]

The voluntary exterior and bodily causes which sadden and afflict the heart are bodily poverty, self-control with regard to food, drink, sleep, and every comfort and self-indulgence of the body. For this reason, on the one hand, St. Mark said: "Without contrition of the heart it is altogether impossible to rid ourselves of evil. Now the heart is made contrite by threefold self-control: in sleep, in food and in bodily relaxation."[479] And on the other hand, the divine John of the Ladder said: "Thirst and vigil afflict the heart, and when the heart is afflicted the tears flow."[480] So just

---

476   *To the Most Reverend Nun Xenia*, *GrPhilokalia*, p. 944; tr. *The Philokalia*, v. 4, p. 314.

477   *No Righteousness by Works* 34, *GrPhilokalia*, p. 102; tr. *The Philokalia*, v. 1, p. 128.

478   *Ibid*, 131, *GrPhilokalia*, p. 106; tr. *The Philokalia*, v. 1, p. 136.

479   *Ibid*, 210, *GrPhilokalia*, p. 111; tr. *The Philokalia*, v. 1, p. 143.

480   Step 6, PG 88, 796B; tr. *The Ladder*, p. 67.

as the things mentioned above give birth to contrition of the heart and compunction, the opposites of these, like riches, luscious foods, excessive sleep, and relaxation of the body, give birth to hardness of the heart and callousness and self-indulgence of the soul. The Fathers mentioned above verify this for us. St. Mark continues: "For excess of these three things leads to self-indulgence; and this in turn makes us accept evil thoughts."[481] St. John of the Ladder says: "Insensibility of heart dulls the mind, and abundance of food dries the fountains of tears."[482] The great Gregory of Thessaloniki seals the words of these divine Fathers saying: "For just as insensibility, callousness and hardness of heart develop as the result of ease, soft living and self-indulgence, so from a way of life marked by self-control and renunciation come contrition of heart and compunction, expelling all bitterness and generating a gentle gladness."[483]

The involuntary causes which afflict the heart and give rise to grief in it are also both interior (of the soul) and exterior (of the body). The interior causes are the obscene, blasphemous, and evil thoughts which the devil hurls toward our intellect like darts and flaming arrows, as are the spiritual and bodily passions which disturb us daily, for we must fight against all of these with all of our strength and not allow our mind to couple with or consent to them. But let us run to Jesus Christ through the prayer of the heart and with His help drive those thoughts away, not allowing them to enter into our heart. How much grief and how much contrition and sorrow this ceaseless and invisible and difficult war causes is truly known only by those who have tasted it through experience. Concerning this war Gregory the Theologian wrote: "This is a terrible war. And this deployment for battle is great. And it is a great trophy."[484] The exterior and bodily causes which afflict our heart are the insults, disgraces, injustices, and other afflictions and various temptations which come from people, from demons, and from our nature, as we have previously said. All of these must be accepted with thanksgiving by the person who truly desires to repent, and

---

481   *No Righteousness by Works* 210, *GrPhilokalia*, p. 111; tr. *The Philokalia*, v. 1, p. 143.
482   Step 6, PG 88, 796B; *The Ladder*, p. 67.
483   *To the Most Reverend Nun Xenia*, *GrPhilokalia*, p. 943; tr. *The Philokalia*, v. 4, p. 313.
484   *Oratio* 11, 5, PG 35, 837B.

for him to receive treatment and forgiveness for his sins. The above-mentioned divine Fathers again confirm this for us. St. Mark says: "The work of repentance is evident from the following three virtues: the withdrawal of thoughts, ceaseless prayer and the endurance of encountered afflictions."[485] And again he says: "Let all involuntary suffering teach you to remember God, and you will not lack occasion for repentance."[486] And elsewhere: "Consider the outcome of every involuntary affliction, and you will find it has been the destruction of sin."[487] John of the Ladder says: "A sign of true repentance is the acknowledgment that we deserve all the afflictions, visible and invisible, that come upon us, and even greater ones."[488] And the divine Gregory Palamas of Thessaloniki says: "[If you] regard yourself as deserving the more drastic remedy of repentance, you will be ready to bear any affliction and will accept any temptation as your due, and you will rejoice when it comes, for you will see it as a cleansing-agent for your soul. In addition, it will spur you to ardent and most efficacious prayer to God, and you will regard it as the source and protector of the soul's health. Not only will you forgive those who afflict you, but you will be grateful to them and will pray for them as for your benefactors. Thus you will not only receive forgiveness for your sins, as the Lord has promised, but you will also attain the kingdom of heaven and God's benediction."[489] Whoever then desires to repent and treat the wounds of his sins, but afterward does not endure the encountered afflictions with thanksgiving but gets upset and complains and seeks revenge, let him know that he neither repents in truth nor treats his sins. St. Mark confirms this, saying: "Without the three aforementioned virtues it is impossible for the work of repentance to be completed." And elsewhere he says: "When a sinful soul does not accept the afflictions that come to it, the angels say: 'We would have healed Babylon, but she is not healed' (Jer. 58:9)."[490]

We all cry out to God: "Lord have mercy," and: "Master pardon our

---

485   *Scholion* 29 on Step 5, PG 88, 792C-792D.

486   *On the Spiritual Law* 57, *GrPhilokalia*, p. 94; tr. *The Philokalia*, v. 1, p. 114.

487   *Ibid.*

488   Step 5, PG 88, 780B; tr. *The Ladder*, p. 65.

489   *To the Most Reverend Nun Xenia*, *GrPhilokalia*, p. 943; tr. *The Philokalia*, v. 4, p. 312.

490   *No Righteousness by Works* 82, *GrPhilokalia*, p. 104; tr. *The Philokalia*, v. 1, p. 132.

transgressions." And when God sends His mercy and the forgiveness of our sins, we reject them. Why? Because when it happens that some temptation or affliction comes upon us, by which hardships God intends to bestow upon us His mercy and the forgiveness of our sins, we do not accept them with joy, nor do we even endure them, but we get upset and distressed and complain. Therefore, in addition to the voluntary and willful afflictions and labors of our repentance, we must also endure the involuntary and unwished-for afflictions and sorrows and temptations which come upon us from the outside, because the voluntary ones, which are much easier, are blessed by the involuntary ones, as much more difficult, as Gregory Palamas says: "For it is through patient endurance of afflictions deliberately entered into and those that are unsought, whether they come upon us from without or assault us from within, that we become perfect... Unless we bear with patience the afflictions that come to us unsought, God will not bless those that we embrace deliberately."[491]

According to the things we have said, brethren, let us take care to acquire pain of heart, because without it we cannot attain true repentance, and this follows a natural and precise order, for every sin has its beginning and is introduced into our soul from the pleasure and gratification of the heart. For this reason sin must be put to death by pain and grief of the heart, thus treating contraries by contraries, according to the physicians, the ethicists, the natural philosophers, and the theologians. And Gregory of Nyssa witnesses to this, saying: "Hence, as sin entered through pleasure, it is exterminated by the opposite. So if men persecute others for confessing the Lord and invent the most intolerable tortures, they bring, through these sufferings, a remedy to souls, for by applying pain they heal the disease caused by pleasure... And so pleasure has left no trace impressed on the heart, for the piercing sensation of pain effaced all the imprints it had stamped on the soul."[492]

Let us forsake verbose and idle talk and vain company, because these things drive away repentance, according to St. Isaac: "Repentance joined

---

491   *To the Most Reverend Nun Xenia, GrPhilokalia*, p. 943; tr. *The Philokalia*, v. 4, p. 312.
492   *De Beatitudinibus VIII*, PG 44, 1297C-1297D; tr. *St. Gregory of Nyssa: The Lord's Prayer, The Beatitudes*, ACW, Westminster, 1954, p. 172.

with conversations is a shattered vessel."[493] Let us love stillness and withdrawal from people, as this greatly helps to attain repentance, again according to St. Isaac: "If you love repentance, love stillness also. For outside of stillness repentance cannot be brought to completion. And if anyone should dispute this, do not argue with him."[494] To this is added the commandment which God gave to Cain after he sinned, saying: "Did you sin? Be still" (Gen. 4:7), meaning: "Understand what you did, and when you do come to understand it, repent for what it is that you have done." This is how the above-quoted passage is explained in the epigram concerning silence and stillness in the book of St. Isaac, where the following is also added: "Whoever cannot find peace, cannot repent, nor can he understand what repentance is." If we are unable to find stillness and silence, then let us at least designate one or two indispensable and mandatory hours, especially during the evening, to withdraw to a secluded and peaceful place and there gather our senses and our intellect into our heart, recalling in detail all of our sins (except the carnal ones, as we said earlier), both the past sins which we committed in deed, in word, or by coupling with thoughts, and the pardonable ones into which we stumbled that very day, and let us repent bitterly with sorrow and grief in our heart because of them and let us ask God for forgiveness. This is how the Holy Spirit directs us to repent through the Prophet David, saying: "Feel compunction upon your beds for what ye say in your hearts" (Ps. 4:5), and this is what Christ Himself said mystically in the Spirit to his servant St. Symeon the New Theologian: "Take care not to commit any of those evil things which will deprive you of those good things which you have been found worthy to receive. If, however, you at some time err, it is to recall you to humility. Endeavor not to leave from repentance, for repentance, together with My own philanthropy, causes both the past and the present transgressions to disappear."[495] And let us not let a single day pass without performing this salvific meditation and spiritual labor, postponing it for another time. For John of the Ladder says: "Do not deceive yourself,

---

493   *Ascetical Homilies,* Homily 51, p. 244.

494   *Ibid.,* Homily 64, p. 316.

495   *Tou Hosiou Symeon tou Neou Theologou ta Heuriskomena,* Homily 86; see *Catechetical Discourses* 16, SC 104, pp. 236-252.

foolish worker, as if one time can make up for another. For the day is not sufficient to repay in full its own debt to the Lord."[496] And Basil the Great said: "Do not make light of a fall even if it be the smallest of faults; rather, be quick to repair it by repentance… In repentance is salvation, but folly is the death of repentance."[497]

Why say so much? God, my beloved brethren, will not arraign us and condemn us in the day of death and judgment because we did not theologize or did not perform miracles or did not become divine contemplatives. No. But because we did not repent and did not grieve over our sins. This is what the aforementioned St. John concludes: "When our soul leaves this world we shall not be blamed for not having worked miracles, or for not having been theologians, or not having been rapt in divine visions. But we shall certainly have to give an account to God of why we have not unceasingly mourned."[498] For this reason we sinners must daily, if not hourly, examine ourselves, if we are in the state of true repentance. And if we suppose that we practiced other virtues and good works with the help of Jesus Christ that day, we must still, however, always remember the virtue of repentance and never ever forget it. And every day that we did not repent and grieve over our sins we must consider as lost, even if we did other good deeds that day. For this reason the aforesaid John said: "He who really keeps account of his actions considers as lost every day in which he does not mourn, whatever good he may have done in it."[499]

In conclusion, I say together with St. Symeon the New Theologian that it is necessary for all of us Christians to be healed of the passions and the wounds of sin, and then also to keep all of the commandments of the Lord and to perform every virtue. If, however, we are unable to perform the other virtues and commandments, let us at least, at least be found completely healed of the wounds and ailments of sin through the commandment and virtue of repentance. For if we die healthy and healed of the passions and sins through repentance, we will go to the kingdom of heaven. But if we

---

496   Step 6, PG 88, 797C; tr. *The Ladder*, p. 69.
497   *De Renuntiatione Saeculi* 4, PG 31, 636B; tr. *Saint Basil: Ascetical Works*, p. 22.
498   Step 7, PG 88, 816D; tr. *The Ladder*, p. 80.
499   Step 5, PG 88, 780A; tr. *The Ladder*, p. 64.

die unhealed, sick, and crippled through unrepentance we will go to Hades.[500] For the kingdom of heaven is not a hospital and an infirmary which receives the sick and the crippled, but it is a home and a palace which receives the healthy and the strong. Therefore, my fellow sinners, let us always cry out to God those familiar supplications of the Church: "Holy One, visit and heal our infirmities, for Thy Name's sake," and: "Heavenly King, receive us in repentance and confession, as Thou art good and lovest mankind." Amen.

To the Accomplisher of good be praise,
glory, honor, and dominion.

---

[500]   *Tou Hosiou Symeon tou Neou Theologou ta Heuriskomena*, Homily 12; see *Catechetical Discourses* 5, SC 96, pp. 374-468.

THE END
TO GOD BE THE GLORY

INDICES

SCRIPTURAL INDEX

OLD TESTAMENT

Genesis

3:4,	302
3:5,	329
3:19,	342
4:7,	347
6:7,	123
9:6,	139
19:17,	144
19:24,	286
19:24,	309
19:26,	321
21:10,	269
21:12,	269
25:34,	286
25:34,	290
27:34,	248
38:10,	180

Exodus

5:2,	282
12:23,	103
14:14,	98
20:2-3,	75
20:4-5,	75
20:7,	76
20:8-10,	77
20:12,	77
20:13,	78
20:14,	79
20:15,	79
20:16,	80
20:17,	81
22:1,	136
22:2,	137
22:3,	136
22:4,	136
22:27,	298
23:3,	137

Leviticus

7:31-32,	104
19:17,	138
20:10,	123
20:13,	124
20:15-16,	124

Numbers

5:7,	150
11:4-5,	325
12:14,	264
16:27-33,	290

Deuteronomy

1:17,	109
6:13,	100
6:16,	100
8:3,	100
16:20,	137
23:19,	212
23:21,	122
32:5,	244
34:9,	107

Judges

16:20,	275

1 Kings (1 Samuel)

14:43,	279
14:43,	286
15:24,	257
15:24,	311
28:20,	249

2 Kings (2 Samuel)

5:14,	272
12:6,	124
12:10,	123

12:13,	131
12:13,	265

4 Kings (2 Kings)

6:18,	309

2 Chronicles

20:12,	118
33:18,	246

Job

2:13,	291
9:28,	319
15:6,	301
15:16,	86
15:25-26,	287
21:14,	281
29:16,	113
31:34,	254
33:14-16,	319
33:14-17,	261
33:27,	294

Psalms

2:11,	77
4:5,	347
6:5,	326
7:5,	322
7:9,	104
9:6,	102
10:5,	123
14:5,	213
16:16,	280
18:13,	281
23:8,	101
24:18,	330
27:7,	250
31:4,	324

NEW TESTAMENT

The ink container of Saint Nikodemos the Hagiorite
(Holy Monastery of Vatopedi, Mount Athos, end of the18th century)

INDEX OF SUBJECTS AND NAMES

UNCUT MOUNTAIN PRESS TITLES

Books by Archpriest Peter Heers

Fr. Peter Heers, *The Ecclesiological Renovation of Vatican II: An Orthodox Examination of Rome's Ecumenical Theology Regarding Baptism and the Church*, 2015

Fr. Peter Heers, *The Missionary Origins of Modern Ecumenism: Milestones Leading up to 1920*, 2007

The Works of our Father Among the Saints, Nikodemos the Hagiorite

Vol. 1: *Exomologetarion: A Manual of Confession*

Vol. 2: *Concerning Frequent Communion of the Immaculate Mysteries of Christ*

Vol. 3: *Confession of Faith*

Other Available Titles

Elder Cleopa of Romania, *The Truth of our Faith*

Elder Cleopa of Romania, *The Truth of our Faith, Vol. II*

Fr. John Romanides, *Patristic Theology: The University Lectures of Fr. John Romanides*

Demetrios Aslanidis and Monk Damascene Grigoriatis, *Apostle to Zaire: The Life and Legacy of Blessed Father Cosmas of Grigoriou*

Robert Spencer, *The Church and the Pope*

G. M. Davis, *Antichrist: The Fulfillment of Globalization*

Athonite Fathers of the 20th Century, Vol. I

St. Gregory Palamas, *Apodictic Treatises on the Procession of the Holy Spirit*

St. Hilarion Troitsky, *On the Dogma of the Church: An Historical Overview of the Sources of Ecclesiology*

Fr. Alexander Webster and Fr. Peter Heers, Editors, *Let No One Fear Death*

Subdeacon Nektarios Harrison, *Metropolitan Philaret of New York*

Elder George of Grigoriou, *Catholicism in the Light of Orthodoxy*

Protopresbyter Anastasios K. Gotsopoulos, *On Common Prayer with the Heterodox According to the Canons of the Church*

Archimandrite Ephraim Triandaphillopoulos, *Noetic Prayer as the Basis of Mission and the Struggle Against Heresy*

The Orthodox Ethos, *On the Reception of the Heterodox into the Orthodox Church: The Patristic Consensus and Criteria*

Select Forthcoming Titles

Nicholas Baldimtsis, *Life and Witness of St. Iakovos of Evia*

The Orthodox Patristic Witness Concerning Catholicism

Georgio, *Errors of the Latins*

Fr. Peter Heers, *Going Deeper in the Spiritual Life*

Abbe Guette, *The Papacy*

Athonite Fathers of the 20th Century, Vol. II

Patrick (Craig) Truglia, *The Rise and Fall of the Papacy: An Orthodox Perspective*

Dn. Matthew Keil, *St Ephraim the Syrian: The Complete Greek Texts*

St. Hilarion Troitsky, Collected Works, Vol. II

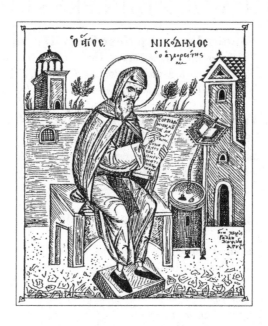

This 2nd (English) Edition of

EXOMOLOGETARION

A Manual of Confession

by Saint Nikodemos the Hagiorite

translated by Fr. George Dokos, typeset in Baskerville and printed in this two thousand and twenty third year of our Lord's Holy Incarnation, is one of the many fine titles available from Uncut Mountain Press, translators and publishers of Orthodox Christian theological and spiritual literature. Find the book you are looking for at

uncutmountainpress.com

**GLORY BE TO GOD
FOR ALL THINGS**

AMEN.

Made in the USA
Monee, IL
14 June 2024

59773914R00218